Stages of Evil

Studies in Romance Languages: 49

John E. Keller, Editor

stages of EVIL

Occultism in Western Theater and Drama

ROBERT LIMA

THE UNIVERSITY PRESS OF KENTUCKY

Publication of this volume was made possible in part by a grant from the National Endowment for the Humanities.

Scholarly publisher for the Commonwealth,
serving Bellarmine University, Berea College, Centre College of Kentucky, Eastern Kentucky University, The Filson Historical Society, Georgetown College, Kentucky Historical Society, Kentucky State University, Morehead State University, Murray State University, Northern Kentucky University, Transylvania University, University of Kentucky, University of Louisville, and Western Kentucky University.

Editorial and Sales Offices: The University Press of Kentucky
663 South Limestone Street, Lexington, Kentucky 40508-4008
www.kentuckypress.com

09 08 07 06 05 5 4 3 2 1

Library of Congress Cataloging-in-Publication Data

Lima, Robert.
Stages of evil : occultism in Western theater and drama / Robert Lima.
p. cm. — (Studies in romance languages ; 49)
Includes bibliographical references and index.
ISBN-13: 978-0-8131-2362-2 (hardcover : alk. paper)
ISBN-10: 0-8131-2362-3 (hardcover : alk. paper)
1. Occultism in literature. 2. Drama—History and criticism. I. Title.
II. Studies in Romance languages (Lexington, Ky.) ; 49.
PN1650.O33L56 2005
809'.9337—dc22 20050283

This book is printed on acid-free recycled paper meeting the requirements of the American National Standard for Permanence in Paper for Printed Library Materials.

Manufactured in the United States of America.

Member of the Association of American University Presses

To John Esten Keller,

in celebration of a life and career

full of achievements

Contents

Acknowledgments

Parts of chapters in this book were conference presentations and were issued as follows: chapter 1 as "The Mouth of Hell: The Iconography of Damnation on the Stage of the Middle Ages," *European Iconography East and West,* ed. György E. Szönyi, Symbola et Emblemata Series (Leiden: Brill, 1996), 35–48; chapter 2 as "The Genealogy of Harlequin as Diabolus," in *The Iconography of the Fantastic,* ed. Attila Kiss, Márta Baróti-Gaál, and György E. Szönyi (Szeged: Jate, 2002), 81–92; chapter 3 as "The Arcane Paganism of Celestina: Plutonic Magic versus Satanic Witchcraft in *Tragicomedia de Calixto y Melibea,*" *Neophilologus* (Dordrecht) 82, no. 2 (April 1998): 221–33; and chapter 9 as "*Nosferatu:* A Play on the Vampire by Francisco Nieva," *Modern Drama* (Toronto) 44, no. 2 (spring 2001): 232–46. All are used with permission of the publishers.

The majority of illustrations in this book are in the public domain. Permission to reprint those that are not is indicated as appropriate. In some cases, correspondence requesting permission has been ignored. I am grateful to Mr. and Mrs. Sandor Korein for permission to use as figure 17 *The Weird Sisters* (1827), by Alexandre-Marie Colin, which is in their collection.

Introduction

The play's the thing. . . .

—Shakespeare, *Hamlet*

Theater has been a mode of expression since the days of prehistory when man first attempted to communicate his experience and emotions, possibly through oral expression, perhaps through dance or mummery, to attentive companions gathered around a fire outdoors, at a hearth in a cave, or within another form of shelter. To magical gods, whom he feared when nature's wrath was stirred but praised when the land came into fruition and the waters provided its nutrients, he made obeisances that may have consisted of ritualized movements, mimetic gestures, and sacred utterances.

The desire to recount, proclaim, and venerate did not disappear with the advent of civilization. The early centuries of history not only witnessed the ongoing role of secular and religious ritual actions but also saw the emergence of drama, the written form of theater. Ancient Greece, gateway to Western culture, came to adhere to the Asian cult of Dionysus, whose ritual practices ultimately led to that form of expression defined by Aristotle as tragedy, with its masterpieces being the extant works of Aeschylus, Sophocles, and Euripides, and to the concomitant form of comedy, with the plays of Aristophanes at the apex. Rome would follow suit with the writings of Plautus and Terence for two. And both cultures built magnificent outdoor theaters in which to mount numerous productions during their religious and secular festivals.

As the Roman Empire waned, Christianity became more powerful. In the process, it confronted the lewd drama and barbaric spectacles that passed for public entertainment. Soon the excesses became intolerable, and, when the church came into its own on the collapse of Rome, it banned all public representations and ordered the theaters to be closed. But the histrionic spirit could not be bested so readily. If the presentation of plays in

---

Previous page: Le grand architecte, Eliphas Levi. Public domain.

theaters was forbidden, the populace continued to enjoy an informal theatrical experience through the peripatetic troubadours, jongleurs, minstrels, *juglares,* and other such purveyors of song, dance, juggling, acrobatics, and storytelling. In effect, it was an underground theater whose house was a town's street, plaza, or courtyard, weather permitting, or a tavern.

In time, the Middle Ages experienced the slow resurgence of theater, ironically first in the churches themselves as manifestations of the liturgy. An example is the Mass, a daily representation of Jesus Christ's Last Supper, in which there are a leading actor (the priest who acts the role of Christ); supporting actors (the acolytes); a stage (the sanctuary with its altar); movement, gesture, and dialogue (between the priest, the acolytes, and the laity); and an audience (those in attendance at the service). But there were other liturgical observances that permitted greater participation by the laity, often leading to abuses that would prove intolerable. When too many secular elements crept into the liturgical observances, the church excised them, retaining only the sacred. As a result, the religious festivals of a laical nature came to be celebrated on the church's steps or on its plaza under the patronage of craft guilds. An extension of these religious productions occurred with the introduction of pageant wagons, each of which mounted a scene of the seasonal mystery, miracle, or morality play. Slowly, Europe created a new theater with written texts that grafted the sacred and the profane in what is called *religious drama.*

The next development was of greater import. The spirit of Italian humanism (*Umanesimo*) in the fourteenth and fifteenth centuries led to the Renaissance in that country and elsewhere, making accessible classical sources once prohibited. The theater was reinstated as a cultural activity and flourished on all levels of society. Among its patrons were members of the nobility and of the church's hierarchy—bishops, cardinals, and popes. These political and religious dignitaries installed theaters or allocated areas for performances of plays in their palaces.

European theater showed a vigorous life thereafter. Italy exported its popular improvisational commedia dell'arte, giving the world such comic characters as Arlecchino, Colombina, Pantalone, and Pulcinella; Spain enjoyed what has become known as its Golden Age and saw the innovative dramas of Lope de Vega (creator of the three-act play), Cervantes, Calderón, Tirso de Molina, and Ruiz de Alarcón; England produced the genius of Shakespeare and the bountiful talents of Marlowe and Jonson; France boasted the comic perspicacity of Molière and the highly crafted works of Corneille and Racine; the works of Gozzi and Goldoni graced continental stages; and so on. European drama had reached a very high level of excellence.

The centuries that followed proved less fulfilling because succeeding literary movements such as neoclassicism, romanticism, realism, and naturalism superimposed their tenets or perspective on the drama, generally to its detriment. These movements had their small triumphs, but the playwrights whose works stand out in the panorama of the eighteenth and nineteenth centuries are Goldoni, Goethe, Zorrilla, Ibsen, and Strindberg, with Chekhov's successes coming later.

It was the twentieth century that ushered in another burst of dramatic activity akin to that of the Renaissance, but this time authors from the New World had to be counted among major contributors to such avant-gardist movements as surrealism, the theater of cruelty, and the theater of the absurd. Playwrights such as Shaw, Pirandello, Chekhov, Valle-Inclán, Ghelderode, Lorca, O'Neill, Cocteau, Beckett, Giraudoux, Betti, Brecht, Anouilh, Ionesco, Williams, Genet, Miller, and Arrabal, among others, took the theater into new and exciting venues and forms of expression.

Today, the audience is confronted with the greatest variety and audacity the stage has permitted itself since the days of Rome, stopping short only at human sacrifice. But that may yet come, the actors willing. Modern theater attacks even its public or ignores it, eulogizes and demythifies, militates for or against a cause, explores the realm of the subconscious, improvises like jazz or treads the boards in a traditional manner, swings or is mute, is self-conscious or cocky, rants or bleats. At times it is poetic. And often it simply entertains. The avant-garde and the absurd have become usual fare and seldom shock.

But the play is still a ritual, now substituting for Dionysus some other divinity or cause. Today, as in the past, it is in the play that life can be scrutinized with greatest immediacy. Regardless of trappings and sidelights, the play still holds the mirror up to life and lets us see ourselves in major proportions. There is no more effective artistic communication.

And one of the reflections in that mirror is of humanity's belief since prehistory in the occult, a hidden, supernatural dimension whose denizens—from gods to demons[1]—can and do intervene in human affairs of their own volition or at the behest of an individual adept in the arts of summoning them, either in a religious or in a secular venue. Shaman, celebrant, magus, or witch, all essentially perform rituals to evoke the supernatural being(s), for purposes of worship, emulation, or service. And, when involuntary possession of a human by such a being occurs, the tribal healer, shaman, *curandero,* rabbi, priest, or minister is called on to perform a rite of exorcism. Whatever the period or setting, it is all theater.

The encounter of the natural and the supernatural worlds has fascinated creative writers, among others, in the Western cultural tradition from Homer on, not to speak of biblical narrators. Particularly moved to address the multifaceted theme have been the dramatists, from antiquity to the modern era. The works that I have chosen to discuss herein show that some prominent dramatists have focused on the interaction of the two planes in the context of evil, inherent or perceived as such by society.

The personification of evil in the Devil, a syncretic being, a collage of remnants from Indo-European myths, pseudepigraphal texts, rabbinic literature, and folk traditions, who is the rationalization for the baser instincts that man discerns in himself, has been with Christianity since its inception, tempting even its founder. Over the centuries, Satan has attained a status close to that of the Zoroastrian Ahriman owing to the church's concern with damnation theology. It is, in fact, impossible to conceive of Christianity without the Devil, so intimate is the intertwining of the purveyor of evil—the word itself forms the larger part of his name—in the life of the church.

The Devil, be he in the onomastic guise of Lucifer, Satan, Beelzebub, Old Nick, or another of his nearly countless appellations, is also an actor in much of the Western dramatic tradition, as many of the chapters that follow demonstrate. But the Christian Devil is not the only manifestation of evil to have a large presence on the stage. Thus, other chapters emphasize various non-Christian personifications of evil: Euripides is so bold as to represent the god Dionysus as the vengeful purveyor of a cult that promotes blood sacrifice (sometimes human), orgiastic excesses, and madness; Harlequin's persona emerges as the result of a complex evolution out of pagan daemonic beings; Rojas presents Pluto, Lord of Hades, as a malefic deity; in many plays dealing with witchcraft and magic, pre-Christian gods and goddesses such as Hecate are the empowerers of evil actions; An-Sky introduces to the stage the Hasidic manifestation of evil in the form of the dybbuk, a concept out of mystical Jewish lore known as cabala; O'Neill entraps his protagonist Brutus Jones in the psychological web of Caribbean Voodoo and a primordial African god who demands human sacrifice; and Miller eschews the Devil altogether when he interprets the killing ways of Salem Village and surrounding communities as an evil greater than any alleged to have been committed by those whom the Puritans prosecuted or by Tituba's Caribbean pagan spirit; Nieva follows suit by demonstrating that the evil being termed *vampire* is less so than the decadent, nihilistic society in which he functions, wherein eros and death are juxtaposed. Evil has been given many names and identities within and beyond the pale of Christianity.

Evil is concretized in many ways in theater and drama. The multifaceted aspects of evil reflected in the histrionic mirror are what *Stages of Evil: Occultism in Western Theater and Drama* depicts. The theater and drama studied here have been selected as major manifestations of the theme throughout Western culture. The book is intended as a representative, in-depth comparative study of Western mythological, folkloric, and religious beliefs regarding evil as expressed in theater and drama from classical times to the modern era. As such, the text brings together works that show the diversity of treatments of evil as manifested through early theatrical history and written texts that make up the representational tradition of Western culture. The phases of that evolution on the stages of the Western world are expressed in the title of this book. The chapters contained herein, while selective in their subject matter, give a broad overview of the theme.

Part 1, "The Matter of the Underworld," focuses on the Mouth of Hell motif so prominent in religious representations in the Middle Ages and thereafter. The fear of being swallowed by a monster is an age-old one, found in both Eastern and Western cultures. Christianity employed that fear to foster the terror of eternal damnation among the faithful, and, thus, medieval representations of eschatological subjects, both in art and in theater, often featured a Mouth of Hell as the receptacle for those who died in mortal sin. The most grotesque devils imaginable came forth through the miasmic emanations out of the Mouth of Hell to drag their prey into the abyss of everlasting suffering. The iconography of this motif is extensive, as evidenced by the illustrations accompanying chapter 1, among which are depictions of medieval representations most often positioned stage left as befitted the sinister locale.

Part 2, "Metamorphoses of Gods," consists of two chapters. Chapter 2 explores daemonic antecedents of Arlecchino, the most memorable and enigmatic figure of the improvised Italian Renaissance theater known as the commedia dell'arte. Harlequin has very strong links to Northern European and other demonic beings from antiquity, among them the Wild Man, the Green Man, Herne the Hunter, the Erl King, and the like. Both in his manner (acrobatic, sexual, devious) and in his dress (gnome-like mask, patchwork costume, *phallos*, slapstick), Arlecchino showed traces of classical fertility deities and chthonic beings from Nordic climes. The evolution from pre-Attic demon to antic mountebank is shown with illustrations of the antecedents of the character. In chapter 3, Plutonic magic is contrasted to Satanic witchcraft in Fernando de Rojas's *Tragicomedia de Calixto y Melibea.* Magic and witchcraft are two distinct and mutually exclusive esoteric pursuits, the one being ritualistic and the other religious, albeit highly unorthodox. After both are defined and their histories traced, the distinction is applied to the *Tragicomedia de Calixto y Melibea* in order to rectify the traditional conception of Celestina as a witch in the popular sense of a person who has made a pact with Satan and is, thus, empowered to affect human life through supernatural means. But Celestina's "power" derives from a different source. On the basis of the internal evidence of words and rites, Celestina is here revealed as a practitioner of magic, the object of her incantations being the pagan Pluto, not the Christian Satan.

Part 3, "Possession and Exorcism," consists of six chapters. It first looks in chapter 4 at the primal spirit as manifested in the sacred frenzy in Euripides' *Bacchae.* The clash of the Apollonian and the Dionysian polarities, as posited by Nietzsche, is at the core of Euripides' tragedy, the only extant play in ancient Greek drama with Dionysus as the protagonist. Possessed by his spirit (or controlled mentally by him), the Bacchantes dismember the body of Pentheus, who had persecuted Dionysus and his cultists. This chapter assesses the controversial role of Dionysus (nature deity or deranged mortal?) and the unparalleled events that result from the interaction of the deific being with the celebrants of his ghastly rites of orgiastic "mysticism."

In chapter 5, the focus is on An-Sky's *The Dybbuk.* The masterpiece of Yiddish drama is based on the mystical life of the Hasidic Jews, whose foundation is the cabala. The actions of the characters are motivated by their deeply rooted belief that the world of the living and that of the dead are intertwined. Thus, the play is centered on the cabalistic doctrines of metempsychosis, possession, and exorcism. It ends in a remarkable apotheosis that attests to the validity of the belief in the supernatural ties between the two worlds.

Chapter 6 deals with Eugene O'Neill's *The Emperor Jones,* in which the protagonist is about to be deposed by the natives of a Caribbean island. Brutus Jones, the brutal self-styled emperor, enters the nearby forest with confidence at the start of his prepared escape. But he is soon haunted by Voodoo drums beating in the night, and his civilized veneer begins to erode. His primal fears emerge as the incessant drumming seems ever nearer. He starts to regress to the primitive state of the natives he had mocked, ultimately undergoing possession in an ironic triumph of superstition.

Chapter 7 looks at Arthur Miller's *The Crucible.* The historical record shows that some in Salem Village, as elsewhere in colonial America, attempted to traffic with Satan and perform rituals forbidden by the laws of the Massachusetts Bay Colony, thus leaving themselves subject to punishment. But Miller's play clearly attacks the infamous witch-hunt, showing that the Salem nightmare was brought on by a repressive society that impeded the search for personal freedom, including that of sexual expression, because of its superstitious fear that Satan was in its midst as a result of God's abandonment. A case of mass hysteria, the supposed possession could not be remedied by formal exorcism; only the inequity of the legal process and of the executions themselves provided a catharsis that ultimately brought to an end this formidable chapter in American history.

Chapter 8 focuses on *The Devils,* a play by John Whiting, assessing the life and times of the Reverend Urbain Grandier, renowned priest, fiery preacher against government excesses, and confessor to a group of cloistered nuns in the seventeenth-century France of Louis XIII, which was controlled by Cardinal Richelieu. This is the basis for Whiting's study of a persecution and execution founded on political premises but carried out through the accusation against the priest of trafficking with the Devil through a demonic pact (which was produced at his trial, along with one signed by numerous devils) and of sexually possessing the nuns through demonic agency. Political might and popular credulity in superstition made it impossible for the priest to win his case. Urbain Grandier was convicted, sentenced to death, and duly executed by being garroted and burned at the stake.

Chapter 9 offers a dark subject that has long fascinated readers and the theater public, particularly since the publication of Bram Stoker's *Dracula* and the film version, *Nosferatu,* by F. W. Murnau. The vampire was not a motif in Spanish literature until Nieva's play *Nosferatu* appeared. Nieva's is a heterodox stance, a departure from the canonicity established by the early assessors of the tradition. Nieva eschews fundamental elements of the tradition to *play* on the theme in a surrealistic, absurd manner, placing front and center the malign decadence of society.

Part 4, "Cauldron and Cave," has two chapters. Chapter 10 deals with witchcraft on the Elizabethan and Jacobean stages. The three Weird Sisters in Shakespeare's *Macbeth* are the best known of the witches on the Elizabethan stage, but there are numerous other practitioners of the black arts depicted in the works of the period, among them the homegrown Lancashire Witches, Mother Shipton, Mother Bombey, and Mother Sawyer; the classical world's Medea, Erictho, and Hecate; among others. Thomas Middleton's *The Witch,* Thomas Dekker et al.'s *The Witch of Edmonton,* and John Kirke's *The Seven Champions of Christendome* are treated here, along with Shakespeare's *Macbeth,* as representative of these several currents of witch lore.

Chapter 11 explores the topos of the cave and its frequent use in European drama whenever magic was concerned. This may have been because the cave satisfied an intellectual need in the dramatist and addressed an intuitive curiosity in his public—the former saw the motif as an entertaining way to delve into human psychology by assessing the desire for power and control through supernatural means in an appropriate venue, while the latter was awed by the chthonic setting and the magical occurrences within and without its confines. However, as the church became increasingly more powerful, both in spiritual and in political terms, it interpreted as heterodox and, therefore, sinful all attempts at empowerment or knowledge outside what Christianity promoted as acceptable. Magic and magicians became associated with the Devil, as had witchcraft and witches. And the caves that they used were seen as malevolent places, without regard to the type of magic practiced or its ends.

The appendix provides a bibliography of European and American plays. In the first section, European and American playwrights are listed alphabetically, with their pertinent works. In the second section, plays are listed according to category, for example, *alchemy, astrology, demonic pact, fairies, Faust, Last Judgment, lycanthropy, magic, Mouth of Hell, possession and exorcism,* and *witchcraft,* with author, date, and nation as well as any annotation deemed pertinent. This extensive bibliography attests to the hundreds of plays that have been written in Europe and the Americas on the subject of evil, especially on its preeminent figure, the Devil. The division of these works into thematic categories will facilitate the research of those who wish to pursue a particular line of inquiry.

To my knowledge, no other critical study has ranged as widely in time or assessed so many works on the subject of occult thematics in Western theater and drama.

Note

1. Throughout this study, the Greek *daemon* and *daemonic* are employed when the entity in question is a subordinate deity, genius of a place, or chthonic being, *demon* and *demonic* (because of their unfortunate association with *devil* in the Judeo-Christian tradition) when the entity in question is simply an evil spirit.

Part I

The Matter of the Underworld

1

The Mouth of Hell

Damnation on the Stage of the Middle Ages

> Who can force open the doors of his mouth, close to his terrible teeth? . . . Out of his mouth go forth firebrands; sparks of fire leap forth. From his nostrils issues steam.
>
> —Job 41:6, 11-12

The "Mouth of Hell" is a motif out of the ancient world that first became manifest iconographically in Christianity during patristic times and continued to increase in importance thereafter, reaching its apogee in the European Middle Ages. As Christianity increased its spiritual and temporal power in post-Roman Europe, it superimposed its beliefs on the pagan traditions of the Continent. Building on Greek ideas of the underworld, the church began to promote its conception of what awaited the Christian after death: either sanctification in heaven or damnation in hell. The concept of the place of eternal punishment soon caught the imagination of medieval man, and representations of the place of torment became plentiful.

The Christian Mouth of Hell motif appeared in religiously oriented frescoes, mosaics, architectonic elements, and sculpture in churches and cathedrals as well as in illuminated manuscripts, among them antiphonaries, apocalypses, Bibles, books of hours, breviaries, lives of Christ and the saints, and psalters. The motif is particularly prevalent in written and visual works dealing with the fall of Lucifer and the rebel angels, along with those on such eschatological matters as Christ's Harrowing of Hell and the Last Judgment. The Mouth of Hell is likewise prominent in the staging of those medieval secular dramas known as mystery and miracle plays.

The pervasiveness of the Mouth of Hell image can be understood in that its impact lent itself to the needs of a church combating what it saw as the evils of a pagan world. In its mission of impressing on the faithful the dire consequences of leading an immoral life, the church had the alliance of visual artists, mostly anonymous, whose imagination was unfettered in the interpretation of the eternal punishment due those who died in origi-

---

Previous page: The Mouth of Hell, *Book of Hours of Catherine of Cleves*, Utrecht, ca. 1440. By permission of the Pierpont Morgan Library, M.945, fol. 168v.

nal or mortal sin. And the figure that appeared with increasing frequency in their works was that of the sinner being cast into hell through the maw, gaping jaws, or mouth of a grotesque beast. The motif ranged from simple line drawings of the Mouth of Hell to the masterful complexity depicted in the *Book of Hours of Catherine of Cleves.*[1]

Whence came the concept of the Mouth of Hell? There are two distinct concepts that contribute to this traditional Christian motif. The first is that of a great beast swallowing a living human being; the second is the belief in punishment for evil in an afterlife. Through the strange symbiosis that occurs frequently in religion, these disparate images out of classical, biblical, and other lores formed a syncretic bond, creating one of the symbols that not only proved frightening to the medieval mind but continued to fascinate churchmen, laity, and artists well into the seventeenth century.

Swallowed by the Beast

A possible source of the first concept may be traced to intrepid ancient mariners who feared the huge creatures that sometimes destroyed fishing boats or dragged pursuers to the depths of the ocean. The monsters, perhaps whales or man-eating sharks, undoubtedly were attempting to free themselves from the nets and harpoons of marauders or were attacking targets of opportunity in their watery domain. Even the large Mediterranean dolphins of Minoan fame might qualify as probable sources of the mariners' real or imagined concerns. Sea charts, from ancient times to the days of Columbus, often depicted unknown waters as pullulating with grotesque beasts, a warning to those who might wish to traverse those stretches.

The Jonah of the Old Testament,[2] for one, was swallowed by such a sea monster, a "great fish" (Hebrew *dag gadol*) now usually identified as a whale. But, when Jonah cried "out of the belly of hell" (Jon. 2:1), God heard his plea. Jonah emerged unscathed through divine intervention, and perhaps similar miraculous escapes from the gaping mouths of sea creatures led to such encounters being thought of as symbolic of the rite of passage from death to rebirth. The Jonah story thus may disguise the initiation ritual of an ancient mystery religion. In the theatrical context of fifteenth-century Florence, there is among the *sacre rappresentazioni* the play of the Feast of the Purification of Mary (*Purificazione*), whose records list a *peccie di Giona,* a papier-mâché whale to be used by Jonah (and, perhaps, other prophets; see Newbigin, 285).

However, the deep-seated terror of a living entombment ultimately gave precedence to tales of people who, having been swallowed alive by a beast, were never seen again. Whatever the positive overtones that had attached to the Jonah image, they were eroded under the greater impact of the horrific death by bestial assimilation. In the Old Testament, the name given the embodiment of such human-devouring monsters was Leviathan, probably under the influence of Oriental sea dragon or marine serpent myths. The Book of Job makes many references to the great beast:

> Let them curse it who curse the sea, the appointed disturbers of Leviathan. (3:8)

> Can you lead about Leviathan. . . . (40:25)

> Who can force open the doors of his mouth, close to his terrible teeth? Rows of scales are on his back, tightly sealed together. (41:6)

> When he sneezes, light flashes forth; his eyes are like those of the dawn. Out of his mouth go forth firebrands; sparks of fire leap forth. From his nostrils issues steam, as from a seething pot or bowl. His breath sets coals afire; a flame pours from his mouth. (41:10–13)

The Book of Job's description of the beast has the aspects traditionally descriptive of a dragon, but, somewhat surprisingly, the Leviathan described therein has been surmised by some commentators to be a Nile crocodile. On the other hand, the later Book of Isaiah states: "In that day the Lord with his sore and great and strong sword shall punish Leviathan the piercing serpent, even Leviathan that crooked serpent; and he shall slay the dragon that is in the sea" (27:1). Serpent and dragon are the explicit referents in this text, which prophesied how on Doomsday the might of Yahweh, the "new" god of the Hebrews, will be deployed against that of the more ancient divinity that the same Semitic people had worshiped long before him. Indeed, Levi, the name of those who belonged to the priestly caste known as Levites, meant "son of Leviathan." Before becoming the priests of Yahweh, the Levites had served Leviathan in that capacity.

The antipathy of Yahweh toward Leviathan can be understood in the light of the stature of the monstrous deity among the Hebrews. As any new god, Yahweh was intolerant of the deity and the tenets of the earlier religion. The old god had to give way to the new, so Yahweh exercised brutal reprisals against the once-powerful predecessor. Leviathan had become the enemy, as narrated in Psalms:

> Thou didst divide the sea by thy strength: thou brakest the heads of the dragon in the waters. Thou brakest the head of Leviathan in pieces, and gavest him to be meat to the people inhabiting the wilderness. (74:13–14)

> Thou hast broken Rahab in pieces, as one that is slain. (89:10)

Rahab,[3] here, is another personification of the sea dragon, as in Isaiah's exhortation to Yahweh to act once again on behalf of his people: "Awake as in the ancient days, in the generations of old. Art thou not it that hath cut Rahab, and wounded the dragon?" (Isa. 51:9). But Leviathan, although defeated, was not to disappear from the biblical scene. Once conquered, Leviathan became the servant of Yahweh.

The Hebrew etymon for Leviathan, meaning "that which twists around" or "the wriggly one," is also associated with the great serpent Nehushtan,[4] which, at the instigation of Yahweh, Moses had made into a healing icon for his followers, as narrated in Numbers: "And the Lord said unto Moses, Make thee a fiery serpent, and set it upon a pole: and it shall come to pass, that every one that is bitten, when he looketh upon it, shall live. And Moses made a serpent of brass, and put it upon a pole, and it came to pass, that if a serpent had bitten any man, when he beheld the serpent of brass, he lived" (21:8–9). That the efficacious brass *saraph* (or seraph) came to be revered is evidenced by its place of honor in the Temple, where it was still being worshiped more than five centuries later when the righteous King Hezekiah ordered its destruction: "He removed the high places, and brake the images, and cut down the groves, and brake in pieces the brasen serpent that Moses had made: for unto those days the children of Israel did burn incense to it: and he called it Nehustan" (2 Kings 18:4).

Yahweh's hostile associations with Leviathan would imply that the Hebrew's god was distinct from the dragon-serpent deity. But Yahweh's ties with ancient Ophism could be imputed from the Nehushtan episode and other dragon-serpent motifs throughout the Old Testament. Indeed, the Hebrew *saraph,* for a divine fiery serpent, became the source of *seraphim,* "the burning ones," six-winged serpent spirits who hovered above the throne of Yahweh, whom they served (Isa. 6:2–3). Earlier, in Exodus, Moses was instructed by Yahweh on what he should do before the power of Pharaoh:

> And the Lord said unto him, What is that in thine hand? And he said, A rod. And he said, Cast it on the ground, and it became a serpent; and Moses fled from before it. And the Lord said unto Moses, Put forth thine hand, and take it by the tail. And he put forth his hand, and caught it, and it became a rod in his hand. (4:2–4)

> And thou shalt take this rod in thine hand, wherewith thou shalt do signs. (4:17)

> And Moses took the rod of God in his hand. (4:20)

> And the Lord said unto Moses, When thou goest to return into Egypt, see that thou do all those wonders before Pharaoh, which I have put in thine hand. (4:21)

Turning Yahweh's rod into a serpent before Pharaoh, Aaron and Moses witnessed a similar miracle performed by the court magicians. But Yahweh's serpent *swallowed* all the other serpents (Exod. 7:10–12). Thus, Pharaoh's serpents, symbols of the Egyptian god Thoth, were devoured by the serpent of Moses and Aaron, symbol of Yahweh. Furthermore, Jewish medallions of the first and second centuries B.C.E. represented Yahweh as a serpent god, while Jews of Asia Minor said that their Yahweh was the same as Zeus Sabazius, the serpent god of Phrygia (Enslin, 91).

In time, as Christianity began to establish its hegemony in the world of the declining Roman Empire, it unwittingly or otherwise incorporated into its allegorical tradition many diverse Mediterranean and adjacent concepts, among them the far-reaching role of serpents in the affairs of God and man. As attested in the Gospel of John (3:14), the healing "crucified" serpent of Moses is identified with the redeeming crucified Christ (see fig. 1). Here, Saint John uses the Old Testament image in a positive prefigurement of Christ.[5]

But the best-planned symbolism can sometimes go awry, as in the case of Christian Ophites, who claimed Moses as the founder of their tradition and worshiped his brass *saraph* strung on a tau cross, both in itself and as a manifestation of Christ-Ophion. So pervasive was the association of Moses' serpent and the crucified Christ that, in 1415, in his *Ordo paginarum ludi Corpus Christi*, Roger Burton comments on the eleventh pageant of the medieval play cycle: "Moses raising the serpent of bronze in the desert. King Pharaoh, eight Jews in admiration and expectancy" (Nagler, *Medieval Religious Stage*, 60). And, as late as 1583, Renward Cysat's plan for the stag-

Figure 1. *The Serpent of Moses on the Christian Cross,* provenance unknown. Public domain.

ing of the Lucerne *Osterspiel,* the Passion play, included instructions for the central location on the playing area of the Old Testament *saraph:* "Moses' Brazen Serpent and its cross shall have their place for insertion 7 feet away from the Savior's cross. It comes almost in the middle of the square. There a piece of pipe is put upright into the ground, level with the surface" (Meredith and Tailby, 86).

Although the dragon and serpent were often beneficent—as Jesus himself acknowledged when he said: "Be ye therefore wise as serpents" (Matt. 10:16)—they came to be considered as evil beasts in patristic Christianity. First, the serpent identified in Genesis as the purveyor of forbidden knowledge and the instigator of the Fall[6] was transmogrified by Yahweh: "And the Lord God said unto the serpent, Because thou hast done this, thou art cursed above all cattle, and above every beast of the field; upon thy belly shalt thou go, and dust shalt thou eat all the days of thy life" (Gen. 3:14). Second, dragons and serpents either were symbols associated with "false gods" or were gods themselves in many pagan systems of belief. Third, those monstrous deities had become absorbed into the Christian conception of evil personified, the Devil. Therefore, the beast—be it dragon or serpent—had to be slain by a Saint Michael the Archangel, a Saint George (the patron saint of England and, as Sant Jordi, Catalonia), and a host of Christian knights-errant in epics, ballads, and novels of chivalry. As Meredith and Tailby (121–22) record it, in the Valencia Corpus Christi processions of the early fifteenth century, salaries were paid in 1404 "to hire the men who walked in the dragons (*los drachs*)," in 1407 "[f]or repairing the wild beasts (*les figures de les besties feres*) of the blessed St. George," and in 1407 and 1408 "to the man who walked inside St. George's dragon (*la cucha de sent Jordi*)," while, in an indoor performance at the Aranzo estate in Jaén, Spain, in 1461, there was a fire-breathing dragon: "In front of the place where the Countess was seated, there then appeared the head of this huge dragon (*serpiente*). It was made of painted wood, and a device inside it (*su artificio*) propelled the boys out through its mouth one by one, and it breathed huge flames at the same time." And, in the 1510 Saint George celebration at Newcastle-upon-Tyne, various merchants were paid for providing accoutrements for the dragon.

The dragon or serpent also had to have his head crushed underfoot by the Virgin Mary[7] in accord with the exhortation in Genesis: "And I will put enmity between thee and the woman, and between thy seed and her seed; it shall bruise thy head, and thou shalt bruise its heel" (3:15). The suppresion of the beast by the Virgin Mary was meant to provide the faithful with continuing visual evidence of the triumph of the Christian God over more ancient deities. A medieval play that incorporated the prophecy was Hildegard of Bingen's very early morality play in Latin, *Ordo virtutum,* wherein Chastity (read the Virgin Mary) literally oppresses the Devil:

> In mente altissimi, o Satana, caput tuum conculcavi,
> et in virginea forma dulce miraculum colui . . .
> et nunc gaudeant omnes qui habitant in celis
> quia venter tuus confusus est. (Axton, 98)
>
> (In the mind of the Highest, Satan, I trod upon your head
> and in virgin form I nurtured a sweet miracle . . .
> and now let all who dwell in heaven rejoice
> that the fruit of your innards has been confounded.)

A later play with the same motif is *The Presentation of Mary in the Temple* (*Festo praesentationis Beatae Virginis Mariae in Templo*), performed in Avignon in 1372,[8] in which the archangel Michael points to the chained Lucifer and says to Mary: "Behold the rebel against God. . . . You, indeed, have received from God the power of treading underfoot, of overcoming and tormenting him on behalf of God Almighty. He is placed under your sentence, is given over to your will, and is bound under your feet" (Meredith and Tailby, 220).

Yet even such Christian attempts at the subjugation of evil through a symbolic act could not eradicate ancient superstitions. Credence was still given to the belief that many of the mythic beings of old were unspeakable monsters and deities who devoured sinful humans. Christianity affixed all such expropriations to Satan, as in the New Testament Book of Revelation, where an angel of the Lord "laid hold on the dragon, that old serpent, which is the Devil, and Satan" (20:1). *Dragon* and *serpent* appear to have been nearly synonymous terms as well in sacred scriptures out of antiquity and in the early years of the common era. This equating of the dragon-serpent with the Devil indicates the attempt to eradicate traces of Ophiolatreia by associating it with the evil entity of the Christian pantheon.

That such identifications of Satan with dragons and serpents were remnants of Ophic worship is evident in many instances in Christian Europe. In the *Moralia* of Pope Gregory I (the Great; 540–604), Satan is said to be a shape changer, being different beasts under different circumstances: "[I]n those whom he inflames to do malicious injury, he is the dragon" (Galpern, 142). In the Gerona *Apocalypse* (ca. 975), a full-page miniature (fol. 17v) depicts a tripartite hell with a seated Satan entwined with serpents (Galpern, 149). An eleventh-century Icelandic woodcut of a snakelike monster devouring a human (Milosevic, 31) shows that the motif had crossed wide expanses of ocean. The twelfth-century Resurrection and Last Judgment mosaic at Torcello shows Satan astride a serpent that devours sinners. In the thirteenth century and the early fourteenth, the relationship is frequently manifest elsewhere on the Italian Peninsula, particularly in representations of the Lord of Hell seated on a chair made of dragons and serpents "in the pulpits at Siena and Pisa, in the Arena Chapel in Padua, and in the Florentine Baptistry" (Frye, 138) (see fig. 2). And there are many other similar examples throughout the Middle Ages.

So it was that the motif of the sea beast who swallowed humans came to be depicted in medieval treatises in terms of a dragon or some hybrid monster out of Middle and Far Eastern mythology. Thus, Pope Gregory I could write in his commentary on Job in his *Moralia:* "But it was no wonder that this, Behemoth . . . drank up, with the yawning gulph of his deep

Figure 2. *Satan on a Throne Devouring a Sinner,* mosaic after the *Inferno,* Baptistery, Florence. Photograph by the author.

persuasion, the river of the human race. . . . [H]e seizes many with his open mouth, that even after heavenly sacraments he hurries them away to the depth of hell." And he could also describe Leviathan as follows: "For in this abyss of water, that is, in this boundlessness of the human race, this whale was rushing hither and thither with open mouth, eager for the death, and devouring the life of almost all" (Galpern, 143). More often than not, a dragon's mouth was the receptacle for the discomfited human being. However, the whale motif continued to survive in some instances, as in the Anglo-Saxon heroic poem known as *Genesis B,* where Satan is "represented as chained to the teeth of a giant whale, while his followers are shown falling pell mell into the whale's jaws" (Frye, 139). Yet another such Anglo-Saxon association is in the late-tenth-century fragment *The Whale,* from a bestiary in *The Exeter Book,* where the devouring of mariners by the sea beast and that of sinners by Satan are paralleled, equating the jaws of the whale to those of hell:

> When the deceiver, practiced in evil,
> has brought into that prison
> where the fire is renewed, those who, loaded with sins,

adhered to him, and who once listened
eagerly to his teachings in the days of their life,
he then, after their death, clashes
fast together those grim jaws
the gates of hell. Those who enter there
have no return or escape, no egress ever,
any more than those fishes, swimmers in the sea,
may return from the grasp of the whale. (Galpern, 143)

Jonah's escape was, indeed, singular, but he was involved, nonetheless, in a circumstance within a natural framework, if one with miraculous overtones. Medieval man labored under the belief in the supernatural application of being swallowed forever by the zoomorphic Mouth of Hell.

Perhaps the classical and Oriental conceptions of exotic beasts that had informed the apocalyptic vision of Saint John the Divine early on had been strengthened in the European consciousness through the travel accounts of such as Marco Polo. Perhaps it was through the Crusaders, especially the Templars, who, according to their accusers, had become imbued with esoteric Aryan, Islamic, and other heterodox beliefs. Perhaps it was through the symbolism of alchemical and cabalistic practices in the Middle Ages or even through the diffusion of such Oriental tales as those Scheherezade told her sultan. Whatever the provenance, the theme of the whale-dragon-serpent that swallowed living human beings was widely spread throughout medieval Europe.

Punishment in the Afterlife

The second concept, punishment in the afterlife, is equally diverse in origin. It can be traced most effectively to the growing infiltration of Christianity by the plethora of superstitious beliefs that had come together in the Roman Empire, among them some from ancient Greece, themselves derivative from Far and Near Eastern sources.

In book 11 of Homer's *Odyssey,* entitled "The Book of the Dead," Odysseus learns from his mother that, in Hades, "all is consumed by the fierce heat of the blazing fire" (177), while the other shades who come before him are mournful in their deprived condition within "the wide portals of the House of Hades" (186). Odysseus describes the torments suffered by Tityos, Tantalus, and Sisyphus, thus presenting Hades as a place of suffering not only for common men but also for figures of renown.

In the fifth century B.C.E., Democritus, who posited in his atomic theory that something once destroyed cannot exist again, speaks of the false belief held by many that those who enter the netherworld having done wrong in life are punished: "Those who know nothing of the dissolution of our mortal nature, but are aware of having done wrong in life, experience tormented lives in the confused fear of the fables they have fabricated concerning life after death" (fragment 297, pp. 206–7 [my translation]). Those very fables are reflected in book 1 of Plato's *Republic,* where the aged Kephalos tells Socrates of one of the great fears that his waning life has seen emerge into consciousness: "Think of the tales they tell of the next world, how one that has done wrong here must have justice done him there—you may have laughed at them before, but then they begin to rack your soul. What if they are true!" (128). And Aristophanes, Socrates' contemporary, also depicts that interpretation of Hades in *The Frogs,* but in varied comic ways ranging from Heracles' account of "snakes, and armies of wild animals, [and] monsters" (17) such as Empousa through the enumeration of types of punishment. The very mockery of Hades and its personnel presumes the Greek audience's long familiarity with the serious aspects of the underworld. But, whether serious or comic, the thought of Hades as a place of retributive punishment would continue to haunt the Greeks and their inheritors in Rome.

Consequently, a century before Christ, Lucretius could speak of the jaws of hell (*infernus*)[9] in book 3 of *De rerum naturae* (The nature of the universe) with the intent of dispelling what he saw as an unfortunate superstition:

> There is no murky pit of Hell awaiting anyone. (125)
>
> As for all those torments that are said to take place in the depths of Hell, they are actually present here and now, in our own lives. (126)
>
> As for Cerberus and the Furies and the pitchy darkness and the jaws of Hell belching abominable fumes, these are not and cannot be anywhere at all. (127)

Lucretius goes on to explore the basis for the superstition in terms of human psychology, attributing it to a sense of retributive justice: "But life is darkened by the fear of restitution for our misdeeds, a fear enormous in proportion to their enormity. . . . Even though these horrors are not physically present, yet the conscience-ridden mind in terrified anticipation torments itself with its own goads and whips. . . . It is afraid that death may serve merely to intensify pain. So at length the life of misguided mortals becomes a Hell on earth" (127).

The fear of the torments to which Lucretius refers had long standing in the ancient world prior to Rome and Greece. Although the tenets of Egyptian, Babylonian, Mesopotamian, and Judaic religions, among others, did not posit that the realm of the dead was a place of torture in itself, the popular mind had less than orthodox ideas on the subject of the netherworld. For one, it misconstrued Egyptian depictions of fire pits in Amenti (the underworld; also Khert-Neter, Tuat), where the supernatural enemies of hawk-headed Ra (the sun god) were tortured, as a punishment awaiting all such wrongdoers. For another, it was awed by the Zoroastrian idea of postmortem tortures, particularly for women who erred, in an underworld setting of fire, scorpions, snakes, and other vile life-forms that devoured the victim under the eyes of Ahriman, Lord of Darkness, manifest as the Great Serpent.[10]

Besides drawing on varied classical sources, Christianity relied on Old Testament texts as evidence of the belief's antiquity. In Numbers, it found the words of Moses on the fate of the rebellious Korah (Core), Dathan, and Abiram:

> But if the Lord make a new thing, and the earth open her mouth, and swallow them up, with all that appertain unto them, and they go down quick into the pit; then ye shall understand that these men have provoked the Lord. And it came to pass, as he had made an end of speaking all these words, that the ground clave asunder that was under them. And the earth opened her mouth, and swallowed them up, and their houses, and all the men that appertained unto Korah, and all their goods. They, and all that appertained to them, went down alive into the pit, and the earth closed upon them: and they perished from among the congregation. And all Israel that were round about them fled at the cry of them: for they said, Lest the earth swallow us up also. (16:30–34)

In the Psalms, a long cry of anguish contains the words: "Let not the waterflood overflow me, neither let the deep swallow me up, and let not the pit shut her mouth upon me" (69:15). In his fifth-century commentary, Caesarius of Arles emphasizes the closure of the process, that is, the finality of being swallowed and not having the possibility of release à la Jonah (*Saint Caesarius of Arles*, 406–7). And in Isaiah is found a reference to Sheol, the Hebrew netherworld: "Therefore hell hath enlarged herself, and opened her mouth without measure: and their glory, and their multitude, and their pomp, and he that rejoiceth, shall descend into it" (5:14). Such passages, interpreted literally, undoubtedly gave rise to early Christian beliefs in the yawning abyss that awaited the unrepentant sinner.

In a greatly distanced era and setting, the Norse goddess of the underworld, Hel (whose name means "The Concealer"), was symbolized as a cauldron, a metaphor for the womb, both as life-giving and as purgative. In Nifleheim, the goddess presides over a realm distinguished by ice, cold, and darkness, as appropriate to the harsh reality of northern climes in winter. And the entrance to that realm was named Nágrind, gate of the dead. When the Danelaw was extended to parts of England, such beliefs were amalgamated to the indigenous traditions of death and punishment in the hereafter.

The Christian idea of eternal punishment in the fires of hell emerged out of such diverse religious and folkloric beliefs, factoring out of pagan and biblical sources any positive aspects that the image might have had. It would appear that the earliest extant depictions of the abyss in a Christian text are from a sixth-century Greek manuscript preserved in a ninth-century copy[11] (Milosevic, 13).

Symbiosis

The overlord of the torment and discord in the Christian hell was Lucifer (the name being a misinterpretation of Isaiah's reference to Nebuchadnezzar in Isa. 14:12), transmogrified from the leader of the fallen angels (like the Persian Ahriman) into a sadistic being half goat, half human (like the Greek Pan) who, just as Pluto had ruled Hades, was the lord of the underworld (*hell* was a later name derived from the nether kingdom of the Norse goddess Hel).

This syncretic being, a demoted deity in the Christian pantheon, the Devil (from the Aryan *daeva*), was often depicted in art as swallowing the sinner whole, a conception no doubt influenced by the myth of the Greek god Kronos (Saturn), who cannibalized his male offspring because he feared that they would depose him someday.[12]

The descent of the anthrophagous image from Kronos on the Greek Olympus to Satan in the Christianized Hades ultimately led to its expansion. Then it was but a short leap of imagination to transfer the image of Satan (Lucifer, the Devil) ingesting sinners to that of hell itself receiving the damned through a fissure in the earth.[13] It was perhaps inevitable in that scheme of embodiment of evil to hold that the mortal being brought into the place of punishment would experience the nefarious rite of passage through a monstruous mouth that was zoomorphic in its configuration, particularly with the precursory foundation laid by the vivid imagery of the Old Testament, Greek religion, and other pagan belief systems.

What can be interpreted as evolutionary stages in the process are evident in two early texts. The *Life of Saint Guthlac,* written in Latin by the English monk Felix between 730 and 740, contains an episode in which the saint is taken "to the accursed jaws of hell" (*ad nefandas tartari fauces*), there to be faced by a spectacle more frightening than that witnessed by Virgil's Aeneas: "Behold: the fiery entrances of Erebus gape for you with yawning mouths . . . the bowels of Styx long to devour you and the hot gulfs of Aacheron gape with dreadful jaws" (Galpern, 139). Then there is the *Utrecht Psalter,*[14] a mid-ninth-century treatise where several of the illustrations show a so-called death's-head in the pit of hell. Both these medieval texts mark a transition between the inanimate fissure of classical times and the zoomorphic maw of later centuries.

In time, the whale, dragon, or serpent—all Christian metaphors for evil—metamorphosed into yet another and more poignant guise: the exotic beast became the literal Mouth of Hell in written and visual depictions throughout medieval Christendom. The earliest-known illuminations or drawings depicting the actual Mouth of Hell are from the beginning of the eleventh century, and they were made by Anglo-Saxon artists in such manuscripts as the *Liber vitae* (New Minster, Winchester, ca. 1020–30),[15] the *Bury St. Edmunds Psalter,*[16] and others, perhaps inspired by Felix's vivid description of the jaws of hell in his *Life of Saint Guthlac.* The first illustration of the Mouth of Hell in the shape of an *animal* head with open jaws appeared in the Harrowing of Hell scene of an Anglo-Saxon-inspired Gospel book (ca. 1000) from the monastery of Saint Bertin in northern France.[17]

The texts that were to consolidate the motif and promulgate it throughout Europe began to appear once the dreaded millennium had passed without incident and doomsayers began to make verbal and pictorial reassessments of the Last Judgment and other eschatological concepts. The date of the projected catastrophe too was readjusted with frequency, giving vent to ongoing concern over the end of the universe and the punishment awaiting the condemned.

The motif seems to have taken root in France in the twelfth century, as attested by the powerful relief carved on the tympanum of the abbey church of Sainte Foy at Conques-en-Rouergue, featuring the open maw of Leviathan surging through the gate of hell (see fig. 3). The pilgrims who stopped

Figure 3. *Maw of Leviathan and Gate of Hell,* west portal tympanum (lower right), Church of Sainte Foy, Conques-en-Rouergue, France. Photograph by the author.

at Conques on the route from La Puy to the shrine of the apostle James at Santiago de Compostela in northwestern Spain looked up at the Last Judgment images on the tympanum and were taken by the depiction of devils dragging sinners to the Mouth of Hell.

Thereafter, the Mouth of Hell appears elsewhere on the Continent in a variety of written, artistic, and architectonic manifestations (see fig. 4). The transition from classical, biblical, and other lores to Christian tradition was complete, having gone through three stages: an unfortunate human being swallowed by some sea or land monster (the Jonah motif); the association of a vindictive deity with the serpent-dragon (the Yahweh motif); and the Devil gorging himself on sinners in hell (the Kronos motif). These led ultimately to the Christian Mouth of Hell so prominent in Last Judgment scenes in medieval Europe.

Figure 4. Capital, Church of Sainte Pons, France. Photograph by the author.

Stage Left: The Sinister Place of Hell on the Medieval Stage

Since the church promoted the Mouth of Hell with such frequency and immediacy, it is not unexpected to find that the theater of the Middle Ages used the same motif in the mise-en-scène of Last Judgment (or Doomsday) and Harrowing of Hell[18] plays, among others of the mystery and miracle genre (French *mystères,* Italian *sacre rappresentazioni,* Spanish *misterios* and *autos sacramentales*) staged during such important feasts in the church calendar as Corpus Christi, held sixty days after Easter.[19] These were the first "stages of evil" in the European Christian tradition.

Religious treatises may have focused most often on the Leviathan image, as in the exegesis of the Book of Job in Pope Gregory I's *Moralia:* "[T]his whale then, who is lying in ambush. . . . But what man can escape from the mouth of the Leviathan?" (Galpern, 146). But the primary metaphor for the entryway to the place of eternal damnation on the medieval stage was the dragon or serpent.

While the entrance to hell was held by some to be in Palestine, on Golgotha (where the hellish crime of executing Christ took place),[20] for the medieval European who attended the stagings of mystery and miracle plays, the Mouth of Hell erected on pageant wagons, on platforms over secrets (i.e., trapdoors) in town plazas, in courtyards, in corrals, or in the "rounds" (earthworks similar to those of the Iron Age wherein the play was performed) was there in front of him, so terrifyingly re-created was this most dreaded of places.

Many medieval plays incorporate this horrific element. The *Sponsus,* a French miracle play dated ca. 1096–99 and said to be from Saint-Martial de Limoges, is the earliest extant example of demons on the medieval stage. In it, the Bridegroom, Christ, addressing the Foolish Virgins first in Latin and then in the Limousin dialect of *langue d'oc* (Provençal), consigns them to damnation at play's end:

> Amen dico, vos ignosco, nam caretis lumine,
> Quod qui perdunt procul pergunt huius aule limine.
> Alet, chaitivas, alet, malavreas!
> A tot iors mais vos so penas livreas;
> En efern ora seret meneias!
>
> (Amen I say, I know you not, for you lack light;

Those without it lose the path to this hall.
Go, you wretches! Go, accursed!
All your days to come you shall suffer torture.
And now you shall be taken into hell.)

On hearing the judgment, the nonspeaking demons hasten to the Foolish Virgins as hunters would to prey and then cast them into the Mouth of Hell ("Modo accipiant eas Demones, et precipitentur in infernum" [Axton, 103]). This rubric (stage direction) evidences perhaps the first instance of this horrific motif in the staging of medieval drama.

But it was during the twelfth century that the medieval stage in Europe began to represent the Mouth of Hell with frequency. The rubrics of the two versions of the Anglo-Norman Resurrection play *La seinte Resurreccion* indicate the placing of the structure for hell on the playing area. The older Canterbury manuscript states: "Let Hell be put on one side there, in which will be the devils together with the patriarchs who shall be held there in bonds." The later Paris version simplifies even further: "Let Hell be put on this side and the mansions on the other side." The French play of Saint Lawrence, of 1499, says no more than: "On this side is Hell." That of Saints Crispin and Crispinian (*Le mystère de S. Crespin et S. Crespinien*) states: "Then see there stinking Hell!" And the fifteenth-century Last Judgment play from Rouergue likewise assumes knowledge of hell's location: "The devils shall be at the side (*apart*) when they have come from Hell" (Meredith and Tailby, 76–77). The side of the stage on which the Mouth of Hell was to be located was unspecified because of the long-standing tradition in Christianity that all things considered evil were sinister, that is, of the left-hand path. It was unecessary, therefore, for the rubrics to state the obvious: that hell and its devils belonged on stage left, the side of the adversaries of heaven and the righteous.

The best known of the early examples of the Mouth of Hell in medieval drama is found in the twelfth-century Anglo-Norman *Jeu d'Adam.*[21] (The Continental thirteenth-century manuscript titles it *Ordo representacionis Ade.*) In this *mystère,* the anonymous author, commonly held to have been a priest, gives very precise rubrics as to the destination of Adam and Eve on their demise:

> Then shall the Devil come, and three or four other devils with him, bearing in their hands chains and iron shackles, which they shall place on the necks of Adam and Eve. And certain ones shall push them on, others shall drag them

> toward Hell; other devils, however, shall be close beside Hell, waiting for them as they come, and these shall make a great dancing and jubilation over their destruction; and other devils shall, one after another, point to them as they come; and they shall take them up and thrust them into Hell; and thereupon they shall cause a great smoke to arise, and they shall shout to one another in Hell, greatly rejoicing; and they shall dash together their pots and kettles, so that they may be heard without. And after some little interval, the devils shall go forth, and shall run to and fro in the square (*per plateas*); certain of them, however, shall remain behind in Hell. (Nagler, *Source Book,* 46–47)

Just as with the location of hell or the physical aspect of its devilish horde,[22] it was unnecessary for the rubrics to elaborate on the description of the locus because the convention was well established that the place of eternal punishment was entered through the maw of a monstrous dragon or serpent (Chambers, 86). Plays such as *Jeu d'Adam* had elaborate settings that, reading from stage right to left, culminated in a graphically monstrous Mouth of Hell, into which those who had died in mortal sin would be dragged by grotesque demons. The abysmal fires of hell spewed forth as the Devil's minions performed their gruesome labors before a Christian audience awed by witnessing the materialization of the greatest of its fears: a devouring hell, with its everlasting punishment. The visual and auditory[23] lesson of the theatrical experience had a greater impact than the most imposing "fire and brimstone" sermon.

The Mouth of Hell remained a standard fixture of the mise-en-scène in the centuries that followed. A fourteenth-century German version of the story of the wise and foolish virgins, written entirely in the vernacular, was performed at Eisenach in 1322 under the title *Das Spiel von den Klugen und Torichten Jungfrauen;* in it, the condemned women were taken by demons to the Mouth of Hell, as in the *Sponsus.* Another early fourteenth-century Passion play, from Vienna, contains both the fall of Lucifer into hell and a scene in which successive souls are brought there as well.

The Mouth of Hell reached its apogee in fifteenth-century plays, sometimes manifest in innovative, sometimes in colossal ways. The manuscript of the English morality play *The Castle of Perseverance* (ca. 1425), for one, contains a circular plan that has been surmised to hold the key to its staging (see fig. 5). Beyond the periphery of the outer circle are written five locations, the one on the north assigned to the devil Belial. The placing of the heavenly paradise in the east position, that is, to the left of Belial's abode, would seem to go against the traditional heaven-hell relation; however, on a circular staging area, such a placement is not only tenable but also meaningful when seen as assigning hell a position *counterclockwise* from that of heaven—and, thus, unnatural (read evil). Therefore, Belial is in his proper, if somewhat experimental, place. The setting for the staging of this play in Lincolnshire, England, has been rendered by Southern.

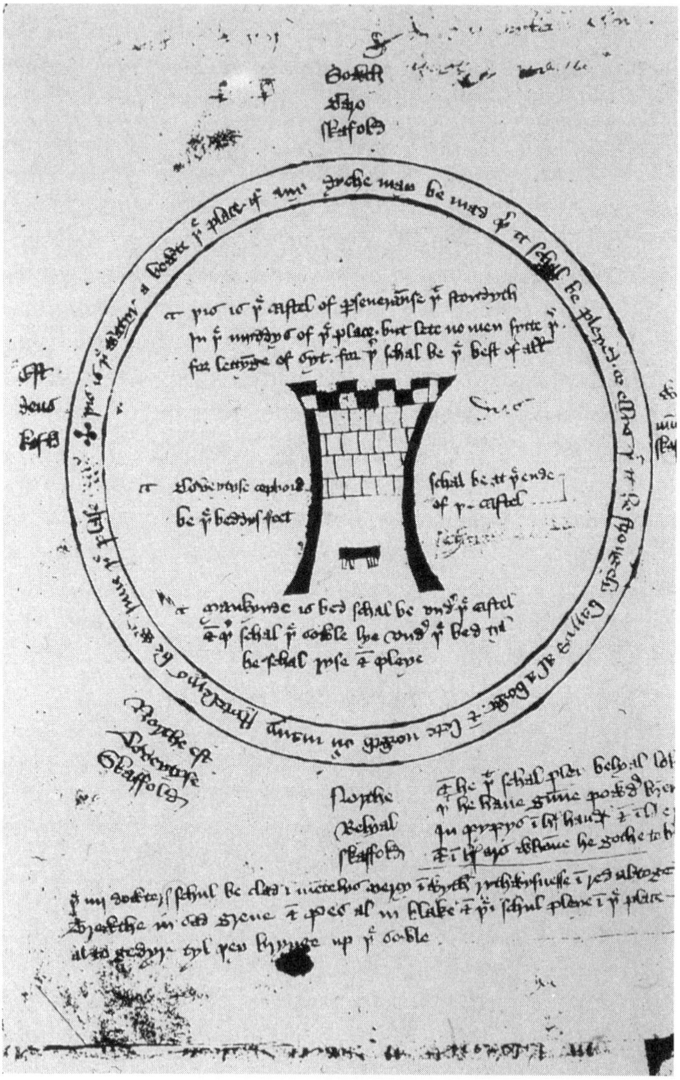

Figure 5. Stage plan for *The Castle of Perseverance* (ca. 1425). By permission of the Folger Shakespeare Library, Washington, D.C., Macro Collection.

The rubrics of fifteenth-century plays, collected by Meredith and Tailby, include a variety of descriptions of hell. The Paris Resurrection play of 1419 associates several elements:

> Here the Anima Christi should shove Satan from the top of the step (*marche*) of the pit (*puytz*) inside, and Satan cries out horribly. This pit should be made between the gate of Hell and the tower of Limbo on the side of the playing space (*champ du jeu*) so as to be more visible, and the said pit must be made in such a way that it seems from outside to be constructed of black dressed stone (*maconné de pierre de taille noire*), and it should be made in such a way that there are formed everywhere inside partitions of mortar (*bousilles*) without them being visible. In one of the sections the Anima Christi shall cast the devils, and from the other shall come forth flaming sulphur, cannon-fire, thunder, and other fearful sounds (*tempestes*) until Satan and the others shall all be cast in. (90)

The Catalan Prades play of the Assumption of Mary, written before 1420, is an example of the motif's use in the Iberian Peninsula; its rubrics read, in part: "Lucifer and the other devils are to make a place which is to be a large Hell (*un loch quey sía infern gran*). And they are to take there an anvil (*anclusa*) and hammers (*mayls*) to make a loud noise when the time comes" (79). One of the more descriptive mentions of the Mouth of Hell appears in the 1437 Metz Passion play: "The gateway and mouth of Hell in this play was very well made, for by a device (*engin*) it opened and closed of its own accord when the devils wanted to go in or come out of it. And this great head (*hure*) had two great steel eyes which glittered wonderfully" (90). In the 1474 Rouen Passion play, the rubric reads: "Hell made like a great mouth (*guelle*) opening and closing as is needful" (90). The Montferrand performance book of 1477 states: "20 March. Item: the said Percheron has given to the said Colas 15d for a bundle of rings (*faysse de cercles*) to make the Hell's mouth. Item: Pierre Noel acknowledges . . . having received . . . the sum of 5s 3d T for the price of a cartload of thorn which was purchased to put round the scaffold of Hell to play the play" (90). And the 1454 Florence celebration of the Feast of John the Baptist included many floats, on one of which the play of the Last Judgment was performed: "Twenty-second, the float of Judgment, with the stretcher for tombs (*barella de'sepolcri*), Paradise, and Hell, and its play (*Rappresentazione*) as in faith we believe it shall be at the end of time" (242).

The stage of the Frankfurt Passion play (ca. 1450), whose text has not been preserved, was "reconstructed" in 1921; the plan shows the traditional throne of God at the top of the Samstagberg and the *portae inferni* at the bottom. The Digby (England) *St. Mary Magdalen,*[24] probably of the late fifteenth century, includes the stage direction: "[A] stage, and a Helle ondyrneth that stage." Other English guild plays, such as that of the Cappers' *Harrowing of Hell* and the Weavers' *Doomsday,* both from Coventry, had a Mouth of Hell (Chambers, 137 n. 3), as did the 1433 Doomsday pageant of York (Johnston and Rogerson, 1:55). But the best visual evidence of the Mouth of Hell in the fifteenth century in what may be a play performance can be garnered from Jean Fouquet's miniature of the play *The Martyrdom of Saint Apollonia* (*Mystère de Sainte Apolline*), painted for a mid-fifteenth-century book of hours.[25] In it can be seen the traditional *loca,* with heaven and hell sited at the extremities of the semicircle, stage right and left, respectively. Two tiered, hell features an upper level with various devils and the lower entrance through the gaping maw in which a demonic host stands ready to receive the damned.

There are many instances in the theater of the sixteenth century where plays continued to focus on the Mouth of Hell.[26] The Belgian *Mystère de la Passion,* held at Mons in 1501, had a Mouth of Hell, as attested by the promptbook of the *meneur de jeu* (production manager), in which were kept records of payments for the plastering of hell (Meredith and Tailby, 91). The 1504 Cornish play *Saint Meriasek,*[27] staged on two days in an earthwork round, provides for scaffolds on the acting circumference. One of these is for the Mouth of Hell, again situated counterclockwise from heaven. In the *Mystère des trois doms* (1509) at Romans, hell's place was in the west, opposite that of heaven, again in a counterclockwise position from the main point of reference; similarly located at the right in Vigil Raber's plan for the church performance is the hell of the 1514 Passion play of Bozen. As in the previous century, the 1526 Doomsday pageant at York included the traditional Mouth of Hell (Johnston and Rogerson, 1:242). The *Mystère des saints actes des Apostres,* presented in 1536 at Bourges, contained a wagon or float on which was erected a huge Mouth of Hell. The description of the pageant is attributed to a local merchant:

> After this infernal crew (*diablerie*) came a Hell, fourteen feet long and eight feet wide, in the form of a rock on which was constructed a tower, continually blazing and shooting out flames in which Lucifer appeared, head and body only. . . . [H]e ceaselessly vomited flames, held in his hands various serpents or vipers which moved and spat fire. At the four corners of the rock were four

> small towers inside which could be seen souls undergoing various torments. And from the front of the rock there came a great serpent whistling and spitting fire from the throat, nostrils, and eyes. And on every part of the rock there clambered and climbed all kinds of serpents and great toads. It was moved and guided by a certain number of people inside it, who worked the torments in the [different] places as they had been instructed. (Meredith and Tailby, 91)

The Passion play of Valenciennes (*Mystère de la Passion*) contains a frontispiece by Hubert Cailleau that gives a total view of the fixed *loca* and *sedes* of the stage,[28] including the grotesque Mouth of Hell in its traditional place on the actor's left (see fig. 6). Not only has this play bequeathed to us the best graphic representation of the motif on the stage of the century in this engraving, but it also prompted a parallel account by Henri d'Outreman of the technical elements that accompanied the 1547 Whitsuntide performance, which lasted twenty-five days: "The machines (*secrets*) of the Paradise and of Hell were absolutely prodigious and could be taken by the populace for magic. For there we saw Truth, the angels and other characters descend

Figure 6. Station stage for the Passion play at Valenciennes, France (1547), frontispiece by Hubert Cailleau. By permission of the Bibliothèque nationale de France, Paris, MS Français 12536.

from very high, sometimes visibly, sometimes invisibly, appearing suddenly. Lucifer was raised from Hell on a dragon without our being able to see how" (Nagler, *Source Book,* 47).

Among the stage sets and properties for the English play *Tobias* (1564), performed in Lincoln, is listed "First, hell mouth with a neither chap" (Craig, 80)—given elsewhere as "First, Hell Mouth with a lower jaw" (Meredith and Tailby, 188)—which item was being stored in a private house. But perhaps the most detailed description of a playing area in the sixteenth century in which the Mouth of Hell appears can be found in the performance record of the Lucerne Passion (*Osterspils*), a two-day event held in 1583 in the city's Weinmarkt.[29] It can be understood better in terms of Renward Cysat's sketch of the setting, with its impressive Mouth of Hell in the southwest part of the playing area:

> 1. Hell at the bottom end of the square towards the *Muligasse,* between the fountain and the Cobblers' Hall, two feet away uphill from the door of said Hall. In front two posts are to be dug in, on which the mouth is hung, drawn up, and lowered, 9½ feet wide. The first post is to be 3½ feet from the Hall. The mouth shall be level with the scaffold (*dem gerüst eben*) beside the fountain on the side facing the square. The length of Hell up to 6 feet away from the door of the Tanners' Hall, towards the fountain. Beside the door (*darneben*) it has a separate closed passageway out. Hell closed in, walled in, also covered over and raised at the rear. The space between Hell and the fountain is to be covered over and also have a stand over it (*verbrügenet sin*) as far as the post on which the mouth hangs—likewise also on the other side, what is free as far (as) the post of the entrance—and forwards it tapers (*werts verloren*) as far as the pillar of the fountain. (Meredith and Tailby, 81)

The Villingen Passion play (ca. 1585) presents a variation on the traditional location of hell. On the extant drawing of the rectangular stage plan,[30] hell appears at the left of the lower register, across from the Garden of Gethsemane, and, thus, is not directly opposite the place of Christ (Golgotha here, the throne of judgment above and behind). The Mouth of Hell also figured in the scene of the Harrowing of Hell. Furthermore, although the text calls for Judas and Beelzebub to glide down to hell together, the stage directions for the suicide of Christ's betrayer are missing, and it is impossible to assess how the lift mechanism worked and where it was located; there is no indication of the point of departure for the aerial journey to the Mouth of Hell.

The motif of the Mouth of Hell was still thought useful as a theatrical device in the seventeenth century, as evidenced, for one, in Spain by Miguel de Cervantes Saavedra's *comedia La casa de los celos y selvas de Ardenia* (see act 2, lines 248–50), wherein the magician Malgesí guards the entrance to the maw, here of a serpent, within which are heard the cries of the damned, and, for another, in England by Christopher Marlowe's *The Tragedy of Doctor Faustus,* in which the magician, uttering, "Ugly hell, gape not" (78), is dragged into hell's mouth on failing to seek God's forgiveness for his pact with Mephistopheles.

From the eleventh century, when the dreaded date of the millennium had passed without incident, the concept of the Mouth of Hell seems to have materialized on the stage to replace the Final Days as a reminder that punishment still awaited the sinner at the end of time. The image derived its power from interpretations in numerous book illuminations, architectural embellishments, and other artistic manifestations that preceded it. Its pervasiveness gives credence to the vulnerability of medieval minds to the idea of eternal punishment for anyone who died in the state of original sin or for a Christian who had not confessed a mortal sin before passing away. And that punishment was believed to begin when the sinner was dragged by devils, as in these plays, into the gaping maw of a great monster, the zoomorphic Mouth of Hell. An image that had its origin in the ancient belief systems of Near and Far Eastern peoples was taken up by medieval Christianity in its religious tracts, church decor, and pageant wagons with unparalleled religious fervor.

Notes

I am indebted to the late Charles Mann, curator of Special Collections, Pattee Library, Pennsylvania State University, Ms. Sandy Stelts, and the rest of the staff for providing me with numerous originals and facsimiles of medieval texts to consult for chapter 1 of this study, as listed below: (1) *Apocalisse,* with extensive wood engravings, analysis by Sergio Samek Ludovici, Latin text from the critical Oxford ed. by J. Wordsworth and H. White, translation and notes by Cesare Angelini (Parma: Franco Maria Ricci, 1969); (2) *The Trinity College Apocalypse: A Reproduction in Facsimile of the Manuscript R.16.2 in the Library of Trinity College, Cambridge* (Cambridge: Roxburghe Club, 1909); (3) *Die Apokalypse*, oldest block-book ed. reprinted in collotype, ed. Paul Kristeller (Berlin: Bruno Cassirer, 1916); (4) *The Dublin Apocalypse,* ed. Montague Rhodes James (Cambridge: Roxburghe Club/Cambridge University Press, 1932); (5) *The Apocalypse in Latin and French: Bodleian Ms. Douce 180,* described by Montague Rhodes James (Oxford: Roxburghe Club, 1922); (6) *Biblia pauperum—Apocalypsis: The Weimar Manuscript,* trans. George Baurley and Leonard

A. Jones (New York: Hacker Art Books, 1978); (7) *Biblia pauperum,* 51, "Codices e Vaticanis selecti quam simillima expressi iussu Ioannis Pauli PP II concilio et opera curatorum Bibliothecae Vaticanae"; (8) *The Sobieski Hours: A Manuscript in the Royal Library at Windsor Castle,* examined by Eleanor P. Spencer (London: Academic, 1977); (9) *Bible Moralisée,* Codex Vindobonensis 2554, Osterreichis-chen Nationalbibliothek; (10) Alfonso X, El Sabio, *Cantigas de Santa María: Edición facsímil del Códice T.I.1 de la Biblioteca de San Lorenzo el Real de El Escorial; Siglo XIII* (Madrid: Edilan, 1979); (11) E. T. Dewald, ed., *The Illustrations of the Utrecht Psalter* (Princeton, N.J.: Princeton University Press, n.d.); (12) Bertram Colgrave, ed., *Early English Manuscripts in Facsimile,* vol. 8, *The Paris Psalter: Ms. Bibliothèque nationale (Paris) Fonds Latin 8824* (Copenhagen: Rosenkilde & Bagger, 1958); (13) *Biblia veteris . . . of Hans Brosamer* (Frankfurt, 1552); and (14) *Vita Christi . . . of Ludolphus de Saxonia* (Venetiis: Guerraeos Fratres et Franciscum, 1581). I am also indebted to Ms. Ingeborg Miller, recent curator of the Slide Collection of the Department of Art History, Pennsylvania State University, for locating and giving me access to numerous Mouth of Hell representations in the university's holdings.

1. *Book of Hours of Catherine of Cleves,* by an unknown master in Utrecht, ca. 1440 (Pierpont Morgan Library, M. 945, fol. 168v). This illuminated manuscript was featured in "The Golden Age of Dutch Manuscript Painting" at the Morgan, March 1–May 6, 1990.

2. The story of Jonah and the whale can be found in the very brief Old Testament Book of Jonah. In it, Jonah had fled by ship to avoid Yahweh's commission to preach in Nineveh: "But the Lord sent out a great wind into the sea, and there was a mighty tempest in the sea, so that the ship was like to broken" (1:4). When the sailors learned from Jonah that his disobedience had caused Yahweh's wrath, they took him and threw him into the sea: "Now the Lord had prepared a great fish to swallow up Jonah. And Jonah was in the belly of the fish for three days and three nights" (1:17). Then Jonah prayed to Yahweh in repentance: "And the Lord spake unto the fish, and it vomited out Jonah upon the dry land" (2:10). Simpson has suggested that the story may be an extended metaphor for an ancient death and resurrection belief. The symbolism of this tale is taken up by Christ as precursory of his own fate when he says: "For as Jonah was three days and three nights in the belly of the whale, so will the Son of Man be three days and three nights in the heart of the earth" (Matt. 12:40).

3. Rahab is a name for Egypt, so the language in Isaiah may be symbolic rather than literal. Rahab is also mentioned in Job 9:13.

4. The name Nehushtan comes from the Hebrew *nahash* or "serpent," from the Vedic serpent god Nahusha, the supreme ruler over all until cast down into the underworld, in yet another variant on the War in Heaven theme (O'Flaherty, 328).

5. Atop Mount Nebo in Jordan, where, tradition has it, Moses was permitted to view the Promised Land, was erected in 1984 a modern iron sculpture of the serpent lifted up by Moses in the desert. The new interpretation of the age-old theme by the Florentine Gianni Fantoni commemorates Moses' act not so much as the Christian version of the serpent on the cross as the prefiguration of the crucified Christ.

6. Having provided Adam and Eve with the means to attain knowledge and,

thus, be like God, the serpent was perceived by Ophites and Gnostics to be as much the benefactor of mankind through its progenitors in the Old Testament as was Prometheus by the ancient Greeks for his daring act of stealing fire from the gods on Mount Olympus to enlighten humanity.

7. Graves (1:27) notes that, in some myths, the Goddess, the Great Mother, punished her consort, the Great Serpent, when he claimed to be the sole creator of the universe by crushing his head underfoot and banishing him to the underworld. The Virgin Mary follows in this tradition, as in Philippe de Mézières's staging of *The Presentation of Mary in the Temple,* performed in Avignon in 1372 (Meredith and Tailby, 220).

8. Biblothèque nationale, MS Lat. 173330.

9. *Hell* is an improper translation of Lucretius's term *infernus,* which in Latin literally meant "an oven placed in the earth." The Roman proverb "The oven is the Mother" can be associated with the Norse Hel, goddess of the underworld, who was thought of "as a cauldron-womb filled with purgative fire" and "may have been related to the idea of the volcanic Mother-mountain" (Walker, 380), as in the Icelandic Hekla, called the Mouth of Hell.

10. Ahriman (from the Vedic deity Aryaman, the creator of the Aryans, i.e., those made of clay), the god of darkness, was the twin brother of Ahura Mazda, the god of light. When his sacrifice was rejected by the supreme deity and his brother's was accepted (as in the Cain and Abel story), Ahriman rebelled against Ahura Mazda and caused the great war in heaven that ended in his defeat and led to his and the *daevas'* fall to the underworld (as in the myth of Prometheus, as in the myth of the fall of the rebel angels). (The *daevas* were beings who supported Ahriman's cause.) Still, Ahriman was considered to be the equal of Ahura Mazda. Out of this dualistic myth emerged the pseudepigraphal account of the fall of Lucifer and the angels in *The Book of Enoch,* later a foundation stone in the patristic view of demonology.

11. Bibliothèque nationale, MS Grec. 923.

12. The theme of a deity that swallows a human being may derive from ancient India, where the monkey god Hanuman is seen emerging from the mouth of the she-devil Surasa. There are also Mongolian images depicting hideous mouths swallowing humans. In a Mogul epic, the mouth of a monster is about to devour Bahman.

13. Besides the maw as an entryway to hell, there are other means of ingress: the pit; the cave; and the gate or portal. All four have extensive iconographies, sometimes related, as at the Abbey of Conques-en-Rouergue, where both the monster's maw and the gate of hell appear on the same relief, with Leviathan emerging through the opening. The "bottomless pit" in which the Dragon (Satan) was imprisoned originates in Saint John the Divine's Book of Revelation (9:1–2, 20:1). Saint John, writing in Patmos, the Greek island, may have been influenced in his conception by the Greek myth of Prometheus, in which the benefactor of humanity, after having been chained to a boulder on the Caucasus, was cast into an abyss for his unbreachable pride in refusing to seek the pardon of Zeus.

14. University Lib. 32, Scrip. Eccl. 484, fols. 1, 9r, 59r, 78r. The sketcher's hand gives ill-defined drawings of hell pits in fols. 1v, 9r, 14v, and 66r. The mid-ninth-century *Utrecht Psalter* resided in England for many centuries, serving as a model

for Anglo-Saxon and later tracts, as in the case of the twelfth-century *Eadwine Psalter* (Cambridge, Trinity College R. 17.1).

15. British Museum, MS Stowe 944, fols. 6v–7r. Part of the manuscript is attributed to the monk Aelsinus. To the right of the lower register is the image of the Mouth of Hell.

16. Vatican Library, MS Reg. Lat. 12. Here, the soul of a sinner is cast into the fiery mouth of a dragon.

17. Pierpont Morgan Library, MS 333, fol. 85.

18. Harrowing of Hell plays seldom employ the Mouth of Hell. Rather, they require the use of gates, which are to fall down or to open on the demand of Christ, as in the apocryphal *Gospel of Nicodemus,* with its "Tollite portas" scene, and liturgical texts used at Eastertide, among them a homily of Augustine and various antiphons. An example is the Middle English (ca. 1250) fragment known as the *Harrowing of Hell* (see Kretzmann). However, the epic poetry of Germany equated the word for door with the mouth of a building, thus the identification in the Anglo-Saxon verses of *The Whale* ("those grim jaws / the gates of hell" [Galpern, 144]) and in *Beowulf* (when Grendel "tore open / the mouth of the hall" [Galpern, 144]). In some instances, the zoomorphic Mouth of Hell awaits the sinner behind the gates of hell, as in the frieze at Conques and the lower register illustration of the Last Judgment in the *Liber vitae.*

19. The feast day celebrating the Body of Christ was instituted in 1264 by Pope Urban IV. The consecrated Host or Eucharist was taken in procession through the streets and then installed on the main altar of the church or cathedral for veneration throughout the day. These public rituals not only reminded the populace of the central mystery of the faith but also demonstrated the power of the church as the sole purveyor of Christianity in medieval society, especially in the light of the encroachments of secularism. In providing a day of rest from labor on the Feast of Corpus Christi, the church gave notice to rulers and populace that it could continue to impose its will on society.

20. Tradition holds that Golgotha was not only the place of the execution of Jesus of Nazareth but also that of the birth and burial of Adam; thus, the blood of the crucified Christ was held to have fallen on Adam's skull and redeemed him (Eliade, 14). The tree used to make Christ's cross was believed to have grown from a seedling taken from Eden and planted on Adam's grave on Golgotha (Hase, 11). A map of Iceland dated 1585 locates the Mouth of Hell at a volcano named Hekla; this is a throwback to classical concepts (Walker, 380).

21. Municipal Library of Tours, MS 927.

22. In the twelfth-century Latin *Dispute of the Body and Soul,* devils are described in anthropomorphic terms as possessing animal characteristics such as wings, claws or talons, tails, and hairy bodies. Furthermore, they exude fire and smoke (à la dragons) since they are denizens of hell.

23. Meredith and Tailby catalog many of the special visual (fire, fireworks) and auditory (drums, cannon, explosions) effects used in medieval plays to convey the awesome nature of hell and its denizens. In Rouen (1474): "Then all the devils cry out together with the drums and other thunderings made by machines (*engins*), and the cannon (*couleuvrines*) are shot off and flames of fire are thrown out from

the nostrils, the eyes, and the ears [of the Hell's mouth]" (157). In Mons, payments are listed for the thunder-making machine: "[F]or two large vellum skins used for a cask of fir wood (*thonneau de sapin*) and a skin of parchment used to cover a cauldron; all this for Hell: 36s. . . . [C]auldron-maker (*caudrelier*) for the depreciation (*amenrissement*) of two large, flat bronze basins (*bachins d'airain*) lent by him for the said Mystery and which were put in Hell to make thunder. . . . [F]or a pound of brass used both for the Pinnacle (*Pinacle*) and for joining together two copper basins (*bachins de keuvre*) for some effect (*secres*) in Hell, 14s. . . . Item: for a pivot of iron and for four pieces of iron and four eyelets to turn on it and two handles (*manevelles*), 16 fasteners (*crampons*) to attach them to two great vats (*keuvres*) to make thunder in Hell, weighing 24 lbs. at 2s the 1 lb., 48s" (157–58). In Modane (1580): "They shall make and supply fireworks for the costume of the play (*des istoires*) for each of the devils every time they emerge from Hell and for Lucifer each time he speaks, each day" (105).

24. Bodleian Library, Digby MS 133, fol. 95.

25. *Livre d'heures pour maitre Etienne Chevalier* (ca. 1452–56), Musée Condé de Chantilly.

26. One case in which the stage plan (in the Landesbibliothek, Kassel) omits hell is the German Alsfeld Passion play, presented in 1501. But the rubrics indicate "that Hell was a large barrel, which had a door that could be closed and a window. Lucifer climbs onto this barrel ('*ascendit doleum*') to make his address to the devils" (Nagler, *Medieval Religious Stage,* 34).

27. *Ordinale de vita sancti Mereadoci Episcopi et Confessoris* (National Library of Wales).

28. Bibliothèque nationale, Paris, MS Français 12536.

29. Original in the Zentralbibliothek, Lucerne.

30. Original in the Fürstlich Fürstenbergische Hofbibliothek, Donaueschingen. For the controversy over the relation of the stage plan to the Donaueschingen Passion play (ca. 1485) in which it was found in the mid-nineteenth century, see Nagler, *Medieval Religious Stage,* 36–47.

Works Cited

Aristophanes. *The Frogs.* Translated by Richmond Lattimore. Ann Arbor: University of Michigan Press, 1962.

Axton, Richard. *European Drama of the Early Middle Ages.* Pittsburgh: University of Pittsburgh Press, 1975.

Bessy, Maurice. *A Pictorial History of Magic and the Supernatural.* London: Spring, 1964.

The Book of the Secrets of Enoch [i.e., *The Book of Enoch*]. In *The Other Bible,* ed. Willis Barnstone. San Francisco: Harper & Row, 1984.

Caedmon. *Archaeologia.* Vol. 24.

Calkins, Robert G. *Illuminated Books of the Middle Ages.* Ithaca, N.Y.: Cornell University Press, 1983.

Cervantes Saavedra, Miguel de. *La casa de los celos o selvas de Ardenia.* In *Obras completas.* Madrid: Aguilar, 1962.

Chambers, E. K. *The Medieval Stage.* Vol. 2. London: Oxford University Press, 1903.

Comay, Joan, and Ronald Brownrigg. *Who's Who in the Bible.* New York: Bonanza, 1980.

Craig, Hardin. "Note on the Home of *Ludus Conventriae.*" *Bulletin of the University of Minnesota,* October 1914, 72–83.

Davidson, Clifford, C. J. Gianakaris, and John H. Stroupe, eds. *The Drama in the Middle Ages: Comparative and Critical Essays.* New York: AMS, 1982.

Democritus. [Moral reflections]. In *Die Fragmente der Vorsokratiker,* ed. Hermann Diels, vol. 2. Berlin, 1936. Reprint, Zürich: Weidmann, 1985.

Dronke, Peter. *Poetic Individuality in the Middle Ages.* London: University of London, Westfield College, 1986.

Eliade, Mircea. *Cosmos and History.* New York: Harper & Row/Harper Torchbooks, 1959.

Enslin, Morton Scott. *Christian Beginnings.* New York: Harper & Bros., 1938.

Frye, Roland Mushat. *Milton's Imagery and the Visual Arts: Iconographic Tradition in the Epic Poems.* Princeton, N.J.: Princeton University Press, 1978.

Galpern, Joyce Ruth Manheimer. "The Shape of Hell in Anglo-Saxon England." PhD diss., University of California, Berkeley, 1978.

Genesis B. See Timmer.

Graves, Robert. *The Greek Myths.* 2 vols. New York: Penguin, 1955.

Gréban, Arnoul, and Simon Gréban. *Relation de l'ordre de la triomphante et magnifique monstre dy Mystère des Saints Actes des Apostres.* Edited by Jacques Thiboust. Bourges, 1836. Geneva: Slatkine Reprints, 1975.

Harrsen, Meta. *Central European Manuscripts in the Pierpont Morgan Library.* New York: Pierpont Morgan Library, 1958.

Harrsen, Meta, and George K. Boyce. *Italian Manuscripts in the Pierpont Morgan Library.* New York: Pierpont Morgan Library, 1953.

Harthan, John. *The History of the Illustrated Book: The Western Tradition.* London: Thames & Hudson, 1981.

Hase, Karl. *Miracle Plays and Sacred Dramas: A Historical Survey.* Translated by A. W. Jackson. London: Trübner, 1880.

The Holy Bible. Authorized King James Version. New York: Abradale, 1959. All citations except those of Job (Job 3:8 in this translation not mentioning Leviathan) are to this edition.

The Holy Bible. St. Joseph New Catholic Edition. New York: Catholic Book Publishing, 1962. All citations of Job are to this edition.

Homer. *The Odyssey.* Translated by E. V. Rieu. Baltimore: Penguin, 1956.

Hughes, Robert. *Heaven and Hell in Western Art.* New York: Stein & Day, 1968.

Johnston, Alexandra, and Margaret Rogerson, eds. *Records of Early English Drama: York.* 2 vols. Toronto: University of Toronto Press, 1979.

Kretzmann, Paul Edward. "The Liturgical Element in the Earliest Forms of the Medieval Drama." *Bulletin of the University of Minnesota,* December 1916, 128–33.

Lima, Robert. "La Gueule de l'enfer: Iconographie de la damnation dans le théâtre de l'époque médiévale." In *Enfer et paradis: L'au-delà dans l'art et la littérature en Europe,* 205–18. Conques: Les Cahiers de Conques, March 1995. For an English translation, see Lima 1996.

———. "The Mouth of Hell: The Iconography of Damnation on the Stage of the Middle Ages." In *European Iconography East and West,* ed. György E. Szönyi, 35–48. Symbola et Emblemata Series. Leiden: Brill, 1996.

Lucretius. *The Nature of the Universe.* Translated by Ronald Latham. Baltimore: Penguin, 1951.

Male, Emile. *Religious Art from the Twelfth to the Eighteenth Century.* New York: Noonday, 1949.

Marlowe, Christopher. *The Tragedy of Doctor Faustus.* New York: Washington Square/Folger Library, 1959.

Meredith, Peter, and John E. Tailby, eds. *The Staging of Religious Drama in Europe in the Later Middle Ages: Texts and Documents in English Translation.* Early Drama, Art, and Music Monograph Series, no. 4. Kalamazoo: Medieval Institute Publications/Western Michigan University, 1983.

Milosevic, Desanka. *The Last Judgment.* Translated by George H. Genzel and Hans Rosenwald. New York: Catholic Art Book Guild, 1964.

Nagler, A. M. *A Source Book in Theatrical History.* New York: Dover, 1952.

———. *The Medieval Religious Stage: Shapes and Phantoms.* New Haven, Conn.: Yale University Press, 1976.

Newbigin, Nerida. "Plays, Printing and Publishing, 1485–1500: Florentine *Sacre Rappresentazioni.*" *La bibliofilia,* November 1988, 269–296.

Nilsson, Martin P. *Greek Folk Religion.* Philadelphia: University of Pennsylvania Press, 1972.

O'Flaherty, Wendy Doniger. *Hindu Myths.* Harmondsworth: Penguin, 1975.

Plato. *The Republic.* Translated by W. H. D. Rouse. In *Great Dialogues of Plato,* ed. Eric H. Warmington and Philip G. Rouse. New York: Mentor/New American Library, 1956.

Preminger, Alex, and Edward L. Greenstein, eds. *The Hebrew Bible in Literary Criticism.* New York: Ungar, 1986.

Rothe, Edith. *Medieval Book Illumination in Europe: The Collections of the German Democratic Republic.* New York: Norton, 1968.

Saint Caesarius of Arles: Sermons 2. Washington, D.C.: Catholic University of America Press, 1964.

Schmidt, Gary D. *The Iconography of the Mouth of Hell: Eighth-Century Britain to the Fifteenth Century.* Selingsgrove, Pa.: Susquehanna University Press, 1995.

Simpson, W. *The Jonah Legend: A Suggestion of Interpretation.* London: Grant Richards, 1899.

Southern, Richard. *The Seven Ages of the Theatre.* New York: Hill & Wang, 1963.

Timmer, B. J., ed. *The Later Genesis: Edited from MS. Junius II.* Oxford: Scrivener, 1948. Includes *Genesis B.*

Walker, Barbara G. *The Woman's Encyclopedia of Myths and Secrets.* San Francisco: Harper & Row, 1983.

Wickham, Glynne. *The Medieval Theatre.* Cambridge: Cambridge University Press, 1987.

Wieck, Rogers. *Time Sanctified: The Book of Hours in Medieval Art and Life.* New York: Brazillier, 1988.

Young, Karl. *The Drama of the Medieval Church.* 2 vols. Oxford: Clarendon, 1967.

Part II

Metamorphoses of Gods

2

The Masks of Harlequin

Daemonic Antecedents of the Commedia dell'Arte Character

Down, down to Hell, from whence ye rose.

—Mercury in *Harlequin Student*

When the god Mercury speaks these words of damnation in the final scene of *Harlequin Student; or, The Fall of Pantomime, with the Restoration of the Drama,*[1] he is addressing Harlequin and his fellows, English pantomime players out of the commedia dell'arte tradition. The Greek god's vituperation speaks to what was once generally known but has lately been forgotten: the origin of Harlequin is demonic and lies within the dark recesses of antiquity. Mercury's words may be ironic in that a pagan deity damns the players to hell, but the anonymous dramatist is, after all, addressing a Christian audience. The damnatory words are, consequently, effective in tying together the various religious and cultural traditions at play in the evolution of Harlequin from pre-Christian daemon to commedia dell'arte and pantomime jester.

The epithet *commedia dell'arte* defines and allies the peripatetic Italian theater companies that, from the sixteenth century through the eighteenth, traversed the continent of Europe performing comic scenarios that were largely improvisational in nature, first on outdoor platforms, carts, or other makeshift stages, and later indoors in the drawing rooms, salons, and theaters of the palaces of nobles and high churchmen. It was largely through the commedia dell'arte troupes, following on medieval pageants, that the secular theater of Europe was reinstated after the long hiatus caused by the church's condemnation of all manner of public entertainments owing to excesses during the decline of Rome. In bringing popular theater back to the populace, the commedia dell'arte in effect revived the Western tradition of comedy, which had been born in ancient Greece and had lain moribund since the fifth century of the modern era.[2]

The outstanding comic figure on the commedia dell'arte stage was the masked, motley-dressed, acrobatic character known as Arlecchino on the

---

Previous page: Masked Harlequin Astride a Bedecked Steed, German and Latin inscriptions, anonymous, provenance unknown. Public domain.

Italian Peninsula,[3] as Harlekin in Germany, as Harlequin in France and England, and as Arlequín in Spain, these being among the most prominent of his stage identities. The doings of Arlecchino and his cronies were promulgated by such as the I Comici Confidenti, the I Comici Gelosi (at one time I Comici Uniti), and the I Comici Fedeli, which, along with the most famed sixteenth-century troupe, that led by Alberto Ganassa, were the leading Italian theater companies of this kind.

Such was the popularity of Arlecchino that the character, who had a secondary role at first (he was usually the second *zanni,* a buffoon or clown), soon took center stage and was often portrayed by the company's leading actor, as in the case of Ganassa. Furthermore, Arlecchino's uniqueness soon made him the subject of both anonymous illustrators and eminent painters from the sixteenth century forward, even to the present era.[4]

Arlecchino was not only the most memorable of the masked characters of the commedia dell'arte but also the most enigmatic owing to the shroud of mystery surrounding his origin, name, manner, costume, and mien. The Italian Arlecchino had existed in other guises and functioned in other venues long before he became the dominant male figure on the stage of the European Renaissance. In previous antique manifestations, he was anything but the zany, doltish servant, said to be from lower Bergamo, who entertained populace and royalty alike at street and court performances.

To fathom the complex essence of Arlecchino, therefore, it is requisite that the elements contributing to the holism of this character be assessed fully. To that end, the delineation of the genealogy, the derivation of the appellation, the conventions of the manner, and the conceptualization of the costume, head cover, and mask of Arlecchino will each be treated separately.

Genealogy

The ancestral lineage of Arlecchino is both ancient and exotic. There are two principal veins in his bloodline, the first being the Central and Northern European barbaric culture, the second the classical tradition of the Mediterranean. Each contributed disparate elements to the evolution of the complex figure that ultimately established itself in the forefront of the commedia dell'arte scenarios.

Belief in nature deities in pagan times often became transformed in the Christian era. There are numerous instances in which such gods and goddesses became transmogrified, being given the role of purveyors of evil in the new faith. Among these is the figure that has come to be known as Harlequin.

The oldest known references that relate to Arlecchino's barbaric lineage clearly show his ancestors to be daemonic. The *Historiae ecclesiasticae libri XIII,* a Norman manuscript by Ordericus Vitalis (1075–1143?), is the earliest extant *written* reference in this context. The Anglo-Norman monk who is its author narrates a legend—perhaps based on a real-life incident—centering on a supernatural encounter experienced by a certain Gauchelin, a French monk, when he was returning late at night to his abode in Bonneval, near Chartres. The text refers to his being accosted by a hellish band: "Haec sine dubio familia Herlichini est" (Vitalis, 3:376). Clearly, the monk in the narrative had been beset by the "family of Herlichin," a "spectral host of relentless demons who marauded the countryside on certain winter nights, at the same time of year as the Carnival celebrations, rampaging through forests and valleys, destroying everything in their path" (Husband, 152–53). Gauchelin recognizes his assailants as the nefarious group that had come to be known among the populace as the Wild Horde, infamous beings out of a very widespread European folkloric tradition.[5] The procession of damned souls is led by a gigantic figure with a club whose proper name is given as "Hellekins." This will prove to be the earliest-known *written* version of the name that would ultimately become Arlecchino.

The fact that this episode, narrated in the twelfth century, is so well delineated indicates that the belief in the Wild Horde and its daemonic leader had currency much earlier. Ordericus Vitalis's account is surely not an isolated one, only the earliest found to date. It is followed by others, narratives that show how deeply embedded was the belief in the Wild Horde and its leader in the imagination of the Middle Ages, particularly in France.

The continuity of the topos can be seen in the thirteenth century, which provides further folkloric and literary references to Hellekin and his cohorts in the works of several church and secular authors. For one, Wilhelm of Auvergne, bishop of Paris at his death in 1248, verifies the wide range of the belief in the daemonic figures when he refers to the tradition in Spain in his *Tractatus de universo:* "De equitibus vero nocturnis qui vulgari gallicano 'Hellequin' et vulgari hispanico 'exercitus antiquus' vocantur, nondum tibi satisfeci, quia nondum declarare intendo qui sint; nectamen certum est eos malignos spiritus esse" (par. 2, chap. 12; Driesen, 239). That the folkloric figure crossed over into literature proper is also evident in the same century. The Norman poet Bourdet narrates in the verse "Lay de Luque la Maudite" the tale of a lascivious old witch of Rouen who on her deathbed calls on "Hellequin" to marry her. In response, the daemon leads three thousand of his hellish kin to the wedding feast and, ultimately, takes her soul into his realm, hell. In this text, as elsewhere, Hellequin has an obvious appeal as a sexual being to a dying woman; in being tied to the lure of death, he also represents the daemon-lover, which is what Hades is in the Persephone myth (McClelland, 100–102).

Another telling identification of Arlecchino with the daemonic in the thirteenth century is found in *Le jeu de la feuillée* (*Li jus Adan ou de la feuillie* [Play of the bower], ca. 1276), a work ascribed to Adam de la Halle (Adam le Bossu), in which "Herlequin," the ruler of the underworld (McClelland, 99; Carré Cartier, 132), seeks to woo the fairy Morgue through the agency of the daemon Crokesot (Croquesot in later texts) rather than in person. Unfortunately, Herlequin himself does not appear on-stage, choosing to remain invisibly ensconced in his nether kingdom.

In this belief system of barbaric origin, the first of the two veins, Arlecchino is seen to derive from a daemon, named Hellequin first and then Herlequin, out of old French (Boulogne) folklore, who becomes manifest in literary texts in the thirteenth century. But this figure is itself derivative.

The ascendant of the medieval French daemon evolved out of Norse and Teutonic mythological beings who came to be known in Germany and adjacent areas as the "Teufel Herlekin" (Driesen, viii) or Hellekin (i.e., "Kin of Hel"), Hel or Hela being the goddess of the Norse underworld. As Hel's consort, Ellerkonge (variant Elverkonge) was the male deity of the sacred alder (elder) tree and of the land of the dead. The mistranslation of the Danish Ellerkonge gave Erlkönig, king of the elves in a Germanic saga. As Erl King, yet another variant, he was a German and Scandinavian spirit or personified natural power akin to Odin who led a band of ghostly riders across the night sky. In Middle English, he is Herleking, while King Herla is the name of another mythical manifestation of the deity in England.

Herlekin is the probable source of Herne the Hunter, the phallic horned god variously known in the British Isles under such names as the Green Man, Jack-in-the-Green, Robin-of-the-Wood, Robin Goodfellow, and Robin Hood.[6] These are all manifestations of the King of the May, the ancient fertility deity whose phallus became the symbolic maypole featured in May Day celebrations held throughout Europe to welcome the rebirth (and impregnation) of Mother Earth in spring. The magical season of nature's fecundity was emulated in rituals of sympathetic magic that culminated in sexual coupling.

Such fertility figures in the British Isles and on the Continent derive from a very early, perhaps Paleolithic, being generally known as the Wild Man,[7] a larger-than-life, often gigantic creature covered in hair, fur, lichen, twigs, or leaves whose primal identity was tied to the woodlands, symbolized by the uprooted tree he carried, usually over his shoulder or in his hand (see fig. 7). Later, in Carnival celebrations, in the wedding-night pandemonium called *charivari* (chivaree), and in rites known as the Wild Man

Figure 7. *Wild Man with Tree in Hand,* Woodhouse type, anonymous, sixteenth century, provenance unknown. Public domain.

Hunt, a massive studded club was often substituted for the traditional tree.[8] Paraphrasing Chrétien de Troyes, Husband describes this elemental being as "an ogrish wild man, black like a Moor, large and hideous, sitting on a tree stump and holding a large club in his hand" (2), while Bernheimer cites the anonymous medieval French *Renaud de Montaubon* for its description of such marginal beings as "black and hairy like a chained bear" ("noir et velu com ours enchainé" [16]).[9]

In one of the strange symbioses that sometimes occur in folklore, the Wild Man came to be associated with mythological beings and himself was held to be daemonic. One of the identities of the savage is Orcus (literally, Wild Man), a telluric deity out of the Gallo-Roman era who led the processions of the dead and who, as a daemon of death, had an association with Pluto or Hades, the lord of the underworld in classical mythology. In the Tyrolean "Virginal," the epic gives the variant Orkise as the name of a cannibalistic hunter in the form of an ogre (Bernheimer, 130). The functions of Orcus as leader of the Wild Horde came to be preempted by the daemon Hellekin, whose name was variously given as Herlekin, Herlechin, Harlekin, and Herlequin or Harlequin in medieval France.

Similarly in the second vein, the complex world of classical and Eastern mythologies, there are several figures who are clearly antecedents of Arlecchino's earliest relative, the Wild Man: "The hairy Enkidu, who, in the Babylonian epic *Gilgamesh,* lives with and protects wild animals and is alternately referred to as a man and a beast, can be viewed as a prototype of the medieval wild man" (Husband, 10). The giant Polyphemus, the leader of the Cyclopes in the *Odyssey,* and the fabled Hercules, who wore the pelt of a lion and brandished a great club, as did the half-animal, half-human Centaurs, were also likely antecedents of the Wild Man. So too were the woodland deities Silvanus, who had the sapling of a cypress in his hand, and especially Silenus, who, like the Wild Man, carried an uprooted tree from his forest realm and was depicted with a thick coat of hair on Greek and Roman kraters, sculptures, and murals.

Besides such prominent deities, there are figures of lesser position in the pantheons of classical antiquity whose similarity to Arlecchino is suggestive of ancestry. Out of the Greek theater comes "an actor dressed now in the skin of a goat, now in the skin of a tiger, variegated in colour, which clung tightly to his body, armed with only a wooden staff, his head shaved, and covered by a white hat, his face by a brown mask; he was called by the vulgar the young satyr" (Sand, 59). Some of these beings of reduced status have survived into the present day in folk festivals and propitiatory rites.

Among them are such fertility figures from across the Mediterranean as Sardinia's Sos Mamuttones or Mamutti (see fig. 8), which means "daemon" or "spirit of the earth," and Kalogeros, from Greece, whose hairy costumes are accompanied by dark masks, large bells, and sticks with animal blad-

Figure 8. Mamuttone, festival at Mamoiada, Nuoro, in Sardinia, Italy. Photograph by the author.

ders.[10] Strikingly similar figures are also found in Germany. To this day, the Venetian Carnevale features such hairy masked relatives of the Wild Man.

In time, the uncivilized behavior of such untamed beings became the object of civilized man's arts. The Wild Man came to play an important role in medieval theater, for one. Richard Bernheimer refers to the *Magnus ludus de homine salvatico,* a major play put on in 1208 during Pentecost, and to another performance in 1224, both in Padua, adding that little is recorded about these productions. The same, he states, is true in the case of later plays about the Wild Man: "We know no more about the *Ludus at virum dictum wildman* acted in 1399 in Aarau, Switzerland. This ignorance is the more regrettable since the Italian plays, at least, are not only among the first instances of theatrical activity in that country since the demise of the Roman theater, but also the first documented examples of wild man plays. But we shall note at least that these performances took place in Italy and in the part of it that is contiguous to the Alps" (51). Another medieval play in which the Wild Man appeared is an English masque of 1348 in which is found a textual reference to "capita de woodewose" (Bernheimer, 71).[11] If this is, indeed, an identification of the chieftan of the satyrs or fauns, that is, the Wild Man, then the English masque is next in the chronology of such plays after the two Italian examples.

This is germane because it demonstrates that ancestors to Hellekin can be found not only in the Wild Man topoi of German folklore but also in theatrical contexts, which are, of course, especially pertinent to the lineage of Arlecchino. In such festivals as the pre-Lenten Carnival, the Wild Man played an important role in connection with fertility dances of pagan origin, such as those performed by the Butchers' Guild and the religious processions that culminated in a "play," as in the 1539 Nuremberg *Schembartlauf,* where there are four manifestations of the Wild Man depicted in the storming of Hölle (hell) along with a fool in a motley costume reminiscent of Arlecchino's.

Such varied Central and Northern European sources in the evolution of Arlecchino are logical in the geopolitical sense since northern Italy was, in fact, largely Teutonic in antiquity prior to Rome and again after the fall of the empire, when hordes of "barbarians," the hirsute elements from beyond the borders, swept into the Italian Peninsula, often resettling ancient sites. Bergamo, northeast of Milan, not only was at the crossroads of the postempire invasions but belonged to the earlier Teutonic sphere of influence. It was to be expected, then, that Arlecchino, said by Italian chauvinists to have been born in lower Bergamo, should possess the name and characteristics of earlier Teutonic deities, whose lot it was to be associated with the Devil under Christianity. In some instances, others were later to be turned into fools on the late-medieval and Renaissance stages, as was the case with Arlecchino.

Within the second vein of Arlecchino's ancestry, the Mediterranean, can be seen additional precursory elements deriving from the mythological, folkloric, and comedic traditions of Greece and Rome (including the Etruscan) in classical antiquity.

The ancient comic theater has provided some historians and critics with grist for the mill of conjecture. But if, in fact, other of Arlecchino's cohorts on the commedia stage have close kinships with such comedic types from antiquity, the same is not true for Arlecchino himself. At best tangential, his associations are limited to stage business and the use of a mask; these are insufficient to establish a sound base for developing a lineage out of the comic characters of classical comedy. Arlecchino's singularity makes any potential equation void de facto.

Other contexts prove more fruitful, however. As has been demonstrated, ancient mythologies of the Mediterranean and its adjacent regions have contributed many antecedents, deific beings in particular, to the genealogy of Arlecchino's earliest human progenitor, the Wild Man. One such is the Greek Hercules, as proposed by Battisti after Nicolini; another is Silenus, along with the additional ancestral figures discussed earlier.

What is verifiable is Arlecchino's rootstock—the daemonic and deific ancestry out of Norse and Teutonic beliefs, on the one hand, and, in a different manner, out of Mediterranean mythology, on the other. His genealogical tree is replete with telluric and cosmic ancestors out of these diverse systems of belief with probable origins at the dawn of humanity. The impact of the daemonic figure that was Herlekin must have been great in the popular imagination for it to have persevered for so many centuries as a myth. But then, having been confronted with modern knowledge and its attendant change in attitudes, which at best tolerated it as fiction, the old belief became transfigured when incorporated in Arlecchino, the outrageous stage character of the commedia dell'arte during the sixteenth century. As Driesen has it, citing in German, the title of the first extant manuscript of a play in which Harlequin actually appears is *Lustige Geschicte von den Handlungen und Heldentaten Harlekins, italienischen Komödianten* (158). The play, discovered in Paris by Emile Picot,[12] had been published in the French capital by Didier Millot in 1585 as *Histoire plaisante des faicts et gestes de Harlequin commedien italien . . .* (Driesen, 249). Its plot directly relates the protagonist to things hellish, if in a comic manner, when he descends into Pluto's realm, charming his way across Styx and into Persephone's bed, and rescuing the madam Mutter Cardine, who had been wed to Cerberus on her death (McClelland, 100–101), in a motif that gives an interesting variant of the thirteenth-century Luque la Maudite's wedding with Hellekin, Lord of Hell.

In effect, Arlecchino became the leader of a very different group, the "wild horde" of masked comedians who began to gambol on sixteenth-century stages throughout Europe and continued thereafter to keep alive, if in a manner more palatable to the times, the ancient traditions of the deific and daemonic figures who were Arlecchino's ancestors.

Etymology

The origin of the name Arlecchino has been problematic to theater historians for centuries, and it continues to be a source of much speculation. Potential antecedents come from a variety of sources and cultures, among them Dante's *Inferno,* Norse and Teutonic mythologies, medieval French tradition, and Italian folklore. Yet there has not been a systematic examination of these toward as definitive an etymology as it is possible to formulate.

The single known use in the Italian Peninsula of a related name prior to the appearance of Arlecchino in the late 1500s is in the *Inferno* (written in the first decade of the fourteenth century), where the minor devil Alichino (canto 21, line 118), later Alichin (canto 22, line 112), appears as a torturer of those damned for barratry in the fifth circle. According to Caffi, Dante could have derived the name of his devil from Allequinus, a Latinate name used by the French Dominican Etienne de Bourbon in his thirteenth-century work *Tractatus de diversis materiis praedicabililus.* What is more important here is that, in both cases, the name is that of a daemonic being. On the other hand, Rossetti posited an etymology, now discredited, founded on Aliotti, the name of a Florentine prior ca. 1303.

The late Italian cultural historian Eugenio Battisti turns to the classical world for a possible source. He sees a relationship between the name of Arlecchino and that of Ercole, the Hercules of Greek mythology: "Questa figura, connessa d'altronde ad una tematica extraeuropea, ebbe una notevole fortuna nel teatro medioevale e nella sacra rappresentazione; entro piú volte mella scultura lignea, e sta, secondo una suggestiva ipotesi, anche etimologicamente al l'origine dell'Arlecchino" (91). The variant Herculinus also supplies suggestive connotations.[13] Elsewhere, in a 1592 source,[14] there is another reference on the speculation Hercules-Harlekin: "Im Jahre 1592 finden wir die entsprechende lateinische Form im Anti-Chopin: '. . . nicht um eine Maskerade aufzuführen oder um die Rolle des Herkules oder Harlekin in der Komödie zu spielen . . .' '. . . non ut faceret mascarandam, vel ut luderet personam Herculis vel Harlequini in Comoedia . . .'" (Driesen, 18).

Also discussing the origin of the name Arlecchino, M. L. Sainéan traces it to the dogs used in the hunt of birds and animals in France: "These popular traditions taken together reveal the predominance of the dog in this legend, which is entirely natural, since the subject is a hunt. Hellequin was in consequence interpreted as *hélechien,* literally a 'dog-caller' (*chien* or dog, taking the form of *quin* in the Norman dialect: a 'haloo-hound' let loose on the game)" (quoted in Duchartre, 138).

Another conjecture appears in *Poussières d'Italie* by Dominique Durandy, who conveys that documents in Bergamo tell of a French lord resident in the vicinity around 1356 who had brought with him a disreputable valet. Wounded in the face while committing thievery, the lout was identified in the indictment as Pietro the Harlequin (for he said that he had been born in Arles) and was forced into exile for his crime: "Dressed in baize, with a wooden sword at his side, and covered from head to foot with as many patches as there are colours in the banners of those whose justice he had defied, he was placed upon a donkey and conducted to the frontier. . . . [T]he following year a band of rowdy drunkards took it into their heads to make themselves up like Harlequin, dressing grotesquely . . . with a wooden lathe and a black mask in imitation of the bandage which the condemned man had worn over his wound" (Duchartre, 136–37).

Yet another proponent argues that the name of the character originated in that of a leader of Parliament, a certain Hachille du Harlay. Having taken under his patronage an actor who played the role of a particular *zanni,* Harlay's name became attached to him, and the comedian was thereafter known as Harlayquino (Duchartre, 137).

The commedia characters themselves often gave outrageous etymologies. For one, the seventeenth-century actor Giuseppe Domenico Biancolelli, known in France as Dominique, gave his own concoction. Having identified himself as Arlecchino Sbrufadelli (lit. "water," i.e., spittle, spitter, thus braggart), he proceeds to tell how his father, fearful that someone would be lying in wait as he traveled with the as-yet-unnamed child, would shout to his donkey: "Ar! lé chin!" (Get moving! He's going to pounce!). The journey safely over, the father laughed at his own antics and christened his son Arlecchino.[15]

There are many other interpretations. Giacomo Oreglia, for one, suggests that the primogenitor of the character's name may be "Hoillequin or Hellequin of Boulogne, a knight who lived in the ninth century and who died fighting against the Normans, giving rise to a legend of damned devils (*chase Arlequin*). This last conjecture is certainly the most probable" (56). There is an obvious confusion here of the knight with the leader of the Wild Horde, thus his unexplained and, therefore, unmerited association with the damned.

But there are more plausible antecedents. In her succinct assessment of Hel, Norse goddess of the underworld, Barbara G. Walker speaks of the Old High German "ancestral ghosts known as *Hella cunni,* 'kinsmen of Hel,' corrupted in the medieval mystery play to Harlequin" (380). She may be referring to the French work by Adam de la Halle, whose own name presents a variant of Hel and Hölle. In the play, Hellekin is the ruler of the underworld, in some dark era having supplanted the classical Lord of the Dead, variously Pluto or Hades. It is from this line that Arlecchino inherits his sometime identification with death and hell in commedia dell'arte scenarios as well as his identity of daemon-lover, as noted by McClelland.

In the same line of folkloric antecedents, Otto Driesen's very thorough assessment early in this century of the origins of Arlecchino posits that the name of the character in the commedia dell'arte was derived from the medieval French daemon Herlequin, apparently first identified in writing as Harlequin in a 1514 French manuscript written in Latin (Driesen, 18, citing Paris, 324). The variant in spelling between the folkloric Herlequin and the manuscript Harlequin may be due to a difference in pronunciation in the Parisian dialect of the period, but the dichotomy is minor since *herle* and *harle* both mean "hair" (from *hure*) in Old French and Old English.[16] Exemplary of this is the thirteenth-century play *Le jeu de la feuillée* (Play of the bower; ca. 1276), in which Crokesot, the messenger of Hellequin, Lord of the Underworld, is described as a *hurepiaus,* a term used to refer to daemons who were said to have uncommonly hairy faces.[17] By association, it has been said that Crokesot's hirsuteness is typical of all his kind and, consequently, of Hellequin himself (Driesen, 72–73). The name of the character may, therefore, have originated in the hairiness of the ancestor, the daemonic Hellequin. Thus, in the evolution toward Harlequin in medieval France, the name was previously Hellequin, with the variants Hellekin, Herlekin, Herlechin, or Harlekin.

It might also be conjectured further on the evidence in the twelfth-century *Lebor Gabála Erenn* (The book of the taking of Ireland)—which tells many Old Testament stories, including that of Lamech, Cain's grandson, shooting an arrow at a hirsute wild man who turns out to be Cain—that the name of the first felon may, with the Old English–Old French *harle,* be seen as Harle Cain (the hairy Cain) and be a possible source of the eventual Herlekin or Harlequin.

Whatever the fanciful variants that have accrued over the centuries, there can be no doubt on the face of the serious evidence that the true etymology of the name Arlecchino has its origin in ancestors out of ancient Norse and Teutonic myths, telluric beings who passed through the crucible of medieval France, where the pagan daemon Harlequin was still found in Christian festivals, into the consciousness of the early troupes of the improvisational theater known as the *commedia dell'arte,* which began to perform in French cities and courts in the sixteenth century. In time, the name of the character in the Italian troupes was to become fixed as Arlecchino, although the French continued to call him Harlequin. Meanwhile, the ancestral daemonic Harlequin continued to have an active and independent presence of his own in French folklore.

THE MANNER

Arlecchino's gestures, movements, poses, and other stage mannerisms serve to characterize him and give him an individuality that has no kin in the commedia scenarios. Recognizing his singularity, Théophile Gautier, who had seen the commedia characters in a pantomime performed at the Funambules in Paris, wrote that Harlequin "represents love, wit, mobility, audacity, all the showy and vicious qualities" (Sand, 54).

Some have seen his stage manner as having evolved from Greco-Roman theater conventions. Although there are no clear matches, sufficient similarities to the *lazzi* (tricks) and attitudes or poses of Arlecchino can be found in the ways of ancient comedic types to make possible an association between his manner and theirs; thus, Duchartre identifies the *lenones* and *phallophores,* as well as others, found in satyr plays of classic comedy with the commedia dell'arte figure. There is no doubt that Arlecchino inherited time-honored ways of representing comic plots from his Mediterranean stage ancestors. But that Arlecchino sometimes expressed his role in ways similar to those of the Greek and Roman antecedents on the comic stage is merely indicative of the continuity of stage traditions. Nonetheless, his are largely coincidental comic manners at best and not indicative of his true nature.

One of the most impressive characteristics of Arlecchino is his ability to perform *cascate*, "devilish capers and backward somersaults" (Duchartre, 125). According to Riccoboni, these physical feats of strength and dexterity constituted the earliest activity of Arlecchino on the commedia dell'arte stage: "The acting of the Harlequins before the seventeenth century was nothing but a continual play of extravagant tricks, violent movements, and outrageous rogueries. He was at once insolent, mocking, inept, clownish, and emphatically ribald. I believe that he was extraordinarily agile, and he seemed to be constantly in the air; and I might add that he was a proficient tumbler" (Duchartre, 125). Some of the engravings in the *Recueil Fossard* document the agility of the sixteenth-century character named Harlequin therein; so do the drawings in the early-seventeenth-century *Compositions de rhétorique*, where the character's name is variously given as Arlequin, Arlechin, and Harlequin. Indeed, physical comedy of all types was one of the most characteristic elements of the commedia dell'arte as a whole.

Again, the ancestral Wild Man, whose physique and strength were associated with the bear (there is a relation between the words *orcus* [wild man] and *ursus* [bear]), also looms large as the potential source of Arlecchino's physical prowess since the gigantic being who uprooted trees or carried a massive club became associated with Hellekin, leader of the Wild Horde, as indicated in Ordericus Vitalis's ecclesiastical history, where the giant Hellekins also carries a club à la the Wild Man, whom he resembles greatly. And the contributory agency of Hercules should also be remembered in terms of Arlecchino's strength.

Arlecchino could also manipulate situations as if he had superhuman powers,[18] albeit in a comic manner. Some have associated these qualities in him with the Roman deity Mercury, who flew between the world of the gods and that of man, often as a messenger (see fig. 9). As well, it may be that Arlecchino's acrobatic ability was derived from his supernatural ancestor's ability to fly, as his winged feet and helmet signified in the ancient world. Indeed, in *Arlequin Mercure galant* (1682), he is dressed as the god and appears in midair mounted on Jupiter's eagle.[19] As Duchartre puts it: "[H]e is without doubt of divine essence, if not, indeed, the god Mercury himself, patron of merchants, thieves, and panders. . . . Arlecchino, transformed into a citizen of Bergamo, made his appearance at the time when the ancient gods emerged from the fertile Latin soil" (124). But the Romans had inherited Mercury from the yet earlier Greek tradition, where the god was named Hermes. The Greeks, in turn, saw their deity as the manifestation of Thoth, the zoomorphic Egyptian god of learning, wisdom, and esoteric arts, naming him Hermes Trismegistus.

Under his many guises, the ancient deity carried his identifying wand or scepter—the caduceus—with the two entwined serpents. Similarly, the Greek Dionysus (Bacchus to the Romans) had a thyrsus, a staff tipped with

Figure 9. Harlequin astride the Devil as a black goat in *Le roy de la Chine,* a seventeenth-century play. By permission of the Bibliothèque de l'Opera, Paris.

a pinecone and sometimes twined with ivy and vine branches. Both symbols of the authority of the deities have been held since ancient times to be emblematic of the male procreative member, the phallus. Male sexual potency is, therefore, paramount in the ancient worshipers' conception of these gods, as the frequent representation of the phallus shows.[20]

A purgated variant of Hermes' caduceus and Dionysus's thyrsus may be seen in Arlecchino's principal stage property, the slapstick, which he often used lewdly after his leather *phallos* was no longer a part of his accoutrements. In this context, the manner of the commedia dell'arte character was openly sexual, and he pleased his audience, high and low, with energetic, satyr-like behavior, à la the Wild Man, of whose tree or club the slapstick is also reminiscent. All Arlecchino's antics were carried out with a keen wit and rambunctious humor.[21]

Arlecchino's manner, therefore, was yet another remnant of his mixed deific and daemonic origins. It mingled elements out of classical Mediterranean tradition and barbaric Norse-Teutonic folklore: Thoth-Hermes-Dionysus on the one hand, Orcus–Wild Man–Hellekin on the other.

The Costume

Arlecchino's chameleon nature is made manifest, not just in his myriad roles, but also in his variegated costume. Originally, on the Renaissance stage, he dressed in a multicolored patchwork resembling tatters (see fig. 10). Indeed, Trivelino, one of his early alter egos, bears a name that means "tatterdemalion," after his ragged costume.[22]

In his early, tattered garb, Arlecchino has an association with the hirsute beings out of the folklore of Scandinavia, Germany, Austria, Switzerland, and Tyrolean Italy—the traditional figure of the Wild Man. In his association with the Wild Man, Arlecchino inherited physical aspects of woodland figures such as Silenus: "Since Silenus, like the wild man, was expected to appear in plays, the alternative to rendering him as befringed and shaggy lay in showing him in his stage costume, a close-fitting garment with glued-on tufts imitating animal fur" (Bernheimer, 94). In time, these aspects became highly stylized:

> More frequent than the replacement of the furs by feathers was the use of close-fitting tights and bodices covered with little bits of colored rags or flax to simulate tufts. . . . The wild men who performed their revels in Basel in 1435 wore green and red tufts; and the wild men and women rendered on the Swiss

Figure 10. Harlequin's tattered costume, *Recueil Fossard* (ca. 1577). By permission of the Bibliothèque nationale de France.

tapestries of the same period wore fluff of any color. . . . [T]he sartorial tradition of the wild man and his daemonic relatives and associates was inherited by the Harlequin of the modern stage. . . . [T]hese rags were systematized into interlocking triangular or lozenge-shaped patches but the original Harlequin of the seventeenth century wore them at random, in a manner similar to a wild demon's garb [see fig. 11]. (Bernheimer, 83–84)

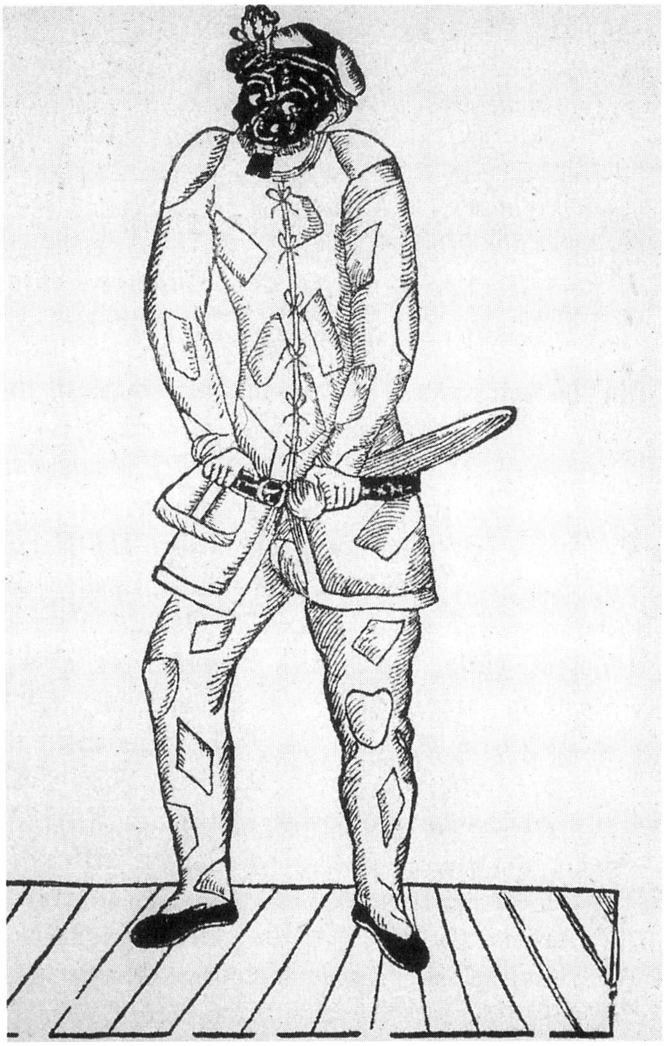

Figure 11. Harlequin's tattered costume, *Compositions de rhétorique* (1601). By permission of the Bibliothèque de l'Opera, Paris.

Making the case for Arlecchino's daemonic identity, McClelland also ties in the costume with its earliest manifestation as part of the physical evidence of the character's origins in woodland daemons, referring to "his multicolored suit, which was originally a skin with patches sewed on to show he was a devil" (101). The color plates and other illustrations in Husband demonstrate visually the changing aspects of the conception of the Wild Man; these can be seen as evolving toward the colorful, patchwork effect associated with Arlecchino on the commedia dell'arte stage.

Many of the Wild Man manifestations are still extant in Carnival celebrations in Europe, as Bernheimer (76) notes. The *Mirabilis urbis Romae,* a medieval text, provides the earliest written record of an event related to the tradition of what came to be known as the Wild Man Hunt; the text cites a pageant occurring in Rome during the Carnival of 1142 where a bear, that is, a man diguised as such, was hunted and "killed." This type of ritual eventually substituted the Wild Man for the bear, who was thought of as "the man of the woods," but, in some areas of Czechoslovakia, Switzerland, and Germany, bear and Wild Man were so closely identified in these rituals that the two were undifferentiated.

In German-speaking areas of Europe, these figures had many names and aspects, among them "the Plaetzlimanli . . . artfully fitted out with small bits of rags sewn on to a garment, so that he may look his name which means 'man in little rags'"; "Flecklegewand, or 'man in patched garment'"; "Fransenkleidle, who like the others imitates shagginess through the fringes on his costume"; and "the Hudler and the Zottler (meaning again 'fringed people'), similar figures in rags." Bernheimer continues: "[T]he incarnation of the Wild Horde would be incomplete without the participation of the fringed revenant" (63). Some variants appear in the British Isles, as in the Sword Dance, which is a symbolic ritual of the death of winter going back at least to *Beowulf.* In some areas, the leader of the mummers wears "a fox's skin, generally serving him for a covering and ornament to his head, the tail hanging down his back" (Wallis, 28), giving him a kinship with the Wild Man. In Elizabethan times, Norton and Sackville's *Gorboduc; or, Ferrex and Porrex* (1561) contains a chorus of "ancient men of Britain" who are none other than the wild men of old.

Duchartre, who does not discuss the Wild Man, traces the costume worn by Arlecchino to the classical theater of the Mediterranean world. To him, the *lenones* or *planipes,* literally "flat feet," the panders of satyr plays, "wore the same sort of motley as Harlequin. It was their master's livery signifying poverty as well as 'neither fish nor flesh,' which indicates the diverse and curious resources of Mercury's proteges" (124). Battisti cites yet another possible provenance of Arlecchino's costume out of antiquity: "Le riesumazioni delle comedie classiche . . . dovettero ridare impulso al mestiere teatrale, e favorire la ripresa di tipi e caratteri antichi, dato anche l'interesse per la fisionomica, per i temperamenti, ecc. Ed ecco rinascere maschere sceniche singolarmente vicine a quelle attestate dagli escrittori antichi: come il mimus centunculus, da cui proverrebbe secondo alcuni il costume di Arlecchino, i tipi delle Atellane, ecc., ma senza che nulla indichi una continuita tradizionale" (121). He adds in the note to that text: "La difficoltà maggiore sta nel costume, che, parrebbe in qualche caso derivare da quelli, di origine culta, adottati in occasione di solenni riesumazioni classiche, a Ferrara, o in spettacoli d'imitazione" (413 n. 55).

In the Twelfth Night celebration of 1515, Henry VIII saw "[e]ight wyldemen, all apparayled in green mosse with sleved sylke, with ugly weapons and terrible visages." By the late sixteenth century, the English Wild Man had acquired the companionship of traditional Roman "fawnz, satyres, nymphs, dryads and hamadryades" (Bernheimer, 71), minor woodland deities all, who were eroding his predominance on the Elizabethan stage, as was occurring at the same time in the masques presented at French courts.

Yet the illustrations in the *Recueil Fossard* (ca. 1577) and *Compositions de rhétorique* (1601) give evidence of the patchwork costumes of the earliest Arlecchinos on the commedia dell'arte stage. In time, stylization set in, and the pattern became that of triangles, until, ultimately, the familiar lozenge pattern in several colors emerged as Arlecchino's distinctive costume (see fig. 12).

The Head Cover

The head covers worn by Arlecchino and his namesakes showed great variety, some reflecting the particular part the character was playing, some having no evident relation to the role or the period, but all thought to be traditional in that they were associated with the overall costume of Arlecchino.

Plumage is frequently associated with Arlecchino's head cover. An engraving from the *Recueil Fossard* shows Arlecchino holding a hat in his right hand: it is a nearly brimless puffed piece whose crown is adorned with two feathers, one broad and curling, the other slim and upright like a quill; the hat, a toque (Italian *tocca*), is typical of that worn in French, Spanish,

Figure 12. Harlequin in *La reverance* by Claude Gillot (1673-1722). By permission of the Bibliothèque de l'Opera, Paris.

and Italian courts of the period as well as of academic attire. To have "a feather in one's cap" was a mark of distinction, as the expression still has it today. In roles such as the Emperor of the Moon and Diana (see fig. 13), Arlecchino wore a variety of feathers as well, perhaps as a way of indicating the aerial aspect of each figure he represented (Cirlot, 98).

Figure 13. Harlequin as Diana. By permission of the Bibliothèque de l'Opera, Paris.

Another item that adorned the head cover worn by Arlecchino was the tail of a hare or fox. The fox was "a common symbol for the devil during the Middle Ages, expressive of base attitudes and of the wiles of the adversary" (Cirlot, 108). In *Compositions de rhétorique* (1601), he is shown cap in hand, while the later Trivelino also wore a soft hat adorned with a rabbit scut.

But a more significant origin for the head cover is the caul, the amnion, the innermost embryonic membrane over a child's head at birth, said to engender magical powers in one so born and protect him from drowning (since the fetus is surrounded by amniotic fluid in the sac). In a study of a Friulian cult from the northern Italian region where German, Italian, and Slav customs meet, Carlo Ginzburg has documented that those born with the caul formed an association, the so-called good walkers, who entered a trance state during planting and harvesting seasons to ensure good crops by battling witches and other malefactors.

The so-called caul of Harlequin indicated the entrance to that underworld once ruled by Herlequin but usurped by the Christian Devil—except in the minds of the populace, who retained the pagan folkloric tradition in the nickname. Later on, and through the nineteenth century, *manteau de Harlequin* was the name given in France to the black curtain behind the apron of the stage (McClelland, 99). In this context, it is interesting to note that, on the medieval French stage, a popular name for the Mouth of Hell was *chape de Herlequin:* "Die Struwelfratze des Holleneingangs, das Teufelgesicht als Wahrzeichen der Hollenbewohner, ist nichts andered als die vergrosserte Struwelfratze des Herlekin Narrenbeisser. . . . Diesr Herle-kinkopf führt selbstverstandlich die beiden Namen, die uns für den Begriff 'Herlekinkopf' vertraut sind: 'Struwelfratze' (hure) und 'Herlekinkappe' (chape de herlequin)" (Driesen, 72–73).

The headdress worn by gods and heroes in Norse and Teutonic mythology also has a possible association with the headgear of Arlecchino: "The most famous magic helmet was called Hildegrim, or Helkappe, or Tarnkappe, or Cap of Darkness. It was given by Mother Hel (Hilde) to her favored heroes. It made them invisible so they could enter the rose gardens of paradise as if they were dead, yet return alive to the earth. The wearer of the mask (sic) became like the Lord of Death, able to reincarnate himself. . . . Some said this magic Helkappe was made of dog skin, since dogs were sacred to the death-goddess, and it was the same mask worn by Hades, the Lord of Death" (Walker, 617).

The Mask

Consider the following apt description of the curious animalistic half mask worn by Arlecchino since the inception of the stage character in the sixteenth century: "I found myself staring, for the first time, into the pin-sized eyeholes of Arlecchino's early mask: . . . the sly brutish features, the two flamboyant warts, the animal hair of this dark leather face. . . . It was a shock to meet . . . the feral ancestor of the shining Harlequin" (Niklaus, 14). This mask provides the strongest physical evidence of his kinship to daemonic beings out of antiquity. For one, the Mediterranean lineage of Mercury and Hermes originates in Thoth, one of whose manifestations was as a baboon-headed deity. For another, the remnants of Arlecchino's Teutonic and Nordic genes can be seen in his strange feral mask, with its black or dark brown leather, bristle hair, severe wrinkles crowned by the stub of a horn, and minute molelike eyes, below one of which is a wen (see fig. 14).[23]

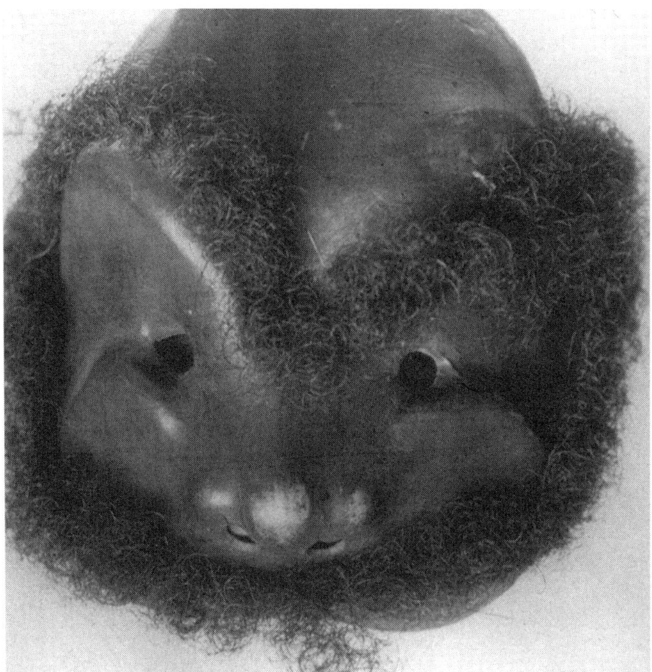

Figure 14. Harlequin's mask, provenance unknown. By permission Bibliothèque de l'Opera, Paris.

Again, Arlecchino's early progenitor, the Wild Man, has passed on one of his characteristics, his distinctive facade. Certainly, the early descriptions of the Wild Man portray him with a virulent black face, usually conveyed in medieval ritual plays through wooden masks that contemporary chroniclers referred to as having "terrible visages" or being "orrende in viso e spaventevole" (Bernheimer, 81–82). Having evolved from Ursus, the great bear of primitive lore, the Wild Man wore a mask that had an undoubted kinship with that animal's features: "There is the Haensele in Ueberlingen on Lake Constance, who wears a fringed suit, a belt of cowbells, and a black velvet mask with a snout. . . . [T]here are the so-called Schuddigs in Elzach, Württemberg, persons all dressed in brownish-reddish costumes and fitted out with masks half-human, half bear-like. They are divided into the 'bear faces' and the 'dead faces' thus manifesting the same connotations which we found universally associated with the figure of the wild man" (Bernheimer, 63–64).

But other accretions ensued over the centuries, including the wen and the stub of a horn, to expand the scope of the mask's origin beyond that initial point of reference in a bear deity out of Neanderthal worship in Paleolithic times.

The stub atop Arlecchino's mask may be the remnant of a horn, as in the black Mamuttones's mask (*bisera*) of Sardinia. McClelland points to the "bestial hairy mask, which even had small horns to leave no doubt of his devilish connection" (101), although none of the extant masks or those portrayed by contemporaries of the commedia show more than the stub of a single horn. It may be that the singularity prompted Ducharte to refer to the growth as "the wart" (135) rather than as the stub of a missing horn.

In this context, Arlecchino may also be associated with the stag-horned god Cernunnos, whose realm was the underworld of Celtic mythology and who functioned in ways similar to Pluto or Hades, or he may have a kinship with a horned deity out of another system of belief, such as Pan or Diana. Thus, in *Arlequin, empereur dans la Lune* (1684), the protagonist is outrageously attired in tunic and cloak, his knees, waist, shoulders, and neck decorated with crescent moons, the goddess Diana's horned symbol. And, in the anonymous seventeenth-century *L'Harlequino bergamasco,* he performs in the role of Diana herself, his visage again identified with the goddess's horns through a large crescent moon that reaches from neck to ears. As Diana, Arlecchino manifests a sometime androgynous tendency, but transvestism was not uncommon on the stage of the commedia dell'arte.

Another interesting conjecture regarding the origin of the stub can be found in *Lebor Gabála Erenn,* wherein the so-called Mark of Cain (briefly referred to in Genesis 4, but without description) is particularized: "God set Cain in a sign, so that no man should slay him—a lump upon his forehead" (1:87). And there is additional commentary in a note: "The 'lump on his forehead' goes back to a lost *Book of Lamech,* which told how Lamech, under the guidance of his son Tubalcain—for he was blind—shot an arrow at a wild man covered with hair, and with a horn growing out of his forehead, who proved to be Cain" (1:237 n. 39). Again, the Wild Man enters the picture, this time with the telling horn on his forehead. And, in the light of the lump on Cain's forehead and the horn of the hairy wild man, Cain himself, there is further support for the conjecture that Cain may have come to be seen as Harle Cain, the hairy Cain, and be a possible source of the eventual Arlecchino with the hairy mask bearing the remnant of a single horn atop its forehead.

Then there is the mask's hirsuteness itself. Discussing Adam de la Halle's *Jeu de la feuillée,* Driesen points to the dialogue concerning the hairy face (*hurepiaus*) of Crokesot, Hellequin's envoy, reasoning, as has been seen earlier, that, since Crokesot has a hairy countenance typical of daemonic beings in the folklore of the time, Hellequin must possess a similar facade (Driesen, 72–73). Unfortunately, the supposition cannot be proved since Hellequin does not appear in the play. Nonetheless, this provides valid evidence for the supposition that this is contributory to the origin of the hairiness of Arlecchino's mask.

Driesen's conception seems valid in the light of the fact that Arlecchino has worn the mysterious dark, hairy mask since his first appearance on the stage and that the mask is not typical of the region of Bergamo, usually given as the birthplace of the comic figure. Rather, as Bernheimer points out, such masks were traditional in depicting the Wild Man in the Alpine region of Italy as well as in adjacent Germany and Austria. That they survived is due to their being integral to folk festivals of pagan origin, be they sacred rituals or profane spectacles, such as the Wild Man Hunt; as they persisted through the centuries, they became so ingrained in the social fabric that they could not be eradicated, even in Christian times.

Since the Wild Man also had strong associations in the popular mind with unbridled sexuality, the prominent long noses on such as the black masks worn in ancient Mediterranean festivals, some still extant, have phallic implications (as in the case of the Mamuttones and Kalogeros). Although Arlecchino's own mask lacks such a protuberance, his lascivious manner gives evidence of his association with such earlier fertility figures.

For Maurice Sand, the blackness of Arlecchino's mask has its origin in the Greek theater, wherein the actor named after his phallic role, as at Sicyonia, had "his countenance blackened with soot or concealed under a papyrus mask" (10) and was the progenitor of the Roman *planipes,* one of the supposed ancestors of Arlecchino out of classical comedy.

Duchartre addresses the blackness of Arlecchino's mask by citing and dismissing as far-fetched various hypotheses, including Carlo Goldoni's statement that its color ("tan," Goldoni calls it) "represents the complexion of the inhabitants of those mountains burned by the fierce sun" and that of Durandy that rowdies recalling how a certain Pietro the Harlequin was ridden out of Bergamo for thievery decided to wear "a black mask in imitation of the bandage which the condemned man had worn over his wound" (136–37). The idea that a black mask was adopted to emulate the blood-stained bandage is one of the lamer aspects of this account of Arlecchino's appearance. Duchartre then posits his own interpretation of the black-masked Arlecchino:

> Perhaps it is because the ancient Harlequin was a phallophore; and, inasmuch as some of the phallophores of the ancient theatre played the parts of African slaves, it is thought that Harlequin might be their direct descendant. . . . Harlequin's authentic mask consisted of a half-mask and a black chin-piece. The eyebrows and beard were bushy and covered with stiff bristles. The forehead was strongly lined with wrinkles which accentuated the slightly quizzical arch of the eyebrows. The eyes were tiny holes beneath, and the *ensemble* gave a curious expression of craftiness, sensuality, and astonishment which was both disturbing and alluring. The huge wen under the eye, the wart, and the black colour completed the impression of something savage and fiendish. (135)

For Duchartre, the stub is termed a *wart,* and, thus, he misses making the connection with the horned figures that contributed to the identity of Arlecchino and that particular aspect of his mask.

For McClelland, the blackness of the mask is indicative of the character's old association with death. Arlecchino's relation with myths of death and resurrection such as that of Pluto or Hades and Persephone, which are often present in one form or another in the *scennari* of the commedia dell'arte, is interpreted as being derived from his "origin in the underworld" (97). Arlecchino is seen as death's seduction personified. Again, Arlecchino's lineage out of Herlekin, leader of the Wild Horde and of the underworld, the walking dead, becomes evident in this speculation.

Conclusions

As has been seen, from the earliest references in the genealogy and etymology, the ancestors of Arlecchino, no matter their provenance, have been associated with the daemonic through the long centuries before his inception as a stage figure. Arlecchino, therefore, has primary primal links to Northern European and other daemonic beings from earlier eras as well as to deific figures from the Greek and Roman worlds, some with zoomorphic aspects. Equally in his stage manner (acrobatic, lascivious, amoral, devious) and in his dress (patchwork costume, gnome-like mask, *phallos*, slapstick), Arlecchino displayed the traces of such chthonic beings as the Wild Man and Herlekin from Nordic climes and such Mediterranean fertility deities as Thoth, Hermes, and Dionysus as well as Hercules, Silenus, and the like.

The devolution of Herlekin from daemon in pre-Roman times to antic mountebank in the sixteenth-century character Arlecchino is typical of the absorption and purgation of ancient deities under the hegemony of Christianity. The remnants of Arlecchino's inheritance from the pagan past are evident in his traditional costume, mask, and other physical accoutrements as well as in the variations in his name. As Cope says while assessing the Cockney character Joey the Clown, named after Joseph Grimaldi, a star of British pantomime: "When we view the character in this light we can see the history of Harlequin's decline in the eighteenth-century popular theater quite differently. The Joey who replaced Harlequin was actually the resurrection of his original form and spirit as the half-man half-daemon who irrupted from the shadowy history of Germanic devils, a carrier of irrepresible [*sic*] irrationality and desire into the fragile forms of social restraint. . . . Arlecchino came from the shades of an older chaos to become its permanent comic voice but one passed from interpreter to interpreter through the centuries" (11, 18).

In conclusion, it has been shown that the tradition of daemonic association of the name Arlecchino is first Norse-Teutonic (Ellerkonge, Elverkonge, Erlkönig, Erlking, Herleking, Hellekin, Herlekin), passing thereafter into France (Herlequin, Harlequin), no doubt throughout the periods of invasions by Germanic tribes on the downfall of Roman hegemony, while the earliest use of a related name in Italy (Dante's Alichino) is likewise that of a daemon.

To the daemonic image out of Central and Northern European folklore was joined the comic spirit out of Attic theater. The commedia dell'arte's

Arlecchino and his namesakes elsewhere in Europe were the inheritors of the symbiosis between the daemonic elements of ancient European lore and classical tradition. Thus, Arlecchino represents a part of the pagan substratum still extant in a world wearing the mask of Christianity. As Driesen summarizes the evidence in his fundamental work on the subject: "Allerdings ist der Harlekin der Teufel" (24). There is, indeed, no doubt that Arlecchino, whatever the period, whatever the variation in his name, wherever he is made manifest, is a being of daemonic nature.

Arlecchino epitomizes the intervention of the supernatural in human affairs. His characteristics are among those that course through much of medieval Christian literature and art, both of which were channels for expressing the varied religious beliefs of the times, be they orthodox or heterodox, Christian or pagan. Undoubtedly with far greater importance in pagan times than in the era of Christianity, the being that came to be called Arlecchino in Italy nonetheless survives in many contexts elsewhere today because in him lies a deep-seated quality that cannot be eradicated: the dichotomy represented by the adjectives *savage* and *deific*, which manifest his telluric and cosmic aspects, respectively. The masks of Harlequin are manifestations of the primal elements of human nature itself.

Notes

1. The full text of *Harlequin Student* can be found in Niklaus, 200–207.

2. For studies of the history and aspects of the commedia dell'arte, see esp. Duchartre; Nicoll; and Sand.

3. There were many variants of the character's name in the Italian Peninsula before it became stabilized as Arlecchino; among these were Harlequino, Harlechino, and Arlechino. Rather than confuse the issue, I will employ the form Arlecchino throughout this chapter when referring to the commedia dell'arte character.

4. From Probus (Porbus) the Elder (Frans or Paul Pourbus), who was the earliest known (ca. 1570–72) depicter of Harlequin and whose work is in the Museum of Bayeux (see Duchartre, 82ff., who identifies two possible Arlecchino figures), through the seventy-two anonymous plates of the *Recueil Fossard* (ca. 1577), the illustrations of the *Compositions de rhetorique* (Lyons, 1601), along with the works of Jacques Callot, Claude Gillot (1673–1722), Antoine Watteau, G. J. Xavery, Edgar Degas, Paul Cézanne, André Dérain, and Pablo Picasso, among many others. For reproductions of some of these engravings, see Nicoll; and Duchartre.

5. The Wild Horde, pagan concept that was adapted in Christian times, was originally a band of spirits under the headship of Diana, Hecate, Herodias, or another female deity out of the Mediterranean world. Belief in it came to be interpreted by the church as heretical and was considered witchcraft. In Germany, the

term *Wild Horde* applies to male spirits under a leader named either the Wild Man or Hellekin (Bernheimer, 78–79).

One of the related manifestations of this motif is the Santa Compaña, a procession of ghosts, spirits, and apparitions of all sorts believed to roam at night and prey on unwary people in northwestern Spain. This is a pre-Christian superstition centered in Galicia, the corner of Spain whose folklore and mythology are largely Celtic. An important parallel with the Wild Horde is that "[a]l frente de esta comitiva de fantasmas acostumbra figurar un espectro de mayor tamaño, según algunos, la Estadea" (Carré Alvarellos, 53). Sometimes known by the name of its leader, Estadea, as well as Hueste (the Spanish for "horde"), the belief was Christianized under Santa Compaña and Procesión de las Animas into a procession of the souls of those undergoing purgation before being admitted into God's presence. Ironically, the belief holds that the Christian dead terrorize the living at night. Any person they encounter is forced to join the Santa Compaña; thus, believers throw themselves to the ground and feign death when they see the approach of the shrouded candle-bearers. But, in other instances, the nefarious group enters houses and drags those sleeping within through keyholes to join the procession of the unholy. Those who see the Santa Compaña despite its invisibility can do so because they are soon to die. In this aspect, the belief resembles that of the Banshee in Ireland, another Celtic land.

6. In Shakespeare's *The Merry Wives of Windsor,* Falstaff dresses as Herne the Hunter to be acceptable to the ladies as a sex partner. Thus attired, he meets Mistress Ford after midnight and dances around the ancient sacred oak before copulating with her. The Wild Man is depicted all in green in Pieter Brueghel the Elder's painting *The Battle of Carnival and Lent.* See also Anderson.

7. Counterparts in other areas of the world include, but are not limited to, the Himalayan Yeti or Abominable Snowman (the descendant of the apelike Gigantopithecus?), the North American Indian Sasquatch (or Saskwatch), and the Northwest U.S. Bigfoot.

8. For a description and depiction of a charivari, see the fourteenth-century *Roman de Fauvel.* The tree-club motif associated with the Wild Man spans many centuries, as exemplified in Boccaccio and Goethe's works. The second tale of the fourth day in Giovanni Boccaccio's *Decameron* narrates how Fra Alberto was punished for posing as the angel Gabriel to carry on a seduction. The good man who assists Fra Alberto in his flight tells him: "'Today we are celebrating a festival in which men are led around dressed as bears, some as wild men. . . . [T]he festival comes to a close with a sort of hunt in St. Mark's Square. . . . I would be willing to lead you along in one of these disguises.' . . . The man smeared him all over with honey, covered him with feathers, and put a chain around his neck and a mask on his face; in one of his hands he put a large club. . . . When he arrived there, he tied his wild man up to a column in a conspicuous and elevated spot, pretending to wait for the hunt. . . . [P]retending to unchain his wild man, he tore the mask from his face" (266–7). The man then announced to all Fra Alberto's crime, whereupon the friar was beset by the mob that had followed them, taken away, and imprisoned by his fellow friars. The traditional uprooted tree is featured in the first act of

the second part of Goethe's *Faust:* "The wild men of the woods . . . [a] fir-tree's trunk in each right hand" (176).

9. Husband is paraphrasing Chrétien de Troyes's *Yvain:* "[U]n vilain, qui resambloit mor, grant et hideus a desmure . . . vi je seoir sor une çache / Une grant maçue an sa main" (lines 288–89, 192–93, cited in Husband, 2). See also engravings of the Wild Man by Jacques Callot.

10. One such figure appears in *Don Quijote,* where the outlandish Cervantine hero crosses paths with an exotically garbed individual: "[V]enía vestido de bojiganga con muchos cascabeles, y en la punta de un palo traía tres vejigas de vaca hinchadas" (pt. 2, chap. 11, p. 1308). (The anecdote is a reference to a traveling troupe about to perform a play, disputedly Lope de Vega's *Auto sacramental de las Cortes de la Muerte*). The association of Arlecchino and similar figures with Death no doubt arises in his ancestor Hermes as Psychopomp, in which capacity he conducted the souls of the dead and is, therefore, thought of as Lord of Death. For an extensive treatment of this aspect of Arlecchino's nature, see McClelland.

11. For an etymology of *woodewose,* see Stratman. *Wose* derives Middle English *wode-wose* from Old English *wasa,* meaning "satyr." Bosworth-Toller, the standard Old English dictionary, defines Old English *wudewase* as "satyr, faun"; the term glosses Latin *silvanus* and *satirus.* See also *A New English Dictionary of Historical Principles,* s.v. "woodwose."

12. Bibliothèque nationale, Paris, Inv. Réserve Ye 4151. Discussed in *Romania* 16: 538ff.

13. "L'ettimologia Arlecchino da Herculinus e stata proposta, convincentemente, dal Nicolini, *Storia di Arlecchino,* Napoli, 1957" (Battisti, 402 n. 130).

14. Carnuti, 1592, p. 23 (Bibliothèque nationale, Paris, L 35 b 351A).

15. Variants of the anecdote can be found in Duchartre, 140; and Niklaus, 30–31. Sand, 58, adds that the character says: "I contrive so well that I now go to Court; I am the Marquis of Sbruffadeli."

16. *Harle* is also the name given a small bird of vibrant plumage (Niklaus, 30–31) and is the root of *harlequin duck,* a name bestowed (after the commedia character's multicolored costume) because of the bird's "blue legs" and feathers "of black, grey, blue and chestnut streaked with white" (Potter and Sargent, 73–74).

17. Crokesot (variants Crokesos, Croquesos) may derive from *croque,* meaning "frappe" (securely bound), and *sots,* meaning "a confirmed drunkard" (derived from Vulgar Latin *sottus*). It may also be related to the English *crock,* for "soot" or "smut."

18. In David Garrick's *Harlequin's Invasion; or, A Christmas Gambol* (1759), Harlequin is interpreted as a French "invader" of the English stage. A diabolical figure who lops off heads and resurrects the victims, Harlequin is eventually undone by the deus ex machina appearance of the god Mercury. As Cope says of Harlequin's role in Garrick's play: "Harlequin was bursting through . . . to speak in his first person to the people about the daemonic bond which had always been implicit in their contract to suspend disbelief in drama in order that it might reinvent its double, as Artaud would say, in the underground of their psyches whence Harlequin had come" (112). The association of Arlecchino with the Wild Man is given a subtle nod through Harlequin's diabolic nature and through his being positioned in a tree in

one scene and in a cave in another, both sites long associated with the woodland deity.

19. The play was presented at the Hôtel de Bourgogne on January 22, 1682, by His Majesty's Italian Players. See the scenario in Niklaus, 194–95.

20. "Hermes's phallic spirit protected crossroads throughout the Greco-Roman world, in the form of *herms,* which were either stone phalli or short pillars with Hermes's head at the top and an erect penis on the front. . . . Saxons worshipped Hermes as the phallic spirit of the Hermeseul, or Irminsul. . . . Other Germanic tribes worshipped Hermes under the name of Thot or Teutatis, 'Father of Teutons.' . . . His caduceus was called a masturbatory symbol, a rod massaged by the serpents that embraced it" (Walker, 397). See also Vanggaard; and Monick.

21. According to Sand: "[I]t was in the seventeenth century that the role of Harlequin was completely transformed by Domenico Biancolelli, . . . who bestowed his own wit upon the character. Thus Harlequin became witty, astute, an utterer of quips and something of a philosopher" (65).

22. According to Cirlot, rags and tatters symbolize "wounds and gashes in the soul" (259). A curious manifestation of this meaning can be seen in the tattered cloaks of medieval and Renaissance Spanish university students, today evident in the musical groups known as *estudiantinas* or *tunas,* whose participants claim that each tatter represents a broken heart.

23. A wen is described in pathology as a sebaceous cyst. *Wen* is also the name of the rune for the letter *w* and derives from Middle English and Old English *wenn;* it has a cognate, *wen,* in Dutch.

Works Cited

Anderson, William. *Green Man: The Archetype of Our Oneness with the Earth.* New York: HarperCollins, 1990.

Battisti, Eugenio. *L'antirinascimento.* Milan: Feltrinelli, 1962.

Beaumont, Cyril W. *The History of Harlequin.* New York: Blom, 1907.

Bernheimer, Richard. *Wild Men in the Middle Ages: A Study in Art, Sentiment, and Demonology.* Cambridge, Mass.: Harvard University Press, 1952. Copious endnotes provide broad documentation on the subject.

Boccaccio, Giovanni. *The Decameron.* New York: New American Library, 1982.

Bosworth, Joseph, and T. Northcote Toller. *An Anglo-Saxon Dictionary.* Oxford: Clarendon, 1898.

Caffi, E. "La questione di Arlecchino." *Rassegna Nazionale* 30 (1908): 210–14.

Carré Alvarellos, Leandro. *Las leyendas tradicionales gallegas.* Madrid: Espasa-Calpe, 1978.

Carré Cartier, Normand R. *Le Bossu désenchanté: Etude sur "Le jeu de la feuillée."* Geneva: Droz, 1971.

Cervantes Saavedra, Miguel de. *Don Quijote.* In *Obras completas,* ed. Angel Valbuena Prat, 1027–1524. Madrid: Aguilar, 1962.

Cirlot, J. E. *A Dictionary of Symbols.* New York: Philosophical Library, 1962.

Compositions de rhétorique de Mr. Don Arlequin. Lyons: Imprimé delà Le Bout du Monde, 1601. Only known copy is in the Bibliothèque de l'Opera, Paris (Rés. Y 2.922).

Cope, Jackson I. *Dramaturgy of the Daemonic: Studies in Antigeneric Theater from Ruzante to Grimaldi.* Baltimore: Johns Hopkins University Press, 1984.

Dante Alighieri. *Inferno.* Translated by Robert Hollander and Jean Hollander. New York: Doubleday, 2000.

Driesen, Otto. *Der Ursprung des Harlekin: Ein kulturgeschichtliches Problem.* Berlin: Alexander Duncker, 1904. Copious footnotes provide excellent documentation on the evolution of the subject.

Duchartre, Pierre Louis. *The Italian Comedy.* Translated by Randolph T. Weaver. London: George G. Harrap, 1929. Expanded ed., New York: Dover, 1966. First published as *La comédie italienne* (Paris, 1929). Contains an extensive bibliography on and numerous illustrations of the commedia dell'arte as well as the *Recueil Fossard* and excepts from *Compositions de rhétorique.*

Dudley, Edward, and Maximillian E. Novak, eds. *The Wild Man Within: An Image in Western Thought from the Renaissance to Romanticism.* Pittsburgh: University of Pittsburgh Press, 1972.

Durandy, Dominique. *Poussières d'Italie.* Paris: Paul Ollendorff, [1911].

Flasdieck, H. M. "Harlekin, Germanischer Mythos in Romanischer Wandlung." *Anglia* (Halle) 61 (1937): 225–340.

Ginzburg, Carlo. *I benandanti: Stregoneria e culti agrari tra Cinquecento e Seicento.* Turin: Einaudi, 1966. Translated as *The Night Battles: Witchcraft and Agrarian Cults in the Sixteenth and Seventeenth Centuries* by John and Anne Tedeschi (London: Routledge & Kegan Paul; Baltimore: Johns Hopkins University Press, 1983).

Goethe, J[ohann Wolfgang von]. *Faust.* Translated by George M. Priest. New York: Covici-Friede, 1932.

Halle, Adam de la. *Jeu de la feuillée* (1276). In *Oeuvres complètes du trouvère Adam de la Halle,* ed. E. de Coussemaker. Paris: A. Durand & Pédone-Lauriel, 1872. An English translation can be found in *Complete Works of the Troubadour Adam de la Halle* (New York: Broude Bros., 1964). A modernized French text can be found in Jean Frappier and A.-M. Gossart, eds., *Le théatre comique au Moyen Age* (Paris: Larousse, n.d.).

Herrick, Marvin T. *Italian Comedy in the Renaissance.* Urbana: University of Illinois Press, 1960.

Husband, Timothy. *The Wild Man: Medieval Myth and Symbolism.* New York: Metropolitan Museum of Art, 1980.

Keightley, Thomas. *The World Guide to Gnomes, Fairies, Elves and Other Little People.* New York: Avenel, 1978.

Lebor Gabála Erenn. Edited and translated by R. A. Stewart Macalister. 5 vols. Dublin: Irish Texts Society/Educational Company of Ireland, 1938. The first redaction of the text is ca. C.E. 1150. These five volumes are nos. 34, 35, 39, 41, and 44 in the Irish Texts series.

McClelland, David C. "The Harlequin Complex." In *The Study of Lives: Essays on Personality in Honor of Henry A. Murray,* ed. Robert W. White. New York: Atherton, 1963.

Mongai, Massimo. *Sardinia.* Olbia: R. Balzano, 1984.

Monick, Eugene. *Phallos: Sacred Image of the Masculine.* Toronto: Inner City, 1987.

Murray, J. A. H., ed. *A New English Dictionary of Historical Principles.* 12 vols. Oxford: Clarendon, 1888–1933.

Nicolini, Fausto. *Vita di Arlecchino.* Milan: Ricciardi, 1958.
Nicoll, Allardyce. *The World of Harlequin: A Critical Study of the "Commedia dell'Arte."* Cambridge: Cambridge University Press, 1963.
Niklaus, Thelma. *Harlequin Phoenix; or, The Rise and Fall of a Bergamask Rogue.* London: Bodley Head, [1956].
Oreglia, Giacomo. *The "Commedia dell'Arte."* New York: Hill & Wang, 1968.
Paris, Paulin. *Les manuscrits de la bibliothèque du roi.* Vol. 1. Paris, 1836.
Pegg, Bob. *Rites and Riots: Folk Customs of Britain and Europe.* Poole: Blanford, 1981.
Potter, Stephen, and Laurens Sargent. *Pedigree: The Origin of Words from Nature.* New York: Taplinger, 1974.
Presta, Vincenzo. "Alichino." In *Enciclopedia dantesca,* 1:125. Rome: Istituto della Enciclopedia Italiana, 1970.
Recueil des plusiers fragments des premières comédies italiennes qui ont esté représentées en France sous le règne de Henry 3. Compiled by Sieur Fossard. ca. 1577. Published for the first time in *Compositions de rhétorique de M. Don Arlequin,* ed. P. L. Duchartre and Van Buggenhoudt (Paris, 1928).
Recueil Fossard. See *Recueil des plusiers fragments* 1577.
Rhulemann, Martin. *Etymologie des Wortes Harlequin und Verwander Worter.* Halle, 1912.
Rossetti, Gabriele. *Commento analitico.* London, 1826–27.
Sainéan, M. L. *Les sources indigènes de l'étymologie française.* 2 vols. Paris: E. de Boccard, 1925.
Sand, Maurice. *The History of the Harlequinade.* London: Martin Secker, 1915.
Stratman, Francis Henry. *A Middle English Dictionary.* Edited by Henry Bradley. Oxford: Clarendon, 1891.
Toschi, Paolo. *Le origini del teatro italiano.* Turin: Einaudi, 1955.
Uribe, María de la Luz. *La Comedia del Arte.* Santiago de Chile: Universidad de Chile/Cuadernos del Centro de Investigaciones de Literatura Comparada, [1963?].
Vanggaard, Thorkil. *Phallós: A Symbol and Its History in the Male World.* New York: International Universities Press, 1972.
Vitalis, Ordericus. *Historiae ecclesiasticae libri XIII.* Edited by Augustus Le Prévost. 5 vols. Paris: J. Renouard, 1838–55.
Walker, Barbara G. *The Woman's Encyclopedia of Myths and Secrets.* San Francisco: Harper & Row, 1983. Excellent compilation of data and illustrations.
Wallis, J. *The Natural History and Antiquities of Northumberland.* Vol. 2. London: privately printed by W. & W. Strahan, 1769.

3

The Pagan Pluto

Touchstone of Celestina's Magic in Tragicomedia de Calixto y Melibea

Demand what you will of me.

—Celestina

Magic and witchcraft have two very different venues and are wholly distinct. The difference is quite marked, magic being ceremonial and witchcraft religious. Magic seeks, through ritual practices, to manipulate the forces and denizens of the supernatural world to the end of personal empowerment. The practices of the magician are prescribed in what came to be known as *grimoires,* among the most famous being the *Clavicle of Solomon* (also the *Key of Solomon*),[1] esoteric texts that contained invocations, words of power, patterns of circles to be inscribed on the ground with esoteric formulas, and descriptions of objects to be used in the conjuration, all of which were meant to enable the individual to control the will of others or affect cosmic forces via the services of supernatural beings. As in the case of a Prospero,[2] the magician uses but does not worship the supernatural entity called on to serve.

Witchcraft (or Wicca), on the other hand, is a religion that encompasses a variety of ancient worship traditions founded on the male and female principles in nature.[3] In Europe, these were deified as the Horned God (e.g., the Greek Pan, the Celtic Cernunnos) and the Goddess (e.g., the Greek Diana and Hecate, the Anatolian-Roman Cybele), whose symbol is the crescent moon.[4] They and the celebrants of their rites, as in Thessaly, predated Christianity by thousands of years. As it grew in influence, the church largely ignored witches and their cult because witchcraft was seen for what it was: the remnant of a nonhierarchical pagan religion that posed no threat. But, in the later Middle Ages, syncretism had confused classical and Christian concepts.[5] Not least among these was the association of benevolent pagan deities with saints and the affiliation of gods deemed sinister with the Devil and his cohorts. Thus, the positive aspects of the Goddess under her varied pagan guises (Diana, Hecate, Cybele, etc.) were subsumed in the Virgin Mary, as her litany reveals; the Horned God of the witches be-

---

Previous page: Pluto and Persephone with Cerberus, provenance unknown. Public domain.

came associated with the Christian Satan, who soon was vested with the physical aspects (the goat's horns and cloven hooves) of the satyr-god Pan. In keeping with the negative attitude of the church toward women, the role of the Goddess was ignored in Christianity—she was not even demonized. If there was only one God of good, there could be only one "god" of evil. Such was the fate of the old deities before the might of the new religion, and resentment of the church's power led many to practice the old religion secretly or to mock Christianity through worship of Satan.

The distinction between magic and witchcraft had been a clear one in antiquity. However, the long-established separation of the two became blurred in the European Middle Ages with Christianity's evolving view that all nonconforming systems of belief and ritual practices that it found to be noxious were under the aegis of Satan. Christianity saw fit to interpret both traditions as evil. *Witchcraft* came to be the term used for what is, in fact, the heretical practice of Satanism, which seeks to elevate (some say restore) the Lord of Darkness to the highest position in the pantheon, no doubt under the influence of Zoroastrian dualism. The accepted idea became that the witch served the Christian personification of evil, the Devil, to whom he or she had made a religious (albeit heretical) commitment through a *professio tacitas* or a *professio expressa* (see Lima, chap. 3). The medieval witch was believed to be in thrall to her deity, the Satan who rebelled against God; consequently, he or she had chosen to follow the path of heterodoxy and had to be punished as a heretic by the Holy Office of the Inquisition. It is due to this Satanic association that the famous King James Bible self-servingly exhorts English Christians: "Thou shalt not suffer a witch to live" (Exod. 22:18).[6]

Similarly, the search for knowledge (i.e., power) by magicians came to be associated by the church with the Devil, and it was held that the conjuror's ability to alter the normal state of things came through a demonic pact, often signed in blood. The most notable of such cases is that of Faust.[7] Not only did such a crossover, associating their practices with Satan through a demonic pact that empowered magicians or witches to seek supernatural alliances, erase the line between magic and witchcraft in the Middle Ages, affecting subsequent conceptions of the two, but it also forced both into the realm of Christian demonology. Thereafter, the confusion was uniform throughout society at all levels.

The secular, that is, nonreligious, work in fifteenth-century Spanish literature that is arguably most representative of the confusion of magic and witchcraft, with the attendant misconception of demonic inspiration, is the *Tragicomedia de Calixto y Melibea* (1502), a twenty-one-act work attributed through an acrostic to Fernando de Rojas. *The Celestina,* as it is generally known after its central character, is a novelesque drama (dramatic novel, according to some) first published in 1499 (but probably composed before 1492)[8] in sixteen acts as *Comedia de Calixto y Melibea,* wherein Calixto's unbridled love for Melibea and later hers for him form the basis for the plot. Such love is defined in the *Malleus Maleficarum:* "Philocaption or inordinate love of one person for another can be caused in three ways. Sometimes it is due primarily to a lack of control over the eyes; sometimes to the temptation of devils; sometimes to the spells of necromancers and witches with the help of devils" (Sprenger and Kramer, 176). This process of philocaption is presented in terms of occult operations at the hands of Celestina that bring about its illicit fruition and, ultimately, the tragic demise of the principal players.

In Celestina, the most outstanding in the cast of players, Rojas created one of the most distinctive characterizations of the medieval old crone. A down-to-earth woman with many side talents, Celestina seems unbounded in the practice of her craft, as Sempronio informs Calixto in the first act: "For a long time I've known a hairy old woman in the vicinity who calls herself Celestina; she's a crafty witch up to every kind of wickedness" (59). Later in the same act, according to Pármeno's description of her doings, Celestina takes in sewing, runs a house of ill repute, repairs the often lost virtue of supposed virgins, acts as a midwife, and concocts all sorts of medicines, cosmetics, and potions, all her services being available at a price to a large and eager clientele from all social classes. Pármeno also refers to her as "a bit of a sorceress," to which description he adds: "It was all mockery and lies" (71).

But Celestina is more than a mere *alcahueta,* a love broker who is "a bit of a sorceress." An unbiased reading of her conjuration and statements pertinent to her arcane work reveals that she is a practitioner of the ancient arts of magic who follows pagan traditions while acting the proper Christian. That she serves the needs of society is obvious in the lack of secrecy surrounding her affairs (although not her occult operations) and in the lucrative manner in which she is repaid. She may be thought of as a witch by those who, like Pármeno and Sempronio, are incapable of properly defining her occult practices, but her rituals are centered on magic and not on the popular misconception of witchcraft as worship of Satan.[9]

The crafty Celestina may function in society under the guise of a devout Christian, but, in fact, she does not have an orthodox identity. This is proved beyond hearsay by her actions. Pointedly in the pivotal third act,[10] in the privacy of her house, Celestina looks to prepare the ingredients that she requires to perform her magical conjuration. First, she instructs Elicia, one of her prostitutes, who is with Sempronio: "Run up to the garret over the sun porch and bring me that vial of snake oil, the one that's hanging from the rope I found in the fields that dark and rainy night. Then open the sewing cabinet; on the right you'll find a piece of paper written in bat's blood, under the wing of that dragon whose claws we removed yesterday. . . . If not there, go to the room where I keep the ointments, and you'll find it in the hide of the black cat, where I told you to put the wolf eyes. Bring down the goat's blood too and a few of his whiskers that you cut off" (109). These instructions leave no doubt that Celestina's pharmacopoeia is replete with ingredients for *hechicería* (i.e., sorcery) as traditionally conceived.[11]

But perhaps more often than is evident, as will be the case here, the services that Celestina provides through her pharmacopoeia are aided by her conjurations of supernatural forces. Yet such magical operations are to be conducted only when she is alone. Thus, when Elicia takes Sempronio upstairs, Celestina proceeds to her task. Using the unsavory (but seemingly effective) ingredients that she had sent Elicia to fetch, Celestina begins the thaumaturgic rite, a summoning of the being whose aid she seeks: not the Devil of Christian tradition but a deity out of classical Greek belief. Her conjuration is of Pluto, Lord of the Underworld:

> I conjure you, dark Pluto, lord and master of the nether depths. . . . I, Celestina, the best of your clients, conjure you by virtue and potency of these scarlet letters, written in the blood of that nocturnal bird; by the weight of the names and signs written on this paper; by the bitter snake venom out of which this oil is made with which I now anoint this thread. Come at once to obey my command, and wrap yourself within this thread; stay wrapped in it so that Melibea buys it at the opportune moment, as she will, and as she gazes at it more and more her heart will soften to my request. Wound her heart, and lance it with base passion and love for Calixto, so that, forgetting her virginity, she will reveal her passion to me and offer just rewards for all my work. Once this has been done, ask and demand what you will of me. (110)

Hers is both a conjuration and an exhortation. She addresses Pluto through a lengthy litany of titles that demonstrates the result of the syncretic process.[12] But it is her command of a deity, something that a witch would neither have the power nor dare to undertake, that distinguishes the ritual as magic.[13]

The offering at the end of the conjuration, being made to a pagan rather than a Christian deity, does not imply the pledging of her soul to eternal damnation. The deity that Celestina deals with is the pagan Pluto, not the Satan of Christianity. Thus, in keeping with her tradition, her statement is a formulaic offer of her services to Pluto—a quid pro quo. For her, there is no Christian damnation in the picture. Nor does her offering qualify as a professed demonic pact in the traditional sense of that entered into by Theophilus or by Faust[14] because it has none of the heretical formulas or public acts of blasphemy (e.g., the *osculum infame,* trampling on the cross, abjuring baptism, the promissory document signed in blood) that Christian tradition associates with such demonic deeds of gift. Nor are there any indications of rites of submission extraneous to the action of the *Tragicomedia.*[15] Internal evidence discloses that Celestina the magician is learned enough in the magical arts to summon Pluto and to manipulate the chthonic deity by having him entwine himself in the thread intended for Melibea.[16]

Pluto, also referred to as Hades in antiquity,[17] is the Olympian who with his brothers Zeus and Poseidon divided the kingdom of Kronos, their father, when they defeated him. Pluto/Hades, who then came to rule the earth and all within its innards, thereafter, with the complicity of Zeus, took the maiden Persephone/Kore while she was gathering flowers and by force made her his consort. Thus arose the seventh-century B.C.E. myth of Demeter's search for her lost daughter and the agreement brokered by Zeus for Persephone's return to her mother, but only if the daughter spent a third of the year in the underworld, owing to her having eaten there a pomegranate offered by Pluto. Demeter, who had avenged herself by keeping the grain hidden so that it would not grow during her daughter's absence, restored the earth's productivity. The myth tied the death of the fields in winter to Persephone's descent into the underworld and the rebirth of nature to her residency in the land of the living each spring and summer. The fructification of the land, a cyclic process, was seen as a double rite of passage. The telluric myth was sanctified in the Eleusinian mysteries.

Celestina's immediate concern is with the swift completion of the appointed task of leading Melibea to her own rite of passage—deflowering—aptly invoking the selfsame Pluto/Hades who had caused the death of Persephone's virtue. And, to assure a satisfactory end to her demand of Pluto, the crone adds a threat to her formulaic invocation: "But should you fail to act with all due speed, I will become your greatest foe. I will pierce your dark and moody dungeons with shafts of light, denounce with venom all your lies, curse with harshest words your hideous name. I conjure you this once and once again. And, trusting in my great power, I set out to my task with this thread, believing that I have you wrapped within" (110–11). The tone of Celestina's words gives a different cast to her role vis-à-vis Pluto. In threatening the Lord of the Underworld, she is, in effect, showing the self-assurance of one who is in control ("trusting in my great power"). Celestina's conjuration and subsequent attitude toward the deity she invokes show her in the guise of potent magician, not subservient witch.

In order to understand Celestina's power and daring in this scene, it is necessary to envision the setting for her incantations and the accoutrements that accompany them. Little or much can be made of the staging of the conjuration scene. The dramatist gives no stage directions to indicate how the scene is to be set (the reader knows only that the locale is Celestina's house), or how the elements used in the conjuration are to be employed or manipulated (we know the things she employs but not their magical meaning in this context), or how the conjuration is to be intoned. Perhaps because the reader of his era knew how such things were done, Rojas felt no need to explicate them In modern times, when the practices once called *magic* or *witchcraft* are no longer so intrinsically related to daily life, interpretative decisions as to how rituals in old works are to be performed on a stage are left up to the reader's imagination or the director's imperatives.

This conjuration scene should be imagined as a ritual of magic—with robe, wand, *grimoire,* and magic circle (as distinguished from the paraphernalia of witchcraft employed by the three Weird Sisters in Shakespeare's *Macbeth*)—in order to give an informed reading of the scene and to extract from Celestina's conjuration (her words of power) its full potential for theatricality.

Celestina's is a subtle magic, neither showy nor pretentious, but highly personal. She keeps the magical operations that she performs private, discreetly avoiding calling on her supernatural connection when people are around. But, when alone, she loosens the bonds of propriety and addresses Pluto with familiarity, showing her control over the deity by words that empower her. It is important, therefore, to convey her power and control over a supernatural being in visual, theatrical terms: through setting, lighting, costuming, props, and ritualized action. Since the dramatist has not given stage directions to achieve this end, it is up to the reader to introduce the stage business necessary to elicit the full theatricality of the scene.

Once alone, Celestina would enter her secret chamber. Magical tradition has it that such were usually caves or other places set apart from prying eyes.[18] Since Celestina is clearly in her house, it would be fitting that she have a secret entrance to her domain; this could be accessed by lifting some floorboards that give access to a subterranean chamber. Lighting a lantern, she would descend some rickety stairs (accompanied by appropriate creaking sounds) and enter the dark confines of her magical laboratory, a setting replete with ominous retorts, *grimoires* full of magical lore and incantations, and other tools of her magical trade. The area must be large enough to accommodate a magic circle, which is to be drawn on the floor each time a ritual is to be performed. But here there are to be none of the objects associated with witchcraft—the cauldron, the broomstick—those are things that belong in the upper world, that of her attic, where she had instructed Elicia to find the ingredients she required. This nether place is closer to the underground realm of Pluto and dedicated to Celestina's magical operations, not to witchcraft.

On reaching the chamber, Celestina should regale her body with the trappings of her calling: she should don the robes of the magician, put on the headdress that vests her with uncommon intuition, and grasp the wand or staff that will extend her power beyond her person into the dark realm of Pluto. This done, she must proceed to make the circle on the ground by standing at its intended center[19] and tracing its circumference with her wand or staff, all the while murmuring a formulaic chant from one of her *grimoires;* once within the circle, she will be protected from the potential harm caused by a spirit brought unwillingly to her presence. It is only after these preparations that Celestina can proceed to vocalize the incantation that will evoke the Lord of the Underworld, Pluto. This is the central moment of the magical work, and Celestina's incantation must be performed with the heightened, hierophantic voice and ritualized gestures that such a daring action requires.

The conjuration scene is larger than life and must be presented as such. It must be highly stylized through setting, lighting, and costuming, for it is ritual. The conjuration itself must be accompanied by sounds and music that enhance its supernatural nature. The presence of Pluto must be made manifest through ambience that suggests rather than defines—the deity must not be visible. Brought together, elements of light and shadow, color and sound, enhance a scene of inherent unreality—or antireality—which, in turn, heightens theatricality.

It is only fitting that Celestina the magician, not the witch of popular misconception, be given a proper interpretation during the one scene in *La Tragicomedia de Calixto y Melibea* in which she allows herself to be seen in the performance of her secret calling. The scene, properly staged (or imagined), would be one of high theatricalism.

Once these magical preparations and rites are over, Celestina proceeds to test her empowerment. Her first visit to Melibea takes place in the fourth act, and the crone is encouraged by the virgin's gracious reception. But later, when Melibea recognizes Celestina for what she is and rants against her for promoting Calixto's cause, the *alcahueta* resorts once more to her sinister ally, calling Pluto in an aside: "How unfortunate my coming here would be if my conjuration fails me! Let's get on with it! I know too well to whom I speak. Go to it, brother, or else all will have been in vain!" (128). Pluto is now addressed as "brother," again showing that Celestina is dealing, not with a deity whom she worships, but with one with whom she is used to dealing, her "brother" in the practice of magic. That she is pleased with Pluto's final assistance can be seen at the start of the fifth act, when, having left Melibea's walled garden retreat, Celestina soliloquizes: "Oh, demon whom I conjured! How well you granted all I asked! I am in your debt. You tamed the shrewish fury of the girl with your power and let me speak to her alone when you got rid of her mother. . . . Bless you, snake oil; bless you, white thread! You've made everything work to my advantage!" (140).

The tone of her mutterings shows that even the experienced magician can be surprised at the efficacy of her conjuration, attested to by Pluto's having "got rid" of Melibea's mother, Alisa, something that Celestina's much-touted rhetorical skills could not have brought about.[20] In the eyes of Celestina, Pluto had accomplished the opportune exit of Melibea's mother by causing the illness that called Alisa to her sister's bedside. He did, indeed, give Celestina the "aparejada oportunidad" that she had asked for toward the end of the third act; she recognizes Pluto's role in an act 4 aside: "That devil is around here creating an opportunity, making that other woman sicker" (44), using *diablo* not in the sense of identifying Pluto with the Christian personification of evil but as a usage of classical origin—*diablo* (from the Late Greek *diabolos* and the Latin *diabolus*) and *demonio* (from the Greek *daimon*). Such terms have been misread as supportive of Celestina's involvement with the Christian Devil. At best, they are employed in the sense of the popular parlance of the era, in the socioreligious context in which she lives, and in order to better communicate with the audience or reader for whom the work is intended, Christians who did not believe in Pluto but knew with certainty that the Devil existed.

The total fulfillment of her Plutonic conjuration with the illicit sexual union of Calixto and Melibea through philocaption further attests to Celestina's powers—both occult and psychological. She has served society once more, as well as Pluto has served her: "Thus you broke down that cruel female with your power" (act 5; p. 52). Despite her success, Celestina does not flaunt her magic. Indeed, she does not mention it at all to others, preferring anonymity in this regard—keeping secret the most important element in her life. She appears to accept society's stigma as witch rather than promote herself as one belonging to a non-Christian magical tradition. It may be that her decision is founded on practicality, for society needs the services of an *alcahueta* and an *hechicera,* both of whom are embodied in Celestina and publicly known. Her persona as magician, however, she chooses to keep private and, therefore, is not evident as are her other facets. Indeed, in *Tragicomedia de Calixto y Melibea,* there is only one ritual of magic—the conjuration in the third act—and that may indicate that such practices are reserved for the most difficult cases, those that Celestina can resolve only through magical intervention.

But, notwithstanding the successful conclusion of the Calixto-Melibea affair in their illicit union, Celestina's achievement as intermediary and magician is marred by the deaths of the lovers and by the avarice of Calixto's servants, who expect to share in the reward that their master has given the crone. In act 12, when Celestina reneges on her promise, Sempronio cannot restrain his ire and, egged on by Pármeno, attacks her with his sword. As he wounds her fatally, the servant shouts out her sentence of infernal damnation. Hedging her bets even at the end (or is she acting the Christian to the end?), Celestina screams for confession. But death has her in its grip, and she dies at the hand of her former accomplice while Elicia looks on. Celestina expires before anyone can bring a priest to her side—or Pluto rescue her.

Celestina may have conjured the pagan Pluto, but, in the eyes of Sempronio, her soul will dwell with the damned in Satan's hell. It is ironic that, despite her craftiness in magic, Celestina has no precognition of the tragic events that her liaison with Pluto will cause, including betrayal by her god, who abandons her at the moment of mortal danger, as he had done with Doña Claudina. Or is it that the Lord of the Underworld has extracted a price for his magical services, calling in Celestina's earlier offer—"demand what you will of me"—by claiming her for his nether kingdom?

Despite the church's misappropriation of ideas that by Rojas's time had led to the conflation of magic and witchcraft, a reading of *Tragicomedia de Calixto y Melibea* informed by the fundamental distinctions between the two practices divulges the intent of the author(s) to present Celestina in two opposing ways: first, as the populace misinterprets her calling, that is, seeing her as a worshiper of the Christian Devil; and, second, as disclosed in her secret identity as magician when she calls on the services of the pagan Pluto. The former identity is presented through the statements of Sempronio, Pármeno, and Melibea, the latter through Celestina's own words and actions in the conjuration scene and in her revelations to Pármeno regarding her training at the side of Doña Claudina: "She would function in a magic circle better and more powerfully than I, even though I was very famous for it then" (176). The magic circle was the protective barrier used by magicians against potential harm by the otherworldly spirits they conjured. Further on, Celestina herself distinguishes what she and Doña Claudina did from the popular misconception termed *witchcraft* when she explains to Pármeno what took place one of the times that his mother was arrested: "Once they brought her up on the charge of being a witch because they found her one night carting earth from a crossroads by the light of candles. They had her tied to a ladder all night, wearing something like painted spun wool on her head. . . . And, without rhyme or reason, as everyone said, they made her confess using false witnesses and cruel torments to being what she was not" (178–79). Like her mentor Doña Claudina, Celestina is taken by society for what she is not. But, rather than a devotee of Satanic witchcraft whose soul will pass into hell, Celestina is a practitioner of Plutonic magic and is, thus, exempt, at least in her own mind, from the punishment meted out to Christian heretics. Thus, her afterlife will be spent in Hades, the underworld ruled by the selfsame Pluto she had conjured, cajoled, and threatened. The prospect is hardly better than that of eternal damnation under Satan's rule.

Notes

1. Although this magical treatise purports to be from the time of the Hebrew king and contains much late Jewish lore, it is of medieval origin, i.e., fourteenth or fifteenth century. Other famous *grimoires* are *The grimorium verum* (1517) and *The Grimoire of Pope Honorius* (Rome, 1629). There is also the *Lesser Key of Solomon* or *Legemeton,* earliest texts of which date from the seventeenth century.

2. For aspects of magic as empowerment through the use of *grimoires,* see Shakespeare's *Tempest* (ca. 1611) and the Peter Greenaway/Sir John Gielgud film *Prospero's Books.* Faust, too, before he signs the demonic pact, is drawn to the power-giving books that the magicians Valdes and Cornelius have brought for his instruction (sc. 1).

3. On the universality and forms of this type of worship, see Murray, *Witch Cult*, and *God of the Witches;* and Hughes. In the English-speaking world, the term *Wicca* is used to denote the religion of witchcraft; its practitioners frequently refer to it as *the Craft.*

4. The moon's crescent is also symbolic of horns, as can be seen on the headband worn by the Goddess in many of her manifestations.

5. Christianity developed many of its tenets and dogmas from Judaic and other Middle Eastern religions, among them Zoroastrianism (with its central doctrine of the dual powers of light [Ahura Mazda] and darkness [Ahriman]), Mithraism, and Gnosticism.

6. The translation is erroneous on two counts. First, the modern term *witch* is how the translator chose to interpret a Hebrew term more properly rendered as *necromancer, soothsayer, seer,* etc.; a more accurate translation would be: "Thou shalt not permit a necromancer to live among you." Second, by deleting the phrase *among you,* the translator has changed the import of the exhortation in the original and given Protestant "witch-finders" the authority to execute those deemed to have practiced what the authorities considered to be the worship of Satan. Yet again the Bible was misused as a tool of power, in this case to purge undesirable elements from society. *The New English Bible* adheres to the perverse sense in the Authorized Version, changing only "suffer" to "allow" (85), as does *The Jerusalem Bible,* which, however, adopts "sorceress" rather than "witch" (84).

7. For a discussion of the Faust tradition and its interpretations in dramatic literature, see Lima, chap. 3.

8. The date of composition is obviously earlier, as ascertainable by Sempronio's statement "Granada may be captured" (act 3, sc. 1; p. 102). The official capitulation of Granada to King Fernando and Queen Isabel occurred on January 2, 1492, when they entered the Alhambra. The siege of Granada had taken eleven years.

9. The confusion is not so much in the text as in the way in which the text has been misinterpreted as regards the meanings of the terms *magic* and *witchcraft*. The vast majority of those who have studied the work use the terms interchangeably, unwittingly following the self-serving practice of the church since the Middle Ages. Such is the case with Lida de Malkiel's treatment of magic in *Tragicomedia de Calixto y Melibea* as Devil oriented. Even Russell, in an otherwise astute rendering of the topic, discusses magic exclusively in the context of Satanism.

10. Numerologists may find significance in the conjuration occurring in act 3, for *3* was a number of great import in the symbology of occultism, as a reading of Cirlot and Biedermann will verify.

11. On potions, cures, herbs, and other elements employed by Celestina in her *hechicerías,* see Laza Palacios, esp. the glossary. Compare Celestina's fifteenth-century list with the ingredients used by the Weird Sisters in Shakespeare's *Macbeth* (ca. 1606).

12. Many of these titles are due to the process of syncretism, which, by the fifteenth century, had taken characteristics of figures from classical antiquity and added them to those of Christian times. One such case pertinent here is that of the Christian Satan (Lucifer, the Devil), who was personified with the goat's horns,

cloven hooves, and lasciviousness of Pan and given the place of Pluto (Hades) as ruler of the underworld, which came to be called *hell* after the Norse deity.

13. In act 7, Celestina tells Pármeno that she learned her esoteric lessons from his mother, Doña Claudina, proceeding to laud her skills and detail their joint practices, including the use of the magician's circle when conjuring the denizens of the supernatural world. Although such a circle is not referrred to in Celestina's conjuration in act 3, its presence may be implied since it was common knowledge that it was always used in such operations.

14. For the demonic pact, see Rutebeuf on Theophilus and both Marlowe and Goethe on Faust.

15. Russell, following numerous critics (from Menéndez Pelayo and Bataillon to more recent writers), errs in two ways in referring to the attempted conquest of Melibea through philocaption when he states that Celestina did so through the "pacto con el demonio hecho por Celestina" (243). In fact, there is no demonic pact of any kind in the *Tragicomedia,* only a verbal statement made by Celestina at the end of her conjuration, as would anyone to someone who has performed a service or done a favor; furthermore, there is no assent from the second party, for there is no Devil involved. Russell and others err also by referring to Pluto as "el diablo" or "el demonio," which is an inexplicable transposition of the pagan god who rules the classical underworld to the Devil, who rules the Christian hell. There is no evidence in the text to warrant either interpretation.

16. Thread, according to the cabalistic text known as the *Sefer ha-zohar* (Book of splendor, sometimes called Enlightenment), is a symbol of the connection between different planes; here, as the skein that Pluto inhabits, it ties the physical world of Melibea and the supernatural plane of the classical deity. The cabalistic symbolism is particularly germane in the Spanish context because the *Zohar* is a compilation by the thirteenth-century scholar Moses de León of the teachings on the Pentateuch by Rabbi Simeon bar Yohai, a second-century Tanna. Also known as *The Midrash of Rabbi Simeon bar Yohai,* the *Zohar* circulated in manuscript form from the thirteenth century until its publication in 1558. The author(s) of the *Tragicomedia de Calixto y Melibea* may have read this text in manuscript. Russell (260) sees the coiled thread as a symbolic snake, making the association because he, like previous critics, sees Pluto as the Devil, whose original manifestation was as the Edenic serpent coiled around the Tree of Knowledge.

17. According to Bernstein (whose sourse is Burkert, 200): "In Hesiod there can be no confusion between Hades and Pluto, yet as time wore on, these figures fused: Hades as lord of the dead became associated with the earth as storehouse of seed; Pluto as a personification of Plenty (that is seed and produce in an agricultural society) took on attributes of rulership." Bernstein goes on to say: "The Homeric *Hymn to Demeter* helps explain this overlap between the underworld as grave (necropolis, city of the dead, catacomb) and granary, the connection between the inner earth and the fertility of its surface, the relationship of Hades/Pluto, Persephone, and Hecate" (39).

18. See the numerous plays listed under the "Cave of Salamanca" motif in Lima, 160.

19. In some traditions, the magician draws the circle while standing outside its

confines, leaving a "gate" through which to enter; this opening is closed once the magician is inside.

20. It has become fashionable of late to consider Celestina less an *hechicera* than a rhetorician, promoters of this view seeing the seduction of Melibea to the life of sin as the result of the crone's art of persuasion through words rather than as that of her art in arcane operations. While it is self-evident that Celestina is a gifted verbalizer on behalf of Calixto's passion as well as a masterly user of indirection and intrigue, the rhetorical devices that she employs in winning over Melibea's sympathy to the suitor's plight are, thanks to modern interests, now being put forward as the real (some say sole) reason for her success in opening the damsel to seduction. Among those who hold this interpretation are Fraker, "Rhetoric" and "Declamation"; Friedman; Handy; Morgan; and Valbuena. It must not be forgotten, however, that Rojas's work has to be considered first and foremost in the context of its own period, wherein supernatural operations by magician or witch were held to be efficacious by the majority of the populace on all social levels, as witnessed by the scope of the Inquisition in Catholic Europe and the Americas as well as that of the subsequent Witchcraft Panic, which gripped much of Protestant Europe and the English colonies in the New World. The fact is that, in the context of the work, Celestina herself attributes her powers to a supernatural agency, while her employer and his lackeys—not to mention all those who have dealt with her—believe her to be able to affect the natural world through unnatural rites.

Works Cited

Bernstein, Alan E. *The Formation of Hell.* Ithaca, N.Y.: Cornell University Press, 1993.

Biedermann, Hans. *Dictionary of Symbolism: Cultural Icons and the Meanings behind Them.* New York: Facts on File, 1992.

Burkert, Walter. *Greek Religion: Archaic and Classical.* London: Blackwell; Cambridge, Mass.: Harvard University Press, 1985.

Cirlot, J. E. *A Dictionary of Symbols.* New York: Philosophical Library, 1962.

Fraker, Charles F. "Rhetoric in the *Celestina:* Another Look." In *Aureum Saeculum Hispanum: Beitrage su Texten des Siglo de Oro,* ed. Karl Hermann Korner and Dietrich Briesemeister, 81–90. Weisbaden: Franz Steiner, 1983.

———. "Declamation and the *Celestina.*" *Celestinesca* 9, no. 2 (1985): 47–64.

Friedman, Edward H. "Rhetoric at Work: Celestina, Melibea and the Persuasive Arts." In *Fernando de Rojas and "Celestina": Approaching the Fifth Centenary,* ed. Ivy A. Corfis and Joseph T. Snow, 359–70. Madison, Wis.: Hispanic Seminary of Medieval Studies, 1993.

Goethe, Johann Wolfgang von. *Faust: Part One and Part Two.* Translated, with an introduction and notes, by Charles E. Passage. New York: Bobbs-Merrill, 1965.

Greenaway, Peter. *Prospero's Books: A Film of Shakespeare's "The Tempest."* London: Chatto & Windus, 1991.

Handy, Otis. "The Rhetorical and Psychological Defloration of Melibea." *Celestinesca* 7, no. 1 (1983): 17–27.

The Holy Bible. Authorized King James Version. New York: Abradale, 1959.

Hughes, Pennethorne. *Witchcraft.* London: Longman's, 1952.

The Jerusalem Bible. Garden City: Doubleday, 1970.

Laza Palacios, Modesto. *El laboratorio de Celestina.* Málaga: Instituto de Cultura, 1958.

[Léon, Moses de]. *Zohar, the Book of Enlightenment* [i.e., *Sefer ha-zohar*]. 1558. Translated by Daniel Chanan Matt. Classics of Western Spirituality. New York: Paulist, 1983.

Lida de Malkiel, María Rosa. *La originalidad artística de "La Celestina."* Buenos Aires: Editorial Universitaria de Buenos Aires, 1962.

Lima, Robert. *Dark Prisms: Occultism in Hispanic Drama.* Lexington: University Press of Kentucky, 1995.

Marlowe, Christopher. *The Tragedy of Doctor Faustus.* ca. 1588. New York: Washington Square, 1965.

Morgan, Erica. "Rhetorical Technique in the Persuasion of Melibea." *Celestinesca* 3, no. 2 (1979): 7–18.

Murray, Margaret. *The Witch Cult in Western Europe.* 1921. Oxford: Oxford University Press, 1967.

———. *The God of the Witches.* 1933. New York: Doubleday/Anchor, 1960.

The New English Bible. Oxford: Oxford University Press; Cambridge: Cambridge University Press, 1970.

Rojas, Fernando de. *Tragicomedia de Calixto y Melibea.* Madrid: Aguilar, 1968. The *Comedia de Calixto y Melibea* was first published in 1499. An amplified version appeared in 1502 as *Tragicomedia de Calixto y Melibea.* It is popularly known as *La Celestina.* All English translations given in the text are mine.

Russell, Peter E. *Temas de "La Celestina" y otros estudios del "Cid" al "Quijote."* Barcelona: Ariel, 1978.

Rutebeuf. *Le miracle de Théophile.* ca. 1261. Paris: Librairie Ancienne Edouard Champion, 1925.

Shakespeare, William. *The Tragedy of Macbeth.* ca. 1606. Edited by Nicholas Brooke. Oxford: Oxford University Press, 1990.

———. *The Tempest.* ca. 1611. Edited by George Lyman Kittredge. Boston: Ginn, 1939.

Spies, Johann. *Faustbuch.* Frankfurt a.M., 1587. Amsterdam: Rodopi, 1970. Also known as *Volksbuch.*

Sprenger, Jacobus, and Heinrich Kramer [Henricus Institoris]. *Malleus maleficarum.* ca. 1486. Translated by Montague Summers. Edited by Pennethorne Hughes. London: Folio Society, 1968.

Valbuena, Olga Lucía. "Sorceresses, Love Magic, and the Inquisition of Linguistic Sorcery in *Celestina.*" *PMLA* 109, no. 2 (March 1994): 207–24.

Part III

Possession and Exorcism

4

The Primal Spirit

Sacred Frenzy in Euripides' Bacchae

> Through pity and fear it achieves the purgation of such emotions.
>
> —Aristotle, *The Poetics*

While this segment of Aristotle's famous definition of tragedy as it became manifest in ancient Greece opts, like many other translations, for the term *fear,* in the case at hand it would be much more appropriate to render the Greek *phobos* as *terror* or *panic,* for either of these heightened states of fear better conveys the emotional extreme elicited by the horrific events that Euripides set before his audience in *Bacchae,* his unique interpretation of Dionysian worship in Hellas.

Euripides' tragedy is at the end of a long evolution of the form, which began with the dithyramb, a choral song in honor of the god Dionysus. That mode of ritual expression was vehement in character and irregular in form, as befitted the orgiastic and intoxicating nature of the Dionysia, Attic festivals in honor of the god of wine out of which formal Greek drama would emerge, Attic tragedy being its preeminent scion. But, as Nietzsche posits, the evolution of the form was not unilateral; rather, it resulted from the interaction and opposition of two "creative tendencies" (19), represented by the gods Apollo and Dionysus.[1] In the spirit of competition, better yet the struggle referred to as *agon,* between the two symbolic deities, the dramatic mode of expression underwent a process of change through the formalization of its elements, the addition of the chorus and an increasing number of actors in dialogue, as well as through eschewing the representation of violent events on stage. It sought through a tragic action involving high-status individuals to move the audience to experience *katharsis,* the purgation of the emotions of pity and terror, on witnessing *peripeteia,* the reversal of fortune or the fall of the mighty through *hamartia,* the so-called tragic flaw, often that excessive pride termed *hubris.* A recognition scene, *anagnoris,* marked the tragic hero's coming to grips with his situation. Fur-

---

Previous page: Dancing Bacchantes, Greek frieze, provenance unknown. Public domain.

thermore, the ritualistic nature of tragedy was enhanced through propitiatory rites, including animal sacrifice, at an altar that occupied the center of the *orchestra*.

Bacchae adheres to the basic tenets of tragedy as delineated by Aristotle yet at times follows a digressive course. It is an odd piece of writing for a dramatist who did not believe in the gods and who sought in many of his works to demonstrate to his fifth-century B.C.E. Athenian audiences how religion had corrupted their minds and put them in thrall to false divinities.[2] But *Bacchae* is unique, not solely as a manifestation of an unpopular position, or as the last of Euripides' plays, but as the only work of those extant in ancient Greek drama in which Dionysus is the protagonist.[3] As such, the tragedy seems to be ironic in the light of its creator's atheism, for it would appear to proclaim the divinity of Dionysus and his righteous vengeance on King Pentheus for opposing the introduction of his cult into Thebes, for persecuting its followers, and for demeaning his godship. The struggle between the Apollonian and the Dionysian is not an *agon* of the first order, for Pentheus is a mortal, and a weak ruler at that, whose antagonist, a god, manipulates him and the populace of Thebes at will.

And it is the deity, albeit in the role of Stranger ("*a very young man in foreign dress*"), who speaks the first lines as he stands before the royal palace at Thebes. He declaims his true nature at the start of his soliloquy:

> I, Dionysus, to the Theban land have come,
> The son of Zeus by Cadmus' daughter, Semele,[4]
> Who was delivered of me in a lightning-flash;
> My form divine discarding for a mortal shape. (330)

Next he states the mission he has in mind:

> This is the first Hellenic city I have reached
> And yonder started dances with my ritual,
> To prove my god-head in the eyes of mortal men.

Then he expresses the reason for his entry on the scene in human form and trappings:

> [B]ut if angry Thebes attempt
> to drive the Bacchae from the mountain-side by arms

I shall join issue, I will be their general.
And with this purpose I have taken mortal shape;
For a man's nature I have changed my form divine. (331)

The Stranger, Dionysus, son of Semele and grandson of Cadmus, has returned to his homeland, seeking to install his cult in Thebes and to right the wrong done his mother. In his righteousness can be seen the seeds of the demagoguery that has characterized many a leader, religious or political, since time immemorial and that was a hallmark of many denizens in the pantheon of the gods. This quality will confront the haughtiness of Pentheus, with dire results for the Theban king.

Taken over by the spirit of Dionysus (or controlled mentally by him), his followers, the Chorus of Bacchae, described as "*women of Asia,*" enter on the invitation of their god. Their choral chant is first a tale of Dionysus's origins, then becomes an ode to the joys of the life, merriment, music, dance, hunting, and the eating of raw flesh, as well as other natural pleasures of the god's cult, with segments punctuated by the cry "Evoi, evoi!" (334). These are the women who have followed Dionysus from Phrygia, not those Theban women whom he describes as follows:

I've stung these women out of house and home
With madness; on the mountain they abide distraught,
Under compulsion wearing Bacchanalian dress.
And every woman of the seed that Cadmus sowed
I've driven frenzied from her home, yes, every one. (331)

So begins the god's revenge on Thebes for having cast doubt on his divine birthright and for having caused his mother's death. Semele's sisters, Ino, Autonoë, and Agave, the latter being the king's mother, have been specially selected by Dionysus for gruesome roles in his play within a play. And, when Pentheus, the young king, returns to his city, he finds that the women have gone to Mount Cithaeron, there to dance and perform other erotic rituals of the Dionysian cult; he then sees limping Cadmus and blind Tiresias, dressed in fawn skins and wielding thyrsi,[5] as the old men too prepare to join the revels. The Apollonian has ceded to the Dionysian, even among such as the former ruler and the prophet. But Pentheus will not adhere to the lure of the new cult; he has had some of the demented women arrested, and, despite the old seer's exhortation and Cadmus's supplication, he orders that the Stranger be arrested.

The guard who brings him before the king reveals that the Stranger has freed the incarcerated women through magic and, like an oracle, dares to warn Pentheus: "The miracles are many that this man has brought / With him to Thebes. Be wary of what are to come" (341). The initial encounter of god and king, both young, both haughty, both powerful, foreshadows their later confrontation; as well, their kinship as cousins, unrecognized by Pentheus, will bind them in a strange sacrificial rite. Unaware of the Stranger's true nature as god and kin, Pentheus heaps scorn on him as an effeminate and lascivious charlatan and orders that his golden curls be shorn. Then he orders the Stranger incarcerated "with nothing for him visible but dark and gloom" (342). The place is a symbolic tomb and the imprisonment a virtual death. The king sees his actions as fitting, for they have been taken against one whom he perceives to be a poseur, dangerous both to his people and to his status. But, unwittingly, he has committed sacrilege by offending the person of a god, and he has sinned against familial tradition by abusing his kin.

Dionysus permits the offenses against his deific nature, but he soon rebels against imprisonment. He frees himself as he freed his imprisoned followers, but his miraculous self-deliverance is characterized by greater pomp and circumstance, as befits a deity. Set to the background of the Bacchae's threnody, an extended lamentation over the fate of their god, the earth begins to quake, Semele's tomb emits flames, and a section of the royal palace collapses. Dionysus emerges from the chaotic setting, returning to a light of day that is enhanced by the glow of fires. Having feared him dead, the Bacchae face him with joyous disbelief.[6]

The second encounter between king and god is very different. Pentheus is amazed at the Stranger's escape but plans yet to keep him from leaving the palace precincts. But he is distracted by a cowherd's tale of the wild actions of the Bacchae on Mount Cithaeron, superhuman feats made possible by the magical powers of the god they worship:

> The Bacchae fell
> Upon the grazing heifers—not a knife had they.
> You could have seen Agave holding in two parts
> A heifer near to milking and it lowed the while;
> And the young cattle others tore to bits and shreds.
> . . .
> Less time was spent in stripping carcasses of flesh
> Than it would take you, sire, to shut your royal eyes.
> . . .

Here, there, and everywhere they scattered all there was;
They snatched up children from their homes; . . .
. . . On their clustered hair
They carried fire that burnt not. Then the folk enraged
And harassed by the Bacchae, rushed to take up arms;
On this there followed, sire, the strangest spectacle.
The pointed arrows did not draw a drop of blood

Out of the Bacchae; they but threw their thyrsus wands,
With these they wounded, turned their adversaries back,
Women with men contending, not without some god. (347–48)

The carnage at the hands of human women become Amazons is seen as possible solely under the spell of some deity. The foregrounded savagery serves as a prefiguration of even more dire behavior toward play's end. This is hinted at when yet another commoner, the cowherd, advises Pentheus to receive Dionysus as a mighty god and when the god himself, as the Stranger, gives a veiled warning to the king not to persist in ordering an attack against the Bacchae.

The action of the tragedy takes a strange turn then. As if under the spell of the Stranger's words, Pentheus decides that he wants to journey to Mount Cithaeron to spy on the Bacchae. The disguised god offers to lead him, but only if the king will also don a disguise, the trappings of a woman—gown, wig, and hat—along with a thyrsus and a fawn-skin cloak. Dressed as a woman, Pentheus will become like the Stranger, taking on feminine characteristics akin to those he had mocked in the god. His curiosity having gotten the better of him, or the Stranger's power having overcome his common sense, Pentheus agrees to the ruse despite the affront to his person that the disguise will bring about. There is no doubt that the Stranger has altered the king's enmity and caused his capitulation through magical control of his mind. Before joining the king in the palace, where the transformation is to take place, Dionysus declares his plan to his followers:

Women, the man is swimming well inside the net.
He'll join the Bacchae, death will be his punishment.
. . .
Now I intend him for the laughing-stock of Thebes,
Female-impersonator, through the city led.
. . .

When from his mother's hands he passes into Death,
By those hands slaughtered. Zeus's son he then will know,
Dionysus; at the end he is the fiercest god,
Though very gentle in his ways with humankind. (350)

Notwithstanding the self-proclaimed gentleness, this statement is a broad depiction of the ghastly events that will befall the king on Cithaeron. Only the details are missing. But this is a technique of economy since keeping the public in suspense was not the point of Greek tragedy. The audience already knew the story of the god and the king; their emotions would be affected, as in any tragedy, by the foregrounding of the character's fate, the terrible consequences attendant on his actions against the god. Even if highborn, the individual was in the hands of powers beyond his control; how, then, could the common man not expect a similar fate? The audience watched with fascination as Dionysus manipulated the king, turning him into a marionette, readying him for sacrifice.

In a parallel to Pentheus's earlier mockery of the god, Dionysus now leads the king out of the palace, a cross-dresser of ridiculous mien who is unaware of his comic condition—or of the destiny that awaits him. As the Stranger tells him: "You are not ordinary and your lot will be / Not ordinary. Fame will lift you to the skies." And, on the termination of a choral ode on the fate soon to befall Pentheus as "[o]ne who knows no law, no right, / Knows not god" (353), a Messenger comes to report to the Chorus, thinking them to be Thebans, what has transpired on Mount Cithaeron.

The Messenger first recounts how the Stranger brought down the top of a fir, as if by miraculous means, on which to seat Pentheus that he might spy on the Bacchae while unseen once the tree was released to gain its full height. The elevation of Pentheus is a physical manifestation of the god's own ascension, as his myth proclaims. Then, the intended victim secured on the perch, the voice of Dionysus rang out from the ether:

"Maenads, here I bring
The man that makes of you and me a mockery
And of our ritual; now avenge yourselves on him!" (355–56)

The Bacchae react almost instantly; led by Agave and her sisters, they stand and hurl stones, javelins, and thyrsi at Pentheus. When their efforts fail, Agave orders that they ring the tree and pull it out by its roots. The

Herculean effort succeeds, and Pentheus finds himself slammed to earth. The Messenger recounts the ghastly actions that took place thereafter as "first his mother, priestess of the sacrifice, / Fell on him," not recognizing her son, not listening to his filial pleas:

> But she, with foaming at the mouth and rolling eyes
> In frenzy, thinking as a mind should never think,
> Was held by Bacchus; his entreaty touched her not.
> She took his wrist, the left one, in her hands and stood
> With her feet pressing on his ribs, poor helpless man,
> And wrenched his shoulder from its socket—not by strength,
> But the god gave it to her hands an easy prey. (356–57)

The mother then killed her son, thus creating a life-death cycle.[7] Ino and Autonoë, her sisters, helped in the rending of the body as the rest of the horde of Bacchae attacked with uncontrollable passion. Body parts were scattered everywhere as a result of the feeding frenzy. As the Messenger narrates:

> [B]ut the wretched head
> His mother chanced on and she took it in her hands
> And fixed it on her thyrsus, thinking it to be
> A mountain lion's—through Cithaeron this she bears. (357)

The occurrences narrated by the Messenger took place off-stage owing both to the difficulty of their representation and to the aesthetic sensibility of the Greek tragic theater. Practicality and sensibility united to banish from the stage all action of a violent nature. Nonetheless, the impact of such deeds was heightened by the narration, on which each member of the audience could impose his or her own horrific interpretation as imagination permitted.

The events surrounding the death of the king qualified for exclusion from the stage owing to their savage nature. Pentheus, signified as a lion in the frenzied mind of Agave and the other Bacchae, becomes a stand-in for the god since the lion is a symbol of Dionysus, along with the bull and the snake. It is not the proper time of year for the god to die, dismembered parts falling to Hades, where his mother Semele (Demeter, Ceres) will reconstruct her son for his rebirth in spring, as his myth stipulated,[8] hence the need for a "scapegoat" who will serve as substitute victim in the off-season, whose blood will fertilize the vines, and who will also satisfy the god's need for revenge on the enemy of his cult. As the Messenger reports, Dionysus himself watched while his surrogate was torn to pieces by his followers as if Pentheus were, indeed, the animal they perceive in their deluded state. Owing to his condition and the rapid progression of events, Pentheus does not have the opportunity to realize that the Stranger is divine and, consequently, acknowledge his offense. Thus, he is deprived of a recognition scene; not even the pitiful words that he utters as his mother tears him apart can be interpreted to constitute such an acknowledgment since there is no mention of his having identified the Stranger as the god, much less of his having wronged Dionysus. His immediate concern, and a very human one at that, is self-preservation. First, he removes the wig so that his mother will know him; then, he seeks through words—since he is otherwise physically unable—to stop his mother's savagery. Failing in both attempts, he becomes a filicidal sacrifice.

The death and resurrection of Dionysus had to recur yearly for natural cycles to be fulfilled, but here the events are outside those seasonal demands, so it is a surrogate, not the god, who must undergo the transition from life to death. Pentheus is portrayed as that surrogate, and Euripides has drawn him as perfectly suited for the part: he is close in age to Dionysus; he is the son of Agave, sister of Semele, and, thus, a first cousin to Dionysus; he is also the grandson of Cadmus, as is Dionysus. And, when he dons female garb, Pentheus takes on the very female characteristics of the god that he had derided in the Stranger.[9] Their identification is so valid that Pentheus qualifies as the ideal substitute victim in the savage rite of passage. As Dionysus said to him: "You are not ordinary and your lot will be / Not ordinary."

And it is Dionysus who choreographs the Bacchae's homicidal frenzy that will lead to Pentheus's death on the mythic geography of Mount Cithaeron. The *sparagmos* (tearing apart)[10] and the *omophagia* (ingestion) are akin to the age-old ritual of the Eating of the God,[11] the consuming of raw flesh that allows the initiate to assimilate "the essence of the god" (Jung, 339 n. 58). In the evolution of that religious practice, the earliest sacrifice and cannibalization was of the king, himself a manifestation of the deity, often in a cycle of seven years, to guarantee the ongoing fructification of the earth and of women of childbearing age. In later rites, the king-god had a surrogate, a victim either chosen at random or, more typically, selected carefully and prepared for the honorable sacrifice so that he would resemble the ruler in his trappings. In the period of the great theater festivals in ancient Greece and its colonies, an animal, typically a goat, took the place of the human victim.[12] The final stage of evolution was the symbolic eating of the flesh and drinking of the blood of king or god through the substitutes of bread and wine, as in the Dionysian mystery at Eleusis, as in the Mithraic rite, as in the Christian sacrament of Holy Communion (but in the Mass, Roman Catholic Church dogma holds, the bread and wine *are* the transubstantiated Body and Blood of Christ, as Christ's words at the Last Seder attest, not mere symbols thereof). Evidence of the survival of the *sparagmos* can be seen in that the bread or Host of Holy Communion is broken into several pieces before ingestion by the celebrant.[13]

However, in their state of ecstasy, the Bacchae are incapable of making any rational connection to the ritual tradition. They dismember the body of Pentheus, not because he has persecuted Dionysus and his cultists, but because they believe the king of Thebes to be a lion and, consequently, the object of a normal hunt, as Agave proclaims on returning to Thebes. The mother and aunts of the victim are unaware of their having been used by the deity to slay his substitute—unaware, that is, until they are released by Dionysus from the spell and told of their horrific deed by Cadmus. It is only then that Agave has a recognition scene, arguably the most dire in Greek tragedy, herself a stand-in for her son. Yet her words to Dionysus are acrimonious:

> Agave: Receive our worship, Dionysus, we have done you wrong.
> Dionysus: Too late you know me; when you ought, you would not learn.
> Agave: That we acknowledge, but your blow is too severe. . . . The gods in anger should not copy mortal men. (362)

The god, speaking from atop his celestial perch, is relentless in his vengeance, banishing Cadmus and his daughters to an exile among barbarians; his actions prompt Agave's dictum against him: "He surely wrought an evil thing" (363).

These unparalleled events result from the interaction of the deific being with the celebrants of his ghastly rites of orgiastic "mysticism," some of whom were unaware of their participation—or of the import of the ritual. Neither Agave nor Cadmus comprehends the meaning behind the words of Dionysus, who is now apotheosized above them: "My sanction came from Zeus, my father, long ago" (362). The execution of Pentheus had to take place because it had been preordained, as in the prior case of his cousin

Actaeon, son of Autonoë, who had been turned into a stag (a horned animal appropriate as a sacrifice) by Artemis and torn to pieces by his own dogs; he, like Pentheus, had been atop a tree on Mount Cithaeron. What fails to occur in either case is resurrection. Despite his remnant body parts being brought together by Cadmus and his head restored to the torso by Agave, there is no reconstitution of the wholeness of being of Pentheus, as in the death and resurrection myth of Dionysus; Pentheus is another substitute victim for the god, not the god himself.[14] Euripides may here be mocking the very foundation of the cult of the god of wine and drama by showing the futility of its beliefs and practices.

The clash of the Apollonian and the Dionysian polarities, as posited by Nietzsche, is at the core of the clouding of reason by blind adherence to the emotions. Or, as Jaynes has it, the superimposition of the god on the celebrants is indicative of an approximation to the bicameral state of the mind that was dominant prior to the fifth century B.C.E. (see Jaynes, chap. 2). Dionysian rapture, then, is equated to the ancients' ability to commune with deity, that is, with what Jaynes terms the *god-side* of the brain. In the context of modern life, that state of consciousness in which a supernatural entity is said to be controlling the human mind and dictating its actions is defined as *possession,* a term that has both religious and psychiatic dimensions.

From the very start of the play, through the autobiographical soliloquy of Dionysus, there is posited the question about the real nature of the being who utters the words. Is he indeed divine, as he proclaims, a Phrygian god who has taken human form to accomplish a mission in support of his cult and its followers in a new land? Or is he merely a charlatan, a poseur, a false claimant to divinity, even a deranged mortal, who recognizes human gullibility and preys on it to his egotistical ends? There is no clear answer. Ambiguity may have been what Euripides sought to instigate in order to create a reasonable doubt in the mind of his audience about the nature of religion and the deities worshiped under its aegis. The play confronted his first audience with this uncertainty as it does those who witness its macabre action in later times.

But is the tragedy a condemnation of false prophets who make deific claims for themselves and a negative depiction of those who blindly follow their dictates? Is it a direct attack on Dionysus, the controversial nature deity? Or is it meant strictly as a representation of how a sector of Greek society practiced its religious beliefs with shocking extremism? Or, even, is it intended as a serious satire on Greek mores in an innovative and audacious final thrust by Euripides against the staid nature of tragedy in his age?

As a tragedy that pits the Dionysian and the Apollonian aspects of human nature against each other, the work shows the destructive nature of the Dionysian as it overcomes the Apollonian. Are the negative actions that Euripides has represented to be construed as evil? So it appears to the Messenger, who brought the news that Pentheus had perished, an act that he calls "evil so complete" (355), and so it appears to Agave as she recognizes: "He surely wrought an evil thing." Yet how valid is it for humans to judge the deeds of a god? His actions are beyond comprehension even though presented in the context of human emotions. But, to the followers of Dionysus, the king's execution is cause for joy since their god has triumphed and his worship has been established in the first Hellenic city. No doubt the example set in Thebes—founded on fear of the deity, as Euripides has it—would help foster the cult of Dionysus throughout the Greek world.

Then as now, *Bacchae* is a powerful portrayal of sacred frenzy and its horrific repercussions. To modern sensibilities, the blind force of instinct, the primal spirit of chaos, the Dionysian, may be perceived as a manifestation of evil, while rationality, the civilized pragmatism of order, the Apollonian, may be held to represent the good. But, since both aspects are manifest as intertwined in Euripides' tragedy, it is, perhaps, proper to assert that the dramatist's intention was to capture the duality of the human psyche—the Apollonian and the Dionysian—and to make his work both a cautionary tale against fanatical adherence to religion and a paean to the primal spirit.

NOTES

1. Nietzsche refers to them as manifestations of "the separate art realms of *dream* and *intoxication*" (19). He adds: "This deep and happy sense of the necessity of dream experiences was expressed by the Greeks in the image of Apollo. Apollo is at once the god of all plastic powers and the soothsayer god. He who is etymologically the 'lucent' one, the god of light, reigns also over the fair illusion of our inner world of fantasy" (21). He represents "the cognitive mode of experience." Dionysus, on the other hand, is the god who empowers rapture: "Dionysiac stirrings arise either through the influence of those narcotic potions of which all primitive races speak in their hymns, or through the powerful approach of spring, which penetrates with joy the whole frame of nature. So stirred, the individual forgets himself completely" (22). As a result: "Man now expresses himself through song and dance as the member of a higher community; he has forgotten how to walk,

how to speak, and is on the brink of taking wing as he dances. Each of his gestures betokens enchantment; through him sounds a supernatural power. . . . He feels himself to be godlike and strides with the same elation and ecstasy as the gods he has seen in his dreams" (23–24).

2. Karl Marx would adopt a similar stance on calling religion *the opiate of the masses.* That Euripides' position in this and other matters was unpopular may perhaps be gauged by his having been awarded only five first prizes at theater festivals during his career. *Bacchae* was written ca. 405 B.C.E. but was not presented on-stage until Euripides' death the following year, when it was performed at the Dionysia.

3. The deity appears in Aristophanes' *The Frogs,* also written in 405 B.C.E., but there he is not the protagonist. Dionysus has been identified with many death-and-resurrection gods of antiquity and has had many identities and names as a result. Among these are Bacchus, Zagreus, Sabazius, Nyetelius, Isodaites, Adonis, Ampelus, Antheus, Orpheus, Zalmoxis, Pan, Liber Pater (Liberator), and Osiris. His followers were also variously identified: as Bacchae or Maenads.

4. Semele was, as Guthrie puts it, "made into a woman by the Thebans and called the daughter of Kadmos, though her original character as an earth-goddess is transparently evident" (56). Semele was the Phrygian Zemelo, herself an incarnation of the Great Mother of the Gods, the Phrygian Cybele. In other versions of the myth, she is also associated with Demeter, with Ceres (the Italian counterpart of Demeter), and even with Persephone (daughter of Zeus and Demeter, who returns yearly from Hades in spring).

5. As we have seen, the thyrsus was a staff topped with a pinecone and garlanded with ivy and vines; it was borne by Dionysus and his votaries. As a staff of active power and propagation, it was a phallic symbol.

6. There are striking parallels between the aspects of Dionysus's life presented in the play (and other elements of his myth collected elsewhere) and the events associated with the birth, ministry, Passion, and Resurrection of Jesus Christ, including: the role of a precursor (Orpheus) who is beheaded; the supernatural aspect of his birth as the son of a human mother and the principal deity; his divine nature changed into human form to accomplish an end; his being perceived as a stranger bearing an exotic message to potential converts; his self-promotion as a deity; the working of miracles; his arrest, questioning, humiliation, and incarceration by the authorities; the natural phenomena that take place on his perceived execution; his having overcome death; his postmortem appearance to the women and their verification of his being alive; his descent into Hades; and his ascent to the world of the gods. In these characteristics of his myth, and especially as a savior god who dies and is resurrected (and whose rite of passage continued to be celebrated), Dionysus is a prototype of Jesus Christ. Unlike Christ, however, Dionysus avenges himself on those who have vilified his mother and blasphemed against him.

Another of numerous examples of the Christian adoption and adaptation of pagan ideas is the labarum, the monogram on Emperor Constantine's battle banners, which he said he saw in a dream prior to battle, and which, as a result of his victory and conversion, came to be interpreted as the Greek letters X (chi) and P (rho) for *Christos.* The symbol was, in fact, the Roman legions' emblem of the god

Mithras, itself having evolved from the Egyptian *ankh.* Mithras was a resurrection-savior god.

The labarum, a *signum Dei,* is affiliated with another emblem of Christ, IHS, often surmounted by a cross. According to Scott: "IHS are Greek characters, by ignorance taken for Roman letters; and Yes, which is the proper reading of those letters, is none other than the very identical name of Bacchus, that is, of the Sun, of which Bacchus was one of the most distinguished personifications; and Yes, or IES, with the Latin termination US added to it is Jesus. The surrounding rays of glory, as expressive of the sun's light, make the identity of Christ and Bacchus as clear as the sun" (169).

7. The mother as life giver and as destroyer has a counterpart in Indian myth in the archetypal Kali Ma, or Dark Mother of all, in whom all things begin and end (see Walker, 488–94). This concept is allied to that of the devouring female, whose symbol is the *labia dentata,* one of the images associated with the Mouth of Hell motif.

8. For the parallel myth of Osiris, see Jung, 233ff. In *De E Delphico* (9, 388 E), Plutarch discusses this aspect of the myth: "We hear from the mythographers, both prose writers and poets, that the god is by nature indestructible and eternal, but yet, under the impulsion of some predestined plan and purpose, he undergoes transformations in his beings. . . . But when the god is changed and distributed into winds, water, earth, stars, plants, and animals, they describe this experience and transformation allegorically by the terms 'rending' and 'dismemberment.' They apply to him the names Dionysus, Zagreus, Nyetelius, Isodaites, and they construct allegorical myths in which the transformations that have been described are represented as death and destruction followed by restoration to life and rebirth" (Linforth, 317–18).

9. His bisexual nature was indicated by his virginal beauty, on the one hand, and by his aspect as a horned deity, the bull, on the other. Euripides acknowledges both sides of the god's nature in *Bacchae.*

10. Dionysus being the god of wine makes more understandable the necessity of this ritual practice, for the dismemberment of the god is but a way of representing the process of creating the end product of the grape: tearing it from the vine, crushing it for its juice, separating out its skin and seeds, and letting the remnant liquid ferment. The process toward fruition of the grape as wine is one of death, dismemberment, putrefaction, and rebirth.

11. The wine produced as a result of the processing of the grape is meant to be ingested, thus this aspect of the consumption of the "god." For an excellent, thoroughly documented account of the ritual practiced in *Bacchae,* see Kott, the title of whose book, *The Eating of the Gods,* has the double meaning of humanity being eaten by the gods and of humanity eating the gods.

12. The Greek *tragoidia,* the etymon of *tragedy,* means "goat song," i.e., the bleating of the animal as it was sacrificed prior to the performance of the play. According to Walker: "Later Theban rites of Dionysus centered on killing and eating a fawn named Pentheus, and the Maenads wore fawn skins" (237). Whatever the animal, it had to have horns (even if vestigial, in the case of a fawn), the symbol of male fertility, and these were often gilded and crowned with a garland or wreath.

13. Although, unlike his prototype Dionysus, Christ was not dismembered, through the breaking of the consecrated bread he is meant to be associated with that rite of the sacrifice of the pagan god. As Hardison notes: "In the liturgy of Good Friday, Christ emerges as the supreme instance of the Divine Victim, the 'lamb' led to the slaughter of the original Passover. The agon of the preceding weeks leads with ritual inevitability to abuse, defilement, torture and destruction, the Christian embodiment of the *sparagmos* of pagan religion" (130).

14. Another surrogate for Dionysus was Orpheus, who, like Actaeon, is also mentioned by Euripides in *Bacchae.* The Bacchae (Maenads), at the behest of Dionysus, killed the priest and poet of his cult, tore his body to pieces, and cast his head and lyre into the river, from whence they floated out to sea. Again, the severed head of the substitute victim plays an important role in the myth of Dionysus.

In the context of Christian mythology, there is a parallel substitute victim. And, again, it was women—Salome and her mother, Herodias—who brought about the death of John the Baptist by having his head severed and placed on a tray. Despite the victimization of John the Baptist, his intended surrogate, Jesus Christ, could not avoid being sacrificed. Although, unlike his prototype Dionysus, Christ was not dismembered. Christ had to die, John the Baptist's beheading notwithstanding, because he was the substitute victim for God the Father, who did not act when Christ prayed for him to "remove this cup."

Works Cited

Aristotle. *The Poetics.* In *Aristotle: On Poetry and Style,* trans. G. M. A. Grubbe. Library of Liberal Arts. Indianapolis: Bobbs-Merrill, 1958.

Euripides. *Bacchae.* Translated by Henry Birkhead. In *Ten Greek Plays,* ed. L. R. Lind, 325–63. Boston: Houghton Mifflin, 1957.

Guthrie, W. K. C. *The Greeks and Their Gods.* Boston: Beacon, 1955.

Hardison, O. B., Jr. *Christian Rite and Christian Drama in the Middle Ages: Essays on the Origin and Early History of Modern Drama.* Baltimore: Johns Hopkins University Press, 1965.

Jaynes, Julian. *The Origin of Consciousness in the Breakdown of the Bicameral Mind.* Boston: Houghton Mifflin, 1990.

Jung, C. G. *Symbols of Transformation.* Translated by R. F. C. Hull. 2nd ed. Vol. 5 of *The Collected Works of C. G. Jung.* Bollingen Series 20. Princeton, N.J.: Princeton University Press, 1976.

Kott, Jan. *The Eating of the Gods: An Interpretation of Greek Tragedy.* Translated by Boreslaw Taborski and Edward J. Czerwinski. New York: Random House, 1973.

Linforth, Ivan M. "Myth of the Dismemberment of Dionysus." In *The Arts of Orpheus,* 307ff. Berkeley: University of California Press, 1941.

Nietzsche, Friedrich. *The Birth of Tragedy and The Genealogy of Morals.* Translated by Francis Golffing. New York: Doubleday/Anchor, 1956.

Scott, George Ryley. *Phallic Worship.* Westport, Conn.: Associated Booksellers, n.d.

Walker, Barbara G. *The Woman's Encyclopedia of Myths and Secrets.* San Francisco: Harper & Row, 1983.

5

Rites of Passage

Metempsychosis, Possession, and Exorcism in S. An-Sky's The Dybbuk

Truly, all souls must undergo transmigration. . . .

—*Sefer ha-zohar*

Sholem An-Sky's play *Der Dibbuk*[1] details the daily life of a group of Hasidic Jews in Eastern Europe, recording in the process a wealth of traditions, legends, superstitions, and other beliefs.[2] But the purpose of the play is not to be merely a faithful folkloric document of a colorful religious community. *The Dybbuk* is the tale of Channon, a young scholar in the Hasidic synagogue of Brainitz, and Leah, the daughter of the congregation's wealthiest member. The love between them stems from their youth, when the orphaned Channon was sheltered by Leah's father, Sender. But, facing the reality that Channon has no prospects for an inheritance, Sender seeks to betroth his daughter to the son of a wealthy man. Channon leaves the household in an effort to raise enough money to satisfy Sender, hoping and praying that the betrothal contract will not be signed in the meantime. However, Channon returns disillusioned by his search for material wealth. Unable to satisfy Sender's monetary stipulations, Channon turns to unorthodox methods to achieve his goal. The illicit nature of his pursuits endangers his life, and, ultimately, he dies.

The Dybbuk is yet another in the stages of evil. An-Sky's drama has as its central motif a love that circumvents the encumbrances of life and finds fruition beyond the grave. This is achieved through a torturous, unnatural process: the transmigration of the soul of the lover (Channon) into the living body of the beloved (Leah); the total habitation therein of the dybbuk (or possessing soul); and the expulsion of this migrant soul through the debilitating rites of exorcism, with an unprecedented and exhilarating outcome. *The Dybbuk* is the literary work most representative of the concepts of metempsychosis, possession, and exorcism in Jewish tradition.

Previous page: Exorcism of Leah, watercolor by Jennifer Coleman, in S. Ansky, *The Dybbuk* (South Bend, Ind.: Regnery/Gateway, 1979). Courtesy of the publisher.

1

Metempsychosis, or soul transmigration, is a belief as old as animism and characteristic of many sophisticated religions of the ancient world. It was a central tenet in Egypt, as attested by *The Book of the Dead;* it was at the heart of Buddhism and Brahmanism; it was fundamental to the Greek mysteries, to Pythagoreans, to Zoroastrianism, and to the cult of Mithra; it was a belief not uncommon among the early Christians, as witnessed by Saint Jerome and Origen, among others; it became prevalent among some Gnostics, Manichaeans, and Cathars; even certain Islamic sects upheld the doctrine.

Living as they did at the crossroads of civilization, and having in their variegated history the Egyptian and Babylonian captivities, the Jews could not help but be influenced by foreign beliefs through religious syncretism and cultural diffusion. Yet there is no viable proof that belief in metempsychosis was extant even in the latter part of the Second Temple era (ca. 516 B.C.E.–70 C.E.). Neither the Scriptures nor the Talmud asserts the concept of soul transmigration; indeed, rabbinic thought held metempsychosis in contempt as a despicable superstition. And, without rabbinic approval, soul transmigration could not attain orthodox status in the philosophical tradition of Judaism.[3]

Despite the lack of official sanction, metempsychosis continued to find adherents in the enclaves in which the doctrine had been reared. For centuries it was taught to initiates as part of the esoteric wisdom requisite for advancement to the highest degrees of mysticism. The sacred and occult nature of the belief mandated secrecy about its deepest mysteries; consequently, communication of this special knowledge was through oral means. It is for this reason that the Judaic belief in metempsychosis cannot be traced to its origin.

The first written expression of the doctrine is not made until the promulgation of one of the major texts of the cabala.[4] The *Sefer ha-bahir,* or Book of Brilliance, defines the belief in a matter-of-fact way, without explication of its genesis or theological foundation, as the transmigration of the soul of a former human being into the body of a newborn male or female child.[5] This is known in Hebrew as *gilgul,* but the term itself was not employed in the *Bahir* or in orthodox philosophy; it made its first appearance in a cabalistic text in the *Sefer ha-temunah,* published in Gerona.[6] The *Bahir* holds that the process of reincarnation may transpire over and over through a thousand generations.[7] *The Dybbuk* also expresses the general belief in reincarnation, but its view of *gilgul* contains a variant: "When the soul of a human being not yet dead is about to enter a body not yet born, a struggle takes place. If the sick one dies, the child is born—if the sick one recovers, a child is born dead" (42). As stated in the *Bahir* and in this segment from *The Dybbuk,* the doctrine of soul transmigration concerns only reincarnation.

But the *Sefer ha-zohar,* or Book of Splendor, the most extensive and influential of the cabalistic texts, transcribes what became the definitive ideas on soul transmigration. Rabbi Simeon bar Yohai, the protagonist of the *Zohar,* expounded on the complex theme by interpreting key verses from Exodus in terms of predestined levels of worthiness:

> When a human being is born into the world he is given a soul (nephesh) from the primordial "animal" sphere, the sphere of purity, the sphere of those who are designated "Holy Wheels"—namely, the supernal order of angels. If he is more fortunate he will be endowed with a spirit (ruah). . . . Should he possess still greater potential merit he is given a soul (neshamah) from the region of the Throne. These three grades of personality are the "maid-servant," the "manservant," and the "bondwoman" of the King's daughter. And if the newly created being deserves still more, the soul which is put into his bodily form derives through a process of emanation (aziluth) from the sphere of the "Only Daughter," and is itself called "the King's daughter." If his merit is still greater he will be endowed with a spirit (ruah), deriving through emanation from the sphere of the "Central Pillar," and its owner is then called "The son of the Holy One." . . . Should he be of even greater worth he is given a soul (neshamah) from the sphere of Father and Mother. . . . But if he should acquire still greater merit, the Holy Name Y H V H is granted to him in fulness. (3:283–84)[8]

These degrees or levels of worthiness existed prior to the human assignation, for all souls had had an ideal existence. This concept is not the creation of the author of the *Zohar;* it is a basic Platonic doctrine, had currency in the Talmud, and was even implied in the Scriptures. But it is the *Zohar* that gives it the most ample expression within Judaic tradition:

> When the Holy One, blessed be He, came to create the world, it pleased Him to form all the souls which were destined to be allotted to the children of men, and each was shaped before him in the very outline of the body she was afterwards to inhabit. He examined each one, and saw that some of them would corrupt their ways in the world. When the time of each was arrived, the Holy

> One summoned it, saying: "Go, descend into such and such a place, into such and such a body." But ofttimes it chanced that the soul would reply, "Lord of the world, I am satisfied to be here in this world, and desire not to leave it for some other place where I shall be enslaved and become soiled." Then would the Holy One respond: "From the very day of thy creation thou hast had no other destiny than to go into that world." At this the soul, seeing that it must obey, would descend against its will and enter into this world. (3:291)

Consequently, there is a ratiocination behind the original pairing of soul and body.

Similarly, soul transmigration is not a random process in the *Zohar:*

> Now as for the soul which is doomed to undergo transmigration, if she is the daughter of the Holy One, blessed be He, we cannot suppose that she is sold to an alien body that is under the domination of the evil spirit emanating from the side of Samael, since it is written: "I am the Lord, that is my name, and my glory will I not give to another." (Isa. 42:8)
>
> Nor is it to be thought that the body which harbours the daughter of the king shall be sold into the power of earthly crowns of defilement. Against this the Scripture says: "And the land shall not be sold in perpetuity." (Lev. 25:23)
>
> Which is the body of the King's daughter? Metatron; and this same body is identical with the handmaid of the Shekinah. Nevertheless, the soul that is the King's daughter is held prisoner therein, having to undergo transmigration. (3:283)

Even on these planes of merit, then, transmigration is requisite. But there are limitations to the process, both in number (as opposed to the plenary view of the *Bahir*) and in type:

> When a soul is doomed to undergo transmigration, should it be one which has emanated from the side of the Servant, Metatron, who represents in himself six aspects, then the successive revolutions of that soul will not be more than six years (i.e., times) until it shall have completed the six stages which lead back to the region from whence it came. But if the soul has emanated from the sphere of the Shekinah Herself, who is symbolized by the number seven, it "shall go forth free," because its owner is righteous, and is not subjected to labour or servitude. . . . This verse assuredly speaks of the soul of the

> Righteous One, teaching us that even though she may have to undergo transmigration in any of these, even in a manservant or maidservant or in any animal, yet "in it thou shalt do no manner of work," or, what amounts to the same thing, "thou shalt not make him serve as a bondsman." (3:282–83)

While the *Bahir* presented its views exclusively in the context of human-to-human transmigration, the *Zohar* expands the cycle to include the residency of a human soul even in an animal. This offhand reference reflects that nonhuman receptacles for human souls had become an accepted concept within the schema of metempsychosis.[9] While there is no attempt to justify such radical metamorphoses, the *Zohar* ascribes varietal transmigration to God's master plan:

> Truly, all souls must undergo transmigration; but men do not perceive the ways of the Holy One, how the revolving scale is set up and men are judged every day at all times, and how they are brought before the Tribunal, both before they enter into this world and after they leave it. They perceive not the many transmigrations and the many mysterious works which the Holy One accomplishes with many naked souls, and how many naked spirits roam about in the other world without being able to enter within the veil of the King's Palace. Many are the worlds through which they revolve, and each revolution is wondrous in many hidden ways, but men neither know nor perceive these things! Nor do they know how the souls roll about "like a stone inside a sling" (1 Sam. 25:29). (3:302)

The Dybbuk verifies the continuity of the belief in metempsychosis, even to the point of expanding on the aspect of metamorphosis: "The souls of the wicked return in the forms of beasts, or birds, or fish—of plants, even, and are powerless to purify themselves by their own efforts" (31).

2

While, in Judaism, metempsychosis at first concerned only reincarnation (*gilgul*), the belief acquired additional aspects over the centuries. The new tonalities reflected a wide variety of folk superstitions and fears. The most important of these, and the most enduring, was *ibbur*.

The concept of *ibbur* impressed itself on both esoterics and populace alike, to the extent that it became second only to *gilgul* within the confines of metempsychosis. *Ibbur* is defined as soul transmigration into a body already endowed with a soul; in effect, it denotes possession. But if *possession* has a connotation of evil, *ibbur* has both positive and negative manifestations.[10]

When *ibbur* is judged to be evil, the possessing soul is called a *dybbuk.*[11] Originally, the dybbuk was thought to be a demon that possessed the body of a person whose moral defenses were inadequate to ward off evil; the entry of the dybbuk was believed possible only because the individual had committed a grave offense. The sin opened the body to possession by the demon and placed the soul in jeopardy.[12] But this aspect of *ibbur* became less important as belief in demons declined, although it has not been eradicated. The principal belief in dybbukim centers on the view that wandering souls (not demons) who could not transmigrate or rest until their mission had been accomplished took possession of living bodies in order to fulfill their destinies.[13]

The teachings of the *Zohar* on *ibbur* are reiterated in An-Sky's *The Dybbuk.* Leah, the play's protagonist, understands the rationale behind the belief; she speaks with a conviction that belies her years:

> [I]t isn't evil spirits that surround us, but souls of those who died before their time, and come back again to see all that we do and hear all that we say. . . . [E]very one of us is born to a long life of many, many years. If he dies before his years are done, what becomes of the life he has not lived? What becomes of his joys and sorrows, and all the thoughts he had not time to think, and all the things he hadn't time to do? Where are the children he did not live long enough to bring into the world? Where does all that go to? Where? . . . [W]hen a candle blows out we light it again and it goes on burning down to the end. So how can a human life which goes out before it has burnt down, remain put out forever? . . . No human life goes to waste. If one of us dies before his time, his soul returns to the world to complete its span, to do the things left undone and experience the happiness and griefs he would have known. . . . It is the same with all the souls who leave the world before their time. They are here in our midst, unheard and invisible. (77–79)

Leah is not merely abstracting; she is concerned with the truncated life of Channon, whom she loved. Her conviction that his soul is nearby is founded on Hasidic tradition and on her sensitivity, which permits her to "see" and "hear" the dead (the assassinated bride and bridegroom buried in the town).

But, despite her intuitive knowledge, Leah is unschooled in the cabalistic refinements of *ibbur;* it remains for the Messenger, a mysterious visitor who presages death, to reveal the necessary addendum to her statements:

> The souls of the dead do return to earth, but not as disembodied spirits. Some must pass through many forms before they achieve purification. The souls of the wicked return in the forms of beasts, or birds, or fish—of plants, even, and are powerless to purify themselves by their own efforts. They have to wait for the coming of some righteous sage to purge them of their sins and set them free. Others enter the bodies of the newly born and cleanse themselves by well-doing. . . . Besides these, there are vagrant souls which, finding neither rest nor harbor, pass into the bodies of the living, in the form of a Dybbuk, until they have attained purity. (81–82)

The Messenger's revelation leaves Leah lost in astonishment. But she soon fixes on the idea of inviting her dead lover to the wedding, as Channon had requested in a dream. In itself charitable and innocent, the invitation nonetheless contains an implicit danger. And, indeed, Leah returns from the graveyard a changed girl, having fainted after an ordeal that her companion is too terrified to explain. Then, as the wedding ceremonies commence, Leah acts wildly and speaks in a voice not her own: "You buried me. But I have come back—to my destined bride. I will leave her no more" (92). The defiant proclamation is in the voice of Channon. Leah has experienced *ibbur,* having been inhabited by the wandering soul of her lover.

Being virtuous, Leah had the protection of her goodness against possession by an evil entity. But that moral bulwark can be breached when an individual desires it or places himself in jeopardy.[14] As her passionate words have attested, Leah believes in and sympathizes with souls who hover near the living because their destinies have been left unfulfilled. Her sympathy opens her heart to Channon's plight; her love instigates an unwitting receptiveness to her lover's soul. She has longed, subconsciously, to be his, but, as this is impossible in normal terms, only a supernatural occurrence can bring about the union of the lovers. And, finally, she extends the fateful wedding invitation.

The *ibbur* that Leah experiences, despite the name of *dybbuk,* is not evil. The rationale for this conclusion is found both in the circumstances of the possession and in the words that Channon uttered while still alive. In the early moments of the play, he expressed his longing in mystical terms: "I wish to attain possession of a clear and sparkling diamond, and melt it down in tears and inhale it into my soul. I want to attain to the rays of the third plane of beauty" (57). Channon's quest is directed to Tifereth (Beauty), one of the four Sefiroth (emanations of God) in the Middle Pillar (Judgment and Mercy being the other two pillars, each composed of three

Sefiroth). The Middle Pillar, which is the Shekhinah, mediates between Judgment (the Feminine, the Left, Darkness) and Mercy (the Masculine, the Right, Light). The Middle Pillar is also referred to by some cabalists as the Tree of Life and the other two as the Tree of Good and the Tree of Evil.

Channon desires to follow the way of the Middle Pillar, the perfect path, which leads to the Shekhinah. But, to achieve that height of perfection, he must fulfill his destiny on earth: marriage to his predestined bride and the procreation of offspring in that union. This mitzvah (commandment) having been denied completion through Sender's obstinacy, Channon's soul must undergo metempsychosis as it is written in the *Zohar:*

> Now the spirit which has left this world without procreation and engendering of children undergoes constant transmigration, finding no rest, and rolling about "like a stone inside a sling" until a "redeemer" comes forward to redeem it and bring it back to the same "vessel" which it formerly used and to which it clave with heart and soul, as to its life's partner, in the union of spirit with spirit. This "redeemer" builds up that spirit again. For the spirit which was left by the deceased still clinging to that vessel has not been lost—since nothing is lost in the world—but it is still there and seeks to return to its basis; and so the "redeemer" brings it and builds it up again in its place, and it becomes a new creation, a new spirit in a new body. (3:303)

In the context of cabalistic mysticism, Channon must seek this redemption through the union of soul and spirit. As the *Zohar* explains it: "[A]ll souls (neshamah) emanate from a high and mighty Tree, from that 'River which goes out of Eden' (Gen. 2:10), and all spirits (ruah) from another, smaller Tree—the souls from above and the spirits from below—and they unite after the fashion of male and female" (3:303). In the symbolism of the play, Channon is the soul and Leah the spirit. Only if their union is achieved can there be attainment of the mystical Shekhinah and, ultimately, of the King's Palace. Thus it is that, in possessing Leah, Channon is seeking only to fulfill that which was his destiny. The habitation of Channon in Leah, therefore, is an earthly attempt to achieve the mystical union and is not evil in itself.

The complication of the motif occurs because Channon, in desperation over Sender's refusal of Leah's hand, turned away from the proper path and sought his end through cabalistic means. Such a process is, as Rabbi Azrael explains, fraught with danger, even for the worthiest of souls: "But it happens sometimes that a soul which has attained to the final state of purification suddenly becomes the prey for evil forces which cause it to slip and fall. And the higher it had soared, the deeper it falls" (81). Channon fits this categorization. He had followed the path of the Middle Pillar, striving to achieve the third of its four Sefiroth. But his lofty intent was defeated by the circumstances that prevented his marriage to Leah. Weakened spiritually by an increasing frustration and pessimism, Channon sought out heterodox means to his physical-spiritual end.

When Channon's body is discovered in the synagogue well after his death, the *Sefer Raziel* is found beside it. The Book of the Angel Raziel is a cabalistic text attributed to Eleazar of Worms, a thirteenth-century C.E. Jewish mystic and magus. The book purports to be an angelic treatise revealed to Adam and transmitted by his heirs to Noah. Thereafter, it was lost. It was discovered in Europe during the Middle Ages, when it became a practical guide to magicians owing to its complex and varied references to the secret names of the Divinity,[15] Solomon's Seal, talismans, potions, incantations, occult symbols, and angelology. With this cabalistic "key" to esoteric knowledge, Channon sought to thwart Sender's plan. But his delving into the cabala for egocentric reasons, no matter how justified, brought him a premature death. However, his demise contains a cruel ambiguity. After reaching the depths of despair, he expires in a state of ecstasy: "So it was all to no avail—neither the fasts, nor the ablutions, nor the spells, nor the symbols. All in vain. . . . So what remains? What is there still to do . . . by what means. . . . (He clutches the breast of his kaftan, and his face is illuminated with ecstasy.) Ah! The secret of the Double Name is revealed to me. Ah! I see Him. I . . . I . . . I have won!" (62–63). Channon dies fulfilled, achieving apotheosis through the revelation of God's Double Name and the beatific vision. Notwithstanding subsequent statements and impressions that define Channon's endeavors as evil, neither his death nor the nature of his wandering soul can be construed negatively in the light of his experience. The ecstatic death of Channon is an important element in assessing the real status of his soul and the validity of its mission.

A further clue in this context is the word *destined.* Neither Channon nor Leah was aware that, before they were born, their fathers had promised each other that, should one have a son and the other a daughter, their children would marry. In the course of time, their wives gave birth to a male child and a female child, respectively. But the friends had parted earlier and did not know of each other's children. When Sender learned of his friend's death, the pact was forgotten. Then destiny brought Channon to his door, but Sender had no reason to think that he was his friend's son and did not ascertain the youth's parentage. Charitably, Sender took Channon into his household, and there Channon and Leah were drawn to each other irresistibly. Sender began to suspect that the love between them was preordained, yet, afraid that, if Channon were his friend's son, his daughter would be bound to a poor scholar, he did not pursue his intuitive leanings. His was a sin of omission.

The pledge of the friends created mutual obligations that were binding on earth and in heaven. Thus, Channon's father returns from the grave to demand a rabbinic trial for Sender and, implicitly, a *tikkun,* or restoration to its proper place in the Soul of Adam, for Channon's soul. At the trial, the accusations are vocalized through the mediumship of Rabbi Samson: "His son had been blest with a noble and lofty soul, and was progressing upwards from plane to plane. . . . [H]is son, growing older, had become a wanderer . . . for the soul to which his soul had been predestined was drawing him ever onward. . . . [Y]ou took him into your house . . . and his soul bound itself to the soul of your daughter" (125–26). Sender's refusal of Leah's hand to Channon has deprived the youth of his destined bride and, consequently, of his rightful place in eternity. Because the rabbinic court sees justification in the charge, it passes judgment against Sender but does not alleviate Channon's plight. Perhaps because of this, Channon's father neither forgives nor concurs in the sentence. Therefore, the fate of Channon's soul rests with Leah, for only she can decide to accept the role in which destiny has cast her.

When all these elements—circumstances and destiny—are measured, it becomes evident that *dybbuk* is a misnomer for the soul that possesses Leah. Its wandering condition is not a punishment for Channon's delving into esoteric doctrines but a final opportunity to obtain restitution so that it may be redeemed. Nonetheless, the rabbis persist in using the pejorative term and demand the immediate liberation of Leah's body. To this the dybbuk replies: "I have nowhere to go. Every road is barred against me and every gate is locked. On every side, the forces of evil lie in wait to seize me. There is heaven and there is earth—and all the countless worlds in space, yet in not one of these is there any place for me. And now that my soul has found refuge from the bitterness and terror of pursuit, you wish to drive me away. Have mercy! Do not send me away—don't force me to go!" (109–10). Because the dybbuk has refused to leave of its free will, and because its cause cannot be sponsored by the living, Rabbi Azrael reluctantly prepares for the process of eviction through exorcism.

3

Exorcism has an old but scattered history in Judaism. It is not founded on doctrinal tenets since the belief in demons is not endemic to the religion; rather, exorcism and its rites derive from case histories found in Scriptures, midrashic literature, and apocryphal or pseudepigraphal writings. The anecdotes in these sources underscore a deep-seated faith in the efficacy of the methods used to cast out possessing entities, be they demonic beings or former humans. The only valid example of what might be termed *possession* in the Scriptures is the series of seizures suffered by Saul. The king's plight was attributed to an evil spirit sent by Yahweh to possess him. This entity could be placated only by the music of David's harp (or lyre): "So whensoever the evil spirit from the Lord was upon Saul, David took his harp, and played with his hand, and Saul was refreshed, and was better, for the evil spirit departed from him" (1 Sam. 16:23). The evil entity returned on several occasions to possess Saul anew, and, in each instance, Saul attempted to slay David; but he was unsuccessful (1 Sam. 18:10–11, 19:9–10). The important feature of the story, however, is the peculiarity of the exorcism, for it does not purport to be such and yet has the same effect as formal rituals with similar intent in other religious contexts, be they Jewish or Christian.

There are two other important examples of exorcism concerning figures from the Scriptures, but the sources are apocryphal. In the first, the Dead Sea Scrolls depict Abraham as an exorcist when he drives out a demon from Pharaoh by invoking God and laying his hands on the victim (Fitzmyer, 58–59). In the second, the historian Josephus recounts the popular view that Solomon had power over demons and that his abilities were God given: "God also enabled him to learn that skill which expels demons, which is a science useful and sanative to men. He composed such incantations also by which distempers are alleviated. And he left behind him the manner of using exorcisms, by which they drive away demons, so that they never return, and this method of cure is of great force unto this day." The prominent historian then refers to Eleazar, "of my own country," who, in his presence (and that of Vespasian and his court), released the demoniacally possessed by using Solomon's name and method: "He put a ring that had a root of one of those sorts mentioned by Solomon to the nostrils of the demoniac, after which he drew out the demon through his nostrils; and when the man fell down immediately, he abjured him to return into him no more, making still mention of Solomon, and reciting the incantations which he composed" (book 8, chap. 2, verse 5; p. 173).

In this context, Justin Martyr, a Greek apologist of the second century, declares: "But though you exorcize any demon in the name of any of those who were amongst you—either kings, or righteous men, or prophets or patriarchs—it will not be subject to you. But if any of you exorcize it in the name of the God of Abraham and the God of Isaac and the God of Jacob, it will perhaps be subject to you. Now assuredly your exorcists, I have said, make use of craft (techne) when they exorcize, even as the Gentiles do, and employ fumigations and incantations (katadesmoi, 'bonds')" (241). Furthermore, some Jewish exorcists incorporated the name of Jesus in their rites because of the well-documented miracles and exorcisms that Christ had performed.[16] The author of the Acts of the Apostles recounts a case that occurred in Ephesus:

> Now some also of the Jewish exorcists who went about, attempted to invoke over them that had evil spirits, the name of the Lord Jesus, saying: "I conjure you by Jesus, whom Paul preacheth." And there were certain men, seven sons of Sceva, a Jew, a chief priest, that did this. But the wicked spirit, answering, said to them: "Jesus I know, and Paul I know; but who are you?" And the man in whom the wicked spirit was, leaping upon them, and mastering them both, prevailed against them, so that they fled out of that house naked and wounded. And this became known to all the Jews and the Gentiles that dwelt at Ephesus. (19:13–17)

As was the case with Solomon and other scriptural notables among non-Jews, Christ was thought of as a powerful magician by non-Christians. In other instances where his name was employed in Jewish exorcisms, accounts relate greater success than in the incident at Ephesus. An apparently effective, if prolonged, Jewish formula in which the name of Jesus is interpolated was discovered in Paris in a papyrus dated ca. 300 C.E.:

> Against demoniacal possession. The tried formula of Pibechis (a celebrated magician). Take of the juice of green fruits, together with the plant Mastigia (?) and lotus-pith, and heat it with marjoram (the colourless kind); then pronounce the following words: "Joel, Ossarthiomi, Emori, Theochipsoith, Sithemeoch, Sothe, Joe, Mimipsothiooph, Phersothi. AEEIOYO, Joe, Eochariphtha; get thee out of N.N." (and other formulae). But write the protecting charm on a tablet of tin: "Jaeo, Abraothioch, Phtha, Mesentiniao, Pheoch, Jaeo, Charsok," and hang it upon the sick person. To every demon it is a thing of fear which he dreads. Place thyself in front of the patient and conjure him. The formula of

> exorcism is the following: "I conjure thee by the God of the Hebrews, Jesus (later interpolation from a non-Jewish source), Jaba, Jae, Abraoth, Aia, Thoth, Ele, Elo, Aeo, Eu, Jiibaech, Abarmas, Jabarau, Abelbel, Lona, Abra, Maroia, Arm, appearing in fire, thou, Tannetis, in the midst of plains, and snow, and mists; let thine inexorable angel descend and put into safe keeping the wandering demon of this creature whom God has created in his holy Paradise. For I pray to the Holy God, putting my reliance in Ammonipsentancho." Say: "I conjure thee with a flood of bold words: Jakuth, Ablanathanlba, Akramm." Say: "Aoth, Jathabathra, Chachthabratha, Chamynchel, Abrooth. Thou art Abrasiloth, Allelu, Jelosai, Jael: I conjure thee by him who manifested himself to Osrael by night in a pillar of fire and in a cloud by day and who has saved his people from the hard tasks of Pharaoh and brought down on Pharaoh the Ten Plagues because he would not harken. I conjure thee, demoniac spirit, to say who thou art. For I conjure thee by the seal Solomon placed upon the tongue of Jeremiah that he might speak. Say therefore who thou art, a celestial being or spirit of the airs." (Oesterreich, 101)

Lucianus Samosatenis (ca. 120–ca. 190), the Greek satirist commonly known as Lucian, cites yet another case of Jewish exorcism. In *Philopseudes sive incredulus,* he quotes the first-person evidence of one Ion:

> I should like to ask you what you say to those who free possessed men from their terrors by exorcising the spirits so manifestly. I need not discuss this; everyone knows about the Syrian from Palestine, the adept in it, how many he takes in hand who fall down in the light of the moon and roll their eyes and fill their mouths with foam; nevertheless, he restores them to health and sends them away normal in mind, delivering them from their straits for a large fee. When he stands beside them as they lie there and asks: "Whence came you into his body?" the patient himself is silent, but the spirit (*daimon*) answers in Greek or in the language of whatever foreign country he comes from, telling how and whence he entered into the man; whereupon, by adjuring the spirit and, if he does not obey, threatening him, he drives him out. Indeed, I actually saw one coming out, black and smoky in colour. (*Lucian,* 345)

Such scattered written examples were supplemented by folktales about possession and exorcism. But the Hasidic beliefs in these subjects relied more heavily on cabalistic teachings of the postzoharic period. The most influential stories and protocols about dybbukim and the exorcism thereof were contained in the works written by the disciples of Rabbi Isaac Luria, who spread his teachings throughout Eastern Europe and elsewhere.[17] The actual rituals of exorcism used in Hasidism were developed from such sources during the seventeenth and eighteenth centuries.

According to Luria's cabalistic doctrines, the power to exorcise a dybbuk was not given to every rabbi. Only one who had attained the wisdom and holiness that comes from a lifetime of dedication to God could be granted the authority to perform the difficult duties of the exorcist. In Hasidism, such a one was a *baal shem* (*balshem, ba'alai shem*), whose saintliness empowered him to perform miracles. Once authorized to act, the saintly rabbi functioned in the presence of a minyan, ten male members of the congregation. He first intoned the Ninety-first Psalm ("He who lives under the protection of the most High . . .") and afterward addressed the dybbuk to ascertain its identity and the reason for its molestation of the victim. If the facts behind its action were valid in the context of the community's moral and social standards, steps were taken to satisfy the demands of the dybbuk. The word of the *baal shem* guarantees this outcome. It was expected that the wandering soul would depart from the victim once its reason for being therein was removed. Such a departure would entitle it to a *tikkun;* in effect, the soul was redeemed.

But, in cases where the possession was of an evil nature or where the dybbuk refused to depart, the ritual continued without mitigation. Prayers for the release of the victim were interspersed with commands to the dybbuk to cease its parasitic existence. As a last recourse, the *baal shem* ordered the blowing of the shofar, the sacred ram's horn. This act was accompanied by prayers from the *Zohar* that ask the angels who are said to reside in the shofar to bear the congregation's prayers to God. The three fanfares of the ram's horn—Tekiah, Shevarim, Teruah—have progressive potency, the last accompanied by "words of power" that pronounce the excommunication of the dybbuk and damn the soul to Gehinnom (Gehenna), the place of torment.

It is this last recourse that Rabbi Azrael employs in *The Dybbuk.* Malediction and anathema are used as threats to bolster the continuing commands to the dybbuk to vacate the body of the girl. But the exorcist also uses the inducement of his promise to work against the evil spirits that wait for Channon's soul to leave its refuge. However, the dybbuk remains adamant, his former pleading for mercy becoming defiance: "I am not afraid of your anathema. I put no faith in your promises. The power is not in the world that can help me. . . . In the name of the Almighty, I am bound to my bethrothed, and will remain with her to all eternity" (111–12). Finally, Rabbi

Azrael orders shrouds, candles, and horns for the decisive confrontation. The seven scrolls and the seven trumpets are each given to different men. Then Tekiah is blown on the ram's horn. The dybbuk reacts with increasing despair but does not depart. The horns then blow Shevarim to no avail. Such is the dybbuk's tenacity. The black candles are lit while the shrouds are vested. With his arms raised, and resembling an Old Testament prophet, Rabbi Azrael pronounces the final invocation. The words of excommunication are followed by the damning sound of Teruah on the sacred horns. The dybbuk is defeated. He submits and leaves the body he possesses, promising never to return to it.[18]

At this moment, Channon's soul is excommunicated from the spiritual body of Israel. But, desirous not only of freeing Leah but especially of providing a *tikkun* for Channon, Rabbi Azrael immediately silences the horns, lifts the anathema, and offers the promised prayer. Channon's soul is freed from the grasp of the demons and is once more redeemable. Yet Channon does not depart from the room when the others leave. He waits until Leah's only companion falls asleep and then, invisible to his beloved, who is protected by a magic circle drawn by Rabbi Azrael, speaks: "I broke down the barriers between us—I crossed the plains of death—I defied every law of past and present time and all the ages. . . . I strove against the strong and mighty and against those who know no mercy. And as my last spark of strength left me, I left your body to return to your soul" (142–43). The promise of the dybbuk never to return to Leah's body has not been broken. Channon's soul has remained, not to repossess the girl, but to assure that he will be in her soul. Channon's desire for this union is shared by Leah. Her passion dissolves the barrier of his invisibility, and, seeing him, she breaches the bounds of the magic circle. As the music of a wedding march is heard, Leah advances to her destined bridegroom. She has opened herself totally to the supernatural world—both physically and spiritually—and crosses the final threshold to be united eternally to Channon as she never could in life. As their two forms merge into one at the spot where he had appeared, a great light enshrines the union of the lovers.

The climactic moment of the drama portrays in visual terms what the *Zohar* indicates verbally: "And when they (soul and spirit) unite, they shine with a celestial light, and in their union they are designated 'Lamp,' as it says. 'The lamp of the Lord is the soul of man' (Prov. 20:27), NeR (lamp) being the abbreviation of Neshamah-Ruah (soul-spirit). Soul and spirit, the union of the masculine and the feminine, bring forth light, but if separate they do not give light" (3:303). The mystical wedding of Channon and

Leah both symbolizes and is the union of the Neshamah (soul) and Ruah (spirit) that the cabalists taught was the supreme moment of Being: "For when the souls ascend from this world in a bright and pure condition, they are entered into the King's archives. . . . [T]here is set a Palace which is called the Palace of Love. This is the region wherein the treasures of the King are stored, and all his love-kisses are there. All souls beloved of the Holy One enter into that Palace. The soul wraps herself in the spirit in order to occupy her station in the upper region, in the hidden Palace, as it is written: 'For the spirit becomes a covering (ya'toph) before me and the souls which I have made' (Isa. 57:16)" (3:292–93, 303).

Despite its concern with ethical values and human sensibilities, *The Dybbuk* is not a didactic treatise. The play focuses on folk beliefs that stem from mystical tenets formulated in Jewish antiquity and conceptualized in the several texts of the cabala. *The Dybbuk,* therefore, evidences the continuity of ancient beliefs in metempsychosis, possession, and exorcism as well as the intrinsic role of the occult in Hasidism.

Notes

1. The original title of *Der Dibbuk* was *Tsvishn tsvey veltn* (Between two worlds). Although written in 1916, the play did not see its first performance until 1920; but it was the 1922 Habimah Theatre production in Moscow, under the direction of Eugene Vakhtangov, that made the work world renowned. The gestation of the play began in 1912 when An-Sky (Solomon Rappoport, 1863–1920) heard a Hasidic folktale about dybbukim. He used that legend and the Hasidic song "Mipnei mah" as the core of his play. Indeed, the work begins and ends with the haunting melody of the chant.

2. Among these are miracles (especially those performed by Baal-Shem Tov, Rabbi Israel, the founder of the Hasidic movement), the reality of Satan (a curious Jewish adoption of a Christian belief), the dark and little people, the evil eye, the cabala, destiny or fate, sin, the dead, and mystic rituals.

3. Metempsychosis was rejected repeatedly in a variety of medieval and later texts: *Sefer ha-orot,* by Jacob al-Kirkisani; *Emunoth v'deoth* (Book of beliefs and opinions), by Rav Saadyah Gaon; *Emunah ramah,* by Abraham ibn Daud; *Ikkarim,* by Joseph Albo; *Megillat ha-megalleh* and *Meditations of the Sad Soul,* by Abraham ben Hiyya; *Sefer kevod Elohim,* by Abraham ha-Levi ibn Migash; and *Ben David,* by Leone Modena. Neither Judah Halevi nor Maimonides discusses metempsychosis.

4. The word *cabala* means oral tradition. It is a general heading given a variety of writings stemming from the oral tradition of Judaism (variously Kabbalah, Qabalah, etc.) and concerned mainly with the mystical exegesis of Scripture. While many writings are called *cabalistic,* these are the principal works: Hekhaloth Books (the remnants of Second Temple era writings concerned with reaching the Merkabah

[the Throne-Chariot of God] by passing through the heavenly halls [or Hekhaloth], among which is included the pseudepigraphal *Book of Enoch*) compiled between the fifth and the sixth centuries C.E.; *Sefer yetsirah* or Book of Creation (a brief collection of writings said to date from between the third and the sixth centuries C.E., dealing with the ten Sefiroth or emanations of God and the mystical meaning of the Hebrew alphabet, as revealed to Abraham the Patriarch in a vision), not published until 1552; *Sefer ha-bahir* or Book of Brilliance (a compendium of random, often nonsequential texts, the most important of which presents the first written expression of the concept of reincarnation), compiled in Provence in the second half of the twelfth century C.E.; and *Sefer ha-zohar* or Book of Splendor (purporting to be the compilation of the teachings of Rabbi Simeon bar Yohai, a second-century C.E. Tanna, by Moses de Leon, a thirteenth-century C.E. Sephardic Jew, a voluminous commentary on the Pentateuch also known as *The Midrash of Rabbi Simeon bar Yohai*), circulated in manuscript in Spain during the thirteenth century C.E. and published in 1558.

5. Transmigration of a male soul into the body of a female child was believed to cause sterility.

6. The *Sefer ha-temunah* was written ca. 1250 C.E. and later attributed to Ishmael the High Priest. It is one of the most difficult of the cabalistic texts to comprehend because its style is deliberately obscure, to disguise the esoteric doctrines promulgated by the author. The most audacious of his teachings concern the theory of cosmic cycles or Shemittot, which interprets God's image in terms of the shapes of the Hebrew letters and the secret name of God. A thirteenth-century C.E. apologia by an anonymous author, when published in 1892, helped clarify some of the obscurities.

7. But the commonly accepted version among cabalists was that only three transmigrations (reincarnations) occurred after the original residency of a soul in a human body, this on the basis of Job 33:29: "Such mercy, not once or twice, God shews to man, rescuing him from the grave, rekindling the lamp of life for him." (The Vulgate reads: "Ecce haec omnia operatur Deus tribus vicibus per singulos." In the *Zohar,* the passage is rendered: "Behold what God does in respect to each man, even to the third time.") Proper burial is a prerequisite for transmigration, and that includes interment within twenty-four hours of death.

8. The soul is tripartite, its aspects being known as Neshamah, which is the superior phase; Ruah, which is the moral seat; and Nefesh, which is the physical side of the spirit, that which motivates the body. Each aspect has as its source one of the ten Sefiroth.

9. Other aspects of reincarnation theory include rebirth in gentiles and in inorganic matter. The rationale in such cases was that the soul, having led a sinful life, had to be punished severely by a radical transmigration; most punishments of this type were associated with sins of sexuality, either expressly forbidden by the Torah or perverse in themselves, or both. Rabbi Isaac b. Solomon Luria (1534–72 C.E.), the founder of the Safed community of cabalists in Palestine, taught that *gilgul* occurs not only through human bodies but also through animals and inanimate objects. Luria himself did not write down his ideas, but they persisted through the oral and written transmission of his pupils, especially Hayim Vital, Moses Cordovero, and Joseph Karo.

10. An example of *ibbur* where the reason for possession is not evil is the granting of an additional soul to one who is close to but needs assistance in attaining redemption (perhaps through the completion of the remaining 613 mitzvoth).

11. The word *dybbuk* itself does not appear in the Scriptures, the Talmud, or the major texts of the cabala; it is first mentioned in writing in a Hebrew document dated 1571 C.E. but already figured in a legend about Rabbi Luria that was later incorporated into the important Yiddish folktale collection *Maaseh Buch* (1602 C.E.). *Dybbuk,* a word common to the spoken language of German, Polish, and Russian Jews, may have derived from *davok,* a verb meaning "to cleave to," used in cabalistic literature.

12. A similar concept appears in Christianity, where it is held that, although a virtuous person may be obsessed (troubled by temptation), as in the case of saints, possession cannot occur unless an individual has sinned gravely.

13. The mission of such a soul could be achieving proper burial, righting of a wrong, paying a debt, collecting on a promise, atoning for a serious sin or sins, or another end of sufficient importance to require possession. But an evil mission, such as vengeance, could also prompt *ibbur.*

14. The best literary examples of this syndrome occur in Bram Stoker's *Dracula,* which is set in the same European vicinity as *The Dybbuk.* Dracula victimizes only those who invite him by word or action and those who place themselves in jeopardy, even if unwittingly.

15. Jewish tradition holds that God has many names. To the cabalists, the most sacred was the Tetragrammaton (composed of the four letters I H V H, transliterated as YAHWEH or JEHOVAH), which was pronounced Adonai since this was the unspeakable name of God. Before the Tetragrammaton, the name was referred to as Shem ha-meforash and consisted of seventy-two syllables made up of 216 letters. There were many other interpretations of God's name among cabalists; they believed that these names, to a greater or lesser degree, held the key to the secrets of the universe.

16. The Gospels set in Judea do not contain acts of exorcism. The casting out of demons by Christ occurs only in those Gospels set in Galilee, where belief in demons was paramount.

17. Reports about dybbukim appear in Samuel Vital's *Sha'ar ha-gilgulim,* Hayim Vital's *Sefer ha-hezyonot,* Manasseh ben Israel's *Nishmat hayyim,* Elijah ha-Kohen's *Minhat Eliyahu,* and in Judah Moses Fetya's *Minhat Yehudah.* Protocols on exorcisms of famous spirits appeared regularly from 1696 C.E. into the twentieth century, the last issued in 1904 in Jerusalem.

18. Folklore maintains that the exit of a dybbuk could be ascertained by the appearance of a bloody spot on the little toe of the victim's right foot and by a tiny break in a windowpane of the room where the exorcism had occurred. There are no such signs in *The Dybbuk.*

Works Cited

Ansky, S. *The Dybbuk.* Translated by Henry Alsberg and Winifred Kazin. New York: Liveright, 1926.

Fitzmyer, J. A. *The Genesis Apocryphon of Qumran Cave 1: A Commentary.* Rome: Pontificio Istituto Biblico, 1966.

Josephus, Flavius. *The Antiquities of the Jews.* In *Complete Works,* trans. William Whiston. Grand Rapids, Mich.: Kregel, 1960.

Justin Martyr. "Dialogue with Trypho, ch. 85." In *The Ante-Nicene Fathers.* 10 vols. New York: Scribner's, 1899.

[Léon, Moses de]. *The Zohar* [i.e., *Sefer ha-zohar*]. 1558. Translated by Harry Sperling and Maurice Simon. 5 vols. London, 1933.

Lucian. Translated by A. M. Harmon. Vol. 3. Loeb Classical Library. 1921. Cambridge, Mass.: Harvard University Press, 1969.

Oesterreich, Traugott K. *Possession: Demoniacal and Other among Primitive Races, in Antiquity, the Middle Ages, and Modern Times.* Translated by D. Ibberson. New York, 1930. Reissued as *Possession and Exorcism* (New York: Causeway, 1974).

6

The Savaged Mind

Voodoo Terror in Eugene O'Neill's The Emperor Jones

Midway through the journey that is life,
I found myself within a darkened wood
On straying from the proper path.

—Dante, *Inferno*

Dante's "darkened wood"[1] is a metaphor for the fallen state of the soul, a condition that impedes taking "the proper path," the way that leads to personal purgation and, in the Christian scheme of the epic journey, to God. Thus, the poet, recognizing that he has strayed from the proper path, must strive to find his way. But he will be able to regain the path only after willingly undergoing the process of integration of the self[2] in the journey through infernal depths. Dante's was an intense rite of passage that required dying to the old ways in order to be born anew. Such is the journey that informs *The Emperor Jones.*

Brutus Jones, the African American protagonist of Eugene O'Neill's extended multiscene expressionistic play, preys on the perceived naïveté of the natives who inhabit the unnamed Caribbean island on which he has established his empire after fleeing from his imprisonment as a murderer in the United States. In his vanity, Jones sees his black subjects as a superstitious and backward lot who have been duped into believing that he possesses a charm whose power is such that his demise can be achieved only through the use of a silver bullet, à la werewolf lore. Jones knows full well, of course, that the poor, ignorant natives he has hoodwinked into serving him have no access to silver and feels quite confident, smug even, about his safety—so smug, in fact, that he has fashioned a silver bullet to show them, indicating that, when the time comes, he will use it on himself. The Brutus Jones of the early part of the play is possessed of a cunning, worldly mind and great self-assurance.

Previous page: Voodoo Drums, anonymous, collection of the author.

Fallen Majesty

The first scene of the play opens on the empty audience chamber of the palace, a building of colonial European style, a remnant of earlier tenancy. Shortly, an old black woman enters cautiously; she is obviously escaping. When she is stopped by Henry Smithers, a Cockney trader dressed in safari gear who has come to see Jones, she discloses that everyone who has served the self-styled emperor has fled to the distant hills while he sleeps. Smithers's face takes on "*an immense mean satisfaction*" as he responds: "Well, I know bloody well wot's in the air—when they runs orf to the 'ills. The tom-tom'll be thumping out there bloomin' soon. . . . 'Es bound to find out soon as 'e wakes up. 'Es cunnin' enough to know when 'is time's come" (sc. 1; p. 10). And, indeed, soon after Brutus Jones awakes, the drums begin to sound. Once introduced toward the latter part of the initial scene, "*at a rate exactly corresponding to normal pulse-beat—72 to the minute*" (sc. 1; p. 24), the drums go on incessantly, beating an unnerving tattoo, an eerie sound unlike any produced by a military band.[3] This is the start of the Voodoo motif.[4]

The news that Smithers gives him about the desertion of the palace staff, who have not only taken to the hills but also stolen the horses, along with the counterpoint provided by the sound of the Voodoo drums, prompts Jones to make his own departure. But his exit is accomplished in seeming self-possessed style: "Does you think I'd slink out de back door like a common nigger? I'se Emperor yit, ain't I? And de Emperor Jones leaves de way he comes, and dat black trash don't dare stop him. . . . (*He puts his hands in his pockets and with studied carelessness, whistling a tune, he saunters out of the doorway . . .*)" (sc. 1; p. 28). Showing his bravado, Jones has left the palace—both locale and symbol of his power and safety as well as of his "civilized" state—to pursue his escape beyond the vast plain into the "Great Forest." In the meantime, his former subjects have taken the high ground, not only physically in the hills, but also symbolically in their superior moral and ethical stance thereon.

After his long trek on the low ground, it is nightfall as Jones approaches the edge of the forest. It is "*a wall of darkness dividing the world*" that he encounters. Jones has, indeed, left his man-made civilized milieu and is about to enter the "*brooding, implacable*" (sc. 2; p. 29) environment of nature. The journey through his own darkened wood will prove highly disturbing and, ultimately, bring about his undoing through a series of experiences to which he reacts with growing fear.

The Haunting

Jones is unsettled first by the sight of the dark forest before him; next by the sound of the drums and the thought of the pursuing natives; then by not finding the food he had stashed outside the forest. Then, as he prepares to traipse through the dense undergrowth, he starts to become aware of his predicament: he is alone in an inhospitable setting full of natural noises and potential dangers. And there is always the pervasive sound of the Voodoo drums. Low at first, yet distinct, the drumming increases in intensity and length as Jones's journey progresses. His bravado and strength diminish as the drumming becomes more pronounced.

Drums have provided a form of communication since primordial times; likewise, through their rhythmic patterns and their timbre, they have been a vehicle for entering a state of trance. In the play, their ongoing and ever-increasing presence has a direct impact on the protagonist. This is first manifest in his earliest encounter with the supernatural. Although he does not see the noisemakers or physically confront the feared denizens of the Great Forest, Jones does experience other disturbing things: "*While his back is turned, the Little Formless Fears creep out from the deeper blackness of the forest. They are black, shapeless; only their glittering little eyes can be seen. . . . From the formless creatures on the ground in front of him comes a tiny gale of low mocking laughter like a rustling of leaves*" (sc. 2; pp. 32–33). The fears that have been welling up during his trek through the darkened wood have come to the fore and taken shape as dark, unfathomable beings.[5] As Jones soon learns, these pose a greater danger to his well-being than any predatory animal. The "Little Formless Fears" rise up before him all at once. With a yell of terror, he yanks out his revolver and fires at the creatures, which scurry into the deeper darkness of the woods. It is then that Jones hastens into the forest proper, the newly risen moon casting eerie beams through the leafy canopy of the very tall trees. The firing of the weapon, symbolic of the power of civilization over the natural world, provides a momentary respite from his fears.

But, as he struggles to make his escape through the massive forest, he loses his hat, his face is scratched, and his gawdy uniform is torn. The Little Formless Fears then manifest themselves one at a time, personifying visions out of his evil past. As such they parallel the beasts—the Leopard, the Lion, the She-Wolf, images representing the capital sins—encountered by Dante in his attempt to climb the serene mountain that they guard. Just as Dante was prevented from attaining his goal because he had not earned such a reward, so Brutus Jones must undergo his own test before he can merit freedom.

The first of the Little Formless Fears to materialize appears in the shape of Jones's friend Jeff, who is dressed in a Pullman porter's uniform and is seen throwing dice. Terrified at seeing again the man he had caught cheating and murdered, Jones fires at the image of Jeff, which disappears instantly. Jones is unnerved by the apparition, the first manifestation of his brutal past.

To the ever-increasing sound of the drum, Jones plunges further into the forest without discerning the path that leads to the sea, on which he has planned his escape from the island. He is lost. His uniform in tatters, he removes his coat and flings it aside. Another vestige of his former state is gone, leaving him stripped to the waist. The spurs are next to go. As if recognizing the stripping away of his civilized veneer, Jones says: "Ha'nts! Yo' fool nigger, dey ain't no such things! Don't de Baptist parson tell you dat many time? Is yo' civilized, or is yo' like dese ign'rent black niggers heah?" (sc. 4; p. 38). But his reasoning cannot stem the tide of apparitions. As he rests in a clearing, a silent gang of black prisoners led by a white guard manifests itself. The guard points to Jones to join the chain gang, and he does so "*in a hypnotized stupor*" (sc. 4; p. 40). Subservient outwardly, but seething within, Jones reenacts his murder of the prison guard, but not having the original weapon—the shovel he had used while on the chain gang—he fires his gun instead; it is his third shot. As before, the apparition disappears. And, again, "*Jones leaps away in mad flight*" (sc. 4; p. 41).

Such are the shapes that beset the haunted man, apparitions that Jones drives away by firing his pistol. Three of his six bullets have been spent in ridding himself of the haunts. He is near the end of his civilized state: "*His pants are in tatters, his shoes cut and misshapen*" (sc. 5; p. 41). And he sees only one recourse left, that of prayer and confession of wrongdoing: "*Suddenly he throws himself on his knees and raises his clasped hands to the sky—in a voice of agonized pleading*" (sc. 5; p. 42). But his is a prayer to be rid of the apparitions, a self-serving turning to God, not a recognition of the evil he has done and a selfless plea for mercy. Religion becomes a crutch in time of need and is no more to Jones than the pistol he has used against the haunts. A means to an end, his prayer is too little and too late to exorcise the demons that beset him.

Once he has undergone the unnerving materialization of his *personal fears*—and their "elimination" through the firing of his weapon—Jones undergoes a second set of hauntings that elicit *racial fears.* He experiences a part of his people's history—the pre–Civil War slave auction—himself becoming the object of the bidding. Now more enraged than frightened, Jones fires twice—once at the auctioneer and once at the planter who has bought him. The scene dissolves as did the other visions when he fires the gun, but, as before, Jones *"rushes off crying with fear"* (sc. 5; p. 45). He has fired five of the six bullets in his revolver, and only the "magical" silver bullet remains.

The Return of the Native

Regression to savage fear and superstition—the very state he had mocked in the island's natives—becomes Brutus Jones's own condition, as manifested in his being physically stripped of white civilization's trappings—*"His pants have been so torn away that what is left of them is no better than a breech cloth"* (sc. 6; p. 46) —and in his joining the swaying, murmuring blacks in his reappearing vision of the chained African slaves. Primal elements have been dredged up from his cultural memory, elements stemming from the subconscious abyss of his being—the African ancestry he had buried by taking on the ways of American life, that is, of the white world.

Soon Jones is unable to stem the regressive swell taking him into African life itself, and he finds himself at the *"foot of a gigantic tree by the edge of a great river"* (sc. 7; p. 47). By the tree is a rough-hewn stone altar, before which he kneels *"as if in obedience to some obscure impulse"* (sc. 7; p. 48). Sobbing hysterically, he crawls away. Suddenly, Jones is confronted by the Congo Witch Doctor, who emerges from behind the huge tree. Jones is awed by this formidable presence out of Africa whose ritual dance and shrill chant are accompanied by the beating of the tom-tom. This sound *"grows to a fierce, exultant boom. . . . Jones has become completely hypnotized. His voice joins in the incantation, in the cries; he beats time with his hands and sways his body to and fro from the waist. The whole spirit and meaning of the dance has entered into him, has become his spirit"* (sc. 7; p. 49).

But there is one crucial element yet to be encountered. Having disposed of the trappings of his personal and tribal life—all externals—in one way or another, there remains only to enter the very soul of Brutus (no longer Jones, but solely the brute that his name has only implied until now). In that depth of his being dwells the creature from the abyss—the Crocodile God. And the horrific monster materializes from the murky depths of the swamp at the beckoning of the Congo Witch Doctor.

The crocodile is vicious and destructive in its physical reality, while in its metaphoric state it represents fecundity and power. Brutus, now Primal Man, is alone with his most basic, ultimate crisis—confronting the creature before him, which is a manifestation of the beast within as well as potential for creative energy. Brutus is to be the sacrificial victim, dying to his old life in order to experience rebirth. In his stupor or hypnotic trance, he is unable to resist the pull of death, and he "*squirms on his belly nearer and nearer*" (sc. 7; p. 50) to the Crocodile God.

Suddenly, as if his last prayer were answered, he remembers the last vestige of his civilized state: the gun that saved him in previous situations of danger. Jones again fires, this time the sixth and last round—the silver bullet—at the intimate nightmare that is the Crocodile God. The beast and the Congo Witch Doctor disappear like the shapes that haunted him earlier. But he has spent his own charm—the silver bullet—not on himself, but on an apparition out of his subconscious.

In a way, he has destroyed himself in annihilating first his personal past, then his cultural or racial memory, and, finally, his own primal self. But he does not replace these with the "new man" that should result from completion of the rite of passage. All that remains of him is his hollow, unfulfilled body. And that will meet its demise in the eighth and final scene of the play.

The Silver Bullet

The natives having accepted the silver bullet myth promoted by Jones, Lem, their leader, patiently collects the precious metal from the chance coins that come his way. When he has enough, he fashions the magical metal into silver bullets with which to execute their despotic superman of a ruler. Accompanied by the deafening beat of the drum, Lem and his tribe track Jones to the very spot at which he entered the Great Forest. They hear his thrashing about in the undergrowth, no doubt having returned to his point of entry by traveling in circles during his phantasmagoric ordeal ("the proper path was wholly lost and gone," as Dante puts it). By this time, Brutus Jones, having escaped execution in the white man's jail, is about to take his final steps in the savages' jungle. He is a dead man walking. Soon, the very superstition that had kept him in power is turned on him: "*The report of several rifles sounds from the forest, followed a second later by savage, exultant yells. The beating of the tom-tom abruptly ceases*" (sc. 8; p. 53). The Voodoo drums have continued beating until the play's last sequence of events. They stop when Brutus Jones has been executed since they are no longer necessary. When they do cease beating, the effect is shockingly dramatic, for they are "heard" even in their absence: their silence is deafening. Like Brutus Jones's life, the natives' plight has been brought to closure by Voodoo magic. Jones has been duly executed. Ironically, the white man's justice that he had mocked has been served under the law of the jungle through the suggestive might of Voodoo and the killing power of civilized man's rifles in the hands of natives who believed in the efficacy of a silver bullet.

A further irony is that Brutus Jones—who, having adopted the white man's perpective,[6] has been right in the supposition that the natives are superstitious—is blind to his own deep-seated credence. What he also fails to realize is how tenacious the natives are in their pursuits. While they hold on to African beliefs that are absurd to the civilized mind of Jones, they also possess what they believe are magical processes that empower them to be rid of adversaries. Their protection lies in traditional supernatural rites that are highly effacious, as the play's denouement makes evident.

The amazement visible on the face and heard in the words of Smithers, the cynical trader, expresses the disbelief that Jones's bravado could have been taken so literally by the natives. But such is the power of age-old conditioning to superstition. The play, which opened with Smithers, has come full circle back to the Cockney trader; too, the path that the bewildered, crazed Jones followed through the forest circled back to the very place through which he had entered it. The circular pattern is emphasized further in the completion of the desire expressed in the opening sequence: "I only 'opes I'm there when they takes 'im out to shoot 'im" (sc. 1; p. 10). In hindsight, Smithers's words are prophetic, for it is Smithers who presides over the body of Brutus Jones when it is brought out by the natives who executed him as if he had, indeed, been a mythic being.

Brutus Jones has undergone a rite of passage, albeit not a salutary one since he has lost his life in the process toward purgation. That rite has its culmination in the encounter with the primal beast. In his association with the Crocodile God, Brutus comes close, if unwittingly, to bringing together the elements of the subsconscious toward the integration of the self. According to Jung (see *Symbols of Transformation*), the animal is a metaphor for the nonhuman psyche, for the level of subhuman instinct, and for the unconscious segments of the psyche. Thus, the more primitive the animal—the crocodile is among the few extant prehistoric life-forms—the deeper the stratum of which it is an expression.

But Brutus fails to immerse himself in the primal swamp out of which the god emerges. Rather than attain rejuvenation at the end of his rite of passage, Brutus dies in the brutish state, unenlightened, unredeemed. He is a failed experiment, like the humunculus of the alchemist, the golem of Jewish legend, or the creature of Dr. Frankenstein.

The mind of Brutus Jones was savaged by the fears latent in his psyche, fears stemming from his murderous acts. These fears were intensified into a crisis by the Voodoo drums, which were not only beating externally but, in his mind, becoming a metaphor for the pace of the regressive quickening within the man. It is through this crisis that the protagonist questions his destiny. Unfortunately for Jones, he was unable to turn the crisis into a positive state by transmuting evil into its opposite through the process of inversion, whereby the potential for change is recognized, followed by the resolution of guilt and, thereafter, rebirth into the new man. He has failed to attain the Jungian integration of the self.

Unlike Dante, who traverses the hell of his own darkened wood and emerges a victor over his fallen human nature, Brutus Jones does not have the will or the deep-seated faith to find the proper path and, as a result, suffers dire consequences in undertaking a journey that he fails to bring to fruition. It is ironic that evil is assigned, not to the Voodoo tradition invoked by O'Neill as a frame for his protagonist's last moments, but rather to the repressive, culpable actions of Brutus Jones, who, having set himself up as a god, has been brought down to his knees by his human nature. In the end, he is just another man, susceptible to the same fears and superstitions as marked the natives he has oppressed. In contrast to Dante's heroic journey, Jones's is a failed rite of passage, a processional to death, both physical and spiritual, a journey to perdition. His life has been extinguished in ironic fulfillment of his own false myth through the savaging of his mind by Voodoo terror.

Notes

1. The translation of canto 1, lines 1–3, used in the epigraph is mine.

2. The process toward integration of the self, i.e., attaining the harmonious relationship of psychological traits, appears in many discussions by Jung. In *Psychology and Alchemy,* e.g., he states: "Natural man is not a 'self'—he is the mass and a particle in the mass, collective to such a degree that he is not even sure of his own ego. That is why since time immemorial he has needed the transformation mysteries to turn him into something, and to rescue him from the animal collective psyche, which is nothing but a *variété.* But if we reject this unseemly *variété* of man 'as he is,' it is impossible for him to attain integration, to become a self. And that amounts to spiritual death" (81).

3. Drums have a fundamental role in African and Afro-Caribbean religious rituals. Depending on the people and their religion, enslaved Africans brought to the Caribbean and other areas made drums reminiscent of African instruments. Since O'Neill does not identify the island on which the play takes place, it is impossible to trace the origin of the natives and, consequently, to define their ritual traditions and the types of drums they use.

4. *Voodoo,* from Haitian Creole *Voudoun* or *Vaudun,* is the generalized term for the religious practices that slaves brought with them to the Caribbean islands and New Orleans from their homelands in West Africa. But each island with slave populations developed its own interpretation of African culture, and the religious rites practiced took on such names as Santería (in the Hispanic islands of Cuba, Puerto Rico, and Santo Domingo), Obeah (in Jamaica), and Ju-Ju (in areas where Hausa slaves were taken), among the most prominent. See Lima, chap. 8.

5. Freudian psychoanalysis was very much in the air when O'Neill wrote *The Emperor Jones.* It was the technique that Freud employed to bring out of the subconscious those matters that affected well-being so that the patient could recognize the source of his or her illness and resolve the problem with the aid of the analyst.

6. While it is clear that O'Neill is writing from the perspective of the white world and that his perception of Brutus Jones is that of an outsider in that culture, the play is not about a confrontation of black and white cultures. O'Neill prompts the character's confrontation with his own roots when he has Jones encounter the enemy within and without in his flight from the civilized world. The playwright has cast Jones in a difficult mold—a black man who must shed the false shell of Western culture and come to grips with both himself and his ancestry—but O'Neill places the *agon* in a non-Western setting, the jungle, and makes the antagonists blacks rather than whites.

WORKS CITED

Dante Alighieri. *Inferno.* Translated by Robert Hollander and Jean Hollander. New York: Doubleday, 2000.

Jung, C. G. *Psychology and Alchemy.* 2d ed. Vol. 12 of *The Collected Works of C. G. Jung.* Bollingen Series 20. Princeton, N.J.: Princeton University Press, 1977.

———. *Symbols of Transformation.* Translated by R. F. C. Hull. 2d ed. Vol. 5 of *The Collected Works of C. G. Jung.* Bollingen Series 20. Princeton, N.J.: Princeton University Press, 1976.

Lima, Robert. *Dark Prisms: Occultism in Hispanic Drama.* Lexington: University Press of Kentucky, 1995.

O'Neill, Eugene. *The Emperor Jones.* New York: Appleton-Century-Crofts, [1949].

7

Satan in Salem

Sex as Grimoire *in Arthur Miller's* The Crucible

I believe that the reader will discover here the essential nature of one of the strangest and most awful chapters in human history.

—Arthur Miller, *The Crucible*

Religious persecution may shield itself under the guise of a mistaken and over-zealous piety.

—Edmund Burke,
"Impeachment of Warren Hastings," 17 February 1788

The realities of fanatical politics in the United States in the early 1950s proved unpalatable to many, among them the playwright Arthur Miller, who was prompted to write *The Crucible*,[1] a work that attacked the perceived evils of McCarthyism under the veil of the infamous witch trials held in the Massachusetts Bay Colony village of Salem in 1692. To the dramatist, the witch-hunt in some areas of colonial America, which condemned those accused as religious dissidents through hearsay and superstitious belief (*spectral evidence*, to use the phrase then current), seemed a perfect parallel to the hearings in which Senator Joseph McCarthy and his Committee on Un-American Activities posited the existence of a Communist conspiracy. This perception led to the undue condemnation of many through circumstantial, often unfounded accusations and charges of guilt by association.

When it opened on Broadway in 1953, *The Crucible*—in effect a modern morality play about repression, guilt, and fear—was seen by critics to be a less than artistic endeavor owing to its topicality. However, the play has, in spite of the dramatist's early insistence on its political intent, become a masterwork of the American theater because it rises above the circumstances that motivated its creation and addresses the universality of human behavior in its search for freedom of choice and expression toward individuation. It is truly qualified to be considered among other stages of evil.

Previous page: Examination of an Accused Salem Witch, artist unknown. Public domain.

Miller entered the skewered world of Salem through its prohibitions. The Puritan code of behavior was rigidly structured and enforced, reaching into all areas of human activity, both social and private. Among things prohibited were leisure reading (only the Bible was held to be valid, but even there certain parts, deemed too risqué, had to be avoided), drunkenness (not even social drinking was tolerated), indolence ("An idle mind is the Devil's workshop" was more than a mere adage), unwarranted laughter, gossip, mischief of any sort, dancing, and falling asleep during church services. The ignorance and superstitious bent of the Puritans ascribed even such uncontrollable actions as epileptic fits and convulsions to the agency of Satan. Moreover, the important Christian holy days, Christmas among them, went uncelebrated since periods of enjoyment were anathema to the Puritan mentality.

But the most abnormal of the Puritan strictures concerned sexuality. In a society where, even in marriage, sexual relations were deemed a necessary evil toward the procreation that God had mandated, there were strict punishments for anyone caught fornicating, committing adultery, or performing acts deemed lecherous, lewd, or bestial. Even impure thoughts were considered sinful. Thus, the attire and deportment of women had to be rigidly regulated so that the female of the species would not become an occasion of sin to her male counterparts through dress, deed, or word (as in the case of Eve's temptation of Adam).

Sexual repression and its attendant repercussions are viewed by Miller as the motivators of the horrific events in Salem Village late in the seventeenth century. *The Crucible* focuses the crisis through the pubescent girls of the community, especially by showing the psychopathology of Abigail Williams, whose "natural" lust for John Proctor is thwarted by "unnatural" social and religious dictums as well as by the married man himself after he has succumbed momentarily to illicit passion. The exposition of their earlier affair is given in their initial meeting in the play:

> Abigail: John—I am waitin' for you every night.
> Proctor: Abby, I never give you hope to wait for me.
> Abigail: I have something better than hope, I think!
> Proctor: Abby, you'll put it out of mind. I'll not be comin' for you more.
> Abigail: I know how you clutched my back behind your house and sweated like a stallion whenever I come near! Or did I dream that? . . . I have a sense for heat, John, and yours has drawn me to my window, and I have seen you looking up, burning in your loneliness. . . .

> Proctor: Abby, I may think of you softly from time to time. But I will cut off my hand before I'll ever reach for you again. . . .
>
> Abigail: I look for John Proctor that took me from my sleep and put knowledge in my heart! (act 1; pp. 20–21)

That "knowledge" had been proffered through the symbolic *grimoire*[2] of sex, a book whose covers Abigail had never opened until John Proctor taught her how to read the secrets in its erotic pages. There she discovered the real wonders and pleasures of physical love, intuited before only in the erotic dreams of her "sleep."[3] She had entered the list of initiates very willingly, indeed, as the dialogue makes clear, as an avid reader of the sexual text. But Proctor's married state and the restrictiveness of Puritan society would not permit their relationship to flourish; yet Abigail wanted to perpetuate her newfound elation in an illicit manner. Nonetheless, Proctor's consciousness of wrongdoing and deep commitment to wife and children prohibited even that. His becomes a crisis of conscience thereafter, a struggle between his unquenched physical desire for Abigail, which represents the Dionysian side of his nature, and his deep-seated commitment to his wife, Elizabeth, which embodies the Apollonian aspect of his personality; in close proximity to the latter are arrayed all the restrictive forces of traditional Puritanism.

When Proctor rejects Abigail, she interprets his reluctance for further intimacy as the result of social and religious prohibitions imposed by the community and its church and decides that the way to overcome his reticence lies in nonorthodox means. Nothing and no one will stand in the way of her libidinal drive; initiated into sexual pleasure but prevented from its further expression, Abigail is not to be denied the man she desires and, thus, turns to heterodox means to assure herself a place in Proctor's life, even if only as his mistress.

Older and more cunning than the other adolescent girls,[4] Abigail leads the group in what turns into a diabolical plot against the socioreligious strictures of Salem Village, enlisting the unwitting accomplices in her plan through intimidation and charisma. Their attacks on the community ultimately lead to her real purpose: to free John Proctor from his ties to his wife through an accusation of her that is tantamount to condemnation in a town made susceptible to innuendo by superstition and fear. Abigail's actions prove the truth of Congreve's poetized observation that hell has no fury like a woman scorned.

Yet Abigail too will ultimately become a dupe and a victim. Her passion leads her into the quagmire of seeking illicit means to attain an end that her society considers immoral. The means that she seeks are provided by Tituba, a West Indian slave belonging to her uncle, the Reverend Parris, the religious leader of the spiritually bankrupt community. Tituba, at first unwilling and afraid of being punished, reluctantly initiates the girls into some of her exotic native traditions at the insistence of Abigail. The girls relish her stories of Caribbean women—she is from Barbados—who drink chicken blood and dance naked in the woods, whose passions are unbridled in the lush tropical island setting, and who meet with "the Dark One" and have sexual intercourse with him without a qualm. Tituba has allowed the impressionable girls a glimpse into an aspect of life they could not even suspect existed; she has shown them the "book of life," as esoteric a text to Abigail and her followers as any secret *grimoire* that might have fallen into their hands. The knowledge that Tituba has given them becomes a powerful aphrodisiac. The tales of the unfettered actions of her people—bred in a tradition of living natural lives—have fired the girls' imaginations. Their fantasies unleashed, Abigail and the girls too dance in the forest, some shedding their clothes in wild abandon as Tituba chants incantations and waves her arms over the fire.

When espied in their Dionysian revels by the Reverend Parris, two of the girls, Ruth Putnam and his own daughter Betty, fall into trance states. Soon the village is awash with rumors of witchcraft, which was the term used erroneously at the time to indicate the worship of Satan.[5] Abigail denies anything other than dancing in the woods, which was punishable by public flogging, but, when Betty comes out of her state, she verifies the truth before the other girls who had been in the woods: "You drank blood, Abby! . . . You drank a charm to kill John Proctor's wife!" Abigail's retort contains both instructions to Betty, Mary Warren, and Mercy Lewis on what they are to declare in public and a direct threat if they reveal anything more: "We danced. And Tituba conjured Ruth Putnam's dead sisters. And that is all. And mark this. Let either of you breathe a word, or the edge of a word, about the other things, and I will come to you in the black of some terrible night and I will bring a pointy reckoning that will shudder you. And you know I can do it" (act 1; p. 17). Abigail has, therefore, not only admitted what Betty has stated, but evidences an involvement in secret rites, "the other things," and an implicit mastery of such that she makes the girls cower before her nefarious power. The threat will no doubt also be conveyed to the other girls, for there were more in the group, as Parris states: "I discovered her—*indicating Abigail*—and my niece and ten or twelve of the other girls, dancing in the forest last night" (act 1; p. 35). The number hints at a group of thirteen, the total generally believed to constitute a coven of witches (see Murray, *Witch Cult,* and *God of the Witches*);[6] if indeed there were ten other girls involved, then Abigail and Betty would make twelve, with Tituba as the leader, the thirteenth person.

When the Reverend Hale, a "witch-finder" from another village, questions Abigail about the events in the forest and asks whether she called the Devil, she denounces Tituba: "I never called him! Tituba, Tituba. . . . She spoke Barbados. . . . I didn't see no Devil!" (act 1; pp. 39–40). Tituba, as a "heathen," is highly vulnerable to accusation. When she is brought before Hale, Abigail points to her and begins the denunciation: "She makes me drink blood! . . . She sends her spirit on me in church; she makes me laugh at prayer! . . . She comes to me every night to go and drink blood! . . . She comes to me while I sleep; she's always making me dream corruptions! . . . Sometimes I wake and find myself standing in the open doorway and not a stitch on my body! I always hear her laughing in my sleep. I hear her singing her Barbados songs and tempting me with—" (act 1; pp. 40–41). Unable to convince Hale and the others of her innocence, Tituba becomes Abigail's first victim. But the slave, terrified at the prospect of being hanged as a witch, falls to her knees before Reverend Hale and "confesses" to having been with the Devil, on the promise that admitting her guilt will save her from execution. Following the promptings of the inquisitors, Tituba tells them what they want to hear, confessing to "trafficking" with Satan and seducing the girls into his service. Once Hale's protection is assured, Tituba names the Devil's accomplices in Salem, denouncing the same two women whom Putnam had put forth as candidates for prosecution.

Seeing that Tituba's confession has saved the slave from being sent to the gallows, Abigail then turns attention to herself again to make her own purgative declaration: "I want to open myself! . . . I danced for the Devil; I saw him; I wrote in his book; I go back to Jesus; I kiss His hand. I saw Sarah Good with the Devil! I saw Goody Osburn with the Devil! I saw Bridget Bishop with the Devil!" (act 1; p. 45). And Betty, waking from her trance state as if triggered by Abigail's confession, adds other names to her accomplice's list. The first act ends with their ecstatic litany of accusations and the promise of the inquisitorial complications that their actions will inspire in the credulous Puritan community. The conflict in the play has become larger than the tension between the desires of two individuals—Proctor and Abigail. What began as a private confrontation swiftly turns into a public affair in which others will be consumed.

Soon, the other girls begin the "crying-out." In the process, Abigail and her coconspirators accuse men and women who have slighted them or their families, along with social misfits perceived as suitable victims and whose aberrations the community would gladly condemn publicly. Abigail and her young cronies are like the avenging Furies of classical mythology in their vindictive antisocial acts and unremitting hysteria.

And so the reign of terror is under way. The girls' hysterical remonstrances against supposed malefactors bring about numerous incarcerations. The men and women accused of persecuting the girls at the bidding of Satan are imprisoned under the charge of witchcraft. Ironically, while Tituba, Abigail, and the other girls are saved from prosecution as a result of their "confessions" of guilt, those who, because their religious conscience does not permit them to lie, even to save their lives, continuously insist on their innocence are summarily adjudged and sentenced to death, as Proctor points out when Hale makes much of those who have confessed: "And why not, if they must hang for denyin' it? There are them that will swear to anything before they'll hang; have you never thought of that?" (act 2; p. 66).

Hale then informs Proctor that the name of his wife, Elizabeth, had been mentioned in that day's proceedings. While John reacts with fury, his wife is not surprised. Knowing of Abigail's unrequited lust for John after their brief liaison, Elizabeth has had reason to fear that the girl would cry her out in court. Shortly, a warrant is presented at the house charging Goody Proctor with the attempted murder of Abigail by means of a needle inserted in a "poppet." Mary Warren, who had given Elizabeth, her mistress, the doll, admits to having made it and inadvertently having left the needle stuck in it: "Why, I meant no harm by it, sir. . . . Let you ask Susanna Walcott—she saw me sewin' it in court. . . . Ask Abby, Abby sat beside me when I made it" (act 2; p. 73). Yet even the self-evident fact that Abigail had taken advantage of that knowledge to feign an attack that she could blame on Elizabeth Proctor proves insufficient to quash the warrant. Elizabeth becomes yet one more detainee, dragged away in chains as the second act comes to a close. The true nature of Abigail's baseness is then evident to the Proctors, although the minds of the civil and religious authorities present remain clouded by superstition and unquestioning acceptance of circumstantial evidence, especially when presented by innocent girls, as the accusers are perceived by the judges and the populace to be.

But the matter of Abigail's innocence is ironic in view of her lasciviousness and vengefulness. Having been first rejected and then scorned by Proctor, Abigail had sought other means to her lustful ends: the secret knowledge she had garnered at Tituba's side. She had opened yet another *grimoire,* the Devil's own book, learning therein the formulas for vengeance against the society that had frustrated her sexual need and against the woman who stood in the way of her union with the man she desired.

But branding Elizabeth Proctor a witch did not effect the release of Abigail's former paramour; instead, Proctor became a man driven by his conscience to free his wife, whose suffering—indeed, the suffering of the entire community—he saw as having been brought about by his transgression. Ironically, Elizabeth Proctor would be saved by John Proctor, while he would himself stand accused of serving the Devil. In a strong, passionate stand for personal freedom, he rebuked the court and chose to go to the gallows, purging the guilt that he felt through an honorable death rather than saving his life through the contrived confession that he had signed earlier.

The two important women in Proctor's life would have very different destinies as a result of his decision. Elizabeth would have her three children and the memory of her husband's ultimate goodness to accompany her; Abigail, her hopes of union with Proctor crushed, would have nothing. She left Salem in the company of Mercy Lewis, never to be seen again in the Puritan community. It was said of Abigail years later that she had become a prostitute in Boston,[7] but that may have been wishful thinking on the part of those who saw the need for justice: as a prostitute her soul would be damned in hell.

Twenty of the accused were condemned to death between June 10 and September 22 in that fateful year of 1692 before the governor of the colony, Sir William Phips, called a halt to the proceedings when his own wife was "cried out upon." A hundred and fifty men and women had been imprisoned during the process, fifty-five of them confessing to having practiced witchcraft; of these, nineteen had been led to the gallows,[8] and one, Giles Corey, was pressed to death under the weight of boulders while refusing to answer the indictment of the Court of Oyer and Terminer, which Phips had instituted (see chapter 11, n. 20).

In this repressive system, where "hellfire and brimstone" was the principal topic of such sermons and religious tracts as Cotton Mather's *The Wonders of the Invisible World* (1693) and Increase Mather's *Cases of Conscience concerning Evil Spirits Personating Men* (1693),[9] there was no acceptable outlet for personal expression. But, in a society where the establishment—in Salem church and state were as one—would not satisfy human needs outside the orthodoxy, there are usually heterodox means of which individuals might avail themselves. In Salem, as elsewhere in the English colonies, witchcraft provided a means, albeit secret, of circumventing the Puritan orthodoxy, if under pain of prosecution. That some people in Salem practiced what was held to be witchcraft is a matter of record, and, consequently, the punishment that they received was justified under the code of law dominant at the time.[10] No matter how unpopular the idea, especially in the light of Miller's sympathetic interpretation of the condemned, the facts show that some in the Puritan community practiced what was forbidden by law and risked their lives knowingly for their heterodox "faith."

While the witch-hunt and the executions in Salem and nearby communities represent a shameful chapter in American history, theirs was not a singular aberration, for there was an important direct precedent for such intolerant and cruel behavior. The mother country, England, saw the beginnings in the 1640s of what has come to be called the Witchcraft Panic, which lasted many years. During this execrable period, untold numbers were persecuted, prosecuted, and executed as witches, especially under such as Matthew Hopkins, the infamous self-proclaimed "Witchfinder General."[11]

The Protestant colonial communities, Salem among them, simply caught the spirit of the times, if somewhat belatedly, and carried out their own witch-hunts, which meted out physical punishment for spiritual crimes, even if the evidence was circumstantial (which, more often than not, it was), based on hearsay, or both. There may have been only twenty deaths owing to the inquisitorial process in Salem, but the methods employed in obtaining the confessions of the victims and in taking their lives did not fall short of those used in the homeland. Both societies were successful to a degree in ridding themselves of undesirable elements.

The Crucible is a study of evil as a way of life in a society that prided itself on acting under God's law for the common good. But God had been ill served by these self-righteous people. Satan had been abroad in the Salem Village of the play, and the adolescents who caused the panic of 1692 that the play depicts had read his esoteric *grimoire* and learned in its forbidden pages the nature of his worship and attendant orgiastic rites. The havoc that they caused and the lives that they destroyed give strong evidence of the result of frustrating natural instincts and drives through the imposition of unnatural strictures. *The Crucible* is admittedly a version of the story of Salem, but its impact lies in its foundation in truth: the Witchcraft Panic of the seventeenth century *is* history, and human behavior *is* ever the same.

NOTES

1. *The Crucible* was first presented at the Martin Beck Theatre in New York City on January 22, 1953.

2. *Grimoire* is the term used to identify books of magical formulas, incantations, and other esoteric writings used to gain power over human beings and supernatural or cosmic forces (see chapter 3 above). Although said to have been used by magicians, who were not practicing any religious cult, these texts began to be associated in the popular mind with witches, who were held to be devotees of Satan, thus the infamous black book in which they inscribed their names in blood (see Francisco Goya y Lucientes's painting of a priest signing such a book). The term is used here in a metaphoric way.

3. Such sexually oriented dreams in a woman were held to be the result of a visitation by an incubus, an evil supernatural being in the shape of a man; if a pregnancy outside wedlock were to occur, it would always be charged to that demonic agent.

4. Miller has taken poetic license in changing the ages of the girls; as he has said in one case: "Abigail's age has been raised" (2).

5. Witchcraft is, as we have seen, a *pre-Christian* religion whose deities embody primal natural and cosmic principles. There is no Satan or Devil in witchcraft. When Christianity became the "establishment" religion of Europe, it superimposed its conception of evil on pagan beliefs, effectively personifying Satan in some deities of the ancient religions that it could not assimilate into its benefic pantheon of saints. Thus, the Old Religion, Wicca, the Craft of the Wise, witchcraft, came to be perceived as worship of the Devil. Properly, however, Satanism is the worship of the Christian personification of evil, thus a heretical cult, not witchcraft.

6. Owing to a misreading of European court records of witchcraft trials, Murray misunderstood handwritten references to "convent" to mean "coven," thus the origin of the term for a group of witches convening to perform their rites. The number thirteen in such a group was taken as a mockery of Christ and his twelve disciples.

7. In "Echoes Down the Corridor," a postscript to *The Crucible,* Miller states: "The legend has it that Abigail turned up later as a prostitute in Boston" (140).

8. Two dogs were hanged as well.

9. Such sermons continued into the next century. Their most notable producer was Jonathan Edwards (1703–58), whose most famous sermon was "Sinners in the Hands of an Angry God" (1741).

10. Hansen's controversial study debunks the popular view "that there was no witchcraft practiced at Salem . . . that all of those executed for witchcraft at Salem were innocent" (226).

11. Hopkins began his career as a witch-finder in his native Suffolk in the early 1640s, extending his range into Norfolk, Essex, and Huntingdonshire during the years 1644–46. Such was his reputation for success that he was invited by town fathers and clergy wherever witchcraft was suspected. Hopkins and his accomplices never failed to identify one or more persons in the community in question as the culprit, using trumped-up means of detection. Most infamous was the prick-

ing tool, which retracted its point when pressed against the flesh, thus causing no outcry from the accused, who was then held to be immune from pain through supernatural (read Satanic) aid. Perhaps worse, because of its lascivious nature, was the practice of thoroughly searching the bodies of comely women in order to locate the "marke" that, according to King James, the Devil left on his devotees.

In 1647, Hopkins published a pamphlet on his life in which he styled himself "the Witchfinder." In time, he was apprehended by an irate public and subjected to the water test that he himself had used to damn many of his victims. When he floated to the surface—a sure sign of the witch's ability to survive as well as a rejection of the evil person by the symbolic waters of baptism—Hopkins was driven off and never pursued his career again. He had not had any official mission and yet had filled many jails with those whom his trickery had condemned as witches.

Works Cited

Hansen, Chadwick. *Witchcraft at Salem.* New York: Brazillier, 1969.

Levin, David. *What Happened in Salem?* New York: Harcourt, Brace & World, 1960.

Mather, Cotton. *The Wonders of the Invisible World.* Boston, 1693.

Mather, Increase. *Cases of Conscience concerning Evil Spirits Personating Men.* Boston, 1693.

Miller, Arthur. *The Crucible.* New York: Bantam, 1968.

Murray, Margaret. *The Witch Cult in Western Europe.* 1921. Oxford: Oxford University Press, 1967.

———. *The God of the Witches.* 1933. New York: Doubleday/Anchor, 1960.

Starkey, Marion L. *The Devil in Massachusetts.* New York: Doubleday, 1969.

8

A Matter of Habit

The Politics of Demonic Hysteria in John Whiting's The Devils

> The universe is such that it bears witness everywhere to a lost God in man and outside him and to a fallen nature.
>
> —Pascal, *Pensées*

When Aldous Huxley issued *The Devils of Loudun* in England in 1952, he drew on a substantial number of sources, some published as early as 1634. This was the very year in which culminated the strange events that took place in the French city of Loudun concerning the alleged misdeeds of a controversial priest and the nun responsible for initiating a series of accusations that would facilitate the priest's demise at the hands of his political and religious adversaries.

The life and times of Father Urbain Grandier, a Jesuit-trained secular priest who was renowned for his decadent and amorous lifestyle, who preached fiery sermons against government excesses from his pulpit at Saint Pierre du Marché, and who is forever associated with the convent of Ursuline nuns in Loudun in the France of Louis XIII, form the basis for the cultural historian's work. *The Devils of Loudun* is a study of a persecution and execution founded on political premises through the machinations of Cardinal Richelieu, who controlled the king and all of France. The high churchman's opposition to Grandier stemmed from the priest's resistance to the centralization of power in Paris (in Richelieu's hands) at the expense of local autonomy. Unable to proceed against Grandier on political grounds, Richelieu carried out his agenda through the trumped-up charge that the priest had trafficked with the Devil. More specifically, Grandier was accused of having made a demonic pact (which at the time was said to have been produced at his trial, along with one signed by numerous devils)[1] and was charged with sexually possessing the mother superior, Sister Jeanne des Anges, and other nuns through demonic agency (see figs. 15–16). The cardinal's political prowess and the populace's credulity in the reality of demonic intervention and other superstitions made it impossible for the

---

Previous page: Urbain Grandier Burned at the Stake, provenance unknown. Public domain.

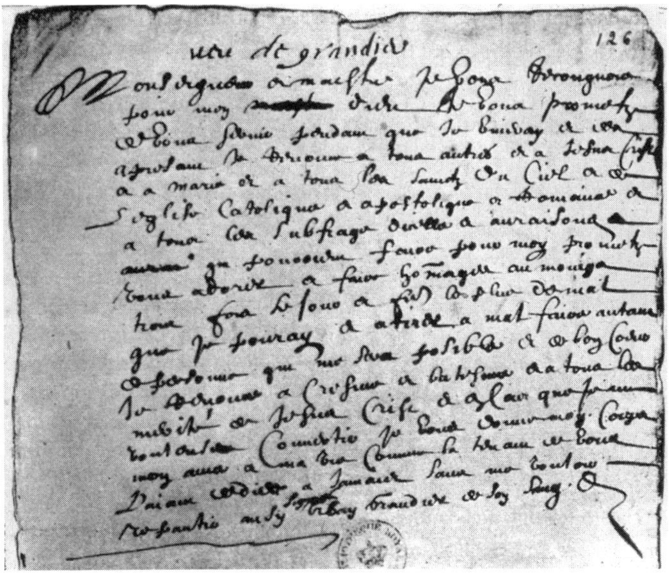

Figure 15. *Father Urbain Grandier's Supposed Pact with the Devil,* provenance unknown. Public domain.

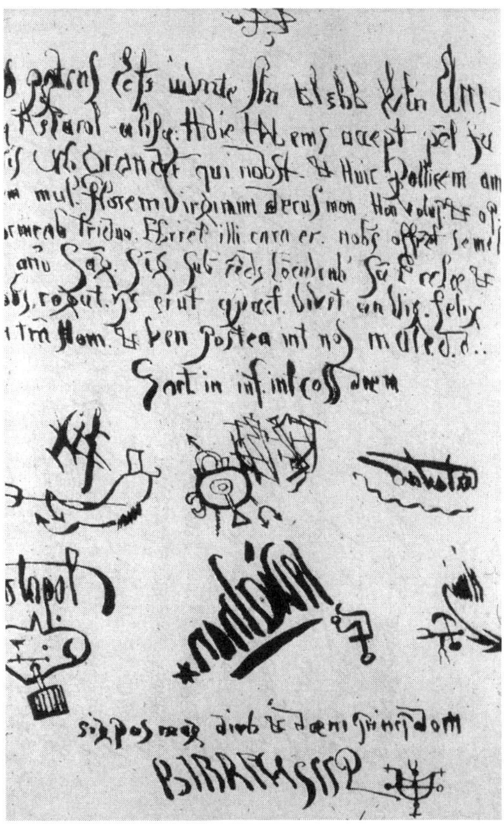

Figure 16. *Devils' Supposed Pact with Father Urbain Grandier,* provenance unknown. Public domain.

priest to overcome these outlandish charges. Father Urbain Grandier was convicted, sentenced to death, tortured, and duly executed by being burned alive at the stake in 1634.

Huxley's account of these events prompted the British playwright John Whiting to create *The Devils*,[2] in which he adopted some and rejected others in the complex series of events surrounding the priest and his accuser. Early on in the first act of the play, he portrays Grandier as man—sensualist, possessor of women, self-confessor at God's altar of having committed the sins of pride, ambition, and lust. This point of view toward the priestly life as oriented toward self-gratification stemmed, as Huxley posits, from Grandier's reading of Pierre Ronsard's poetry, in two of whose stanzas are found the perfect expression of Grandier's credo:

> Quand au le temple nous serons,
> Agenouillés nous ferons
> Les dévots selon la guise
> De ceux qui, pour louer Dieu,
> Humbles se courbent au lieu
> Le plus secret de l'Eglise.
>
> Mais quand au lit nous serons,
> Entrelacés nous ferons
> Les lascifs selon les guises
> Des amants qui librement
> Pratiquent folâtrement
> Dans les draps cent mignardises. (Huxley, 13)[3]

As yet unaware of Grandier's sexual gamesmanship along these lines, and ire aroused by Grandier's sensuality, the bishop of Poitiers, Grandier's superior, pontificates to his attendant priests about the assault to his idea of propriety on smelling Father Grandier's scented handkerchief: "For all vanities are an assertion of self, and the assertion of self in Man is the ascendancy of the Devil." De la Rochepozay fears that the symbol of the priest's decadence that has proved offensive to his olfactory sense signifies something other than dandyism; he suspects an even greater problem with consequences beyond personal debasement: "[A] banner flung across the world, stinking, enveloping, overwhelming our beloved Church in shamelessness and lust. We are in peril!" (Whiting, 23).

Immediately on the bishop's departure, Barré and Rangier, two of the priests who have listened to the tirade, introduce the name of Satan, speaking of cases of the presence of the Evil One in their respective parishes. Regarding a marriage that he had conducted, Barré states that he recognized a devil in a cow that had interrupted the proceedings:

> Before I could act he had passed from the cow to the bride's mother, who fell to the ground in a kind of convulsion. . . . I began exorcism at once. . . . The spirit screamed from the church like a great wind. A kind of black slime was found smeared on the girl's forehead. She said she'd fallen, but of course I know better. That's not all. Two days later the husband came to me and said he'd found himself quite unable to perform his necessary duty. The usual kind of spell, you know. I've now started investigations into the whole family. (Whiting, 24–25)

Rangier confirms that there has arisen a "great popular interest in evil nowadays," and, in confirmation, Barré discloses that he must set out for a farm where "[t]hey say that something is speaking through the umbilicus of a child. The child herself is now in conversation with it, and I'm told the two voices have evolved a quite astonishing creed of profanation" (25).

The situation is clear: the Devil is abroad in the land, and even God's holy places and innocent children are not immune from his visitations. As the bishop hinted when speaking of Grandier, God's servants are not de facto excluded from Satan's grasp. And, unknown to any but themselves, the chemist Adam and the surgeon Mannoury have set out to keep a record of Grandier's sexual dalliances toward toppling the priest by accusations of debauchery, profanity, and impiety that they plan to bring before the king. Such were the intentions of two "good" men, pillars of society.

In a scene that parallels Grandier's when prostrate before the altar, Sister Jeanne soliloquizes in prayer to God. But, whereas the priest sought to free himself from his passions by imploring God to let him die, the mother superior of the Ursuline convent of Loudun wants to live so as to fulfill a special expectation: "I will find a way. Yes, I will find a way to You. I shall come. You will enfold me in Your sacred arms. The blood will flow between us, uniting us. My innocence is Yours" (Whiting, 29). Small and deformed by a humpback, she begs God to remove her physical burden: "Please, God, take away my hump so that I can lie on my back without lolling my head. There is a way to be found. May the light of Your eternal love . . . " (30). The prayer of this *bride of Christ*—as a woman who takes the veil is termed by the church—is in the language of sexual love. In the *en-*

folding of his arms, she will *come;* her *innocence* is to be his, and the *blood* of that rite of passage will flow, *uniting* both as she *lies on her back,* evoking *love* as in a hymeneal rite. "There is a way to be found," she says, but the suspicion arises that what she desires is other than a mystical union.[4] Her words and ardor introduce the possibility that, if the bonding with God cannot be effected, then an appropriate physical substitute is to be found. That this is, indeed, her meaning will become clear later in the play, when she decides on Grandier, about whom she has heard gossip, as the replacement for the dead confessor and spiritual adviser to the convent, and when, on seeing him on the street from her window, she lets out an anguished cry that he hears but cannot place.

When Grandier refuses her request, if ever so gracefully, Sister Jeanne is visibly shaken. Then, in an act of transference,[5] she fantasizes over the lovemaking between the priest and his pupil Phillipe, daughter of the public prosecutor, Trincant. Her expectations shattered by Grandier's refusal, she "sees" the lovers and describes the vision as if she were participating in their intimacy, ultimately agonizing over an act that she knows she will never perform. Weeping, she cries out: "This frenzy, this ripping apart, this meat on a butcher's slab. Where are you? Love? Love? What are you? Now. Now. Now. . . . O my God, is that it? Is that it?" (Whiting, 42). Hers is a strange recognition scene, for, rather than achieve the purgation of emotion and a liberating self-awareness, it instigates depression. The vision of the lovers fades away as the reality of her pitiful situation puts her in a state of shock. She falls to her knees as if in prayer, but, convulsed, she is unable even to breathe properly. Sister Jeanne is suffocated by her unfulfilled passion and near despair over its ever being brought to fruition. It is clear that the deformed nun has become obsessed with the priest.

It is this moment that marks a turning point in the nun's life and, unbeknownst to Grandier, in his as well. The repercussions of such people intruding into one's existence are foregrounded in the scene that follows immediately. There, Baron Jean de Martin Laubardemont, the king's official emissary to the governor of Loudun, D'Armagnac, communicates the sovereign's demand that the city's walls be razed (what is unsaid is that the order stems from a national program to destabilize local autonomy); when unsuccesful in his attempt, Laubardemont exits. D'Armagnac then declares to his supporter Grandier: "My dear fellow, we are all romantic. We see our lives being changed by a winged messenger on a black horse. But more often than not it turns out to be a shabby little man, who stumbles across our path" (Whiting, 44). The governor's decision to oppose the king's mandate as communicated by his envoy will bring dire consequences to both governor and city, while Grandier's own fate will be tied to them through his unwitting refusal of the delusional nun who has crossed his path. The woof and warp have begun to interweave on the loom of destiny.

The repercussions that this creates are soon to be evident. Sister Jeanne is next seen in conversation with an elderly priest, described as *"a foolish old man,"* who has assumed the duties at her convent in lieu of Father Grandier. Walking with Father Mignon, the mother superior discusses the state of things in the convent, revealing her own troubled state: "I have myself recently suffered from visions of a diabolical nature. . . . I managed to resist the vision. Several hours of prayer and I was myself again. But the visitation. . . . The dead Canon Moussant, your predecessor, came to me in the night. He stood at the foot of my bed" (Whiting, 45). The priest interjects that the visitation was no doubt "a visit of love," but it soon becomes apparent that the nun's intent is to go beyond the retelling of a spectral event. To the priest's query whether the visitor spoke, she declares: "He spoke filth. Dirt. Jeering, contemptuous, hurtful obscenity. . . . He was not in his own person. . . . He came to me as another. A different man. . . . Grandier. Father Grandier" (46). On mouthing this accusation, tantamount to credible evidence when made by such a "reliable witness" as the mother superior, the nun has become something other than a manifestation of Christian charity: she has turned into a vindictive woman. Beneath the calm with which she makes the accusation lies the hellish fury of a woman scorned.

Father Mignon, joining the chemist, the surgeon, and the king's emissary, who is now investigating Grandier for his opposition to the royal plan, informs them of the state of the prioress in order to enlist their help: "She may be just an hysterical woman. . . . She already complains of a spasmodic but acute swelling of the belly." All agree to visit her in their professional capacities, to be accompanied by Laubardemont as "a disinterested party" (Whiting, 50) and by Father Barré as an expert on matters demonic. The scene is set for the rational examination of Sister Jeanne.

But, when the moment arrives, it is Father Barré who takes charge. As the local priest reputed to have a special talent for exorcising demons, Barré is cast in a mold typical of the period, and his actions reflect the church's attitude toward possession and its cure, as Scott notes in *Letters on Demonology and Witchcraft:*

> The Catholic Church had much occasion to rally round her all the respect that remained to her in a schismatic and heretical kingdom; and when her fathers

> and doctors announced the existence of such a dreadful disease, and of the power of the church's prayers, relics and ceremonies to cure it, it was difficult for a priest, supposing him more tender of the interest of his order than that of the truth, to avoid such a tempting opportunity as a supposed case of possession offered for displaying the high privilege in which his profession made him a partner, or to abstain from conniving at the imposture, in order to obtain for his church the credit of expelling the demon. (168)

Such is the exorcist who addresses the demon, a priest who is convinced, if without real evidence, that such a supernatural being resides in the body of the prioress.[6] Beginning the rite of exorcism, Barré learns the identity of Sister Jeanne's possessor; Asmodeus, the devil, responds in "*peals of masculine laughter*" that "*pour from her open, distorted mouth.*" And, when he speaks, it is in a "*deep man's voice*" (Whiting, 51). The exorcist is proud of (and relieved at) having been proved right and of his great accomplishment in identifying the agent of Satan. Further prodding reveals that Asmodeus entered Sister Jeanne's body through the agency of Father Grandier. The first act closes with the tormenting priest's name shouted out thrice by the nun, followed by "*deep, sullen laughter*" (52).

Although shocking in itself, the revelation pleases everyone present. They now have a vested interest in the disclosure of Grandier's diabolic liaison. Laubardemont has obtained religious grist for his political agenda against the priest, Mannoury and Adam have seen their circumstantial case inflated beyond mere accusations of sexual improprieties, and the two priests now have the sacred mission before them of ridding the town of an agent of the Devil. And what of Sister Jeanne? The vindictive nun has had her first moment of public recognition, and its consequences are to give her the central role in the tragic proceedings against Grandier that are to follow. Exorcism has, in effect, exacerbated the very condition that it was meant to dispel.

The second act opens in St. Peter's Church, where, in the secrecy of night, Grandier is performing the marriage Mass for himself and Phillipe. This holy act performed before the eyes of God by one of his ministers becomes doubly heinous under the circumstances, being a mockery of the church's law on the celibacy of its priests, on the one hand, and a perversion of the sacrament of marriage by having it as a self-administered rite, on the other. On these counts, as well as on his many breaches of the vow of chastity, Grandier is patently guilty. But these are only incidentals to his accusers now that they have a greater charge with which not just to destroy the man but to damn his soul.

The hysteria of the prioress has tainted other nuns. Father Barré, resolved to defeat Asmodeus and thereby set a pattern for freeing the rest of the nuns, diagnoses: "He seems at the moment to be lodged in the lower bowel" (Whiting, 58). Since the devil will not leave as a result of the exorcist's use of Latin formulas, Barré resolves to flush him out with an enema. When Sister Jeanne realizes what he is about to undertake on her person, she speaks in her own voice: "No, no! I didn't mean it!" (59). Her protestations go unheeded because those present choose to believe that Asmodeus is speaking in the nun's voice. Her words are unconvincing as an abjuration. The exorcist and his assistants drag her screaming into a small, dark room to have the chemist administer the purging solution, which has added efficacy, having been turned into sacramental holy water by the blessing of Father Rangier. Thus will a spirit, albeit an evil one, be ousted by physical means; such were the concepts at work during the period. Of course, with Sister Jeanne having faked possession, the enema proves effective in restoring her to God, if in a somewhat diminished state; and the other "possessed" nuns soon mend their ways as well, fearing that, if the unorthodox exorcism could be administered to the mother superior, they would not have a chance of avoiding it.

The self-deluded Father Barré was no doubt a better psychologist than he was an exorcist, as De Cerisay's cynical comments to D'Armagnac and Grandier imply: "It seems that after the Prioress more normal methods of exorcism are proving successful. A little holy water—applied externally—a few prayers, and the devils go" (Whiting, 60). Nonetheless, Sister Jeanne's vengeful game has become all too real to the two observers, but Grandier cannot accept that the matter is as serious as his two friends would have him believe. Yet the affair is not closed, for, as magistrate, De Cerisay must question the prioress, and, while present at the interrogation conducted by Barré, he listens to her recite in her own voice the debauched things that she claims she did with Grandier and his devils:

> Grandier! Grandier! The beautiful, golden lion entered my room, smiling. . . . Six of his creatures were with him. . . . He took me gently in his arms and carried me to the chapel. His creatures each took one of my beloved sisters. . . . That night it was a place of luxury and scented heat. Let me tell you. It was full of laughter and music. There were velvets, silks, metals. . . . Yes, and there was food. High animal flesh, and wine, heavy, like the fruit of the East. I'd read about it all. . . . I forgot. We were beautifully dressed. I wore my clothes as if they were part of my body. Later, when I was naked, I fell among the thorns. (65)

Again, Sister Jeanne's words betray her fantasizing over things missing in her life as a nun: Grandier, the man that she cannot have ("beautiful, golden lion"); food and drink that she cannot consume ("[h]igh animal flesh," "wine," fruit); a lifestyle that can never be hers ("luxury," "laughter and music"); clothes that cannot replace her drab habit ("velvets, silks"); but most of all the sexual behavior that has been forbidden to her ("I fell among the thorns").[7] And her imagination was abetted by an external source: "I'd read about it all." No doubt the passages to which she alludes in her description of orgiastic behavior are from the Old Testament, while the reference to coition ("I fell among the thorns") is from the New Testament (Matt. 13:7). Hers is clearly a case of erotomania prompted by her state of privation and abetted by biblical readings.

There is also evident in Sister Jeanne's words a deep resentment of God, the God of prohibitions, the God who did not come to her as a lover: "[A]nd so we vanquished God from his house. He fled in horror at the senses fixed in men by another hand. Free of Him, we celebrated his departure again and again. (*she lies back*) To one who has known what I have known, God is dead. I have found peace" (Whiting, 66). God, who did not satisfy her sexual craving, was replaced by a man, Grandier, whose presence was made manifest to her by devils. But, in killing God,[8] the nun has, in effect, become an atheist and abandoned her former status, at least in her own mind, although she is still seen by her charges as their mother superior. Furthermore, in positing "the senses fixed in men by another hand," she is ascribing the instigation of humanity's sensual nature to Satan,[9] thus putting forward a variation on the church's prelapsarian doctrine, that is, its view of the innocent status of man prior to Satan's temptation of Adam and Eve into original sin—an act that brought them into the possession of forbidden knowledge, namely, the empowerment to become like God, by creating life through the act of sex. Sister Jeanne has "found peace" in the release of her own sexuality from the bonds imposed by God, as had her sister Eve; similarly achieved through the agency of the Devil is her liberation from God, who is no longer necessary in her life.

De Cerisay recognizes the narrative as the obsessive ravings of an "unhappy woman" (Whiting, 66), but Barré takes as fact statements made by three other nuns that they copulated with devils. Despite the certification by the surgeon Mannoury that the nuns were deflowered, to De Cerisay it is evident that the young women, deprived of an outlet for their sex drive by the vow of chastity, had lesbian relations within the convent walls; "sentimental attachments" (67) he calls them so as not to offend the priest. As a result of what he has observed, De Cerisay prevails on the archbishop to halt further exorcisms and to deny Barré and his colleagues access to the convent. For the time being, the danger to Grandier is allayed.

Although he should rejoice over the turn in his favor, Grandier confesses to De Cerisay and D'Armagnac that he desires to die. And it would appear that, despite his naive belief that the gossip against him will simply dissipate, a part of his being longs for a death like that of others who have suffered under similar circumstances. There is an ironic element of self-destruction in the makeup of a man who had been a brilliant student under Jesuit tutelage but who became a roué[10] in the guise of a secular priest. Aware of the dichotomy, he presents an apologia to D'Armagnac: "All worldly things have a single purpose for a man of my kind. Politics, power, the senses, riches, pride and authority. I choose them with the same care that you, sir, select a weapon. But my intention is different. I need to turn them against myself. . . . I have a great need to be united with God. Living has drained the need for life from me. My exercise of the senses has flagged to total exhaustion. I am a dead man, compelled to live" (Whiting, 73).

Like his antagonist Sister Jeanne, Grandier needs "to be united with God," yet both have turned from him to seek satisfaction in sins of the flesh, imaginary or real. In both, the transcendent life of the spirit has been supplanted by the debased sexuality of the body. Although his spirit is dead, Grandier is unable to gauge that he will, in effect, become a dead man in the physical sense as a result of self-destructive actions, as his friend asserts: "I can see that the obvious short cut, self-destruction, is not possible. But isn't creating the circumstances for your death, which is what you seem to be doing, equally sinful . . . to create an enemy so malignant as to bring you down, and so send you—up?" (Whiting, 73). Perceptively, D'Armagnac has decoded Grandier's intent and his hope for the salvation of his soul. His words foreshadow the end that awaits the priest in this life, if not in the next. And, when the news reaches Grandier that the city walls will be torn down and that he has been accused of sedition by Richelieu, he sees in the prosecution that is certain to result the answer to his death wish.

The situation takes a turn for the worse when Laubardemont and Father Mignon instigate a new avowal of possession by the nuns, who, acting as if inhabited by many devils, shout out their names as in a roll call. Leviathan, Beherit, and Isacaaron, each in a different part of the body, are in Sister Jeanne; Elimi is in Sister Claire; Eazaz is in Sister Louise. And, as the self-satisfied priest and envoy look on, the other nuns present participate, as indicated by the stage directions: "*Clamor of diabolical voices. Derisive laughter: grunts, squeals, howls*" (Whiting, 81).

Sidestepping the archbishop's prohibition against their entering the convent, the principals next gather in the palace courtyard, there displaying the nuns as they perform their animalistic and lewd actions before the masses and the king's representative, Prince Henri de Condé, a sodomite who has brought along his pleasure boys. It has become a public spectacle on many levels. Barré has again taken up the challenge of exorcising the nuns, once more without success, but the prince offers him a reliquary containing the blood of Christ. When the priest applies it to the possessed Sister Jeanne, the nun miraculously is freed of her three tormentors. But the worldly-wise prince "*takes the box from Barré, opens it, and holds it upside down; it is empty.*" And, with cynicism, he queries Barré: "Reverend Sir, what sort of trick are you playing on us?" (Whiting, 89).

As if in response, the priests Mignon and Rangier become possessed, as do several women in the crowd. Barré runs to them, shouting his magical formulas in Latin. Pandemonium reigns in the square. As the crowd is dispersed by the guards and the other nuns are led back to the convent, Sister Jeanne alone stands before the prince, listening to his bemused yet jolting words: "I'd say you'll have your wish about this man Grandier, seeing the way the world goes. But do you know what you must give? (*casually*) Your immortal soul to damnation in an infinite desert of eternal bestiality" (Whiting, 90). Sister Jeanne makes no reply to the fearsome statement, and the prince leaves with his retinue, but thereafter she speaks in the voice of Leviathan: "Now think, my dear. Remember the night time visions. He and—(*obscene giggles*)—oh, that thing—and you, agape—no, no, my darling, not purity, not even dignity. What are you thinking of? Not only all impure, but all absurd. Remember?" (92).

Sister Jeanne and her diabolic consort laugh at once as darkness enfolds the scene. The two simultaneous laughters indicate that, if the obsessed Sister Jeanne had mounted a play in which she acted the part of a woman possessed through the agency of Grandier, she has now become truly possessed by the Devil. Her condition has evolved along the lines that the psychologist Jaynes has noted: "Like schizophrenia, negatory possession usually begins with some kind of hallucination. It is often a castigating 'voice' of a 'demon' or other being which is 'heard' after a considerable stressful period. But then, unlike schizophrenia, probably because of the strong collective cognitive imperative of a particular group or religion, the voice develops into a secondary system of personality, the subject then losing control and periodically entering into trance states in which consciousness is lost, and the 'demon' side of the personality takes over" (348).

Events follow quickly toward the abasement of Grandier and the fulfillment of the prince's words to Sister Jeanne. A council of state in Paris hears both the prince and Laubardemont on the matter of the political and moral accusations against Grandier, but it becomes evident very quickly that the prince's defense cannot overcome the damning words of the priest's prosecutors. Richelieu himself utters the words that ensure the punishment of Grandier: "The Devil must never be believed, even when he tells the truth" (Whiting, 93). One of the priests under Richelieu's pastoral mantle as well as a citizen subject to his despotic rule, Grandier will forfeit his life, ostensibly for leading a life of debauchery that culminated in a liaison with Satan, but actually for having opposed the will of Richelieu. And so Laubardemont proceeds to act on the cardinal's instructions. The king has not uttered a word during the "star chamber" proceedings.[11]

Before Grandier is taken prisoner by Laubardemont at the end of the second act, he has a moment outside his church in which he proclaims to the Sewerman the epiphany that he has experienced after accompanying an old man as he died:

> I created God! . . . I created Him from the light and the air, from the dust of the road, from the sweat of my hands, from gold, from filth, from the memory of women's faces, from great rivers, from children, from the works of man, from the past, the present, the future and the unknown. I caused Him to be from fear and despair. I gathered in everything from this mighty act, all I have known, seen and experienced. My sin, my presumption, my vanity, my love, my hate, my lust. And last I gave myself and so made God. And He is magnificent. For He is all these things. I was utterly in His presence. I knelt by the road. I took out the bread and the wine. Panem vinum in salutis consecramus hostiam. And in this understanding He gave Himself humbly and faithfully to me, as I had given myself to Him. (Whiting, 96)

Again, in a parallel but contrapuntal scene to that in which Sister Jeanne declared the death of God, Grandier declares his existence. His has been a grand holistic act of creation. And the result is that, unlike the peace that Sister Jeanne proclaimed to have experienced in the aftermath of God's death, Grandier rejoices in having found meaning and reason in his creation of God. The street and church may be filled with the mocking laughter of devils as the priest is led away, but the priest's personal discovery of God will sustain him as he undergoes incarceration, torture, and execution.

These come together in the third and final act of the play. The parallelism continues as, first, Sister Jeanne expresses to Father Mignon doubts over her actions against the man whom she has come to love and, second, Grandier, alone in his cell, soliloquizes on the fear that is killing God within him and sheds doubt on the awareness of God that he had experienced earlier that day. But he renews his commitment during a conversation with the old priest who has come to console him; through the simplicity of Father Ambrose he has found that "God is here" (Whiting, 106).

Stern faced and unyielding, the judges, led by Laubardemont, have found Grandier guilty.[12] The clerk reads the sentence: "Urbain Grandier, you have been found guilty of commerce with the devil. And that you used this unholy alliance to possess, seduce and debauch certain Sisters of the holy order of Saint Ursula (they are fully named in this document). You have also been found guilty of obscenity, blasphemy and sacrilege. . . . [I]t is ordered that you be taken to the Place Sainte-Croix, tied to a stake and burned alive; after which your ashes will be scattered to the four winds. . . . Lastly, before sentence is carried out, you will be subjected to the Question, both ordinary and extraordinary" (Whiting, 110–11). The sentence was entered on August 18, 1634. Before the prisoner's plea to be spared the torture inherent in being "subjected to the Question,"[13] Laubardemont offers relief only if he signs a confession. Grandier refuses and is led away to await torture; soon it is administered by the priests who have dogged his path and by the jailor under the watchful eyes of Laubardemont. While Grandier's screams pierce the dungeon as his legs are systematically crushed, Sister Jeanne, a rope around her neck, muses on the events she has unleashed but is easily convinced by her nuns not to kill herself.

Grandier's death march is a processional reminiscent of Christ's. Like Christ, Grandier has been tortured and mocked. Instead of a cross, he is strapped to a chair borne on a litter; instead of the purple garment, he is dressed in a vivid shirt colored yellow by sulphur; instead of a crown of thorns, he has a rope around his neck; and, as in the case of Christ, soldiers guard him. He has his fall, too, here before the convent, but there is no Veronica to wipe his blood, no Mary Magdalene to console him. Instead, for the first time, he sees the woman who has brought him low. There is no remorse in the few words that Sister Jeanne utters, only an expression of her admiration of his manly beauty. Or is it that she recognizes in him a state of grace that she cannot attain? Then he is led away to the place of execution, where, as Rangier says, "I saw his women sitting there, watching" (Whiting, 125), another evocation of the scene at the foot of the cross. Too, as reported on Christ's execution, when nature was convulsed, on Grandier's demise: "*The town seems to be on fire. Distant buildings are silhouetted against a harsh red sky. A church door gapes like a sulphurous mouth. Armed men with banners cross a bridge. A man is climbing a ladder, waving into the distance in hopeless distress*" (124–25). The crowd that had watched the burning at the stake rushes about hysterically. The play ends with a forlorn Sister Jeanne crying out her victim's name.

Father Grandier's immolation, the consummation for which he so devoutly wished, has come to pass. He has been removed from the world of the senses, to which he had capitulated so frequently. And, prior to his demise, he purged his soul through confession, thereby assuring entry into the kingdom of God. But, to those who brought about his downfall and execution, Grandier is damned to hell, or so they would like to believe to assuage their guilt and doubt. Grandier may have suffered a physical death, but is the fate of his accusers less severe? Except for the plight of Sister Jeanne and the remorse of Father Mignon, it would seem so. Yet, within the belief system that triggered these events, Grandier will be saved, while his accusers will suffer the consequences of their crimes only in the world to come. But that will be an eternal punishment. As Dante has vouched, there are special places reserved in hell for sowers of discord, hypocrites, falsifiers, evil counselors, perpetrators of fraud, tyrants, and other such wrongdoers. All of Grandier's accusers fall into one or more of these categories.

Who then are the devils of the play's title? Grandier, who has broken his priestly vows and is so full of himself that he becomes an *Übermensch* in his own sight? Sister Jeanne and her nuns, who have fallen into the practice of feigning possession to achieve the libidinous desires that their habit does not permit them and whose false witness brings about the execution of Grandier?[14] Fathers Barré, Rangier, and Mignon, so full of mistaken zeal and self-aggrandizement that they choose not to see the falsehood and self-interest around them? The surgeon Mannoury and the chemist Adam, whose pompous ethics instill in them a crusading desire to topple Grandier? Ninon the widow and Phillipe the virgin, two of the many women who have given themselves to the priest's insatiable lust? Cardinal Richelieu, who has usurped power and is so corrupted by it that he can condemn a fellow priest to death in order to promote his political agenda? King Louis

XIII, who neither recognizes injustice nor acts to rectify it? The prince, a sodomite who, despite his awareness of the falsehood behind the accusations, takes no action to save a man he knows to be innocent? Laubardemont, who, feigning to cry over their obstinacy to confess, revels in his power to send men to their deaths—and to eternal damnation? Only the devils themselves, who may or may not be real in the context of the plot? Or, in the light of all the false, hypocritical, self-serving human beings arrayed against a defenseless man, is the *devils* in the title meant to be applied collectively, a way of signifying the culpability of all the players in the drama owing to the fallen nature of man: the habit of sin?

Notes

1. On the belief in the accessibility of the Devil through a pact, generally held to have been signed in blood, see Lima, chap. 3.

2. The play was first produced in London at the Aldwych Theatre on February 20, 1961, by the Royal Shakespeare Company. In the previous century, Alexandre Dumas père wrote *Urbain Grandier* (1850), a play in five acts, which may be read in a 2000 English translation/adaptation by Frank J. Morlock available on the Web at www.cadytech.com/dumas/stories/urbain_grandier.php (accessed March 14, 2005).

3. The gist here is that the priest has two faces: the first as the proper servant of God in his house, the second as a wanton in the bed of a lover.

4. Although to convey their striving for union with God mystics often employed language couched in amorous terms, their desired end was clearly a spiritual union, through a transcendence of the physical "prison of the body," as in the case of Saint Theresa of Avila and Saint John of the Cross in Spain.

5. In psychoanalysis, the term *transference* is used to express the conveyance of emotions originally felt or expressed toward one person to another individual. In the case at hand, Sister Jeanne has transferred her erotic passion for God to Grandier, who, as a priest, is his representative.

6. For a concise yet thorough overview of possession and exorcism, see Walker, 807–15 (possession), 293–94 (exorcism).

7. Sexual activity that is both heterosexual and homosexual: "[A]nd her beloved sisters incited her" (Whiting, 66).

8. Whiting has introduced a modern existentialist concept, the death of God, into seventeenth-century proceedings. The idea is both intrusive and distracting because it is out of place on three counts: most obviously, it belongs to a school of thinking based on Nietzsche's tenet; the idea is not in keeping with the theology of the period in which the play takes place; and it is expressed by a nun, albeit a mother superior, who has been portrayed as a hysteric rather than as a theologian and who speaks as herself, not as the possessing entity, to whom such a concept might otherwise be credited.

9. She may be alluding as well to a fundamental tenet of Gnosticism: the differ-

entiation of the unknown (thus, alien) God of Light and the Demiurge, who is the maker of the universe and all that is in it. The Demiurge, equated to Satan/Lucifer in some Gnostic systems of belief, is the one who has quickened the senses of man. Akin to this is the myth of Prometheus, who brought humanity knowledge, symbolized by the fire that he stole from the Olympian gods.

10. The term is not strictly appropriate, although apt, since it was first used in 1720 to refer to the profligate companions of the duc d'Orléans.

11. The original Star Chamber, an English inquisitorial court with jurisdiction over religious and secular matters, sat in secret without a jury. Noted for the arbitrariness and severity of its judgments, the court was abolished in 1641.

12. The actual trial is not seen on-stage. Had it been, the evidence against Grandier would have included two demonic pacts: one signed by the priest and the other by a host of devils. The latter instrument, written backward and from right to left, included the signatures of Satanas, Beelzebub, Lucifer, Elimi, and Astaroth.

13. The Question was the process whereby one adjudged guilty by the Holy Office of the Inquisition was allowed to abjure his or her sinful deeds by signing a confession. Admitting guilt would in no way remove the punishment, but it would save the soul of the individual from eternal damnation, in accordance with Christ's dictum: "Whatever thou shalt bind on earth shall be bound in heaven" (Matt. 16:19). Should the person choose not to sign the document of his own volition, the Question would be put through the application of torture, as in the case of Urbain Grandier, whose legs were crushed. The priest refused to admit guilt for something he had not done and went to his death without signing a confession.

14. The history of Sister Jeanne continued beyond the events covered in the play. Her state deteriorated over the years after the Urbain Grandier episode, and she had to be counseled and exorcised regularly by Father Jean-Joseph Surin, who would himself fall victim to the evil spirits that possessed the nun (see Oesterreich, 49–56, 86–90). In 1644, Sister Jeanne composed a narrative of her possession, and this was published in 1886 as *Soeur Jeanne des Anges.*

Works Cited

Huxley, Aldous. *The Devils of Loudun.* New York: Harper & Bros., 1953.

Jaynes, Julian. *The Origin of Consciousness in the Breakdown of the Bicameral Mind.* Boston: Houghton Mifflin, 1990.

Lima, Robert. *Dark Prisms: Occultism in Hispanic Drama.* Lexington: University Press of Kentucky, 1995.

Oesterreich, Traugott K. *Possession: Demoniacal and Other among Primitive Races, in Antiquity, the Middle Ages, and Modern Times.* Translated by D. Ibberson. New York, 1930. Reissued as *Possession and Exorcism* (New York: Causeway, 1974).

Saint Joseph "New Catholic Edition" of the Holy Bible: Confraternity-Douay Version. New York: Catholic Book Publishing, 1962.

Scott, Sir Walter. *Letters on Demonology and Witchcraft.* London: George Routledge & Sons, 1884.

Soeur Jeanne des Anges: Autobiographie d'une hystérique possédée. Edited by Gabriel Legué and Gilles de la Tourette. Paris, 1886.
Walker, Barbara G. *The Woman's Encyclopedia of Myths and Secrets.* San Francisco: Harper & Row, 1983.
Whiting, John. *The Devils.* New York: Hill & Wang, 1961.

9

The Prey of the Vampire

Malign Decadence in Francisco Nieva's Nosferatu

> In all the darkest pages of the malign supernatural, there is no more terrible tradition than that of the Vampire.
>
> —Montague Summers, *The Vampire: His Kith and Kin*

Until 1961, when Francisco Nieva wrote his play *Aquelarre y noche roja de Nosferatu* (Witches' Sabbat and Red Night of Nosferatu), the theme of the vampire had not been treated in serious Spanish or Spanish American literature. With the play's belated publication in 1991 and production in 1993, the Spanish-speaking public was given an opportunity to experience through the interpretation of one of its dramatists a dark subject that had long fascinated many readers and filmgoers, Spaniards included. In order to achieve his end of informing and interpreting, Nieva steeped himself in the lore of the vampire, derived from sources that, by necessity, were external to Spain. That material, extensive and multifaceted though it is, affected Nieva's conception of the vampire in an unexpected manner, for he found therein an opening to a new view; his is substantially a heterodox stance, a departure from the canonicity established by the first assessors of the tradition.

The lore and literature of vampirism was early on assayed by Montague Summers in *The Vampire: His Kith and Kin,* wherein are discussed numerous novels, stories, poems, and plays on the dark subject. The famed student of the occult devotes many pages to the notorious tale *The Vampire,* reputed to have been written by Lord Byron when published in 1819, but actually penned by his physician, Dr. John W. Polidori.[1] However, the most nefarious, and popular, in its day, Summers notes, was *Varney the Vampire; or, The Feast of Blood,* a novel of 868 pages by either Thomas Preskett Prest or James Malcolm Rymer, first published in 1847. But, be it founded on *Varney* or another early manifestation of the vampire genre, the lore of the undead has generally been presented seriously in literature and other arts,

---

Previous page: Image of Nosferatu by Albin Grau (1922) for press distribution for the silent film *Nosferatu* by Murnau. Public domain.

most notably in Bram Stoker's seminal *Dracula* (1897), from which have come its truncated English stage adaptation of 1924 by Hamilton Deane and its American revision by John L. Balderston in 1927, the elegant and highly romanticized Broadway production of 1977, and, more recently, the works of the contemporary novelist Anne Rice, beginning with the controversial and revisionist *Interview with the Vampire* (1976) and its numerous sequels, among the latest of which is *The Vampire Armand* (1998).

But Nieva is not informed solely by the literary; he is openly indebted to filmography for many of the images of the vampire that his play conveys. In cinematographic culture, the motif was first given visual treatment by F. W. Murnau in his great silent film *Nosferatu* (1922) as a rather loose adaptation of Bram Stoker's novel; thereafter, the motif became a genre as it evolved through the Bela Lugosi era, beginning with Tod Browning's classic film of 1931,[2] and, more recently, devolved into satiric portrayals of the undead in such as Roman Polanski's multipart *The Fearless Vampire Killers* (1967) and *Blackula* (1972). And what can be said of the extravagant and quirky film version of the Dracula story by Francis Ford Coppola or of the long-running television series *Buffy the Vampire Slayer*? The Dracula mystique even invaded the realm of the very young through the cereal manufacturer's Count Chocula and television's counting Count on *Sesame Street*. So heady was the modern reintroduction of Stoker's character into all areas of popular culture that, in 1977, *Time* magazine was prompted to ask: "Is Dracula Really Dead?" Both query and admonition, the question reveals a concern that is even more applicable today.

The topos of Nosferatu[3] has had its greatest literary expression in Stoker's novel. But the tradition of Dracula and his ilk has not fared well in recent years, falling onto hard times through revisionist, often defamatory practices. The latest assault on the serious tradition of vampirism comes from an unexpected quarter, Spain: unexpected because, while that nation has a rich trove of myths and occult lore that has evolved from Iberian, Celtic, Carthaginian, Roman, Suevian (Swabian), Visigothic, Jewish, and Islamic cultures, that panorama of beliefs has not included vampirism, nor has the Spanish imagination been intrigued by the blood, gore, and sexuality on which that aspect of lycanthropy thrives elsewhere. The Spaniards may have read Stoker's classic, but they have not taken Dracula to their bosom.[4] The figure of the vampire remains intrinsically an Eastern European construct that was adopted and adapted by Bram Stoker.[5]

An important contemporary Spanish dramatist, Francisco Nieva[6] has sought to awaken his countrymen, as well as his public in Spanish America, to the lure of the vampire through the curious dramatic exercise that is *Aquelarre y noche roja de Nosferatu*, premiered in Madrid's Sala Olympia on May 26, 1993, when its title became simply *Nosferatu*. It is my intent to show how Nieva's work eschews the traditional concepts of vampirism in order to *play* on the theme in a surrealistic, absurd manner and make the point that society is so corrupt, decadent, and self-serving that it will accept evil as good. Nieva's use of *witches' Sabbat* in the title may stem from the influence of Francisco Goya y Lucientes (1746–1828), several of whose large paintings hanging in Madrid's Prado Museum are entitled *Aquelarre*. Goya used his malign images metaphorically to satirize the credulity inherent in the society of his turbulent era as well as to point out the evil thereby engendered. Nieva follows suit in commenting on his own sphere of time. He does so by replacing Goya's Satan, dressed in the vestments of the Black Goat (the he-goat called in Spanish Macho Cabrío), with his own purveyor of evil, the vampire Nosferatu in his de rigueur black regalia. Just as Goya's Satan is central to the gatherings of witches who serve his cause and benefit therefrom, Nieva's vampire is the focus of the populace, mostly women, who wish to partake of his nefarious schemes for personal gain.[7]

However, Nieva does not allude to this aspect of the title in the text of the play itself; only in its final moments does he refer to a "damned witches' Sabbat of Nosferatu" (57), perhaps mimicking the gathering of women in Goya's paintings, although Goya does not figure in the action except as an allusion in the use of *aquelarre*. It is in the introduction that the playwright states his inspiration and his intent: "The fashion of Nosferatus began when the 1960s were still in their heyday, along with that of melodrama and horror films. . . . It was the time of acid, but, if *Nosferatu* was not made with LSD, it was certainly created to play with many who used it. . . . I am the first to admit to having no doubt that this evocation of the vampire must be a great bit of nonsense" (9). Nieva goes on to make direct reference to the silent films that inspired his mise-en-scène, among them Murnau's *Nosferatu*, Eric von Ströheim's *Queen Kelly* (1928–29), G. W. Pabst's *The Street of Sorrow* (*Die freudlose Strasse*, 1925), and *The Threepenny Opera* (*Die Dreigroschenoper*, 1931), as well as Walt Disney's cartoon creation Mickey Mouse, whose early version had a somewhat sinister facet and whose role in the film *Fantasia* cast him as a sorcerer. These cinematographic influences will be discussed as the study progresses. Queen Kelly becomes the focal point of Nosferatu's attentions in the play, while Mickey Mouse actually appears toward the end and has a destructive role in the action. But, while incorporating many of the cinematic ideas and images of these master filmmakers in his play, Nieva sets out in a new direction that will alter the fundamental aspects of the vampire tradition and make his protagonist into a modern antihero. It is this process and its outcome that are assessed here through a delineation of the play's deconstructive aspects and, in particular, its unorthodox presentation of the vampire as he interacts with men and women on varied levels of society.

A plot summary will help the reader follow the play's often surrealistic twists and conceits. Set in a decadent, cubist city on the Danube, the play opens on the agonizing figure of a man with a knife in his chest; lying on the street, he is approached by Aurora, Dawn personified, who arrives in a flying chariot and offers to save him with a cup of strong coffee and the offer of her body. He climbs into the chariot for both offerings; she removes the knife and proceeds to seduce the failed reporter. They fly off together to oversee the death of the world, which she has predicted. The next occupants of the stage are the four women of the Madrigal (a classical Greek chorus), the bandit Fiacro, and three soldiers. Their interaction would be the stuff of melodrama except for its discordant tone and the introduction of the theme of vampirism with the entrance first of Ottilia, niece of a vampire, and then of Celestino, the vampire's apprentice, who unlatches the coffin in which Nosferatu is housed. Thereafter, Nosferatu maneuvers the various elements of society to serve his ends. When Aurora returns toward the end of the action, the decadent world that Nosferatu has manipulated is ready for obliteration. The skeleton of the reporter that she flings to earth is symbolic of the end that awaits humanity.

The title character of Nieva's play has been given the "surname" Pitiflauti, which is a version of the Spanish phrase (*pito y flauta* = "whistle and flute") for something or someone of a frivolous, devil-may-care nature. This is a Nosferatu who is seen exclusively during the day (the most blatant subversion of the vampire canon). He makes his initial entry onstage in a casket borne by Celestino, a young man described as "*malign and shriveled*" (17). Celestino is a type of Igor or another such assistant to the great malefactors of horror films yet possessed of sufficient strength to carry the considerable burden of a laden casket, albeit with comic difficulty. The vampire's assistant is conceived somewhat in the style of the *zanni* in the improvisational scenarios of the commedia dell'arte or the *gracioso* character in Spanish Golden Age drama.[8]

Initially, the play renders homage to earlier traditions of vampires and vampirism. Thus, when this vampire first thrusts his hand out of the coffin, it is described as "*vinelike and with the vile paleness of Nosferatu*" (18). No doubt it is Murnau's powerful, frightening image that Nieva evokes here. And then the stage directions emphasize the corrupt aspect of dead bodies: "*Nosferatu begins to rise, and he is like a cardboard figure* [*acartonado*] *in his black Macferland dusted with the verdigris of putrefaction. He is like a board encrusted with designs* [*taracea*] *reminiscent of the dank fermentation of cheese. His nails and fangs should be very evident*" (18). The stiff, rising image, first depicted by Murnau's darkly swathed Nosferatu and later by Tod Browning's Bela Lugosi characterization in formal garb and cape, is suggestively employed by Nieva. Yet he immediately adds the folkloric touch of the corrupted corpse, akin to the mindless Eastern European vampires that confront the narrator and his vampire-protégée, Claudia, in Anne Rice's novel *Interview with the Vampire* or the stalking zombies out of the horror film classic *The Night of the Living Dead* (1968). Sophistication and naïveté mingle with abandon in the description of the protagonist of Nieva's play.

Yet, despite his negative physical image, Nosferatu Pitiflauti seems very human in his sentiments, seeking as he does his own happiness despite society's perception of the vampire as a solitary being and as a purveyor of misery and death. Thus, he asks, as if rhetorically: "Who says that Nosferatu cannot be happy?" But his source of pleasure does not follow the human norm nor the accepted quest of the vampire; rather, he finds satisfaction in his utility as a facilitator of the esoteric satisfaction of others: "Every human being who desires something calls me secretly to take a bite. All sell themselves and barter everything they have for an ecstasy they do not know." Such secrecy and bartering are reminiscent of that attendant on human dealings with the Devil through demonic pacts or magical incantations in earlier times, when the inquisitional arm of the church lay in ambush for anyone seeking to fathom cosmic knowledge through means that it considered illicit.[9] But this Nosferatu lives in a different age than a Théophile or a Faust, one in which, as he says, "[a]lready the world is loosening its bindings at breakneck speed." Such liberation from traditional ways is a hallmark of Nieva's *teatro furioso*, in which the struggle for individual freedom is paramount. "How could I not be happy" (19), Nosferatu proclaims while assessing the permissive state of affairs that will soon enhance his clientele.

That he is correct in his optimism is evident from his first appearance on the scene. It becomes obvious that Nosferatu is known and accepted by all in the neighborhood. It becomes self-evident as well that Nieva's play has a democratic side. His is a chaotic, absurd, surreal world in which characters from various social levels that inhabit the neighborhood intermingle freely and without awkwardness—the rabble, the lower middle class, prostitutes, the military, the nobility. And Nosferatu functions as a roving psychoanalyst for the likes of Azul, the violin-playing gypsy hooker who always seeks true love in the next stranger who passes by; Ottilia, his own niece, who periodically lets loose a wrenching scream from inside her house over her dead lover; and Greta, the fruit and vegetable vendor who regularly proclaims that she wants only to die (but not through the bleeding that Nosferatu offers as a tranquilizer).

It is obvious that, as in the neighborhood, Nosferatu has found favor at court, functioning quite openly there as a vampire, and publicly performing minor vampirical incisions on the queen and other willing females. When Queen Kelly, whose identity derives from the Ströheim silent film, first enters, it is to aptly name Nosferatu minister of burials (or interments) and to obtain from him a "kiss" of gratitude on her proffered hand, while saying in a hushed voice: "The kiss, the kiss. . . . Obey! . . . Kiss and pierce that vein. . . . Suck freely without misgiving!" The stage directions denote her exaltation: "*While she allows her hand to be bitten, under cover of the edge of Nosferatu's Macferland, Kelly's face shows her ecstasy*" (28). And her words mark that state: "How delicious it is to reach the lower depths. . . . I'm satisfied, although not sated" (28–29). She and the other women are, no doubt, similarly attracted by the exotic nature of the protagonist and his art of elation; as if they were damsels in distress in some silent film, they swoon as the masterful Nosferatu punctures their veins. On experiencing his pointed "gift," their fling takes an erotic turn, if only comically hinting at the highly charged sexuality delineated in *Varney the Vampire* and *Dracula.*

Beyond the sensual and sexual aspects of encounters in neighborhood and court lies something more sinister. A sardonic image of death is made manifest throughout the play—from the treatment of Greta, who is constantly threatening to commit suicide, through that of the queen, who offers her hand to Nosferatu for blood sucking in public and seems willing to cross over into his world, to that of Fiacro, her ski instructor, who threatens to blow himself and her into smithereens with a cartoonlike bomb with a lighted fuse because she has spurned his love. And, of course, ever present is the putrefactory image of Nosferatu himself, who has it in his power to transport the living into the realm of the undead through means other than explosive. That the living are not repelled by the physical aspect of Nosferatu or what he symbolizes (and is) is indicative of the human fascination with death, greatest of all mysteries of existence. Thus, Queen Kelly's confrontational attitude before Fiacro's death threat as she takes the bomb from his quivering hands is anything but heroic; her disdain of death makes her failure to extinguish the fuse antiheroic. She is defiant of death and reminds the cowering public that death comes to everyone, giving Fiacro what might be interpreted as the kiss of death. Having made an issue of the inevitability of death, she then blows out the fuse. In a sense, however, all of them have experienced death in the interval between the threat and the bomb's defusing.

But, if death brings finality to the human condition as we know it, the state of being undead has the appeal of overcoming that closure through an extended continuance. So certain is Nosferatu of the seductiveness of death after Queen Kelly's bravado performance and the ecstatic reaction of the other women at his touch that he chuckles to himself: "Now they are all mine" (31). And he may be right, for it may well be this realization that first fascinates and then attracts living human beings at all levels of society in the play. But Nosferatu does not take his clientele into his realm of extended existence beyond human life; they are given only the initiatory bite, then left on the threshold of transformation. In this, Nieva's Nosferatu differs markedly from Dracula and his ilk, whose unquenchable preying more often than not leads to a population explosion among vampires.

Yet it could be said that one individual has been singled out for extended treatment by Nosferatu à la Svengali.[10] Enveloped in a mist that suddenly appears, Nosferatu gathers the monarch in his arms and flies with her to the palace. It is his first overt magical act, perhaps a salute to the alate powers of his literary and film ancestors, if without the transmogrification that makes their flight possible. Nosferatu proclaims to the swooning Queen Kelly: "You are flying. Pure evil lifts you as it does all of us above the misery of life" (33). And, indeed, almost all present levitate in flight toward the palace. Only the terrified Madrigal, a chorus of young women reminiscent of their classical Greek counterparts solely in their unison, remains firmly planted on the ground; Nieva describes the group in the introduction as "the chorus of humble women enraptured by and eternal slaves to the fallacious preservation of the past and the present" (10). Also beholding the flight of the damned, Aurora, Dawn personified, proclaims: "They will not awaken; they will never see me again for I am Dawn" (33). And dawn is, indeed, an event that can be experienced only by the living. In the orthodox tradition of vampirism, the rising of the sun will bring the disintegration of the revenant's persona unless the enclosure of the coffin is attained in time—but not in Nieva's conception of Nosferatu, where the coffin is nothing more than a stage prop. Consequently, the finality of Aurora's words is negated in the case of both Nosferatu and those who have come under his spell.

Proving wrong Aurora's prognostication, the characters who are, as Nieva says, "in love with their own misfortunes" (10) begin to interact in a new context when outlandish desires that they share with Queen Kelly permit them entry into the privileged world of court and government through what might be termed the *supernatural mediumship* of the vampire. When Nosferatu next appears, his bedecked figure, powdered face, and painted lips reflect the clownish and decadent life of the court, which he has come to control. Even the chorus of damsels succumbs to his ministrations.[11] Nieva's vampire moves in the context of the court much like Rasputin in the Russian realm of Czar Nicholas II, with a sinister personal design to possess power akin to that which marked the actions of the astute peasant who feigned being a monk,[12] only here the power is wielded by a vampire and not by a mere mortal. The seduction of otherworldliness proferred by Nosferatu far surpasses that of any physical gratification that Rasputin could offer.

Alas, the headiness of sharing power and having license to act immorally in the new realm does not last. The pompous leader of the Queen's Guard attempts to intimidate Nosferatu with the threat of imprisonment, but he is soon suborned by the lure of the queen's favors, leaving with the vampire to partake of the insinuated tryst. Meanwhile, attaining his lustful desire to fondle the queen's breasts, Nosferatu's apprentice falls asleep in the palace. But the other changelings are not as easily satisfied with their newfound boon. Instead of finding happiness, the former have-nots fall prey to greed and disillusionment, and the queen tries to flee their crazed demands but, as the stage directions indicate, is "*trapped by the accumulation of triumphant and malign silhouettes that cackle and complain in a paradoxical combination of sounds*" (43). It is a grotesque, absurd scene out of any one of many of Goya's etchings of human folly. And, with the destruction of illusion, the characters return to their miserable lives, the queen no less a victim than her lowest subject. Yet she tries to restore their faith in her ability to overcome their sad reality by offering them passage on the Orient Express, a symbol of progress, but they find themselves unable to pursue the nonmoving train. Ultimately, they die at the hands of Mickey Mouse, agent of the Decent Nations,[13] who has come to restore the realm and its ruler to their previous status in a unilateral act of political interference in the affairs of a sovereign nation. But, despite the incongruous yet manifest power of Mickey Mouse and his cohorts, Nosferatu rises from among the dead, again to take control of the situation and of Queen Kelly.

The new day brought about by the massacre of the not-so-innocent is made manifest by the brilliant light that frames the return of Aurora, whose reentry is ironic in the context of the finality of her earlier words of exit: "[T]hey will never see me again." The scene of a new beginning echoes the words of Mircea Eliade: it is "the end of one humanity, followed by the apparition of a new humanity" (72). But, if Eliade seems to posit a wholly distinct emanation, *new* in *Nosferatu* is not necessarily *improved.* Both, in fact, indicate a rebirth out of the same source, not a different species, but a new group of *human beings.* The apotheosis in each instance indeed heralds a commencement, but what it in fact constitutes in Nieva's play is a return to more of the same—a cyclic pattern that purports to be the human predicament, the Nietzschean "ewige Wiederkunft" (179), the eternal return, brought to its lowest common denominator.

Nosferatu looks on the surreal scene with the wisdom brought on by years of observing human frailty; he alone wears the face of serenity, for, in allowing himself to be used by queen and commoner alike to attain a different life, he has satisfied his own need for continued existence. His personal satisfaction proves once again the adage "For the blood is the life," and, for the vampire, here as elsewhere, that is the rationale for existence. Unwilling to relinquish his regal source of sustenance, Nosferatu once more departs with Queen Kelly, but this time, an unwilling victim, she screams for help. It is to no avail. Those who are left in this not-so-brave world can only watch as the threesome of the reluctant Queen Kelly, the manipulative Nosferatu, and the deific Aurora fly off in the latter's chariot. It is then that Mickey Mouse removes his mask and, in metatheatrical fashion, addresses to the audience the final words of the play: "And here, ladies and gentlemen, we come to the end of Nosferatu's damned Sabbat, which has been performed especially as a just punishment for our faults" (57).

The reintroduction of the word *Sabbat,* first given in the original title of the play, is either an equivocation or yet another attempt by the playwright to derail the internal logic of *Nosferatu* to which he has led the audience. Vampires have nothing to do with witches or with their craft, either the pre-Christian religion of Wicca or its popular misconception as witchcraft,[14] and it would appear that, by making reference to the principal ritual of witchcraft first in the original subtitle and then in the conclusion, Nieva wants to bring together the two in a way that would never happen in either witchcraft or the tradition of vampirism. And, in point of fact, there is no interaction because there are no witches of any kind in the play, nor is there a Sabbat. It is yet another of Nieva's disorienting techniques, the use of disassociation.

The play also presents the transmutation of the fundamental concepts associated with the vampire since Stoker's Gothic novel and Murnau's expressionistic film. Nieva burlesques age-old beliefs through satire and irony. First, the traditional nighttime activities of the vampire become daytime activities exclusively, and related to this change is his empowerment in both contexts, for the queen has granted the bloodsucker a well-stamped official permit allowing him to go about his business in the daytime. Ironically, such a sanction places supernatural power in the hands of one who is not only the sovereign but also one of the vampire's clients. The accepted belief is that the break of dawn will bring about either the vampire's disempowerment or his demise; such is the case in the dramatic culmination in Murnau's film, where the sun's rays turn the vampire to ashes. But, in Nieva's play, that powerful effect is made ineffectual from the very start of the action, when Aurura appears, and through to its culmination, when Aurora returns. Nonetheless, as Nosferatu says (in a tone that shows his yearning for the way things once were): "Morning vexes me more and more in comparison with liberating night" (18).

Next, fear of the supernatural becomes indifference as the grotesque aspects of the tradition develop into commonplaces of daily life. The vampire, ever present in the day-to-day life of the kingdom, becomes the focal point in the social and political scheme of things, for Nosferatu's reach has risen from the low station of such as Azul and Greta to the heights of power embodied in the queen. And fear has no dominion under such circumstances.

Then it becomes evident that there is no need for garlic, crosses, communion wafers, holy water, pointed stakes, or bowie knives because the vampire in Nieva's *Nosferatu* is perceived, not as a threat, but as an ally in furthering the unorthodox desires of the living. Where Stoker's Count Dracula and Murnau's Nosferatu must be destroyed to protect society, Nieva's vampire is integral to the evolution of that society, albeit in a context of evil.

Neither are there the metamorphoses typical of vampire lore, for the figure of Nosferatu, grotesque though it may be, is readily accepted by commoner and royalty alike. His ends are pursued openly and without the subterfuge of transformation or disguise. Indeed, society is proactive toward the vampire, seeing him as a facilitator of its desires.

Finally, the notion of closing windows against the entry of evil—so important in Van Helsing's list of instructions in *Dracula*—is debunked through the free entry to domiciles and shops that open their sashes and doors, access granted this Nosferatu by the ladies of the barrio (neighborhood) and of the court. Evil has become a commonplace, and it is given entry by one and all, allowing it penetration into their abodes and into their bodies.

The play, however, *is* about metamorphoses, not of the vampire into the bat or wolf of traditional lycanthropic lore, as explicated by Dr. Van Helsing in *Dracula,* but of the varied characters—from the queen down to her lowest subject—all of whom desire to change, to be something other than what they are, to enter into a different state of life. Yet, when these social transformations occur, the newly empowered find no satisfaction in their change of status. Thus, Nosferatu is an agent of change, instilling in his clients the sense that their dreams can become reality through his intervention. Yet, at best, otherness proves wanting, for their transmuted state is but an illusion that lasts for a while, akin to a dream state in which another identity is donned. Nosferatu, more than a Rasputin or a Svengali, has given the populace the opportunity to experience its lust for otherness. As Nieva points out in his introduction: "He represents the vampire of Europe, and I make him the trumpeter of its decadence. *Nosferatu* stands out as the maximum representative of *cupiditas,* sensual concupiscence, and unbridled instincts. At the end, these are violently 'repressed' by a supposed—and nth degree—worldwide deflagration, only to resuscitate anew. With each orbit of the sphere, a world ends, but another equally obnoxious is reborn. The world that ends in *Nosferatu* is that of the old Europe, that of my parents and grandparents, full of the memories of the cabaret and silent films" (9).

Yet what occurs in the aftermath of the conflagration is not a cleansing or a purgation of society at large; and the society that arises, as if from its own ashes, is not one that can be symbolized by the mythic phoenix. Rather, it can be symbolized only by a concept out of science fiction: the parallel universe, wherein things appear to be the same but are not. Nieva has brought about the end of the world of "old Europe" only to posit the stirrings of a *new* society by employing mechanisms and concepts from the very past that he eschews. In Nieva, there is no doubt that humanity is doomed to repeat its errors. And the vampire, who enjoys extended existence until dispossessed by some appropriate act of execution, will be there to oversee and affect the debacle—all over again.

Nieva's play, outrageous in its satire, subversive in its realignment of vampire lore, surreal in its couplings, deceptive in the depths it probes, cruel in its perversion of hope, is either a brilliant tour de force on the unsettled, longing human condition or a great joke played on the theater public and the reader alike, who expected the serious treatment of the vampire implied by the title. The play thumbs its nose at long-held traditions and, in so doing, mocks the very nature of the vampire legacy. But it must be remembered that the Spanish-speaking public that has seen and read the play would not be disturbed by the surgery performed on the vampire and his lore because neither is integral to its belief system. Immune from vampirism, as it were, Nieva (and Spain and Spanish America) can stand back and look with amusement at the same beliefs that have terrified many and fascinated others elsewhere on the European continent and in other venues. Nieva's *Nosferatu* can, then, be accepted on its own terms and recognized as a metaphor for what the playwright perceives to be European decadence. In this manner, Nieva takes Montague Summers's fearsome words and applies them with biting satire to the European scene that he dissects surrealistically.

Notes

1. The inspiration came from a gathering in which Byron, John Keats, Percy Bysshe Shelley, Mary Wollstonecraft Shelley, and Polidori read ghost stories to each other, deciding thereafter that each would compose a frightening tale. Mary Shelley contributed *Frankenstein; or, The New Prometheus.* The preamble to Polidori's work states: "The superstition on which this tale is founded is very general in the East. Among the Arabians it appears to be common; it did not, however, extend itself to the Greeks until after the establishment of Christianity; and it has only assumed its present form since the division of the Latin and Greek churches; at which time, the idea becoming prevalent, that a Latin body could not corrupt if buried in their territory, it gradually increased, and formed the subject of many wonderful stories, still extant, of the dead rising from their graves, and feeding upon the blood of the young and beautiful. In the West it spread, with some slight variations, all over Hungary, Poland, Austria and Lorraine, where the belief existed, that vampyres nightly imbibed a certain portion of the blood of their victims, who became emaciated, lost their strength, and speedily died of consumption; whilst these human bloodsuckers fattened—and their veins became distended to such a state of repletion as to cause the blood to flow from all the passages of their bodies, and even from the very pores of their skins" (quoted in Summers, 282).

2. A Spanish-language version of the same script, but with a different cast, was filmed on the same set after hours under the direction of George Melford. Although

little known, this version has been lauded by critics as superior to the English-language version.

3. Erroneously believed to be a Romanian term for the myth of the undead, *nosferatu* was acquired by Bram Stoker from Emily Gerard, who had misheard a reference (see E. Miller). Nonetheless, the exotic nature of the term has made it synonymous with *vampire* in later literature and criticism. A similar misreading resulted in the term *coven* (see chapter 7, n. 6, above).

4. The verification lies in the fact that there is no *serious* literature on the subject in Spain, no doubt because vampirism is not germane to the nation's belief system (as supported by the data presented in n. 1 above). In Stoker's *Dracula,* when Dr. Van Helsing informs his listeners on the origins and dispersion of the belief in vampires, he does not include Spain (see 285–86). At the Second World Dracula Congress, held in Poiana Brasov, Transylvania, Romania, May 25–28, 2000, there was only one presentation of a paper on a Hispanic topic, a shorter version of the essay at hand. The scholars at the congress were very surprised to learn of a Spanish literary work dealing with vampirism since neither creative nor critical attention to the subject has been evident in that context. Even the Spanish-language film version of *Dracula* to which I refer in n. 2 above was done in Hollywood by an American director. But there has been some contemporary inclination in Spain to address the foreign myth of the vampire. In recent years, the success of the horror film genre has prompted Spanish filmmakers such as the Catalonian Jorge Grau to explore the theme of the vampire, if at a remove, as in the 1972 *Ceremonia sangrienta* (also known as *The Legend of Blood Castle*), about Countess Bathori, who bathed in the blood of virgins in order to rejuvenate herself. England's Hammer Films had earlier released *Countess Dracula* (1970), starring Ingrid Pitt as Elizabeth Bathori; but, despite the title, the real-life countess was not a vampire in the traditional sense established by Bram Stoker in his novel. The countess's blood-bathing rituals only perpetuated the appearance of physical youth; they did not extend her life span.

5. Stoker uses his character Dr. Van Helsing to delineate the aspects of the vampire, if in a quaint, "Dutch-inflected" English: "There are such beings as vampires; some of us have evidence that they exist. . . . The *nosferatu* do not die like the bee when he sting once. He is only stronger; and being stronger, have yet more power to work evil. This vampire which is amongst us is of himself so strong in person as twenty men; he is of cunning more than mortal, for his cunning be the growth of ages; he have still the aids of necromancy, which is, as his etymology imply, the divination of the dead, and all the dead that he can come nigh to are for him at command; he is brute, and more than brute; he is devil in callous, and the heart of him is not; he can, within limitations, appear at will when and where, and in any of the forms that are to him; he can, within his range, direct the elements: the storm, the fog, the thunder; he can command all the meaner things: the rat, and the owl, and the bat—the moth, and the fox, and the wolf; he can grow and become small; and he can at times vanish and come unknown" (283). These are the fundamental elements of the vampire belief as Stoker found them in his research for the novel.

6. Francisco (Morales) Nieva was born on December 29, 1927, in the Spanish

city of Valdepeñas. He has had a distinguished career as a playwright, scenic designer, painter, and theater director and as a professor (*catedrático*) in the Royal School of Dramatic Arts. Having begun his career as a dramatist in 1949, the same year that saw the premiere of the late Antonio Buero Vallejo's engagé play *Historia de una escalera* (Story of a staircase), Nieva has gone on to write plays that range from what he has termed *teatro furioso* (furious theater), conceived as "open" works, free in style and characterization, meant to be susceptible to additions by actor and director alike, to *teatro de farsa y calamidad* (theater of farce and calamity), plays that are highly structured with characterizations that are finely drawn. Where the former exalt the defiance and freedom of the individual, the latter show his disillusionment and defeat. A black humor and a surrealistic touch frequently are manifest in all his works. *Nosferatu* is one of the plays that Nieva has classified as *teatro furioso* and labeled *apocalyptic*. The play, however, does not have an affinity to the much-vaunted theater of cruelty of Antonin Artaud, nor does it follow its premises, even if Nieva's early admiration of the Frenchman has led to that association. That esteem of the aesthetic promoted by Artaud found expression in some of Nieva's critical commentary and in the choice of one of his texts as the introduction to the first version of *Nosferatu;* pointedly, that text was removed prior to the publication of the new version in 1993.

Among many national and foreign awards, Nieva won both the Premio Príncipe de Asturias and the Premio Nacional de Literatura, two of Spain's most prestigious recognitions of literary merit, in 1992. In 1986, he was designated as an electee of the Real Academia Española, taking possession of his seat in 1990.

7. Although men were also involved in the practices that Goya depicts, more often than not his Sabbats show women as the principals in the unholy rites. In so doing, Goya was adhering to the common notion that witchcraft was practiced by women in private and in groups on special occasions such as Sabbats. Since women, but especially those in the lower classes of society, were disenfranchised in most areas of social and political activity, the power inherent in an association with Satan had great appeal. By their acceptance of the Evil One as master, witches gave their souls to the Devil for eternity in exchange for temporal gain and sexual gratification. For numerous assessments of witchcraft in Hispanic drama, see Lima.

8. I am reminded, for one, of Tello in Lope de Vega's *El caballero de Olmedo* (The Knight from Olmedo). Tello is the foil to Fabia, the Celestinesque witch of the play, in nefarious activities carried through with comic terror on behalf of his lovelorn master. In Nieva's play, Celestino's name itself calls to mind Celestina, the malevolent go-between in Fernando de Rojas's *Tragicomedia de Calixto y Melibea* (see chapter 3 above).

9. For an extended treatment of liaisons with the Devil in folklore and literature à la Théophile and Faust, among many others, see Lima, chap. 3.

10. Svengali is the evil hypnotist in George du Maurier's novel *Trilby.* The name has come to refer to a person who, through force of personality, lures another to perform something against his or her will or who enthralls the impressionable and the greedy by promising false rewards.

11. When the virtuous young women of the Madrigal succumb to the vampire, they do so out of despair over the fallen state of society. Seeing that they alone

represent virtue, they cast their lot with Nosferatu, a transference that designates the vampire as a purveyor of good through evil. The futility of being the sole survivors feeds the need to be in society even if that construct has become evil; a similar process of acceptance and transformation was brilliantly analyzed in Ionesco's play *Rhinoceros.*

12. An earlier example can be found in the court of Isabel II, the nineteenth-century Spanish monarch who fell under the spell of a wonder-working nun; Ramón del Valle-Inclán satirized the queen and Sor Patrocinio in his novel *La corte de los milagros* (The court of miracles), which was very well received in Communist Russia because of its attack on a decadent monarchy not unlike that of the czarist regime.

13. The satire on the United Nations (and the United States) via the Disney character, whose magical powers were made manifest in the film *Fantasia,* is but one means that the dramatist employs to discredit the gullibility of his parents' generation. In other instances in the play, he lambastes the Singer Sewing Machine Co. as representative of the dominance of American capitalism and as a contributor to such evils as sweatshops and pollution. The Orient Express, once the symbol of modernity and luxurious adventure—thus, a hallmark of the past—is made manifest as a static anachronism representative of the ineffectual Western tradition.

14. On witchcraft as a religion, see chapter 3 above.

Works Cited

Artaud, Antonin. *The Theater and Its Double.* Translated by Mary Caroline Richards. New York: Grove, 1958. The original French edition appeared as *Le théâtre et son double* (Paris: Gallimard, 1938).

Eliade, Mircea. *Aspects du mythe.* Paris: Gallimard, 1963. All English translations are mine.

Ionesco, Eugène. *Rhinoceros.* 1959. In *Rhinoceros; The Chairs; The Lesson.* London: Penguin, 1962.

"Is Dracula Really Dead?" *Time,* 23 May 1977, 60.

Lima, Robert. *Dark Prisms: Occultism in Hispanic Drama.* Lexington: University Press of Kentucky, 1995.

Lope de Vega Carpio, Félix. *El caballero de Olmedo.* ca. 1615–26. Madrid: Cátedra, 1989.

Maurier, George du. *Trilby: A Novel.* New York: Harper & Bros., 1894.

Miller, Elizabeth. *Dracula: Sense and Nonsense.* Westcliff-on-Sea: Desert Island, 2000.

Nietzsche, Friedrich. *Thus Spake Zarathustra.* 1883–85. Translated by Thomas Common. Amherst, N.Y.: Prometheus, 1993.

Nieva, Francisco. *Nosferatu.* In *Francisco Nieva: Teatro completo,* ed. Jesús Martín Rodríguez, vol. 1. Madrid: Junta de Comunidades de Castilla/La Mancha, 1991. All English translations are mine from this edition.

———. *Nosferatu.* Madrid: Sociedad General de Autores de España, 1994.

Polidori, John. *The Vampire.* London: Sherwood, 1819.

Rice, Anne. *Interview with the Vampire.* New York: Knopf, 1976.

———. *The Vampire Armand.* New York: Knopf, 1998.

Shelley, Mary W. *Frankenstein; or, The New Prometheus.* London: Lackington, Hughes, Harding, Mayor & Jones, 1818.

Stoker, Bram. *Dracula.* London: Constable, 1897. New York: Penguin, 1979.

Summers, Montague. *The Vampire: His Kith and Kin.* New York: University Books, 1960. Originally published in 1928 as *The Vampire.*

Valle-Inclán, Ramón del. *La corte de los milagros.* 1927. Barcelona: Editorial Nuestro Pueblo, 1938.

Varney the Vampire; or, The Feast of Blood. London: E. Lloyd, 1847. The author is either Thomas Preskett Prest or James Malcolm Rymer.

Walker, Barbara G. "Convent." In *The Woman's Encyclopedia of Myths and Secrets,* 175–79. San Francisco: Harper & Row, 1983.

Part IV

Cauldron and Cave

10

Wither'd and Wild

Witches of the Elizabethan and Jacobean Stages

What are these
So wither'd, and so wild in their attire,
That look not like th'inhabitants o'th'earth.
And yet are on't?

—Shakespeare, *Macbeth*

The description of unearthly beings is of "the weird sisters," as the three hags in Shakespeare's *Macbeth* call themselves. They are first glimpsed and heard briefly "*At an open place*" (act 1, sc. 1; p. 858), accompanied by thunder and lightning, as the play opens. As Banquo so tersely describes them in his query, they are the physical prototypes of Elizabethan and Jacobean witches. The folk belief of the times perceived witches as malefactors, thus their decadent, otherworldly aspect, their eerie and secretive behavior, their power to affect human lives and the contexts in which they are lived. Yet, despite the evil that they are held to represent and promote, people seek them out and listen to their pronouncements or ask for their mediation in affairs of the heart, the hearth, or society. So it is even with high-status people, as Shakespeare's tragedy shows so distinctly, baring the dire results to person and state of a nefarious collaboration with purveyors of evil. Shakespeare has captured in his three abnormal characters the popular image and intonation of the witch and the dread that the visual and auditory presence of witches inspire. Yet, curiously, he has them operate under the tutelage and control of Hecate, the goddess-witch of classical antiquity,[1] rather than under bondage to the Christian personification of evil, Satan.[2] In this, the dramatist has chosen to veer from the standard popular belief in witches as devotees and pawns of Satan. Consequently, Shakespeare's creatures, already deemed exotic by Banquo, seem more like mythic demigoddesses than perverse contemporary human beings who have taken the left-hand path.

The Weird Sisters (see fig. 17) reappear two scenes later at a heath,

---

Previous page: Witch at Cauldron Attended by Devils at Sabbat, provenance unknown. Public domain.

again with thunder, where Macbeth, thane of Glamis, and his companion and fellow general Banquo encounter them. Banquo, having described their ghastliness, further queries the strange creatures:

> Live you? or are you aught
> That man may question? You seem to understand me,
> By each at once her choppy finger laying
> Upon her skinny lips: —you should be women,
> And yet your beards forbid me to interpret
> That you are so. (act 1, sc. 3; p. 859)

But it is to Macbeth that the bizarre, androgynous beings respond, wasting no time in foretelling each man's future. And, on the revelation that Macbeth will be thane of Cawdor and king, he is spellbound. The words have the impact of thunder on his imagination. And, when the Weird Sisters vanish, like elementals, both men question the reality of what they have seen and heard until two of the king's courtiers arrive to dress Macbeth in the trappings of Cawdor. He then knows to believe the hellish hags' words: because the first part of their prophecy has come true almost immediately, he

Figure 17. *The Weird Sisters* (1827) by Alexandre-Marie Colin. Courtesy collection of Mr. and Mrs. Sandor Korein.

senses intuitively that their second prognostication will come to pass as well. The twisted words of the Weird Sisters foreshadow the twisted actions that Macbeth's own mind begins to devise and his lady will implement on his and her own behalf. On the treacherous murder of Duncan, his sons flee for their lives, leaving Macbeth heir to the throne as suspicion falls on Malcolm and Donalbain. The witches' second prediction has also become reality in a very short time.

Macbeth has reached the apex of the feudal pyramid. But was he destined to achieve the uppermost level of Scottish society, or was his heady ascent to kingship the result of witchcraft? Did the Weird Sisters motivate the events leading to his investiture as monarch, or were they mere seers, à la Tiresias before Oedipus, who communicated what fate had in store for Macbeth? It would appear that witchcraft, not fate, is responsible for the turn of events since Hecate is not pleased with and berates the Weird Sisters for not having consulted her before they trafficked with Macbeth and altered his life thereby. The goddess of witchcraft orders them to meet her at Acheron,[3] where they will decide the future of the newly crowned king. Shortly thereafter, the three witches are gathered around the boiling cauldron in a cavern, mouthing their chant:

> Double, double, toil and trouble;
> Fire, burn; and caldron, bubble.

And, as they concoct an unsavory brew, the second witch adds new ingredients to the "charmed pot," saying:

> Fillet of a fenny snake,
> In the caldron boil and bake;
> Eye of newt, and toe of frog,
> Wool of bat, and tongue of dog,
> Adder's fork, and blind-worm's sting,
> Lizard's leg, and howlet's wing. (act 4, sc. 1; pp. 873–74)

Hecate makes a brief entrance at the end of the three witches' incantations to praise their toil and urge them to go about the business of creating trouble by complementing the enchantment with singing around the cauldron.[4]

As if in response to the witchery, Macbeth enters the cavern. On his demand to have his questions answered, the Weird Sisters raise up spirits that respond to questions that his mind has shaped. Macbeth listens as each of the three apparitions speaks:

> [B]eware Macduff;
> beware the thane of Fife.
> . . . [L]augh to scorn
> The power of man, for none of woman born
> Shall harm Macbeth.
> . . . Macbeth shall never vanquisht be, until
> Great Birnham wood to high Dunsinane hill
> Shall come against him. (act 4, sc. 1; p. 874)

But Macbeth requires more knowledge, and the witches raise the ghost of Banquo, who points to the seemingly endless line of kings that will come from him. The witches then vanish, leaving Macbeth in amazement at the revelation and fearing its implications. Knowing at firsthand that all they had predicted has lately come to pass, Macbeth has reason to fear that the latest revelations will also become reality—and perhaps as quickly. Their efficacy over, the Weird Sisters are not seen again, but it is fitting to conjecture that Hecate and the three witches, in some dark place, have witnessed the deaths of the usurper to the throne of Scotland and of his fiendish wife along with the subsequent enthronement of Malcolm.

The three crones in *Macbeth* are the best known of the witches on the stages of the Elizabethan and Jacobean periods in England,[5] but there are numerous other devotees of the heretical affiliation with Satan, popularly misnamed *witchcraft*,[6] depicted in the works of both eras, among them the Lancashire Witches, Mother Shipton, Mother Bombey, and Mother Sawyer. But, besides depicting the lives and trials of these native-born practitioners of the black art, the theater of the Elizabethan and Jacobean periods focused on witches whose names have a classical pedigree, including Medea, Erictho, and Hecate.

Such witches as Shakespeare's colleagues present in their plays were held by religious authorities and by the faithful to be in thrall to the Devil for having offered their souls to him for eternity in exchange for supernatural powers during their life on earth. It was not always so. At first, witches were seen as solitary individuals—women primarily but men also—who practiced their peculiar calling in the privacy of their homes and who were accessible to anyone in the community desiring their services. As such, they were perceived as providers of an herbal cure or love potion out of their traditional pharmacopoeia or, perhaps, as persons who could call on pagan deities to promote fertility in women, animals, and land. But this perception of witches as benevolent possessors of esoteric knowledge who could benefit society began to change as the church attempted to organize the life of European society under its religious banner. It found intolerable a secondary level of belief that promoted pre-Christian concepts and usages, such as the worship of male and female principles in nature personified as the Horned God and the Lunar Goddess, each with identities reflecting the area and time in which they were adored. Those men and women who represented the old ways, the Old Religion, came under ever closer scrutiny, and, ultimately, taken for a threat to church and state, they came under attack from religious and secular authorities, often in league against witches, the former passing judgment, the latter administering punishment.

The accusations that led to the persecution and condemnation of witches were multifaceted. It came to be said of witches that they gathered in covens of thirteen (in mockery of Christ and his disciples)[7] as well as at the four major seasonal festivals called *Sabbats*[8] and, with greater frequency, at lesser convocations called *Esbats.*[9] It was thought that witches annointed their bodies[10] and those of the soon to be initiated before flying up the chimney (or another means of egress) to these gatherings mounted on common household besoms, twig brooms whose sticks are symbolic of the phallus of earlier fertility religions.[11] But, as in numerous illustrations in Guaccius's *Compendium maleficarum* as well as paintings, drawings, and etchings of Albrecht Dürer, Hans Baldung-Grien, and Francisco Goya, the witches are seen astride a he-goat. It was widely believed by the populace that the Devil, in the form of a great black goat,[12] presided at the Sabbat, often initiating men and women into his unholy craft on their blaspheming God, renouncing their baptismal vows, signing his black book in blood, and administering the *osculum infame* on their new master's anus. Ironically, thereafter, they celebrated their newfound freedom from Christian bondage by performing lewd and unnatural acts during orgiastic revels, including copulation with Satan or one of his devils. One particularly damning accusation against witches was that unbaptized infants were sacrificed to Satan at these gatherings,[13] their souls, tainted by original sin, being added to the Devil's bounty in hell, both because of Satan's desire to increase his larder at God's expense and because, as the adage has it, "Misery loves company."

Empowered by their alliance with the Lord of Evil, witches took on a different function in society and were looked on with dread, owing partly to the horror inspired by their living outside the grace of God, partly to the manifestion of their fallen nature in their physical grotesqueness. Unlike the time when they were practitioners of the Old Religion, now, when their services were used by king, noble, churchman, or serf to obtain some surreptitious, illicit, or illegal end, they were seen as a necessary evil at best. At worst, they were damned souls who threatened the Christian life and civil order of the community. Causing fear among the populace at large, they were dealt with in the most severe ways.

Rightly afraid of being denounced, prosecuted, tortured, and burned at the stake or hanged, witches worked in the privacy of their homes or in the sanctuary of a cave, where they cast their spells and concocted their unsavory brews (in the same cauldrons used for daily food preparation). Such charms and potions could be employed for medicinal purposes, to facilitate seduction, to cause a change in the weather, or to effect bodily harm, even death. In some instances, witches were consulted as prognosticators, for they were said to be able to foretell the future directly or, as in *Macbeth,* via the agency of spirits raised by their conjuring, to influence the outcome of events. Similar feats were accomplished in the Old Testament by such as the Witch of Endor, who conjured Samuel at the behest of King Saul (1 Sam. 28:7ff.). The machinations of witchcraft, which could be benign (white) or malefic (black), were believed to be achieved by supernatural means and, consequently, were taken to be highly effectual.

Despite their usefulness to unscrupulous individuals at all levels of society, witches and other practitioners of occult arts occasioned widespread dread, prompting James VI/I,[14] for one, to formulate views (in the *Daemonologie* [1597]) and promulgate laws (in an addition to the Witchcraft Statutes) against such social and religious aberrations.[15] James was the very monarch who promoted the 1611 translation of the Bible that has come to bear his name, one of whose dictums is the infamous exhortation from Exodus: "Thou shalt not suffer a witch to live" (Exod. 22:18).[16] Another dictum, this one from Leviticus, proclaims: "A man also or a woman that hath a familiar spirit, or that is a familiar spirit, or that is a wizard, shall surely be put to death; they shall stone them with stones" (20:27).[17] Such texts lent Old Testament authority, and, thus, gave license, to Christians to kill those adjudged or otherwise deemed to be followers of Satan. The result was the execution of numberless women and men, some of them members of the clergy, during the centuries-long period that became known as the Witchcraft Panic.[18]

Witch-hunters, such as the opportunistic Matthew Hopkins, self-styled "Witchfinder General," were at the beck and call of any town or institution willing to pay the price for the discovery and prosecution of witches and other such in their midst.[19] The evidence that these individuals accepted as factual was at best circumstantial, based as it was largely on hearsay and on the authority of the plaintiff, usually a person of higher status than the accused. The methods to which such hired help resorted to obtain physical evidence were often fraudulent (see chapter 7, n. 11, above). Worse, instruments of torture, among them the notorious rack and the boot, and techniques employed to force confessions, such as "floating" and "pressing," were barbaric—but often effective. Floating consisted of weighing down the body of the accused and placing it in a body of water. If the body rose to the surface, it was deemed to have done so through Satanic agency, and the accused was patently guilty. If it stayed submerged (for an unspecified period of time), the accused was exonerated, provided that he or she survived. (King James believed that the pure element, water, could not tolerate the body of anyone who had renounced baptism; witches, consequently, would be rejected and, thus, float.) Pressing consisted of laying stones, bricks, or other great weights on the chest of the accused until a confession was obtained or, as happened frequently, the individual was crushed to death.[20]

The extent to which the church perceived a conspiracy of paganists against its teachings in the Middle Ages and well into the Renaissance, and the need for the suppression of that conspiracy, became evident when it codified the actions deemed evil and ordained the methods for their investigation and eradication. The *Malleus maleficarum*, the "hammer of evildoers," was a textbook for the inquisitor in the fight against the principal malefactor, the witch, in Germany, as its popular name, *Hexenhammer,* makes evident. In 1486, its authors, members of the Roman Catholic Order of Saint Dominic, Jacobus Sprenger and Heinrich Kramer, published their compendium under the patronage of Pope Innocent VIII.[21] The effectiveness of this book as a tool for defining the *maleficia* of witches and assigning methods for its eradication is attested by its numerous editions in Germany through 1669. It soon reached France, Italy, England, and other embattled European states. In Scotland and England the *Malleus maleficarum* would, in time, be assisted by the *Daemonologie* of King James. Germany and the British Isles were both highly suitable arenas for the expurgation of heresy, be it of Roman Catholic or Protestant ancestry.

Such were the horrific folk beliefs in Satan and his agents, the ritual celebrations of low- and highborn in honor of the god of evil, and the gruesome punishments meted out for heretical practices that governed the representation of evil witches on the stages of the Elizabethan and Jacobean eras. But there were many witches of each ilk, positive and negative, portraying major or minor roles in the masques, comedies, tragedies, and tragicomedies of those days.

White witches, that is, those whose craft was seen to benefit society, were treated by major playwrights. Robert Greene's *Alphonsus, King of Arragon* (ca. 1589) contains a sketch of Medea as a white witch, and in his *Orlando Furioso* (ca. 1590) there appears Melissa, a white witch. In John Lyly's *Mother Bombie* (ca. 1590), the title character is a white witch, although identified in the dramatis personae as a "Fortune-teller," to whom the characters resort for advice or to hear prophecies regarding the complex relationships in their lives; however, she affects the action only at play's end, by inducing the confession of the old nurse, Vicinia, that legitimizes the relationship between the lovers. And John Fletcher's *The Faithful Shepherdess* (ca. 1608) has a heroine, the shepherdess Clorin, who is a white witch involved with herbs in a play in which Pan rules the sacred wood where satyrs and nymphs gambol. So too is Delphia a white witch, although listed as a "Prophetess" in the cast of characters; she interacts with Diocletian in Fletcher's *The Prophetess* (1622). Invariably, such gifted females were depicted as using their supernatural powers to help an individual, better a situation, even save a kingdom.[22] But some were perceived to be frauds, prompting Thomas Heywood in *The Wise-Woman of Hogsdon* (ca. 1604) to ridicule as the work of charlatans the quackeries and impostures of those who pretended to be white witches (in this instance fortune-tellers) for some personal gain.

Black witches inspired by classical, that is, Greco-Roman, models appear or are mimicked, as in Christopher Marlowe's *The Jew of Malta* (1592), wherein Barabas the Jew, presented as evil incarnate, parodies Medea's incantation in Seneca's tragedy. John Marston's *The Tragedie of Sophonisba* (1606) has the Greek witch Erictho. The most famous of the type appear as the three Weird Sisters in William Shakespeare's *Macbeth* (ca. 1606), with Hecate thrown in briefly for good measure. Thomas Middleton's *The Witch* (ca. 1613) is a tragicomedy set in Ravenna and centered on the witch named Hecate, after the classical deity. But Ben Jonson outdoes them all in *The Masque of Queenes* (1609), a courtly entertainment in which twelve classicized black witches appear in the first part.

In a historical mode, William Shakespeare, in act 5, scene 3, of *Henry*

VI, Part I, dealt with Joan La Pucelle (Joan of Arc), treating her from the English Protestant perspective as a black witch who conjures familiars and offers to give them suck if they will aid her.[23] Another witch, Margery Jourdain, raises the spirit Asmath at the behest of Eleanor, duchess of Gloster, the conjurer Roger Bolinbroke (who makes a protective circle), and the priest John Hume to foretell the future of the king and his courtiers in act 1, scene 4, of *Henry VI, Part II.* The conjuration scenes in both plays wherein fiends or a spirit appear are marked by thunder and lightning, standard fare for such supernatural manifestations. And, in a quite different style and trajectory, John Kirke's *The Seven Champions of Christendome* (1635) is a melodrama that features Calib, "the most bizarre Elizabethan witch of dramatic literature" (Reed, 179), in the context of the historic titular figures.

Witches who were closer in time and locale to the dramatists were also depicted, as in the aforementioned *Mother Bombie.* Ben Jonson in *The Sad Shepherd* (1637) presented Mother Maudlin, who lived in Sherwood Forest at the time of Robin Hood, had a familiar spirit named Puck-hairy, took the shape of Maid Marian, became a raven or a hare at will, and practiced malefic witchcraft by casting spells against lovers and by making waxen images of intended victims; although forced to leave her abode, she is never brought to justice by her pursuers since the play was unfinished at the dramatist's death. Thomas Dekker, William Rowley, and John Ford's *The Witch of Edmonton* (1621) portrays Mother Sawyer, née Elizabeth Sawyer, "probably the most realistic portrait of a witch in the annals of literature" (Reed, 150). Thomas Heywood and Richard Brome's tragicomedy *The Late Lancashire Witches* (ca. 1634) uses the trials of seventeen second-generation Pendle Forest witches[24] as its basis. This major witchcraft trial and its complex issues of feigned statements, superstition, family hatreds, and greed awakened great interest throughout England, and the playwrights were quick to capitalize on the notoriety of the trials[25] and what Symonds terms "the vulgar and farcical aspects of the subject" (xiii).

Rather than write a play that would be a faithful interpretation of the journalistic reports that abounded, Heywood and Brome brought in outlandish, sensational superstitions that had nothing to do with the trial records, sometimes extrapolating from Reginald Scot's notorious *The Discoverie of Witchcraft* (1584). No doubt seeking to please the audience that would attend the production by the King's Men in London's Globe, they concentrated on the spectacle of the lascivious and illicit practices believed to be performed at the the witches' Sabbat as well as witches' transformations into animals and their involvement with familiar spirits (e.g., the black-clad devil Mamilion). Periodically eschewing the court record, they then focused on the fictitious and genteel Mistress Generous, wife of the innkeeper. A good man who wanted order restored to the community on the outbreak of the witchcraft revelations, which included that of his wife's practice of the craft with her witch cronies Goody Dicconson, Mal Spencer, and others, the innkeeper had given his wife a second chance to abandon witchery, but, when he discovered that her hand had been severed while, metamorphosed into a cat, she attacked a soldier, he turned her over to the authorities for prosecution. It would appear that Mistress Generous was cast in the image of her Pendle Forest predecessor Alice Nutter, who had been executed in 1612, at least so far as, unlike the other witches, both were well-born women. It may be that Heywood and Brome sought to create a character who would elicit pity by giving her a social status well above that of the other witches, whose baseness and ignorance would disqualify them as worthy of sympathy. But, whatever the implied discrepancy in their social status, all six witches who participated in the various episodes are, at the end of the play, led off to jail to await their fate. Nowhere in the play is the confessed hoax perpetrated by the Robinson boy introduced, so the play remains a travesty of the real events, an artistic decision no doubt excusable under the concept of poetic license, which in this instance permitted a more dramatic conclusion than adhering strictly to the record would have.

But it is three other works, Middleton's *The Witch,* Dekker, Rowley, and Ford's *The Witch of Edmonton,* and Kirke's *The Seven Champions of Christendome,* that offer the most varied in range and interesting interpretations of witchcraft and its practitioners as popularly conceived on the Elizabethan and Jacobean stages. Although the roles of the witches in these plays are secondary to those of the main characters, their supernatural powers both facilitate aspects of the action, if sometimes only subplots, and create an esoteric ambience that was dear to audiences of the time.

In the words of presentation of *The Witch* to his enigmatic patron,[26] Thomas Middleton states: "Witches are, *ipso facto,* by the law condemned, and that only, I think, hath made her lie so long in an imprisoned obscurity" (117). The playwright was probably referring to the resting place of the manuscript, which may have lain dormant owing to the legal attitude toward witches and, perhaps, toward anyone who wrote about them, for among the stipulations of the Witchcraft Statute of 1604 we find: "[I]f any person shall practice or exercise any invocation or conjuration of any evil or wicked spirit . . . such offender shall suffer the pains of death as felons without benefit of clergy or sanctuary" (quoted in Middleton, 125). Nonetheless, Middleton resurrected the manuscript for presentation to his patron, saying: "For your sake alone she hath thus far conjured herself abroad" (117). It may have been an act of great courage, and of faith, to release the manuscript of *The Witch.*

The principal character is a witch named Hecate. She is assisted by other witches, Stadlin and Hoppo[27] chief among them; there are also the witches Hellwain and Puckle; Firestone, Hecate's son; and Malkin (diminutive for Matilda), a catlike familiar spirit. Their first manifestation occurs in the second scene of the first act, set in Hecate's cave. It is a witchcraft scene of some interest that seems, along with other elements, to have been modeled on *Macbeth,* but it lacks the eeriness and mystery instilled by Shakespeare in his tragedy through the creation of a macabre setting and memorable dialogue for his bizarre characters.[28] Yet, much more than *Macbeth,* and starting with this scene, in which a charm is created to impede the consummation of a marriage, Middleton's play provides a cornucopia of popular ideas on witchcraft and other superstitions, English and Continental, if largely derived from a close reading of at least Scot's *The Discoverie of Witchcraft,* parts of which are, in fact, transcribed verbatim.

The practice of borrowing material is evident immediately on the witch's appearance on-stage. Hecate conjures at her cauldron as the scene opens, mouthing the names of "Titty and Tiffin, Suckin and Pidgen, Liard and Robin!" (125), familiar spirits listed in a 1582 English pamphlet on a witch trial, *A True and just Recorde of the Information, Examination and Confession of all the Witches Taken at S. Oses, in the countie of Essex,* along with "white spirits, black spirits, grey spirits, red spirits, devil-toad, devil-ram, devil-cat, and devil-dam!" (125). The only exception to the listing is Robin, one of the avatars of the fairy Puck out of English folklore (see chapter 2). The contemporary English imp names and the references to "devil," a Christian appellation, by a classical goddess-witch are incongruous, to say the least; indeed, the witchcraft practices depicted throughout the play are Elizabethan or Continental in origin and have little relation to the majesty and supernatural activities associated with the classical Hecate. In effect, Middleton has misappropriated the name of the goddess of the underworld by attaching it to a vulgar creation without concern for the mythical tradition attendant on it.

In a similar paucity of ingenuity, the dramatist borrows a ritual from an Italian source that Scot incorporates wherein the body fat of an infant is rendered by Hecate and her attendant witches to create a magical ointment that will permit them to fly and more, as Hecate says:

There, take this unbaptized brat;
Boil it well; preserve the fat;
You know 'tis precious to transfer
Our 'nointed flesh into the air. (126)

The balm thus concocted will anoint the naked bodies of the witches; once it penetrates the skin, its chemical properties will make possible many adventures:

When hundred leagues in air, we feast and sing,
Dance, kiss, and coll, use everything:
What young man can we wish to pleasure us,
But we enjoy him in an incubus? (127)

The sexual nature of some witch practices is given briefly here, culminating in the embrace ("coll") of the "incubus" (which, considering the sex of the witches, rightly is the male demon who mounted human females in their sleep for sexual gratification).[29] A witch's sexual passion, not easily quelled through normal human contact owing to her physical repulsiveness, seeks to be satisfied through supernatural measures.

But a witch has other human concerns as well. Hecate's pharmacopoeia comes into play immediately thereafter, for she is involved in the preparation of "magical herbs" already in place within the cauldron, which she personifies:

They're down his throat;
His mouth crammed full, his ears and nostrils stuffed.
I trust in eleoselinum lately.
Aconitum, frondes populeas, and soot—
You may see that, he looks so black i' the mouth—
Then sium, acorum vulgare too,
Pentaphyllon, the blood of a flitter-mouse,
Solanum somnificum et oleum. (127)[30]

While the concoction is brewing, Hecate attends to another matter, hexing. A farmer and his wife will suffer a special kind of vengeance for having denied the witch sustenance:

[T]he heart of wax
Stuck full of magic needles
. . .
the farmer's picture and his wife's
Laid down to the fire. (127)

The first punishment is an attack on the vital organ, while the second guarantees prolonged suffering until the images, made of clay,[31] are consumed by the fire. She gloats over the effect that the spells of her image witchcraft will have on the victims.

It is soon apparent that Hecate's is a practice without cessation, that her work, like a proper mother's, is never done. No sooner has she finished with one preoccupation than another arises. When her son Firestone enters, he requires her help to ride the "Night-mare" to the bed of "a fat parson's daughter," and, like a good mother, Hecate promises to grant the lascivious wish. On his exit, another appears to seek her services. Sebastian—loath to enter the "damned place"—learns that his lovesickness, a melancholy that he seeks to overthrow through philocaption (bringing his beloved to love him by the workings of a spell), cannot be remedied: the woman he desires is already married, and, as Hecate reveals, wedlock, being of "Heaven's fastening," cannot be disjoined by witchery. She can, however, enlist her spell in his cause by giving him serpent skins that she has enchanted:

Knit with these charms and retentive knots,
Neither the man begets nor woman breeds,
No, nor performs the least desires of wedlock. (132)

Sebastian departs a happy man, planning vengeance on the woman who betrayed his love. But Hecate is not yet free from her social obligations. Firestone returns to inform her of the arrival of Almachildes, who is drunk and has knocked over Stadlin and Hoppo. The clumsy young man also seeks a potion or charm to use, in this case on Amoretta, the duchess's woman, but Hecate, who has lusted after him and possessed him as a succubus, invites Almachildes to sup at her table with a fine dinner that she has conjured for him as the act ends.

The long scene has framed a bountiful presentation of Hecate's varied activities and powers as a witch, a catalog transferred from Scot to the theatrical idiom, but, in point of fact, the effectiveness of her conjuring is verified only in the trivial scene (act 2, sc. 2) in which the ribbon that she has given Almachildes, having been placed in Amoretta's bosom, momentarily turns her disdain into passion. When Hecate next appears (act 3, sc. 3), it is in the context of nature—in a field, where she is accompanied by her witches as they prepare to take flight after anointing themselves. A cynical Firestone looks on, wishing that his mother would croak so that he "might have all quickly" (165), his attitude showing a twist on the adage, "There is no honor among thieves." Hecate's final appearance (act 5, sc. 2) is once again in her abode, where, about the cauldron, she entertains the duchess's impatient demand for something to bring "a sudden and a subtle" (186) death to Almachildes, who, in the course of being enlisted in the duchess's murderous scheme against the duke, has been tricked into believing that he has been granted her sexual favors. Hecate assures her that the spell she will cast will take effect within five hours, and, when the duchess departs, she sets about preparing the concoction with the assistance of the other witches and Firestone. Once more, the cauldron receives the foul ingredients for the murderous brew. And, as in *Macbeth,* these witches dance around the fuming pot at stage center, but here Hecate is a participant. However much the witches celebrate beforehand, the spell against Almachildes has no repercussions, perhaps because he is not villanous, having only feigned killing the duke. If such be virtue, then it triumphs here. The play ends with the "revived" duke forgiving the duchess on hearing her words of repentance while he was feigning death.

Despite the importance given her in the work, Hecate has not held sway over the lives and doings of the play's characters and certainly not over the outcome. Nor do her companions in evil have any but a supporting role. Witchcraft may have been present for certain characters to have sought its empowerment toward evil ends, but here, at least, cauldrons, conjurations, and charms have proved to be mere theatrical adornments that are peripheral to the action and wholly ineffectual. No doubt the intent was to entertain through mystification provided by a glimpse into the workaday world of evil that the audience believed was in its midst in real life. However, much that distinguishes Hecate and her crones was foreign to English life and belief.

That world was more realistically captured in *The Witch of Edmonton,* a collaborative effort by Dekker, Rowley, and Ford that differs greatly from its predecessor in its outlook and premise, stemming as it does from an actual case history, "A known true Story" as the subtitle has it. A journalistic play, it is based in part on the pamphlet *The Wonderful Discoverie of Elizabeth Sawyer, a Witch, Late of Edmonton* by Henry Goodcole, as entered in the

Stationers' Register on April 27, 1621, thirteen days after the trial, in which Goodcole recounts his interview with Elizabeth Sawyer in London's Newgate Prison. The journalistic play on Sawyer's life and ordeal was performed in London on December 29, 1621, no doubt to capitalize on her notoriety as a black witch, on the revelations at her trial, and on the publication of the pamphlet earlier that year. The portrait of Elizabeth Sawyer that emerges in the play is of the most English witch of the time, both in character and in the native aspects of her practice.

At the onset, the playwrights state that "[t]he whole Argument is in this Dystich": "Forc'd Marriage, Murder; Murder, Blood requires: / Reproach, Revenge; Revenge, Hell's help desires" (489). But the couplet does not reference the authors' attitude toward the subject. And, indeed, the play presents a sympathetic picture of Sawyer as a lonely old woman, "poor, deform'd and ignorant" (505), who, having been physically abused and accused of witchery by her landed neighbor, makes a pact with the Devil in order to seek vengeance. Furthermore, Farmer Banks is mocked when, under a spell, he involuntarily must approach his cow, lift its tail, and kiss its behind. He is literally at the butt end of the Devil's joke. Nonetheless, Mother Sawyer is portrayed in a historically correct context and in keeping with the statutes of the realm under which she was prosecuted.

Elizabeth Sawyer makes her initial appearance in the first scene of the second act. Gathering sticks for her fire while bemoaning the gossip against her in the town, she is accosted by her principal tormentor, who calls her a witch, beats her, and throws her off his grounds. Thus oppressed, Mother Sawyer soliloquizes:

> I have heard old Beldames
> Talk of Familiars in the shape of Mice,
> Rats, Ferrets, Weasels, and I wot not what,
> That have appeared, and suck'd, some say, their blood.
> But by what means they came acquainted with them,
> I'm now ignorant. (508–9)

In her ignorance of the ways of witches and their familiars lies the evidence of her innocence. But it is too late for her to fight the discrimination alone, and she wonders:

> [W]ould some power good or bad
> Instruct me which way I might be reveng'd. (509)

To accomplish this she goes to extremes that jeopardize her status as a Christian and put her soul beyond salvation:

> Abjure all goodness: be at hate with prayer;
> And study Curses, Imprecations.
> Blasphemous speeches, Oaths, detested Oaths,
> Or any thing that's ill. (509)

In short, she becomes what she has been wrongfully accused of being: a witch. Hers is a very human reaction under the circumstances, for:

> 'Tis all one,
> To be a Witch, as to be counted one. (509)

No sooner has she spoken these words than the Devil appears, in the form of a black dog named Tom, to claim her as his own, reasoning that anyone who curses and blasphemes has thereby joined his infernal ranks. Now she knows firsthand how the "Beldames" came to have familiar spirits.

Mother Sawyer gets over her initial surprise, accepting the presence of a black dog who speaks as a manifestation of the Devil, no doubt putting aside any rational disbelief because it was common knowledge that supernatural agents of evil could materialize in any form they chose. The phenomenon, known as *transmogrification* among the learned, included human to animal metamorphoses as well. Still, she hesitates before the speaking dog, and only when the Devil as Tom threatens, animalistically, to tear her to pieces does she adhere to his demand:

> That uncompell'd thou make a deed of Gift
> Of Soul and Body to me
> . . . Seal't with thy blood. (509–10)

She acquieces by letting him suck her blood. It is a demonic pact with an unusual twist: instead of signing the contract in blood, as in the tradition of Theophilus and Faust,[32] the Devil has performed an action more in keeping with vampirism than demonolatry. Perhaps the fact that a person such as Mother Sawyer could neither read nor write prompted the dramatists to take an innovative approach to the blood pact. No matter the motivation, the introduction of a pact with the Devil is key to the play since Mother Sawyer is ignorant of witchery and can be empowered only through the Devil's agency. Where *Macbeth* and *The Witch* exclude the Devil, using instead a classical point of reference for witchcraft operations, here the folk belief in Satan as the source of the witch's power is foregrounded. And, as that belief system has it, access to the Devil is attainable through some rite of veneration and submission, as in what the church called *professio expressa,* an actual commitment sealed as by such a deed of gift as a blood pact.

Thus initiated, Mother Sawyer takes to her new role immediately. Before the Devil departs, she empowers her revenge through his service, ordering the killing of Banks's cattle and the mildewing of his corn crop. The Devil then teaches her a brief incantation, with a line in Latin, with which to call him, playing the servant, but knowing that, ultimately, he will be master of the witch's soul for all eternity. But she thinks only of the revenge that she has ordered through her personal agent. Moments after his exit, Cuddy the Clown, Banks's son, enters and seeks Mother Sawyer's aid in winning Kate's love; the new witch calls on her familiar with her magic words, and he makes a brief appearance, after which she assures the young man that his wish will come true the next day. But she relishes making the son of her enemy a pawn in her extended revenge.

Mother Sawyer does not enter again until the first scene of the fourth act, but, in the meantime, the Devil, acting as her familiar, has had his way. He sows malice and discord between Carter's daughters, Susan and Katherine, and their suitors, Warbeck and Somerton; cozens Cuddy Banks with a spirit in the guise of Katherine, whom he desires; prompts Frank Thorney to kill Susan, whom he has wed bigamously, Winnifred being his first wife, and to feign being wounded and tied by Warbeck and Somerset while defending her; stills the fiddle at the morris dance; and bewitches the townswomen and drives some mad, setting their husbands, fathers, and masters, Banks among them, against Mother Sawyer.

When fire is set to the thatch of her roof to force her to appear, as the belief has it, the witch confronts her enemies, only to be attacked by them until a justice intervenes and sends them off. She denies being a witch, giving a long, reasoned exhortation on the real witches in society, women who daily seduce men through their feminine wiles, and men in trusted positions who do evil in performance of their duty. Her listeners, at first sympathetic, soon interpret her words as demonically inspired.

Finally, in the fifth act, again in the first scene, Elizabeth Sawyer enters, soliloquizes on her plight, and pleads for the Devil to come to her again. But, when he comes, now as a white dog signifying death, it is to withdraw his power and to taunt her over the death she is soon to suffer. His words ring true when Banks and others take her prisoner. Yet, even as he laughs at her, the trickster is bested by Cuddy, who, having dealt with him in his manifestation as a black dog, now dismisses him without losing his soul. It was characteristic of the time to show the Devil to be a fool, and there was no better way of doing so, save having him anathematized by a saint, than having him bested by a clown.

This final act heads inevitably to its tragic conclusion on two levels. First, Elizabeth Sawyer is taken to her punishment for the real and imagined crimes that she has committed as a witch. Tormented by the crowd through which she is being led to execution, she cries out:

> Bear witness, I repent all former evil;
> There is no damned Conjurer like the Devil. (559)

Next, Frank Thorney is led by guards to the gallows for having assassinated Susan, the procession pausing before his father and his wife as well as others he has wronged. All accept his repentance of his wrongs and express their forgiveness before he is led off to "purge the guilt of blood and lust" (562) in death.

Both Frank Thorney and Elizabeth Sawyer are executed for crimes resulting from their succumbing to the wiles of the Devil. But there is a marked difference in attitude toward their respective antisocial behavior. Frank's admission of guilt and his sincere repentance bring all who listen to tears and to forgiveness; he achieves a secular salvation through his recognition scene at play's end. Mother Sawyer, on the other hand, does not move her judges or the townspeople by her words of repentance and her condemnation of the Devil, both uttered with a proud bravado that alienates rather than unifies those who hear them. In effect, the parallel of the two condemned individuals is altered intentionally in the distinction between the attitude and the outcome of their final appearance on-stage. Both are condemned to die, but one has attained a superior status in the eyes of society despite his having committed murder.

As to Elizabeth Sawyer, in the end, witchery has not provided a good return on the investment. Mother Sawyer sought the death of Farmer Banks for having abused her physically and ruined her name, but the Devil could not accommodate her desire, acting on her behalf only by attacking Banks's goods. Ironically, her much-vaunted powers could not eliminate her enemy, and he persisted in his persecution of her even unto her death. In the Christian context in which she dies, the only question left unanswered pertains to the status of her soul in the hereafter: did the Devil abandon her smug in the assurance that she would be condemned to hell as a result of her pact and the evil deeds prompted thereby, or is the brief repentance that she expresses before being led away sufficient to foil the Lord of Evil and win her God's forgiveness? Ponderous questions for any audience to face, but especially one prone to believe that heinous crimes deserved to be punished with the utmost rigor and that God was decidedly more just than merciful. Unlike those who judged Frank Thorney's uxoricide, those who deal with Elizabeth Sawyer, notwithstanding their awareness of what led her into the practice of witchcraft, cannot find it in their hearts to sympathize with her human frailties or see her indirect actions as meriting a lesser punishment. To them, trafficking with the Devil was a greater evil than committing murder; in making a pact with Satan, Mother Sawyer was perceived as having signed a document that replaced God with the Devil, thereby attacking the very foundation of Christianity.

The defense of that faith is the topos of Kirke's *The Seven Champions of Christendome,* wherein the titular heroes act on behalf of the church in its European manifestation. The seven are Saint George (he of dragon fame) of England, Saint James (the apostle, Santiago the Moorslayer) of Spain, Saint Anthony (the Franciscan) of Italy, Saint Andrew (the apostle) of Scotland, Saint Patrick (the English missionary) of Ireland, Saint David (the bishop) of Wales, and Saint Denis (the first bishop of Paris) of France. Besides these, there are numerous other personages in the cast, including the magician Ormandine, the "Inchanter" Argalio, the "Divell" Tarpax, the giant Brandron, the witch Calib and her son Suckabus,[33] three spirits, and five ghosts (only three are listed). This is arguably the play most populated with saints, magicians, witches, and varied denizens of the supernatural realm in English dramatic literature. But the inclusion of so many occult elements is not wholly original, deriving as it does from *The Famous Historie of the Seven Champions of Christendome,* Richard Johnson's chivalric prose romance of 1596.

Johnson's "Kalyb, the wise Lady of the Woods" and "the fell Enchantress," who "lives by Charms and Witchcrafts" (act 1; p. 1), appears at the very onset of Kirke's play as Calib, the Witch. In her soliloquy, accompanied by the mandatory thunder and lightning, she presents an exegesis of her condition as practitioner of "Arts darke secret, / And bewitching path" and dweller "within the rugged bowels of this Cave": "Yet here inthron'd I sit, more richer in my spels / And potent charmes, than is the stately mountaine / Queene" (act 1; p. 7). She also reveals having stolen and nurtured the baby who she is later to predict will become Saint George, patron saint of England. She then turns to her initial act of witchery, the conjuration of her special "spirit of the Aire / Grand Tarpax, prince of the grisly North" (8). Of him she asks the boon of knowing the length of her life, to which he responds with a riddle:

> Whilst Calib in her powerfull hand
> Holds fast her powerful art,
> So long may Calib by her power,
> Comand Death hold his Dart.
> But where fond Love by dotage shall,
> Blindfold wise Calibs eyes,
> With that great power she did command,
> The great Inchantresse dies. (act 1; p. 8)

Tarpax's riddle does not in itself foreshorten time, as do many prognostications; rather, it offers an either-or perspective, a possibility of extended time that places the outcome—how long she shall live—in Calib's own hands. Whereas Macbeth's lifetime is made subject to a set of developments largely outside his ken and control, Calib's lifetime depends on avoidance of a "fond Love" that will "blindfold" her wisdom. The person who will instill that love has already been identified indirectly in the soliloquy as the future Saint George. But the "wise" woman fails to make the connection and laughs, offering Tarpax her teat to suck[34] as a reward for a prophecy that she interprets as wholly beneficial.

As the first act continues, Calib introduces Tarpax to their son Suckabus, who, despite the tradition associated with the name, plays the clown. They exit as George enters, preceded by the blast of a horn. His heart is set on knowing his parentage, so he extracts from Calib a vow that she will "grant what ere it be" (act 1; p. 9), yet, on learning his desire, she lies about the circumstances of his birth, telling him of his mother's desire to kill her bastard son. And, seeking to reward him for his gratitude and newly stated love toward the woman who rescued and raised him, Calib offers him the services of the six champions she has imprisoned in her cave and, pointedly, the use of her magic wand.[35]

Notwithstanding the picture of his parents painted by Calib's words, George remains curious about them and sets about bringing their ghosts before him through the power of Calib's wand. On materializing amid thunder and lightning, followed by soft music, they disclose their noble status, reveal to their son his legitimacy, and tersely relate Calib's treachery in poisoning them. Before they return to their eternal abode, his father instructs George:

> But now be wise, her power is in thy hand.
> Oh then be swift, be swift to execute
> Thy Parents murder on the damned witch;
> That done, redeeme the Christian Champions, go with them,
> Her cave is not unfurnisht frich Armes;
> Fame holds the Christian Trophy thou must beare,
> Englands Red Crosse shall George, then St. George weare. (act 1; p. 15)

At his parents' behest, George waves the wand, and they disappear as they came—but not before exhorting him to avenge them quickly. George is resolved to do their bidding, which is that of his heart as well. Calib, as a witch, is aware of his intent and calls on Tarpax and her other spirits to shield her from George's wrath, but they are powerless to act on her behalf. Tarpax reminds her of the riddle that portended her death; she has brought about her precarious state, and he cannot go against that which is preordained. She climbs the crags to escape, but George enters to execute his vengeance. Tarpax and the other spirits leave her to her inevitable end as George waves the wand once more. Calib cries out: "Now cleaves the Rock, and I doe sinke to Hell; / Roare wind, clap Thunder for great Calibs knell" (act 1; p. 17). The thread of the prophecy has come unraveled, and its secret meaning clear, as Calib dies at the hands of the avenger of the family she had wronged. George, now wholly liberated, both from ignorance of his ancestry and from the illicit hold of the witch, goes on to fulfill his destiny as one of the seven champions of Christendom despite the ongoing attempts of the forces of evil, led by Tarpax and the magicians, to thwart their heroic work. Truth and the Christian faith triumph in the end.

That triumph is at the core of the Elizabethan and Jacobean plays dealing with witchcraft, for, in a sense, their end was twofold: first, to entertain through the creation on-stage of an exotic social type whose life of nefarious activities intertwined with that of everyday folk and, second, to promote a position deemed beneficial to society as a whole, the Protestant ethic and morality that would overcome the repercussions of the witch's evil actions. As a consequence, witches in Elizabethan and Jacobean drama led a mixed existence: although they were used frequently in a variety of serious and comic contexts, witchcraft was considered of insufficient consequence to dominate the plot. Before 1600, the roles of witches were minor and peripheral to the central action. But, with the advent of *Macbeth* in 1606, witches came to be seen as highly theatrical and, thus, more important. Sometimes, as in *The Witch of Edmonton,* they were the focal figures of plays, if not their sole protagonists. Their enhanced position on the stage was no doubt the result of Shakespeare's masterful characterization of the Weird Sisters and the impact of their actions on the protagonist—but also of the ongoing belief in witches and their ability to perform evil deeds, as evidenced by the infamous witchcraft hysteria that marked the seventeenth century and the next. But, while the witch sometimes figured as the less than effective tool of the Devil and herself generally suffered his betrayal and abandonment, she also served the didactic purpose of the dramatists, who portrayed her as a sinner who was justly punished by society for acts against individuals and property, on the one hand, and by God for her transgressions against the laws that the deity had promulgated in the Old Testament, on the other.

Witches of all hues—classical or contemporary, white or black, comical or serious—who were either incidental or consequential characters in the Elizabethan and Jacobean theater represent yet another important element among the numerous examples of sinister occultism on the European stages of evil.

Notes

1. The ancient Greeks called Hecate goddess of the moon, the earth, and Hades, the infernal realm, her trinitarian nature a metaphor for the heavenly body's journey from the sky to the earth and into the underworld. For the genealogy of the goddess and her association with other female deities, see Walker, 378–79.

2. Some critics have rejected the role of Hecate as spurious (see Adams's edition of *Macbeth*), but, if Hecate were omitted, there would be no supernatural agent above the witches, and the origin of their power would be undefined. Such a situation would not coincide with the belief system in place at the writing of *Macbeth:* people could accept the classical divinity of Hades in lieu of the Christian Lord of Hell, but not the omission of a source for evil.

3. Acheron, the river in Hades across which Charon ferried the souls of the dead, is used here to indicate the underworld. However, its usage is metaphoric since the cavern where Hecate next addresses the witches, being accessible later to Macbeth, cannot be in Hades.

4. For a discussion of the witches' song and dance as popular elements that detract from the tragic in *Macbeth,* see Barber, 25–26.

5. The designations *Elizabethan* and *Jacobean* are more appropriate to this study than are *Tudor* and *Stuart* because the plays discussed here fall under the reigns of Elizabeth I (1558–1603) and James I (1603–25). The term *Tudor* encompasses the period of rule by descendants of Sir Owen Tudor, i.e., the reigns of Henry VII, Henry VIII, Edward VI, Mary, and Elizabeth I. *Stuart* refers to the Scottish royal house, from the reign of Robert II through that of James VI (i.e., from 1371 to 1603), who inherited the English throne in 1603 as King James I of England and Scotland; the Stuart era ended in 1714 with Anne.

6. The distinction between witches and magicians is put very succinctly by King James VI in his *Daemonologie:* "Witches ar servantes onelie, and slaves to the Devil; but the Necromanciers are his maisters and commanders" (book 1, chap. 3, p. 9). On the difference between witchcraft and Satanism, see chapter 3 above.

7. On the misreading that resulted in the term *coven,* see chapter 7, n. 6.

8. There were four Sabbats, each representing a seasonal change of great import: Samhain (October 31–November 1), which marked the end of the old year and heralded the new; Embolc (February 1–2); Beltane (April 30–May 1); and Lugnasa(d) (July 31–August 1). The origin of the term *Sabbat* is unknown, and a witches' Sabbat should not be confused with the Shabat or Sabbath of the Jewish faith or its Christian counterpart.

9. The origin of these names, though much debated, is unknown.

10. The balms used have been shown to contain hallucinogenic agents, such as aconite (monkshood, wolfsbane) and belladonna (*solanum somniferum*), which may account for the witches' own belief that they could fly. In an era when the church proclaimed the fallen state of the body after original sin, the attention lavished on the body by witches in their anointings was held to be sinful.

11. The broomstick, symbolic of the male generative member, ironically was associated with Hecate, who, as the Triple Goddess, presided over marriage and births. Jumping over the broomstick was a common practice at marriage ceremonies in many traditional European communities (see Walker, 119–21).

12. Sometimes called the Goat of Mendes (see de Givry, 78), it was at one time associated with the Templars, the influential order of knights accused of worshiping the Black Goat as the deity Baphomet. For Eliphas Levi, the image was a symbol of occult knowledge. The personification of evil as a goat is the result of the transmogrification of the Horned God when the physical attributes of Pan, the principal deity of the Old Religion, were superimposed on Satan; the Christian image thus assimilated the horns, body hair, tail, and cloven hooves of the goat-god Pan, becoming a synthesis for the figuration of the antidivinity.

13. Francisco Goya y Lucientes depicted such rites and offerings in his paintings (e.g., *Aquelarre*) and etchings. The subject inspired many other painters, among them Hans Baldung-Grien.

14. He was king of Scotland (1567–1625) as James VI and king of England (1603–25) as James I.

15. For an assessment of the rationale behind James's views regarding witchcraft, see Notestein, chap. 5. To his credit, James sometimes looked into accusations and judgments against those brought to trial as witches (see Barber, 11).

Witchcraft statutes were passed in 1542 (repealed in 1547), 1563, and 1604 (repealed in 1736). For a thorough study of these statutes and their implementation, see Macfarlane. For a chronological list of those brought to trial, executed, acquitted, or pardoned from 1603 through 1717, see Notestein, 383–419. The last of the English laws against witchcraft were not repealed until the 1950s, an occurrence that brought about a "coming out" of many practitioners of Wicca and effected a resurgence of the Old Religion in the British Isles. The impact was felt in Europe and in North America as well.

16. On the erroneous translation on which the mandate is based, see chapter 3, n. 6, above.

17. The version of Lev. 20:27 in *The New American Bible* reads: "A man or a woman who acts as a medium or fortuneteller shall be put to death by stoning; they have no one but themselves to blame for their death" (116). A related Old Testament text is Deut. 18:10–11: "There shall not be found among you anyone . . . that useth divination, . . . or an enchanter, or a witch, or a charmer, or a consulter with familiar spirits, or a wizard, or a necromancer."

18. In the British Isles, the period of the Witchcraft Panic extends from the mid-sixteenth century into the early 1700s. Ewen studied cases tried at the Home Assize Circuit—which included only the counties of Essex, Hertfordshire, Kent, Surrey, and Sussex—between 1558 and 1707. His numbers (18 n. 38) show that there were a total of 790 indictments resulting in 112 executions, with decreasing numbers in both categories in the later years.

In the English colonies in North America, particularly in Salem Village, there were similar dire circumstances that tore the social and religious fabric of many communities (see chapter 7 above). It has been suggested that many of the European and American cases of popular delusions concerning witchcraft stemmed from ergotism, a toxic condition caused by eating grain and grain products infected with ergot fungus. Such a demented state of mind may have led to the widespread hysteria associated with the "calling out" of witches.

19. On Hopkins, see chapter 7, n. 11, above.

20. The extension of this practice to the British colonies can be seen in the fate of Giles Corey in the settlement at Salem, to which Puritans had imported the same fears and prejudices then commonplace in their native England. Giles Corey, indicted as a wizard, "stood mute, refusing to answer to his indictment. And under both English and New English law a man who refused to answer could not be tried. He could, however, be tortured. . . . Accordingly Giles Corey was pressed: placed upon the ground with gradually increased weight piled upon him. It took him two days to die" (Hansen, 154).

21. Prior Heinrich Kramer (sometimes Latinized as Henricus Institoris) prevailed on the pontiff to issue a papal bull, *Summis desiderentes affectibus* (December 5, 1484), shortly after his ascension to the papacy. This decree was printed in full at the beginning of the *Malleus maleficarum* (see Hughes).

22. During the Second World War, English witches made a concerted effort to raise "a cone of power" as a shield for the British Isles against bombardment by German airplanes and rockets.

23. The scene does not appear in Holinshed's *Chronicles,* but Shakespeare's interpretation of the political enemy of England as a black witch is derived from the

historian's work. Joan of Arc was born in 1412 and burned at the stake by the English in 1431; she was canonized by the Roman Catholic Church in 1920.

24. The earlier generation was convicted of witchcraft in this wild and bleak area overlooking the Yorkshire moors in 1612 when two recusant (i.e., non–Church of England) families, the Demdyke-Devices and the Chattox-Redfernes, began hurling accusations of malefic deeds, including murder through bewitchment, at each other. The nine-year-old Jennet Device was a principal witness against members of her own family, who were arrested on numerous complaints, as were friends and relatives who had gathered to plot a defense strategy. Some died while in custody, but many others were executed during the witchcraft hysteria that ensued, among them the highborn and wealthy Alice Nutter, who refused to confess even at the moment of death.

25. Barber (38–69) gives an extented account of the events preceding and surrounding this prolonged case and its aftermath as a foil against which to judge the verisimilitude of the play. In reality, the boy Edmund Robinson in time confessed that he had made up a story about witches in order to explain an absence from home that would have brought severe punishment from his father (65–66). Barber (71) also states that internal evidence in the epilogue (lines 2803–20) indicates that a verdict had not been entered and, thus, that the play was produced before the case against the accused witches ended. Indeed, the accused were still in jail in 1637 without a resolution, pro or con, in their cases.

26. The identity of "Thomas Holmes, Esquire" has yet to be uncovered.

27. These names, like many other aspects of *The Witch,* are taken from Reginald Scot's massive 1584 treatise *The Discoverie of Witchcraft,* in which he attacks witchcraft, its practices, and the superstitions attendant on it.

28. Reed (173) argues convincingly that two songs, "Come away, come away" and "Black spirits and white," that appear in both Shakespeare's and Middleton's plays, and possibly Hecate's role, were borrowed from *The Witch* and added to *Macbeth* by producers of the latter.

29. For contemporary interpretations of the incubus and the succubus, see James VI, *Daemonologie,* book 3, chap. 3, pp. 66–69; and Sprenger and Kramer, *Maleus Maleficarum,* vol. 1, chap. 1, p. 10.

30. The modern equivalents of these ingredients are mountain parsley ("eleosinum"); monkshood or wolfsbane ("aconitum"); poplar leaves ("frondes populeas"); yellow watercress ("sium"); common myrtle ("acorum vulgare"); cinquefoil, clover, or some other five-leafed plant ("pentaphyllon"); a bat ("flittermouse"); and deadly nightshade or belladonna ("solanum somnificum"); and oil ("oleum"). According to Scot, who cites Johannes Baptistus of Naples, when witches add these ingredients to the rendered fat of the "unbaptized brat" and rub it on their skins: "By this means (saith he) in a moone light night they seeme to be carried in the aire, to feasting, singing, dansing, kissing, culling, and other acts of venerie, with such youths as they love and desire most" (126 n. 1).

31. Such was the testimony in *Examination of John Walsh touching Witchcraft* (1566), cited in Bullen, 369 n. 1.

32. For a full discussion of the demonic pacts of Theophilus and Faust, among others, see Lima, chap. 3.

33. There is a confusion in the use of *succubus* and *incubus*. The idea of the succubus is used erroneously; Suckabus, being a male, should be named after the incubus.

34. As in *The Witch of Edmondton*, devils and other familiar spirits were believed to be rewarded by sucking the witch's blood from her "Devil's teat."

35. Magicians, not witches, use wands to work their spells. Kirke has borrowed the motif from Johnson without concern for overstepping the boundary between magic and witchcraft. However, the wand provides the playwright a prop with which to effect the appearance of the ghosts of George's parents and, most theatrically, the downfall of Calib.

Works Cited

Barber, Laird H., ed. *An Edition of "The Late Lancashire Witches" by Thomas Heywood and Richard Brome.* New York: Garland, 1979.

Bullen, A. H., ed. *The Witch.* Vol. 5 of *The Works of Thomas Middleton.* Boston, 1885.

de Givry, Emile Grillot. *Picture Museum of Sorcery, Magic and Alchemy.* Translated by J. Courtenay Locke. New Hyde Park, N.Y.: University Books, 1963.

Dekker, Thomas, William Rowley, and John Ford. *The Witch of Edmonton.* 1621. In *The Dramatic Works of Thomas Dekker,* ed. Fredson Bowers, 3:481–568. Cambridge: Cambridge University Press. 1958.

Ewen, C. L'Estrange. *Witchcraft and Demonianism: A Concise Account Derived from Sworn Depositions and Confessions Obtained in the Courts of England and Wales.* London: Heath Cranton, 1933.

Goodcole, Henry. *The Wonderful Discoverie of Elizabeth Sawyer a Witch, Late of Edmonton.* London: W. Butler, 1621. Reprinted in *The Works of John Ford,* ed. William Gifford, 1:lxxxi–cvii. London: Lawrence & Bullen, 1895.

Guaccius, Père M. Mar. *Compendium maleficarum.* Milan, 1626. See the illustrations in de Givry.

Hansen, Chadwick. *Witchcraft at Salem.* New York: Braziller, 1969.

Heywood, Thomas. *The Wise Woman of Hogsdon.* ca. 1604; printed 1638. In *The Best Plays of the Old Dramatists: Thomas Heywood,* ed. A. Wilson Verity, with an introduction by J. Addington Symonds. Mermaid Series. London: Vizetelly, 1888.

Heywood, Thomas, and Richard Brome. *The Late Lancashire Witches.* ca. 1634. See Barber 1979.

Hopkins, Matthew. *The Discoverie of Witches.* London, 1647. Edited by Montague Summers. London, 1928.

Hughes, Pennethorne. Introduction to *Malleus maleficarum,* by Jacobus Sprenger and Heinrich Kramer [Henricus Institoris], trans. Montague Summers, ed. Pennethorne Hughes. London: Folio Society, 1968.

James VI, King of Scotland. *Daemonologie, in Forme of a Dialogue, Diuided into three Bookes.* Edinburgh: Robert Walde-graue, 1597. Reprint edited by G. B. Harrison. London: John Lane the Bodley Head Ltd. and New York: E. P. Dutton, 1924. Original in the Bodleian Library (Douce. 1, 230).

Johnson, Richard. *The Famous Historie of the Seven Champions of Christendome.* n.p., 1596.

Jonson, Ben. *The Masque of Queenes.* 1609. In *Ben Jonson,* ed. C. H. Herford, Percy Simpson, and Evelyn Simpson, 7:337–56. Oxford, 1941.

Kirke, John. *The Seven Champions of Christendome.* 1635. With an introduction and notes by Giles Edwin Dawson. *Western Reserve University Bulletin* (Cleveland) 32, no. 16 (15 September 1929): 1–82.

Lima, Robert. *Dark Prisms: Occultism in Hispanic Drama.* Lexington: University Press of Kentucky, 1995.

Macfarlane, A. D. J. *Witchcraft in Tudor and Stuart England.* New York: Harper & Row, 1970.

Marlowe, Christopher. *The Jew of Malta.* 1592. In *The Complete Plays of Christopher Marlowe,* ed. Irving Ribner. New York: Odyssey, 1963.

Marston, John. *The Tragedie of Sophonisba.* 1606. In *The Works of John Marston,* ed. J. O. Halliwell. London, 1856.

Middleton, Thomas. *The Witch.* ca. 1613. In *The Best Plays of the Olde Dramatists: Thomas Middleton,* ed. Havelock Ellis, vol. 2. Mermaid Series. London: Vizetelly, 1890. All quotations are from this edition.

The New American Bible. Camden, N.J.: Thomas Nelson, 1971.

Notestein, Wallace. *A History of Witchcraft in England.* 1911. New York: Thomas Y. Crowell/Apollo, 1968.

Reed, Robert R., Jr. *The Occult on the Tudor and Stuart Stage.* Boston: Christopher, 1965.

Scot, Reginald. *The Discoverie of Witchcraft.* London: W. Brome, 1584. Edited by Brinsley Nicholson. Totowa, N.J.: Rowman & Littlefield, 1973.

Shakespeare, William. *Macbeth.* ca. 1606. In *The Complete Works of William Shakespeare,* 858–84. Oxford University Press, n.d. All quotations are taken from this edition.

———. *Macbeth.* Edited by Joseph Quincy Adams. Boston: Houghton Mifflin, 1931.

Sprenger, Jacobus, and Heinrich Kramer [Henricus Institoris]. *Malleus maleficarum.* 1486. Translated by Montague Summers. Edited by Pennethorne Hughes. London: Folio Society, 1968.

Symonds, J. Addington. Introduction to *The Best Plays of the Old Dramatists: Thomas Heywood,* ed. A. Wilson Verity. Mermaid Series. London: Vizetelly, 1888.

A True and just Recorde of the Information, Examination and Confession of all the Witches Taken at S. Oses, in the countie of Essex. London, 1582.

Walker, Barbara G. *The Woman's Encyclopedia of Myths and Secrets.* San Francisco: Harper & Row, 1983.

11

The Cave and the Magician

Chthonic Sanctuaries in Early European Drama

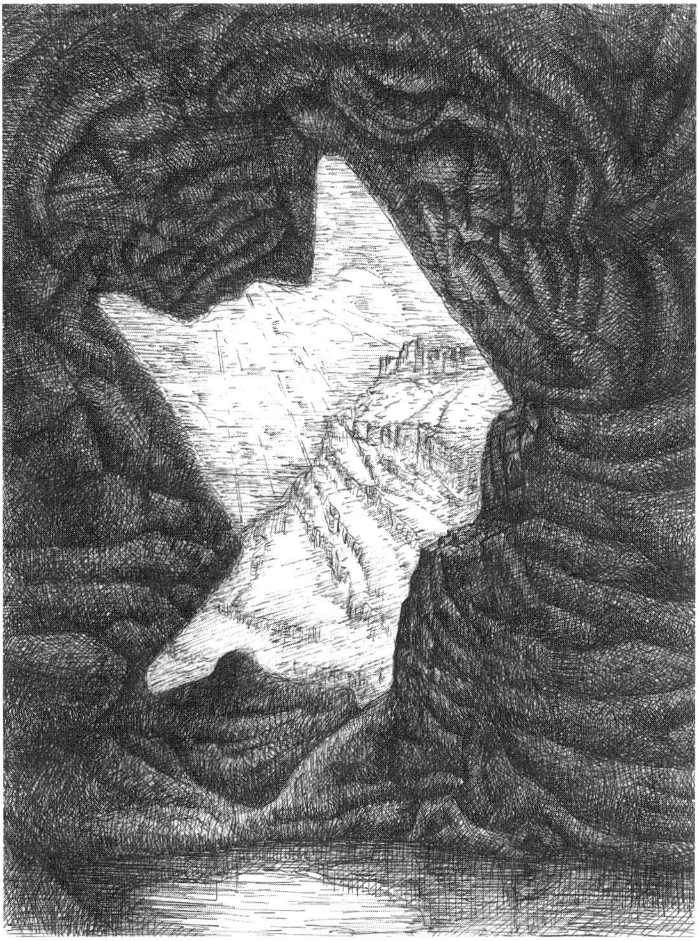

> As the child is conceived in the womb, so is the spirit of the earth engendered within the subterranean depths.
>
> Caves were residences of the earth spirit before they were inhabited by men.
>
> —John Michell, *The Earth Spirit*

There is no certainty about the use to which caves were put in the first instance. But, when they began to be inhabited by human beings at a time lost in the abyss of prehistory, their function was to provide shelter at night and whenever the elements proved inhospitable; to enfold shamanistic practices that would propitiate the spirit(s) of the place, ensure the fertility of nature, abet the hunting strategy, involve the tribal group in the unmanifest dimension, and initiate the youth in the ways of the earth; and, finally, to entomb within the womb of Mother Earth those felled in battle, in the hunt, by old age, or by disease. Or so we surmise on assessing the scant evidence at hand—the human bones, the pottery shards, bone and stone implements, the hearths, the kitchen middens, and especially the magnificent cave art at such sites as Spain's Altamira and France's Lascaux and Chauvet,[1] some of whose images (abstract to us) may symbolize the vulva of the same fertility deity whose effigies have been found in these and other caverns. The cave was sacred since primordial times, and it was used accordingly by our forebears, for they seem to have known intuitively that "the earth is a living entity animated by spirit" (Michell, 12).

Evidence from later eras shows that caverns were revered in Western culture since recorded antiquity as entrances to the underworld (or Erebus, or Tartaros, or Hades, the realm of the chthonic deity Pluto), as passageways for the ascent of spirits to the overworld, and as sites for the mysteries, the celebratory and initiatory rituals of many pagan cults in classical Greece. The underworld is both the source of the life of the earth (as in the myth of Demeter [who symbolizes life], Persephone [who represents death

---

Previous page: Merlin's Cave at Tintagel, Cornwall, England. Drawing by Keith Lima.

and resurrection], and Pluto) and the destination at the end of every life; like the Indian goddess Kali, the cavern is a metaphor for life giving and life taking. But, in the Greek mysteries, the process continues into reincarnation, thus creating a cyclic pattern, what has been termed the *eternal return,* whose analogy is the planting, harvesting, and reconstitution cycle in agriculture, which was revered as magical in the telluric rites held at Eleusis.[2] Caverns were also the locus of such prognosticators as the Pythia, Apollo's oracle at Delphi,[3] of the oracle of Trophonius near Mount Helicon (Boeotia),[4] of the Phrygian Cybele (Sybil) at Cumae,[5] and of the lyric poet Orpheus, he of the descent into Hades (the greatest cavern of all) as well as the focus of the mystery religion termed *Orphism* (see Walker, 218 [Delphi], 745–48 [Orpheus]). In the Acropolis in Athens, a cavern with a spring was a shrine dedicated to Aesculapius, the god of the healing arts. And a cavelike labyrinth was the habitation of the Cretan Minotaur, whose rites of propitiation centered on periodic human sacrifice. In some areas of the Mediterranean, caverns were emblematic of the womb of the Earth Goddess or Mother Goddess (see Michell, 3–23; and Walker, 154–56), as in Crete, where Zeus was hidden in her cave by his mother, the goddess Rhea, who feared that Cronus would devour yet another of their sons, one of whom was prophesied to overthrow him. Important men—kings, political leaders, heroes—were buried in tombs that often resembled caves, as in the *tholos* (so-called beehive) tomb at Mycenae. Caves were also associated with poetic inspiration, as in the writings of Homer and Euripides, for two.[6] The cave was a fundamental element in the mythic, ritualistic, and creative life of the Greek world in antiquity as well as in its conception and expression of the afterlife. Thus, it has passed down through time as an archetype.

Arguably the best-known assessment of the cavern's deeper meaning lies in Plato's allegory in book 7 of the *Republic,*[7] in which the human condition is presented through individuals chained from their youth within abysmal darkness, the imprisoned unable to see themselves or others except in the shadows cast on the uneven walls by a fire at their backs. In such a context, they would be unable to recognize reality as it is, only the shadow of that reality—the illusion of reality. If set free and allowed to climb out of the cave into sunlight, their confrontation with the real would be difficult at first to comprehend and adapt to, just as returning to the darkness of the cave would inflict once more the negativity of that existence.[8] Man's soul, too, is imprisoned in a cavern, that of the body,[9] which is merely an inert substance owing to its lack of knowledge; only when infused with mind or reason would the soul become *nous,* a rational, active entity.[10] Plato does not concern himself in the parable with the cave or cavern as a locale for magical practices, positive or negative. But what is pertinent is Plato's cavern as a symbol of the ignorance of the human condition without the infusion of *gnosis,* that is, knowledge. Inversely, perhaps though a serious misunderstanding of Plato's image of the cave, the magician sought to possess that knowledge by inhabiting a real cavern rather than seeking the transcendental through introspection.

In Roman times, the cave continued to be a locus for the same types of beliefs and rituals. It was logical that, with such a prehistory, caverns should continue to be looked on as residences of spirits, telluric or otherwise, wherein such deities of place (*lares,* the Romans called them) could be worshiped as in ancient times, and wherein humans could find assistance in their search for fulfillment through esoteric knowledge. But, distanced from the magical worldview by the superimpositions of civilization, humans considered it necessary to have an intermediary—an initiate in the mysteries—between the seeker and the desired end. Thus, in writing the fictional history of Rome, Virgil follows the ancient myths of Greece, among them the descent into the underworld, here Avernus ruled by Dis, and has his hero, Aeneas, seek the aid of the Sybil, the priestess of Phoebus at Cumae, for entry into and safe return from the great cavern. Virgil, who by the Middle Ages had earned a reputation as a white magician for this feat, then served as guide to Dante in the Florentine's descent into the infernal depths. But Dante's epic journey was into, not the classical realm of Pluto, but the Christian hell,[11] the cavern that held the great fallen angel Lucifer, his cohorts, and those who had died in mortal sin. Because Dante faced his fear, overcame the baseness of his human nature, and attained wisdom, his *catabasis* is comparable to that of such classical heroes of myth and literature as Theseus, Orpheus, Homer's Odysseus, and Virgil's Aeneas.

Under the Christian hegemony, the cavern was no longer the mythical seat of wisdom, abode of male and female deities, orifice of the Mother. And magic was no longer seen as *scientia,* which sought to unravel the secrets of the universe through the so-called scientific method of experimentation toward proof of a theorem. Similarly, magic pursued the search for wisdom, that is, knowledge, although not through the same process; all too often the knowledge sought by practitioners of magic was thought to be accessible early on through sybils whose prognostications were made in caverns or, later, through the manipulation of spirits or demons in similar grottoes. With Christianity, magic was transmogrified. Its former legitimacy came to be perceived as a ploy to garner forbidden knowledge, a blasphemous attempt at usurpation of God's omniscience. Thus, in canto 20 of Dante's *Inferno,* sorcerers are punished by having their heads twisted backward, "all power of looking forward being denied" (195). The condemnation here is not just of sorcerers who sought to know the future, but of all magic as a perversion of knowledge to satisfy the ego through the domination of individuals and of nature, thereby intruding into God's realm, magic's powers lying beyond the natural abilities given man by his creator. The adage "Knowledge is power" speaks to the perception that the magician's arcane quest would lead to a position of control that was *contra natura.* Thus, places wherein conjurations were held had to be thought of as evil, thus the unnatural, contorted condition of the sorcerers in the *Inferno.* Caverns came to be associated in the popular mind with nefarious magical practices, for they were believed to be entrances to the abode of Satan and the other fallen angels, in a typical superimposition of the church's myths on those of pagan antiquity.[12] Caves were, therefore, taken as mouths or maws of hell, ready to receive those who defied God, and became important features of Last Judgment plays in medieval Europe (see Lima, "La Gueule de l'enfer"; and chapter 1 above). The magician who performed his secret rituals in the bowels of the earth was seen to be within the Devil's dark domain itself, his nefarious acts all the more efficacious owing to his proximity to the Lord of Evil.

The Devil is the great purveyor of evil in the Christian tradition. As such, Satan seeks to employ free will by encouraging human frailties into moral corruption. In the end, he hopes to collect a human soul to enhance his nether kingdom, both because misery loves company and to thwart Christ's work of salvation. Consequently, Satan has made himself the most accessible supernatural entity in the Christian pantheon. The Devil's accessibility particularly appeals to those who seek a knowledge beyond that normally attainable by human endeavor. Practitioners of goetic magic,[13] that is, so-called black or diabolic magic, are among those who call on Satan and his cohorts for the assistance necessary to attain their desired ends; thus, Marlowe's Faust deeds his soul to Mephistopheles in a pact written in blood, what the Scholastic philosopher Albertus Magnus in the thirteenth century termed *professio expressa.*[14] In so doing, Faust opts for the world of shadow over that of substance.

However, unlike witches and Satanists, the magician did not worship the Lord of Shadows but only used his own knowledge of secret formulas, incantations, and words of power found in magical texts known as *grimoires* and other esoteric writings to bring before him denizens of the netherworld to do his bidding.[15] But, as Mephistopheles explains to Faust in Marlowe's *Tragedy of Doctor Faustus*, the reason that he materialized is quite different than what the prideful magician surmises: "For when we hear one rack the name of God, / Abjure the Scripture and His Saviour Christ, / We fly in hope to get his glorious soul" (sc. 3; p. 16). Yet, to achieve this end, as in Faust's situation, the magus was often required to make a binding contract in which his soul was held in escrow by the Devil. Faust and other magicians did so as a means to an end rather than as an act of worship. The magician was a paradox, however. As one empowered by supernatural forces under his command, the magician had horizons that were seemingly limitless; but the magician was, after all, only a mortal whose quest for knowledge, and, thus, power, could not forestall his natural end as a human being. It was a matter of supernatural aspirations and physical limitations. Nonetheless, perhaps in a self-delusory, naive manner, he delved into his occult work with a gusto and expectation that rivaled those of his fellow seekers after the secrets of the universe, the practitioners of the alchemical arts.[16]

Once vested, the magician proceeded to his esoteric endeavors, performed alone, often in a cavern, within a circle whose cabalistic, astrological, and other symbols protected him from potential harm at the hands of the demonic beings he was conjuring. Or so he believed. The Devil and his minions, of course, performed as commanded by the magician, knowing only too well that those who dabbled in the occult sciences were going against God's natural law and had put their souls in jeopardy of eternal damnation, whether a pact had been signed or not. When the twenty-four years of Marlowe's Faust's empowerment are over, Mephistopheles and his aides are at hand to drag the unrepentant magician into the Mouth of Hell, prompting Faust's near-to-last words: "Ugly hell, gape not."[17] In the context of Christian belief, it was a matter of free will, and the magician who conjured evil spirits had chosen the sinister path that, in the eyes of the church, leads to eternal damnation in hell.

Curiously, Marlowe's Faust does not repair to the traditional setting of the cavern, within whose chthonic venue magicians were believed to perform their unholy rituals, opting instead to seek empowerment through his newly learned magical skills in "some lusty grove" (sc. 1; p. 9), that locale perhaps selected by the playwright under the influence of Druidic practices in sacred woods, as typical of England and other parts of the Celtic world. In scene 3, although the setting is not specified, the outdoor locale and its seclusion are evident as the neophyte magician soliloquizes:

Faustus, begin thine incantations,
And try if devils will obey thy hest,
Seeing thou hast prayed and sacrificed to them.
(*He draws a circle on the ground.*)
Within this circle is Jehovah's name
Forward and backward anagrammatized,
The 'breviated names of holy saints,
Figures of every adjunct to the heavens,
And characters of signs and erring stars,
By which the spirits are enforced to rise. (14)

The choice of an outdoor rather than an indoor setting for the conjuration may have another rationale behind it. In the highly charged religious atmosphere of the time in which Marlowe is writing, it would have been dangerous for a scholar to have magical texts in his house. Marlowe may have thought it more in keeping with the cultural ethos of the period to change the venue. Thus, Faust's library does not contain the *grimoires* that provide the formulas for his ritual; he does not possess them until his magician friends put them into his hands. It is understandable in this context that Faust seeks a secluded place beyond his domicile rather than conjuring in his library.[18]

In the case of Goethe's *Faust,* however, the conjuration scene early in the first part of the work occurs in the scholar's study, or library, a setting that can be interpreted as a metaphor for the magician's cave of less-sophisticated times. Since Faust is a learned and renowned academician, it is fitting that the place of conjurations should be the library in which his magical texts are housed alongside other books. Goethe is far removed in time from his protagonist's era, and he is not constrained, as was his English predecessor, by popular expectations to have his magician perform in the formulaic setting of the cave or even in another natural setting. Nor in the more liberal times in which he writes is Goethe under religious impediments similar to Marlowe's.[19] The German's Faust, consequently, functions in a manner different from the Englishman's. And so, suspecting that a shape-shifting spirit has taken the form of the stray dog that he has welcomed into his house, Faust turns to the *Key of Solomon*[20] in his collection of books and utters one of its spells until the transformation from dog to spirit has occurred, a distraught Mephistopheles appearing in disguise and also refusing to identify himself,[21] thus not offering "a name to conjure with," as the saying goes. But Faust correctly defines his diabolic nature by calling him "Corrupter, Liar, God of Flies" (pt. 1, study room; p. 49).[22]

As Marlowe's and Goethe's plays show, it was not necessary to perform magical rites in a cave for them to be efficacious.[23] Indeed, caves as such seldom appear in plays on magic in the Tudor and Stuart eras, in itself a curious omission considering their presence in the lore and narratives on such as Merlin, the famed magician of the Arthurian cycle, said to have been born of a princess-nun and an incubus, thus his inherent powers, as in *The Birth of Merlin* (ca. 1612). But a later play, *The Birth of Merlin; or, The Childe Hath Found His Father* (1662), written by William Rowley, debases the early life of the magician through coarse humor and, in effect, perverts the details soberly delineated by Geoffrey of Monmouth in the twelfth-century *Historia regnum brittaniae.* Nonetheless, Merlin's magic is paramount in the plot of the play. His first magical act is the besting of the Saxon magician Proximus. His second is the besting of the dragons—the pivotal episode of the magical cave. Through his art, Merlin conjures two dragons, one white and one red, whose nightly battles in the cave have weakened the foundation of King Vortiger's castle. When Merlin disposes of them, thus saving the king's abode, his magic is proved infallible, and his reputation as a magician is assured throughout the realm. Although the cave in the play is not the lair of the magician, it is at least evinced in terms of the magical creatures who do battle in its confines and of Merlin's power.

Shakespeare does not avail himself of the cave per se as a stage setting, but he does create a few magicians in his plays, from histories through comedies to tragedies.[24] There are, however, veiled suggestions of caves in several of these works. In *King Henry the Sixth, Part 2,* the magician Roger Bolinbroke, his apprentice John Southwell, and the witch Margery Jourdain enter the duke of Gloster's garden at the behest of the duchess to perform a magical ceremony. In preparation, Bolinbroke ordains: "I have heard her reported to be a woman of an invincible spirit; but it shall be convenient, Master Hume, that you be by her aloft, while we be busy below. . . . Mother Jourdain, be you prostrate, and grovel on the earth; —John Southwell, read you; —and let us to our work." The earth is the crucial element here, for, in having the witch "be . . . prostrate, and grovel on the earth," Shakespeare recognizes the importance of the telluric dimension in the magical tradition. And it is out of the depths of the earth, its caverns, that the magician and witch will raise a demonic spirit to make prognostications concerning the fate of the kingdom's leaders. In preparation, Bolinbroke addresses the lady:

> Madam, sit you, and fear not; whom we raise,
> We will make fast within a hallow'd verge. (act 1, sc. 4; p. 37)

The "verge" here is the limit of an area contained within a ceremonial circle drawn by the magician; a geometric figure without opening, the circle will constrain the spirit or demon "whom we raise" from escaping or bringing harm to humans.[25] This is the magical work that takes place *below,* where the witch is ordered to "be . . . prostrate, and grovel on the earth." *Aloft,* the duchess has her own verge: the limited, safe area of the balcony from which she can view the magical work *below,* as if from the rim of a cavern. The *aloft/below* axis is a metaphor for the upper world of reality and the underworld of magic; the cave is, therefore, implied as both the setting in which Bolinbroke and the witch perform their ritual and the setting out of which the demonic spirit Asmath emerges from even lower depths.

Another marked possibility of a veiled reference to a cave occurs in Shakespeare's *Tempest* (ca. 1611; published 1623), which situates its protagonist, Prospero, in what is termed a *cell* on the island of his forced banishment. What means the term *cell?* Does it relate to the Latin *cella,* which was the name of the inner enclosure in a Roman temple—the sanctuary modeled on the Greek—wherein the statue of the divinity was placed? If so, it could be said that Prospero is the lar, the genius of the island, and that the figure of the white magician moves within his *cella,* attended by his virginal daughter, Miranda, and the neutral spirit Ariel,[26] while outside it lies the grotesque Caliban, offspring of the witch Sycorax and the Devil.[27] The cell then becomes the inner sanctum and, as such, can be interpreted as an encoded site that stands for the cave traditionally used by magicians.

Similarly in Robert Greene's earlier *The Honorable History of Friar Bacon and Friar Bungay* (ca. 1589),[28] the conjurations occur in another kind of cell, the type found in the friars' monastery. Such cells provide seclusion from other brethren for prayer and meditation and the occasion, if so sought by the wayward, for less orthodox practices, such as the magic rituals of Friar Bacon. And, indeed, when Friar Bacon welcomes to his cell the "masters of our academic state, / that rule in Oxford," he asks them: "Why flock you thus to Bacon's secret cell [?]" (sc. 2; p. 173). The cell is *secret* because of the occult uses to which it is put, not because it is in a secret place (since it is part of the monastery that Friar Bacon inhabits and accessible to many). His cell, then, is an acceptable place for a magician's conjurations under the friar's circumstance, as efficacious a site as the formulaic cave. This is evident in the power of the magic that he performs there, as the friar proclaims proudly:

> Bacon can by books
> Make storming Boreas thunder from his cave,
> And dim fair Luna to a dark eclipse.
> The great arch-ruler, potentate of hell,
> Trembles when Bacon bids him or his fiends,
> Bow to the force of his pantagonon. (sc. 2; p. 174)

And he proves his claim by conjuring up a devil and transporting an innkeeper before the astonished guests as the scene ends.

Later, when Bacon invites King Edward to his cell, the setting is described in the stage direction as *"the study."* This study/cell is the place where the friar offers the king a magical sight (but without sound) in his crystal ball ("prospective glass"):

> Here tempers Friar Bacon many toys,
> And holds this place his consistory-court,
> Wherein the devils plead homage to his words.
> Within this glass prospective thou shalt see
> This day what's done in merry Fressingfield
> 'Twixt lovely Peggy and the Lincoln Earl. (sc. 6; p. 188)

At the jealous king's behest, the magician halts the impending wedding of the pair by immobilizing Friar Bungay, who is intent on performing the rite. Then, Bacon has a devil take Bungay on his back to Oxford. His is, indeed, long-distance magic, from his cell in the university town to far afield where the lovers met. Later, in a confrontation before the king with the magician Vandermast, whom Friar Bungay failed to best in conjuring, Bacon defeats the German and has him transported magically to the European mainland.

But Bacon's days as a conjuror are numbered. The next time he is seen in his cell (sc. 11), the Brazen Head he has fashioned as an oracle ironically speaks of the passage of time while the friar is asleep. When his student awakens him, the oracular bust has already been destroyed: *"[L]ightning flashes forth, and a hand appears that breaks down THE HEAD with a hammer"* (sc. 11; p. 222). Subsequently, when two young scholars enter his cell to gaze into the crystal ball, they stab each other to death, just as in a vision they had seen their fathers do in a duel. Now it is Bacon who, in the presence of Bungay, destroys his last access to magic, repenting his seven years of countervailing God:

Bungay, I'll spend the remnant of my life
In pure devotion, praying to my God
That he would save what Bacon vainly lost. (sc. 13; p. 230)

Yet, in a curious anticlimax to Bacon's abjuring magic, the devil Plutus materializes two scenes later, stating that he has come at the behest of Bacon to seek out his student, and, when he encounters him, Miles is quite content to ride on the devil's back to hell. The play draws to a close with a hymeneal celebration of Margaret and Lacy's love; this is followed by Bacon's heightened prognostication of England's great future, in the preamble to which the friar discloses his authority:

I find by deep prescience of mine art,
Which once I tempered in my secret cell. (sc. 16; p. 238)

When Bacon makes this final reference to his "secret cell," he is, in effect, coming full circle to his first reference to it in scene 2. In a sense, then, the gifted friar has brought closure to his art by closing the circle of his magical practices in his symbolic cave.[29]

In George Chapman's tragedy *Bussy d'Ambois* (ca. 1607), the matter of the cave and the magician is again but a simulacrum of itself, for the former has become a vault and the latter a friar. A vault is an arched space—a chamber or passageway—especially one underground. It is in this subterranean guise that it is used in the play. Here, the vault opens, seemingly of its own accord, before Tamyra, who, distraught by her passionate inclinations, exclaims:

I fly, my sex, my virtue, my renown
To run so madly on a man unknown.
See, see, the gulf is opening that will swallow
Me and my fame for ever; I will in,
And cast myself off, as I ne'er had been. (act 2, sc. 2; p. 30)

Tamyra's use of the terms *gulf, opening, swallow, in,* and *cast* leave no doubt of the subterranean nature of the vault that has mysteriously opened before her; for her sin of lust, she seems resolved to plunge herself into that vault, and, in that context, by allusion it becomes the pit of hell.[30] Yet, having said her speech, she exits without casting herself into the unholy abyss. Furthermore, as the stage directions make obvious, "*Friar and D'Ambois ascend*," no doubt the cause of the vault's opening earlier through their agency (or magically). Later, having brought D'Ambois and Tamyra together for the tryst, the pandering friar "*descends*" (act 2, sc. 2; pp. 30, 33), as the stage directions have it, once more entering the vault. If the vault is, indeed, a device that stands for the cave, how is it that it can be present in Tamyra's chamber without causing surprise, wonder, or fear? It is taken totally for granted as belonging where it is, for no explanation is given in the stage directions or in the dialogue. Appearance or reality? It is possible—although this is not indicated in the text—that theater convention of the period would accept the set piece as "invisible" when not in use and permit the vault to "appear," that is, become visible, as occasion demands, as when in Tamyra's and Bussy's presence Friar Comolet, now clearly the magician, puts on his ritual robe, explaining to the lady:

> To which ends, honoured daughter, at your motion,
> I have put on these exorcising rites,
> And, by my power of learned holiness
> Vouchsafed me from above, I will command
> Our resolution of a raised spirit. (act 4, sc. 2; p. 56)

Empowered by heaven, Comolet's conjuration of Behemoth, Cartophylax, and other devils is fittingly in a formula in Latin.[31] When they materialize, they too ascend from the selfsame vault that the friar and Bussy had used, but the devils' entrance is accompanied by thunder—and by a torch, ever a symbol that indicates the underworld. Once their prognostications and other services have been rendered, Behemoth and his hellish companions return to their abode through the vault. After their magical entrance and exit, there can be no doubt, not only that the vault is the way to the magician's cave, but also that, in turn, it provides access to the depths of hell.

On three other occasions do the vault and its emanations figure in the plot. When Friar Comolet enters brandishing a sword, defending Tamyra from the attacks of her jealous husband, he ascends from the vault as before; and, when the friar dies suddenly in shock at seeing Tamyra's bloody body on the rack, Montsurry comments wryly:

> Since all earth's pleasures are so short and small,
> The way t'enjoy it, is t'abjure it all.
> Enough! I must be messenger myself,

> Disguised like this strange creature: in, I'll after,
> To see what guilty light gives this cave eyes. (act 5, sc. 1; p. 66)

Having placed the friar's body in the vault, Tamyra's husband dons his garb, intent on delivering his wife's letter to Bussy in that disguise. He then proceeds into the innards of the vault, which he has termed a *cave.* His recognition of the vault's real identity verifies earlier suppositions of its function as a magician's cave, but its deeper nature is hinted at by the "guilty light" that "gives this cave eyes," lightly veiled references to the fires of hell that glow from the vault's opening.

The next appearance of the vault/cave takes place in the following scene when the ghost of Friar Comolet appears to Bussy in his residence amid strange occurrences, as Bussy notes:

> What violent heat is this? Methinks the fire
> Of twenty lives doth on a sudden flash
> Through all my faculties: the air goes high
> In this close chamber, and the frighted earth
> Trembles, and shrinks beneath me; the whole house
> Cracks with his shaken burthen. (act 5, sc. 2; p. 67)

The heat from the fires (of purgatory or of hell?) herald the brief visit of the friar. Promising to meet Bussy in Tamyra's chamber, he exits as he came. Bewildered, Bussy recalls Behemoth's promise to appear should he be needed, and, although he lacks "[t]he powerful words and decent rites of art," he calls on the "Prince of Darkness" (67), ironically, to enlighten him. As before, Behemoth appears from the vault and warns him of the danger he faces if he follows the summons in Tamyra's letter. But, when the Devil disappears and Montsurry enters as the friar, Bussy resolves to go to his love anyway.

Following immediately, in the last scene of the play, the ghost of Friar Comolet reappears in Tamyra's chamber, and soon Bussy enters, there to be murdered by hidden assassins while he struggles with Montsurry. The friar's ghost has come to right the wrongs he has caused, and he succeeds in inducing Bussy to forgive his murderers and in effecting a "Christian reconcilement" between husband and wife, although Montsurry repudiates his love for Tamyra while forgiving her trespass. The ghost of Friar Comolet, his mission accomplished, exits to face his own accounting in the hereafter, as his near final words declare:

My terrors are struck inward, and no more
My penance will allow they shall enforce
Earthly afflictions but upon myself. (act 5, sc. 3; pp. 77–78)

That his end will be purgation rather than damnation is also evinced in his exit, which is not indicated as a descent into the vault. Indeed, the vault/cave is not mentioned in the stage directions at all. All that is indicated at his departure from the scene, theatrical and human at once, is simply "*Exit*" (p. 78). The magician will not return to the cave to dwell therein eternally, for he has not performed any acts that call for the damnation of his soul; empowered "from above" as a friar, he has unabashedly manipulated the lower powers through the access provided by the vault/cave in order to know the flow of things in the world of the court that he frequents. In effect, he has practiced benevolent magic with admirable control over the negative forces that he has conjured, yet he emerges as flawed in his inability to rise above mere curiosity in seeking to know what is hidden from the human condition.

But traditionally written plays were not the only expression of the cave and magician topos in Elizabethan and Jacobean England. Dramatists such as Ben Jonson, who gained favor at court during the reign of James I, were invited to produce court masques. This genre was conceived initially, not as drama, but as an extravagant presentation of song, dance, and instrumental music on a theme and performed on elaborate sets by such distinguished designers as Inigo Jones. Playwrights of the quality of Ben Jonson were entrusted with yearly productions of such spectacles. Many court masques celebrated a king or queen's status and accomplishments (real or imagined) by associating the monarch with, or even having him or her onstage as, mythic beings and deities. Magic and other occult activities were frequently incorporated into these celebratory pageants.[32]

Representative of such entertainments, as well as exemplary of the motif of the cave and the magician, is William D'Avenant's *The Temple of Love* (1634), an elaborate court masque conceived and performed for Queen Henrietta Maria. It features a group of magicians who have cast their spells against young lovers, imprisoning them in a false temple of love. When these magicians emerge from their cave, they are concerned over the approach of a greater magician, who will overturn their evil spells. They raise up spirits, who appear in the company of an unsavory lot of lowlifes. But the arrival of Indamora (the queen) cannot be impeded, and she clears the mists, reveals the true temple, and vanquishes the grotesque magicians, who are consigned to a sector of the stage (the sinister side) away from goodness triumphant.

The motif of the magician's cave has, perhaps, its last manifestation in the curious form of English theater known as the *pantomime,* a popular form of entertainment with music and miming wherein romped characters derived from the Italian commedia dell'arte, among others. The *harlequinade,* as these presentations were often called, and the theme of the magician's cave come together in the anonymous 1741 production entitled *Harlequin Student; or, the Fall of Pantomime, with the Restoration of the Drama.* The pantomime to end all pantomimes opens on the magician Tenebroso's cave, his student Harlequin sitting in the hollow of a rock, Tenebroso himself leaning on the rock. But, after Harlequin is sent into the world armed with a magic wand, the cave is not featured again, although Tenebroso returns to magically instigate the appearance of Elysium, with its cast of Cupid, Mercury, and "the Heathen Gods." Thereafter, Mercury invokes the spirit of Shakespeare and the attendant return to Great Britain's greatness in the drama. In the process, the god damns Harlequin and his crew: "Down, down to Hell, from whence ye rose" (Niklaus, 206).

In Renaissance Italy, where the improvisational theater known as the commedia dell'arte flourished as a popular expression of satire and mockery of pomposity, hypocrisy, and stupidity in individuals and institutions, the comedic formula reigned on-stage in such written masterworks as *The Mandrake* (*La mandragola*) by Niccolò Machiavelli and *Ruzzante Returns from the Wars* (*Il reduce*) by Angelo Beolco as well as in the plays of a later era, for example, *The Servant of Two Masters* (*Il servo di due padrone*) and *Mirandolina* (*La locandiera*), both by Carlo Goldoni, and *The King Stag* (*Il re cervo*) by Carlo Gozzi. But, in this broad array, there is only one practitioner of magic. Durandarte, the magician in Gozzi's commedia-inspired play, years before created a plaster head for King Deramo's use in deciding all kinds of matters, including at this juncture the choice of a wife. The head will laugh in disdain of hypocrisy and subterfuge or remain impassive in recognition of sincerity and truth as the candidates pass in review. Pantaloon's daughter Angela passes the test and is proclaimed queen, to the chagrin of Tartaglia, the king's prime minister, whose daughter was rejected along with thousands of others.

Having fulfilled its mission, the plaster head is destroyed by Deramo, who declares a holiday and orders preparations for a royal hunt in the forest of Roncislappe. However, Tartaglia promises secretly to avenge himself there, saying: "[I]f the devil stand by me!" (act 2, sc. 1; p. 320). In the forest, Cigolotti releases a parrot who is his master Durandarte, transformed by Oberon, the king of the fairies, and kept in a cage for having revealed their secrets to Deramo, including that of the plaster head. The second magical secret permits the one who pronounces a secret formula to possess the body of a dead animal and then return to human form. Through deceit, Tartaglia gets the king to reveal it to him in the forest, and, when they shoot two stags, Deramo becomes one, leaving his own dead body behind. Tartaglia then possesses the king's body and attempts to hide the second stag when an old man appears. Tartaglia kills him. Having assumed the body of the king, he orders that the other, revivified stag be killed and offers a reward. Thereafter, Deramo enters the old man's body when he cannot find his own and proceeds to the palace. Meanwhile, the parrot allows itself to be captured by Truffaldino in order to enter the queen-to-be's presence. There, during the confrontation of Deramo in the old man's body and Tartaglia in the king's, the spell is broken, and Durandarte returns to his own, human shape. Controlling the scene with his wand, he transforms the changelings back to their real forms. All ends happily, except for the evil Tartaglia, and the magician, his task ended, gives up his powers, also to become a normal human being.

The clever transmutations in the play may be the result of Durandarte's magic, but the magician himself, transformed into a parrot for his transgression against the fairy realm, cannot function freely early on and has to rely on Truffaldino to take him into the palace in a cage in order to complete the process of his liberation. Thereupon, the spell is broken, and he is free of the enchantment, free as well to perform the magical acts that restore order and happiness to the kingdom. Just as metamorphosis is the foundation of the plot, once again, as in plays analyzed earlier, the motif of the cave has been transformed: here, the loss of Durandarte's identity has imprisoned the magician in a symbolic cave from which he cannot escape until events dictated by Oberon come to pass. Unlike the typical magician's cave, which is the setting for empowerment, this "cave" has deprived Durandarte of his ability to perform magic.

The French seem not to have had a propensity for caves and magicians in their plays, although there are two medieval works that can be seen as using the motif, the first without a magician. Adam de la Halle (Adam le Bossu, ca. 1250–ca. 1288) in *Le Jeu de la feuillée* (Play of the bower; ca. 1276) depicted the demon Crokesot (variously Crokesos, Croquesos, Croquesot) and fairies (Morgue, Maglore, Arsile), along with witching and hexing at the behest of Hellequin (variant Herlequin), Lord of the Underworld, who seeks to woo the fairy Morgue through the agency of his fiend. But Hellequin never appears on-stage, nor is his cavernous kingdom ever seen; it is referenced only through such terms as *là-bas* (beneath, below, or down under) and *inférieure.* But the popular imagination needed little to envision the place of torment, abode of the Devil, whatever his name.[33]

In one of France's most celebrated medieval plays, Rutebeuf's *Le miracle de Théophile* (ca. 1261), the first in which a pact with the Devil signed in blood appears, the place where the act of fealty takes place is unspecified. This may be because, in the lore of the period, such sacrilegious actions were to occur out of the sight of God, thus in a recess in the earth, a cave. Rutebeuf may have felt it unnecessary to specify the locale in that context of popular knowledge. So, when Théophile approaches Salatin, the magician who is held to be Jewish but whose name is Arabic, the setting is not described. Rather than an omission, failing to identify the setting is as conscious a technique as a poet's elision; in so doing, Rutebeuf leaves us merely taking for granted that, as the reader and spectator of his time would have come to expect in such cases, the setting is, indeed, a cave. Certainly, the magician's conversations with the devils he has conjured, including Satan himself, cannot take place in any but a secret place, and none is more secret than a cave. And, when Théophile again seeks out Salatin, the magician informs him that the Devil awaits, instructing: "Descends là-bas, sans tarder. . . . On t'attend là-bas" (sc. 5; p. 9). The fallen churchman descends into the pit, there to make his pact with the Devil.[34]

Nowhere in European drama is the topos of the cave and the magician foregrounded more directly or with greater frequency than in Spain during its Golden Age (1492–1680). The dramatists of the era were fascinated with the various aspects of the subjects related to it, most notably the demonic pact, said to have been executed by scholars à la Faust or, earlier, by clerics such as Theophilus of Adana.[35] But not all who practiced magic did so in a formal contractual involvement with the Devil, and many of the plays of the period concern magicians both within and outside Christianity. But, even in cases such as those of Moors and Jews, magicians' powers were interpreted as emanating from the Devil. Zoroaster, e.g., appears in Juan de la Cueva's *Comedia de la constancia de Arcelina* and José de Cañizares et al.'s *El anillo de Giges, y mágico rey de Lidia,* while Merlin has the leading role in Andrés Rey de Artieda's *Los encantos de Merlín* and appears, too, in *La casa de los celos y selvas de Ardenia* by Miguel de Cervantes. Juan Ruiz de Alarcón's *Quien mal anda en mal acaba* deals with Román Ramírez, a Moor who was arrested and punished by the Inquisition on charges of being a magician, in a typical *comedia* (a full-length play of any type) of intricate plot and superimposed identities maneuvered by Satan. Ruiz de Alarcón also portrays a Moorish magician, Amet, in *La manganilla de Melilla.* Another reputed magician, Pedro Vallalarde, is the subject of Juan Salvo y Vela's *El mágico de Salerno,* while the eighteenth-century dramatist Antonio Valladares de Sotomayor wrote numerous plays in which magicians are protagonists, among them *El mágico de Mogol, El mágico en Cataluña,* and *El mágico de Tetuán.* There are also numerous plays on magic by anonymous authors.

In Golden Age Spain, many of the magicians portrayed in literature—with the possible exception of Celestina—performed their rituals in caves or had their lessons therein.[36] Such is the case in Pedro Calderón de la Barca's *El mágico prodigioso* (1663).[37] Almost at the conclusion of act 2, Cipriano, a pagan, heeds the offer of a stranger, pretending first to be a traveler and later a magician, to help him in his quest to possess the chaste Justina, whom he has glimpsed in a vision proffered by the disguised Devil. At his behest, Cipriano signs a contract in his own blood. Thereafter, Cipriano listens to the terms of the stranger, whom he does not know to identify as the Christian personification of evil, the Devil:

> [Q]ue en una cueva encerrados,
> sin estudiar otra cosa,
> hemos de vivir entrambos. (832)

As the act ends, Cipriano enters the Devil's cave, secreted in a forest, to learn the necromantic arts that will help him effect his seduction of the virtuous Christian woman Justina.[38] Perhaps relying on folk belief to inform the public's imagination, Calderón does not describe the interior of the cave; in fact, Cipriano's lessons in goetic or black magic are not staged at all. All that is evident is what Cipriano declares in act 3 on emerging from the cave after a year of instruction:

> Este monte elevado
> en si mismo al alcázar estrellado,
> y aquesta cueva oscura,
> de dos vivos funesta sepultura,
> escuela ruda ha sido
> donde la docta mágica he aprendido,
> en que tanto me muestro,
> que puedo dar lección a mi maestro. (833)

The "monte elevado" rises toward heaven, the place of salvation, as the "cueva oscura" is sited toward the opposite polarity, the place of death and damnation.[39] The symbolism may stem from Dante's *Inferno,* in which the mountain in cantos 1 and 2 is contrasted to the abyss of hell, which the poet enters in canto 3. But, in this *comedia de magia,* the very mountain that thrusts toward the firmament contains the cave in which unholy rites have been performed and taught by the Devil. There is little irony in this union of positive and negative in the context of Cipriano's pagan world, where dualism was commonplace; however, Christianity's dictate that good proceeds from God and evil from the Devil presents a dichotomy that becomes highly ironic when the symbols of the two polarities are intertwined, as here.

The cave in *El mágico prodigioso* is nameless and has no tradition, nor, as noted earlier, is it described. This is not the case in other plays of the period. Most notable among magician's caves of the Golden Age are two notorious settings: the Cave of Toledo and the Cave of Salamanca. The renowned eighteenth-century Spanish critic and encyclopedist Fray Benito Jerónimo Feijoo addressed the matter, referring to what he termed popular *fábulas* (fables) that

> entre los magos gentiles era circunstancia del rito destinar cuevas o sitios subterráneos a sus sacrílegas imprecaciones. La especie de que en un tiempo hubo escuelas de las artes mágicas en varias partes de España, señaladamente en Salamanca, Toledo y Córdoba (algunos ponen en vez de Córdoba a Sevilla), no sólo se derramó en el vulgo, más también logró asenso en algunos graves escritores. . . . Créese que nos trajeron esta peste acá los moros, los cuales, aún hoy, se supone que son muy prácticos en toda hechicería. Es verosimil, pues, que juntando el vulgo una noticia con otra, la de ser circunstancia de las imprecaciones mágicas el celebrarse en cuevas, y la que en algunos lugares de España se enseñaban las artes mágicas, sin otro fundamento destinase para escuelas de ellas las cuevas de Toledo y Salamanca." (376–77)

What prompted Feijoo's critical discourse is that each of these caves had a long association with the magical tradition in Spain long before his time. Toledo, a seat of power and learning in Moorish times and after the Christian Reconquest, had the legend of the Cave of Hercules on which dramatists and others could draw. According to the legend, as promulgated in the *Crónica del moro Rasis,*[40] Hercules foresaw that Toledo would become a great city and so erected a great tower that his fame might prevail despite the passage of time.[41] The tower endured for centuries. Here the story takes a different turn, for, by the eighth century C.E., the tower had been transformed into an enchanted palace that Hercules had kept locked; stories about great treasures buried within its keep persisted until the time of Rodrigo, king of the Visigoths, who set out to unearth them, as Feijoo recounts: "[A]lgunos creen, que aquel palacio encantado, que dice el arzobispo don Rodrigo había en Toledo, y estaba siempre cerrado por no sé qué predicción creída, de que cuando se abriese se perdería España; pero el infeliz rey don Rodrigo le mandó abrir, entrando en él, halló un lienzo en que estaban pintados hombres armados de hábito y gesto de moros, con esta inscripción: *Por esta gente será en breve destruída España,* digo, que algunos creen que aquel palacio encantado no era otro que la cueva de que hablamos" (378). It was said after Rodrigo's defeat at the hands of the Muslim invaders that his kingdom fell as a result of his desecration of the ancient tower/palace erected by the Greek hero. Somehow, over time, when the tower was no longer extant, the legend transformed it into the cave over which, according to some accounts, it had been erected.[42] And so it was the Tower or Palace of Hercules first and, ultimately, the Cave of Toledo, a transformation for which Feijoo finds a classical antecedent: "Que se diese nombre de palacio á una cueva, no se debe extrañar, pues palacio real llamó Virgilio a la cueva de Caco" (378).

The influence of Virgil, considered at the time a white magician in Spain as elsewhere in Christendom, should not be underestimated, for he foreshadows much supernatural lore in the Middle Ages and the Renaissance, of which the first canto of the *Inferno* is but one example. When Dante encounters the shade of Virgil, he acknowledges the author of the *Aeneid* as his master and inspiration and asks his help in overcoming the travails that lie before him in his journey through the netherworld. And Virgil leads him into the pit, in a sense making Dante a disciple as he teaches him the lore of hell and exposes him to its secrets. As the work progresses, the abilities that made Virgil a magician in Dante's time manifest themselves through the words of power that he employs to open paths and keep his charge from being harmed by demons and souls alike as the two delve ever deeper into the abyss.[43] In another context, Virgil conjures the Greek hero Ulysses with an economy of language that demonstrates his self-assurance as a magus (canto 26, lines 78–84). Through his empowerment from heaven-granted words of power, Virgil proves to be the facilitator through the cavern of the damned. It is easy to see how he came to be viewed as a great purveyor of theurgic, or white, magic.

It is perhaps owing to this positive image of Virgil that many practitioners of the art of magic in subsequent times were seen in a favorable light. One such magician was Don Illán de Toledo, whose story can be traced to Don Juan Manuel's medieval collection of didactic texts in which Patronio instructs his master, Count Lucanor, on affairs of state and on human nature.[44] In the best known, "Exemplo XI: De lo que conteçió a un deán de Sanctiago con don Illán, el grand maestro de Toledo," Don Illán tells his clerical visitor from Santiago de Compostela that the occult arts he wishes to learn "non se podía aprender sinon en lugar mucho apartado e que luego esa noche le quería amostrar dó habían de estar fasta que hobiese aprendido aquello que él quería saber" (83). The appropriate place is the magician's cavern, the infamous Cave of Toledo, into which they descend shortly thereafter: "[P]or una escalera de piedra muy bien labrada e fueron descendiendo por ella muy grand pieça, en guisa que paresçia que estaban tan baxos que passaba el río de Tajo por çima dellos. E desque fueron en cabo del escalera, fallaron una posada muy buena, e una cámara mucho apuesta que y había, ó estaban los libros el estudio en que había[n] de leer" (84).

The descent into the cave here is not fraught with dire implications, as in classical accounts. Neither is Don Illán's cave presented as a hellish setting. It is impressive in its unsuspected location beneath his house, in its great depth, in its comfortable appointments. But is it only an enchantment, a magical illusion? At the end of the tale, having shown the dean his future in the church and the ingratitude that he would show his host and teacher, Don Illán has everything return to the same setting as before the descent into the cave, and he sends his would-be apprentice back to Santiago de Compostela, without satisfying his desire to advance in the knowledge of magic, but having taught him a lesson nonetheless, one that leaves him shamefaced and without response.[45] In the tale, Don Illán, the master of occult arts, emerges as a principled man and the setting in which he performs his magic as a nether intellectual haven away from the mendacity and hypocrisy of the overworld.[46] The reason behind this sympathetic portrayal is that natural magic was considered a science and its practitioners were generally thought of positively in the European Middle Ages, as in the case of Virgil.

Such a view was reflected in the *comedias* of the Golden Age, in which magicians were not infrequently portrayed as wise men who brought benefits to society by the application of their esoteric knowledge to practical situations, as in the resolution of political, religious, or personal dilemmas. One such example is *La prueba de las promesas* (ca. 1618), a *comedia de magia* with moral overtones by Juan Ruiz de Alarcón, which uses "Exemplo XI" of Don Juan Manuel's book as its foundation, giving the classic tale an effective adaptation for the stage (see Fadrejas Lebrero).[47] The playwright keeps as his protagonist the selfsame Don Illán who taught his apprentice a lesson through magic, but the dean of Santiago de Compostela does not appear herein, his role having been assigned to Don Juan de Ribera, a gentleman in love with Doña Blanca, the daughter of the magus in this version. Similarly, none of the other characters proceed from Don Juan Manuel's tale. Also missing from the *comedia* is the setting of the Cave of Toledo in which "Exemplo XI" is set. For reasons that the playwright did not divulge in the play, the magical illusion performed by Don Illán to test Don Juan de Ribera's character and love occurs in the study of the magician's house in Toledo; there is no descent into the depths of a cavern as in the medieval tale. The omission may be a reflection of the dramatist's fear that hearkening back to that topos might bring on him the wrath of the Holy Office of the Inquisition, either in his native Mexico or in Spain. Nonetheless, the enchantment that makes Don Juan believe in his good fortune and that demonstrates how success can make an individual eschew his avowed love and solemn promises is as effective as that cast in the Cave of Toledo in the medieval version of the plot.

But Toledo, once the most important gem captured in the early stages of the Reconquest, lost its privileged position, and, as Feijoo notes, Toledo's cave passed from public lore, to be replaced by Salamanca's seat of magical operations:

> La especie de la cueva de Toledo ya casi enteramente se ha desaparecido de el vulgo; mas la de la cueva de Salamanca echó hondas raíces en él, y aún se halla apoyada por algunos escritores demonógrafos. . . . Lo que tiene aprehendido el vulgo es que en la cueva de Salamanca el demonio por sí mismo enseñaba las artes mágicas, admitiendo no más que siete discípulos por cada vez, con el pacto de quedarse con uno, aquel a quien tocase la suerte, destinado luego en cuerpo y alma a las penas infernales, y aquí entra la historia del Marqués de Villena, aquel mismo de quien creyó toda España ser un insigne mágico. . . . De éste dicen que, habiéndose hecho consumado mágico en aquella escuela, entre los siete le tocó la suerte infeliz, pero el engañó al demonio, dejándole su sombra con la aprehensión de que era su cuerpo. (377)

The Cave of Salamanca, then, provides the second major setting for magic in the Golden Age theater. And one of the more fascinating historical figures associated with that site who became prominent in the works of the Golden Age was the marqués Enrique de Villena, the Aragonese nobleman born about 1384. He published a study on astrology (*Tratado de astrología*) and an influential treatise on the evil eye (*Libro de aojamiento,* 1425), which caused him to be branded a sorcerer and moved the church to burn his library on his death in 1434. The confrontation between the Devil and a member of the Spanish nobility could not help but be dramatic, and its appeal to the major playwrights of this period is evident in the works that they created on this theme: Ruiz de Alarcón wrote the full-length *comedia de magia La Cueva de Salamanca,* Calderón *Los encantos del marqués de Villena* (presumed lost), and Rojas Zorrilla *Lo que quería ver el marqués de Villena.*[48] For his part, Cervantes used the motif in a satirical manner in the *entremes* (short play) of feigned magic *La Cueva de Salamanca,* excluding the marqués de Villena from the cast of characters. Instead, a university student, claiming to have been robbed on the road, takes the occasion of Pancracio's entrance to inveigh against the poor shelter given him by his wife, Leonarda, in his absence and regrets not being able to use the *ciencia* that he learned in the Cave of Salamanca to better his situation for fear of the Holy Inquisition. But, as if suddenly inspired, he changes his resolve and hoodwinks Pancracio into believing that the sacristan and the barber, who had secretly come to woo Leonarda and her maid, are, in fact, demons. The student orders them to bring in a hamper of food destined for the bacchanale that Pancracio's unexpected return had squelched. Elated by the encounter with the pleasant "demons," Pancracio leads all into the dining room, there to feast and hear of the wonders of the the Cave of Salamanca.

While Cervantes eschews the cave and magicians as topics worthy of high consideration in his *entremes,*[49] Ruiz de Alarcón gives each his serious attention in *La Cueva de Salamanca,* often demonstrating a philosophical knowledge of occult traditions as well as a sound grounding in Catholic doctrine. The *comedia de magia* features two magicians, the marqués Enrique de Villena as a *galán* (young man) and one Enrico, an old Frenchman who, wherever he finds himself, has devoted his life to studying, on this occasion at the University of Salamanca.[50] The latter is the first magician encountered (sc. 6) when some gallants fleeing the law after vengefully killing some of its officers are helped to "disappear" by the elderly magician, who later reveals to them his background as a pupil of Merlin in Italy, who taught him chiromancy, astrology, and necromancy. The young men decide to enlist among Enrico's apprentices. When the marqués de Villena makes his entrance (sc. 13), he too divulges his credentials as a magician, curiously coinciding with Enrico in that he studied with Merlin as well and in Italy. What will bring the two magicians together is the Cave of Salamanca, as Villena reveals to Don Diego, one of the gallants rescued by the old magician:

La parlera fama allí
ha dicho que hay una cueva
encantada en Salamanca,
que mil prodigios encierra;
que una cabeza de bronce,
sobre una cátedra puesta,
la mágica sobrehumana
en humana voz enseña;
que entran algunos a oírla,
pero que de siete que entran
los seis vuelven a salir,
y el uno dentro se queda. (410–11)

The marqués has come to Salamanca in search of the cave, and his investigation has led him to Enrico's minute house:

La cueva está en esta casa,
si no mintieron las señas;
pero que verdad dijeron
muestra el hallaros en ella,
porque, si no es por encanto,
imposible es que cupieran
dos hombres que son tan grandes
en casa que es tan pequeña. (411)

Don Diego, now versed in the history of the cave as a result of his training, interprets what the marqués has heard as allegorical imagery and proceeds to explicate that the bronze oracular head symbolizes Enrico:

[Y] porque excede a la naturaleza
frágil del hombre su saber inmenso,
se dice que es de bronce su cabeza. (412)

And this is the sage who freely teaches his magical arts in his one-room windowless house, wherein the sun can enter only through the door, which setting is a metaphor for the famed cave. To Don Diego, what had seemed the humblest of abodes has become glorious, as he explains to his beloved, Doña Clara, in scene 14:

> No ya humilde la llames, pues ha sido
> oriente celestial de luz tan nueva. (415)

Don Diego's description juxtaposes, first, the preconception of the image of the dark cave and the revelation that it is a place that provides light, in other words, enlightens with new knowledge; next, the nether locale of the cave and its celestial dimension, both as an orientation and as a reference to the East, from whence esoteric knowledge comes; and, finally, the old lore and the new wisdom. Both Enrico's teachings and the place in which they are imparted are presented in a positive manner. Yet, when in act 2, scenes 5 and 6, the magicians are in Enrico's cave, there is no description given nor any indication in the dialogue of its aspects; the playwright, who had given detailed stage directions in the previous scene for the magical tricks played on Don Diego's servant, Zamudio, has nothing to say concerning the cave. As is the case in Calderón's *El mágico prodigioso,* the omission leaves the reader (and the director) to his or her own imaginings. But these are subvented by popular belief, which is influenced by a long oral tradition concerning the aspect of magical caves since antiquity as well as by written descriptions.

Don Diego is the bridge between the supernatural inner realm of the cave and the external world of reality. His interest in entering the grotto to learn magic stems from practical needs in the world he inhabits: to secure his and his fellow conspirators' freedom, on the one hand, and to sexually possess Doña Clara since he lacks the financial means to be an acceptable suitor for her hand. When, in the last scene of act 2, Don Diego's passion for Doña Clara drives him to attempt to take her illicitly, his action vitiates magic's positive aspect, as William Blake has it: "When thought is closed in caves, then love shall show its root in deepest Hell" (*The Four Zoas*, 344). Having forgone love for lust, courtliness for dishonor, Don Diego has also perverted the esoteric knowledge provided by his study of natural magic when entering Doña Clara's bedroom through the ruse of assuming the shape of the bronze statue that he has had delivered in a large wooden box. When Clara first opens the box, the statue is, indeed, inside; but, when she returns after an interruption and again accesses it, Don Diego has taken the place of the statue through his magical prowess. To her fear that he is an apparition, and to protestations of his presence in her bedroom, he proclaims:

> Yo soy la verdad, señora;
> que el bronce fue la ilusión.
> Por estar aquí Lucía
> aquella forma tomé . . .
> te escriví que si quisieras
> saber nuevas verdaderas
> de amor y misterios raros,
> en pasando la mitad
> de la noche, sola hablaras
> con la estatua. (442–43)

When he attempts to impose his nefarious will on her, she fights him, exclaiming that his hellish magic cannot overcome her free will. But the act concludes ambiguously, without indication of whose will will triumph.[51]

The last act commences with Don Diego's declaration to Villena of his resolve to use the aid of Enrico's magic to free Don García, imprisoned as a result of the murderous conduct of the gallants early in the play. But the marqués offers instead to intervene with the king. Yet, no doubt by magic, Don García's prison is open and unguarded when Don Diego arrives to rescue his friend. Having freed other prisoners as well, Don Diego magically sets fire to the prison records and orders the warden, who has been forced to provide them, to tell the corregidor that he will burn as well if he does not pardon him and his cronies. Instead, the corregidor imprisons Enrico.

The confrontation of the power of magic and the power of the state has come to a head. The king orders a convening of all concerned before a tribunal of theologians at the University of Salamanca, during which Enrico will present his arguments pro magic as a natural science. In scene 15, the last in the play, the magician proceeds with great eloquence to delineate the positive aspects of his art, his long disquisition founded on a syllogistic statement:

> Propongo desta manera:
> toda ciencia natural
> es lícita, y usar della

es permitido; la magia
es natural: luego es buena. (461)

While his reasoned arguments ring true for many, the rebuttal by the learned Doctor is longer and more convincing; its efficacy relies on church doctrines concerning the role of the Devil in human affairs. He posits that Satan uses those types of magic deemed licit, those founded on natural laws or on artifice, to his own ends:

[M]as con capa de las dos
disimulada y cubierta,
el demonio entre los hombres
introdujo la tercera.

He goes on to define this illicit form of magic:

La diabólica se funda
en el pacto y convenencia
que con el demonio hizo
el primer inventor della. (464)

Following the rhetorical practices of argumentation then prevailing, he proceeds to a series of proofs of his position, with the intent of influencing the thought and future conduct of his listeners:

Pruébolo así: por virtud
de palabras esta ciencia
obra prodigios, que admira
la misma naturaleza;
luego los obra en virtud
del pacto implícito en ellas,
contraído del demonio. (464–65)

At the end of the Spaniard's lengthy presentation on magic as diabolically inspired and implemented, the French magician Enrico admits that the arguments have convinced him of his error; he will abandon the practice of magic, acknowledging that it is evil and perverse.[52] Through the confrontations of these two philosophies—one pagan, the other Catholic—Ruiz de Alarcón brings to bear his knowledge of both and resolves the matter of magic's place in the scheme of Christian society. In a time and place in which the church holds the dominant position, the debate is won by the learned doctor, a member of the Order of Saint Dominic, which was in charge of the Holy Office of the Inquisition. Whatever the playwright's personal inclination, the *comedia,* as a public vehicle of entertainment and instruction, had to adhere to the tenets of the church.

Curiously, in the light of the importance of the cave, there is no mention of it in the doctor's oration, nor does Enrico say anything in regard to the place where he conducted his magical operations. Is the expectation that, since Enrico will no longer function as a magician, the cave will simply be abandoned? Or will it cease to exist, as if it had been an illusion sustained by the magician? Or will it simply cease to be effective without its tenant, returning to its natural state? Or is it valid to assume that the cave will continue to be a magical setting awaiting another who will enter its recesses to seek personal empowerment?

And what of the famed marqués de Villena? Will he be the next occupant of the nether premises? It is ironic that, while Enrico is imprisoned and then made to defend his cause, the marqués remains untouched by the authorities, no doubt untainted by his association with magic because of his social and political stature. Ruiz de Alarcón felt it necessary, at least, to address the issues of the cave and the marqués, for he has the actor who played that role step out of character to address the public:

> Y porque es justo
> que el noble auditorio sepa
> por qué dicen que engañó
> el gran Marqués de Villena
> al demonio con su sombra,
> oíd: la razón es ésta.
> Como el Marqués estudió
> esta diabólica ciencia,
> tuvo el infierno esperanza
> de su perdición eterna;
> mas murió tan santamente
> que engañó al demonio; y ésa
> es la causa porque dicen
> que con la sombra le deja. (469–70)

It is strange that, while the marqués de Villena plays a secondary role, both as a character and as a magician and has been presented more as a man of reason than as a necromancer, Ruiz de Alarcón felt it necessary to address the lore regarding his involvement with the Devil in the practice of goetic magic and his ultimate mockery of his master, although the latter is a mere accommodation to Christianity rather than a valid interpretation of the magical operation behind the popular belief. Having dealt with that matter, however inadequately, the playwright has left only the cave, and he deals with that in the *comedia*'s final speech:

> Y con ésto demos fin
> a la historia verdadera
> del principio, y fin que tuvo
> en Salamanca la cueva,
> conforme a las tradiciones
> más comunes y más ciertas. (470)

It should be noted that the lines "principio, y fin que tuvo / en Salamanca la cueva" imply either that the *comedia* finalizes the "historia verdadera" of the cave (meaning that it will thereafter cease to be other than a natural setting) or that the play has delineated the purpose ("fin") or reason for the existence of the cave. Whether the cave will remain as a venue for magic is moot. In a sense, then, the dramatist has left an open ending while seeming to bring the play to closure.

Ruiz de Alarcón's *comedia de magia* is one of the two most representative plays on the Cave of Salamanca motif, for it deals directly with the magical setting. It is also the most moral, for it presents the marqués de Villena as one who has learned magic but does not succumb to the Devil's wiles, rather tricking the Old One as payment for his services. Making a fool of the Devil, such as deceiving the deceiver, is a practice much admired in Christianity.

The other play in which both the Cave of Salamanca and the marqués de Villena are manifest is Francisco de Rojas Zorrilla's *Lo que quería ver el marqués de Villena.* Well into the first act, the marqués de Villena enters as the wooer of Serafina, who immediately defines him as:

> Unico sois en las ciencias,
> Dueño de las experiencias
> Sin la costa de los años.
> Sois en la escuela el mayor
> Sugeto della, esto sé. (323)

The term *ciencias* covers, not only the traditional academic areas, but, as the conversation that follows indicates, also astrology. The marqués has attained the superior status at the University of Salamanca because of his broad knowledge, having accomplished this "[s]in la costa de los años," which implies both that he gained knowledge very quickly and that the years have not taken their toll, that is, that his aspect is that of a young man rather than of a man who has been worn by having toiled over a long time to gain intellectual distinction.

But, as in *La Cueva de Salamanca,* the marqués gives way to another figure associated with supernatural pursuits, the masterly magician Fileno. As with Villena's appreciation of Enrico in Ruiz de Alarcón's play, Rojas Zorrilla's marqués is delighted by the encounter with the older magician at the *tertulia* in Serafina's house, a gathering of minds that she calls her *academia.* In the engaging discourse that ensues, Fileno posits:

> Digo que la magia es
> La ciencia más necesaria,
> Más útil y más perfecta.
> . . .
> Digo que la magia es una
> Filosofía perfecta,
> Y es una ciencia evidente,
> Que si el hombre la alcanzara,
> Todo cuanto deseara
> Consiguiera facilmente.

His brief apologia troubles the marqués, who retorts: "La magia está prohibida." In reply Fileno, like Feijoo later on, divides the field into categories:

> La natural no lo está,
> La diabólica será
> La que lo es.

Villena immediately resolves to learn this science as well, saying: "Eso es lo que yo he de ver" (323). It is this curiosity that the title of the play echoes and that Fileno will satisfy. As the act draws to an end, the magician invites the marqués to visit his abode the next day.

Act 2, then, opens with Villena and his servant Zambapalo[53] at the cave of the magician Fileno. The *gracioso* is afraid even to knock on the door:

Porque deste hombre me cuentan
Que tiene en una redoma
Un demonio.

The idea of a demon in the flask seems outlandish to Villena, but his servant's fear is based on his experience of having been in the cave, whose configuration he gives in great detail:

Es larga como señor
De otros tiempos; es estrecha,
Como mercader de ahora,
Y oscura como conciencia
De letrado que recibe
Cualquiera pleito que venga.
Está en el zaguan la sala
Y la alcoba en una pieza,
Y aunque no hay cocina, es
Todo el cuarto chimenea.
Hay en aquesta espelunca,
Alcázar de la Noruega,
Un lampión, que desde el techo
De un cordel de lazo cuelga,
Que no alumbra tanto cuanto,
Mancha á los que salen y entran;
Sola la puerta es un ojo
Por donde un rayo aún no entra.
. . .
No tienen polvo sus libros,
Pero como es la cueva
Tan húmeda, tiene lodo,
Ya podrida la madera. (328)

How Zambapalo got to enter the cave is not explained here, but the impact of that visit left an indelible impression, as his description makes clear. For the marqués, the aspect of the cave and its contents elicits, not fear, but admiration for the man who has chosen to live in such humble surroundings despite his magical powers. Nonetheless, Zambapalo appears to have cause to warn his master not to cross the threshold of the cave, both for the dangers it may contain and for the negative association that doing so would create in anyone who saw him. But the marqués de Villena will not abandon his quest for esoteric knowledge. The mystery of the magician and the cave lures him on, and he enters the cave's confines as the door opens without human agency.

A moment later, Villena and his servant are greeted by Fileno, accompanied by Bermúdez, one of the competitors for a *cátedra* (chair) at the university. When he leaves, Fileno promises his distinguished guest:

> Hoy no ha de salir de aquí
> Sin que antes experimente
> Si hay magia
> . . .
> Pues pida
> Imposibles vuecelencia,
> Que á imposibles se prefiere
> Mi ciencia.
> . . .
> Pues sin salir desta cueva
> Ha de ver cuanto quisiere. (331)

Villena asks to see all that occurs that night in the city, and Fileno obliges by showing him the events in a mirror—first a comic scene in which hungry university students steal a turkey, next a scene with Bermúdez hiding in a lady's bedroom, then a scene in Serafina's house, and finally a return to Bermúdez as he discovers the lady's secret and is in turn discovered—through which the marqués sees unraveled before him all the complex interpersonal relationships and learns that he is desired by two women. Yet, despite the magical display that he has witnessed, he is loath to admit that magic exists, and the act ends when Fileno waves his wand and the vision disappears.

In the third and final act, Fileno invites Zambapalo and the student Cetina to visit his cave in the morning, adding as an explanation:

> Mis discípulos no más
> Son á los que yo convido. (341)

Thus, it becomes clear that Zambapalo's first visit to the cave was in his role as sorcerer's apprentice. Now he has been asked back, as Fileno explains: "[P]ero en llegando el día / Veréis. . . . / *Lo que quería / Ver el marqués de Villena*" (341). Fileno has convened his four disciples of the moment:

Zambapalo, Cetina, Bermúdez, and the marqués de Villena. When they have come to the cave, Fileno locks the door, tells them of the past master who taught him magic, and informs them of his intent:

> Ese, cuando me enseñaba,
> Con condición me enseñó
> Esta ciencia no adquirida,
> Que aquí venís a aprender,
> Que su esclavo había de ser
> Como en la muerte en la vida,
> Y que de cuantos mi engaño
> Engañase la magia,
> Un discípulo le había
> De dar por feudo cada año,
> Y como faltar no puede
> Este paso. . . .
> . . .
> Cada año se ha de sortear
> Uno que conmigo quede;
> Todos suertes han echado
> Para esta satisfacion;
> Trece discípulos son
> Los que en trece años le he dado;
> Y así, si hoy os conformais
> A obedecer lo que os digo,
> Uno de los cuatro que aquí estaís. (345)

When the four disciples voice their disbelief at his diabolic plan, since none had made a pact, the magician voices his last dictum:

> Aquí ha de quedarse uno
> O los cuatro han de quedar. (345)

Resigned to the magician's power, each of the four selects a slip of paper from a pot proferred by Fileno. The one who selects the unmarked piece will be the loser. And that lot falls to the marqués de Villena. Nobly, Bermúdez wants to revoke the decision, but Villena insists on its execution. Unknown to all, he has formed a plan. He grabs Zambapalo before he can exit with the other two and speaks his intent:

El sol he de escurecer,
No me he de apartar de aquí:
A la noche semejante,
Vario el dia quedará;
Ninguno conocerá
Propio ni ajeno semblante.
. . .
Pues ahí queda mi sombra. (346)

Suddenly, all is dark. And when Fileno attempts to grab the marqués, his arms enfold Zambapalo instead. The marqués de Villena has disappeared. He has left behind his "shadow," his servant, who proclaims in recognition, as if of a great truth: "En efeto, los criados / Son sombra de los señores." Unlike the lame explanation in Ruiz de Alarcón's *La Cueva de Salamanca,* the motif of the shadow rings true here as a feasible substitution in magical terms. The self-assurance that Fileno had demonstrated throughout now abandons the magician as he comes to his own recognition of what his failure portends when, as the stage direction indicates, he sees that "*salen por debajo de la tierra diferentes animales con luces,*" the lights that the creatures bear being the torches traditionally symbolic of the underworld. Fileno cries out in despair at the terrible fate that awaits him:

¡Ay, el Marqués me engañó!
Vive mi pena inmortal,
Con la magia natural
La diabólica burló.
. . .
Y al espíritu también
Que me gobierna ha burlado. (346)

Fully cognizant that he has failed to keep his diabolical vow, Fileno resigns himself to his damnation. There is no soul-searching, as with Marlowe's Faust, no hedging one's bets by calling for confession, as with Celestina. Momentarily, as the stage direction has it, "[*h*]*úndese debajo de la tierra*" (346), he is swallowed by the earth, going into depths beyond those of any cave. His descent is into hell, for, in exclaiming the word *Infierno* as he falls, the entire magical context of the *comedia* leading up to his demise takes on the aspect of the Devil's work. Except for a few exclamations of the word *Diablo* by the *gracioso,* Satan had been excluded from the proceedings. But now, with Fileno's final utterance, the purveyor of goetic magic is identified as the Devil, and, in that context, Fileno's damnation to hell is established.

The aftermath of this theatrical *desenlace* (unraveling) is the promised reappearance of the marqués at Serafina's house, where others have gathered at his earlier behest. The event is not anticlimactic, for there are still concerns and problems to be resolved. To the many questions that the company poses, the marqués replies:

> Burlé al mágico Fileno,
> Porque tiene tanta fuerza
> La natural magia, que
> La demoniaca mesma
> Quedó burlada con ser
> Espíritu quien la enseña. (346)

The spirit, of course, is the Devil. In mocking his servant Fileno, the marqués has mocked the master as well. But that was not the reason for his quest. Finally, the marqués de Villena reveals through individual disclosures what it is that he wants to see: the truth. And, as each masquerader is uncovered, each sentiment expressed, each desire made manifest, it becomes clear that illusion disguised in falsehood or in courtly manners cannot be rewarded. Just as the falsehood of the magician Fileno came to an end, so too the play ends with none of the principals achieving their convoluted goals. Love does not triumph in the end, for it was perverted by all kinds of subterfuge. Even the marqués de Villena partakes of the general disillusionment, for he has, indeed, seen the truth that he wanted to see and, hereafter, must sublimate both sexual and intellectual expectations.

The topos of the cave and the magician, foreshadowed in Spanish literature in Don Juan Manuel's exemplum, attained its frequency in the *comedias* of the Golden Age because it satisfied an intellectual need in the dramatist and addressed an intuitive curiosity in his public—the former saw the motif as an entertaining way to delve into human psychology by assessing the desire for power and control through supernatural means, while the latter was awed by the chthonic setting and the magical occurrences within and without its confines. However, as the church became increasingly powerful, both in spiritual and in political terms, it interpreted as heterodox and, therefore, sinful all attempts at empowerment or knowledge outside what Christianity promoted as acceptable. Magic and magicians became associated with the Devil, as had witchcraft and witches. And the caves that they used were seen as malevolent places, without regard to the type of magic practiced or its ends.

In a Christian context then, the crucial element in *comedias de magia* became the struggle between good and evil, whose result for human beings could be salvation (à la Cipriano) or damnation (à la Fileno).[54] In Calderón to a large degree, and in Rojas Zorrilla to a lesser, the religious aspect of the *agon* was the climactic moment: the decision of the individual to persist in his nefarious ways or to use his *albedrío* (free will) to reclaim his Christian status (to emerge from the cave, as it were). In the plays by Cervantes and Ruiz de Alarcón, the focus is different: a burlesque on people's gullibity without recourse to magic or religion in the first and a largely secular treatment, although with an intellectually motivated conversion to "the right path," in the second.

The plays discussed here are exemplary of the several dimensions of the theme. To a greater or lesser degree, directly or through subterfuge, with positive or negative attitudes, all of them reify evil through the topos of the cave and the magician.

The sophistication of the Renaissance prompted a reassessment of medieval thought, and this, in turn, may have brought about the eschewing of *catabasis,* thus of the cave associated with the descent since classical times. The growing impact of science and the scientific method no doubt infringed on superstition and slowly eroded its premises, although the presence of astrologers and alchemists persisted. Another form of sophistication, the Protestant Reformation, may have contributed to the elimination of the topos as well since the cave had affinities with the Catholic theology that many new rebellious congregations had abandoned, even condemned as hellishly inspired. Such generalizations may help explain why the magician's cave is absent as such from the English stage in Elizabethan and Jacobean times as well as from the plays of the same era in France, Italy, and Germany—but not why it remains in place in the Spanish Golden Age. Since it was Spain that led the Counter-Reformation with such entities as the militant Society of Jesus, founded by Ignacio de Loyola in 1534, it could be argued that the staunchly Catholic nation remained a repository of the medieval religious heritage and that motifs such as the cave with its association with the Devil were important in promoting the dangerous proximity of the Lord of Evil. The stories of blood pacts with the Devil signed in his caves by magicians, priests, nobility, and the general laity were simply too valuable as exempla to be dismissed, and the playwrights of the Golden Age, many of them members of religious orders or otherwise affiliated with them, did their best to maintain a tradition that had served the church so well.

Notes

1. These and other Paleolithic cave sites in Southern Europe contain many chambers on whose walls and ceilings are depicted bison, reindeer, mammoths, horses, bulls, and rhinoceros, many of which are pregnant, others shot through with arrows or spears. In a few instances, there are human figures, as at Lascaux in France (the ithyphallic warrior or shaman) and Addaura in Sicily (figures of dancers or acrobats), but they are line drawings without the detail and coloration that distinguish the animal figures. Some caves also contain stenciled human hands. In southern Spain, black "stick" figures of hunters appear in many caves.

2. The dominance of agriculture over the pastoral way of life may be implied by the importance of its ritual tradition in ancient Greece, but, in the biblical context, Yahweh accepts the blood sacrifice proffered by Abel and disdains the burnt offering of the earth's produce made by Cain.

3. *Delphi* means "vagina." Before its conquest by Apollo, Delphi was the site of Pytho, the oracle of Ge or Gaea, the Earth Goddess, who is today's Gaia. Emanations from a cleft in the hillside induced the state of prophetic trance (see Harpur, 196–201; and Michell, 86).

4. As Michell tells it: "The experience of the descent and confrontation with the goddess was so dreadful that whoever underwent it was said never to smile again" (80).

5. Sybil was the Latin form of Cybele, the Phrygian's Great Mother of the Gods, whose name means "cavern dweller." In Crete, she was known as Rhea, who gave birth to Zeus and hid him from Cronus (Saturn) in her cave. Her cult was brought to Rome in 204 B.C.E.

6. The Greek tradition, which seems to occur first in Pindar, continues in Roman times with Propertius, Horace, and Virgil (see Berg, 116–17).

7. I have referred to three different translations, each with commentary: the Lee, Jowett/Buchanan, and Cornford editions.

8. There is a parallel in Calderón's *La vida es sueño,* in which Segismundo has been imprisoned in a tower by his father, the king of Poland, and kept ignorant of reality and his place in it as man and as heir to the throne.

9. This image retains its power in many mystical systems, notably in the concept *cárcel de barro,* which defines the entrapment of the soul as it strives toward God, in the writings of Saint Teresa of Avila and Saint John of the Cross in the Spanish Golden Age.

10. For a discussion of the soul and its relation to matter, see Plato's *Timaeus.*

11. Christianity named the abode of Lucifer after the Norse goddess Hel, perhaps in an attempt to sever the bonds with the classical underworld, which was a place of the dead, not of eternal punishment, and its lord, Pluto or Hades.

12. However, catacombs in Rome and other locales served early Christians as

refuges from persecution, as secret places of worship, and as secure resting ground for their dead. In Cappadocia, in central Anatolia (Turkey), the natural upheavals of stone and tufa brought about by volcanic activity made possible the creation of cave dwellings for prehistoric peoples and Christian monks alike (as at Goreme) as well as extensive underground cities that were entered through narrow, cavelike corridors and that were serviced by air shafts, water wells, and other amenities.

13. After *goetia,* the Greek term for a wizard, necromancer, or magician who practiced malevolent magic. Goetic magic is sometimes associated with the Wandering Jew topos. Agrippa posited that there were two kinds of magic—goetic and theurgic—the latter being empowerment through positive forces that he called *angelic, celestial,* or *planetary* spirits.

14. While this was a solemn act, i.e., one performed in the context of Satanic worship, its counterpart, the *professio tacita,* was a private profession, usually through heretical actions or by commitment of service to the Devil through another individual. Tradition has it that Theophilus of Adana was the first to sign a demonic pact in blood. For the history of the Devil pact, see Lima, *Dark Prisms,* chap. 3.

15. Magicians are not only males. Celestina, the central character in *Tragicomedia de Calixto y Melibea,* is herself a magician, although perceived by society as a witch (see chapter 3 above).

16. Alchemists sought to accomplish the "great work" through physical agency rather than via demonic forces. They are, in their distinct way, magicians as well. Plays dealing with alchemy are not discussed in this book because they do not fit the topic and are generally of a mocking tone.

17. Another damned magician is Pope Alexander VI (Roderigo Borgia) in Barnabe Barnes's *The Divils Charter* (ca. 1607), an anti-Catholic play in which the papacy is attained by the agency of bribery and a demonic pact. Perhaps fearing that the pope will repent the avarice, incest, and murder that he has committed, Lucifer switches a poisoned cup, and Alexander dies without the benefit of confession, his soul damned to eternal punishment in hell.

Quite the opposite occurs in two other Elizabethan plays. In the anonymous *Merry Devil of Edmonton,* the magician Peter Fabell comes to the end of his tenure under the demonic pact that he has signed, but, when Coreb comes to drag him to hell, he philosophizes so brilliantly that he convinces the demon of his need to stay alive:

> The infinity of Arts is like a sea,
> Into which, when man will take in hand to saile
> further then reason, which should be his pilot,
> Hath skill to guide him, losing once his compasse,
> He falleth to such deepe and dangerous whirlepooles,
> As he doth lose the very height of heauen:
> The more he striues to come to quiet harbor,
> The further still he finds himselfe from land.
> Man, striving still to finde the depth of euill,
> Seeking to be a God, becomes a Deuill. (prologue [induction], lines 50–58; pp. 110–11)

Through the process of induction, he is granted another seven-year term on earth.

Similarly, if with better results, Friar Bacon argues with the demon Astrow in the anonymous *John of Bordeaux* that he has no power over a Christian's faith, and the spirit accedes by continuing in his service rather than dragging him to hell. The supposition is that Bacon's stature as a friar will prevent his damnation (see Traister, 51–52).

18. In his treatment of Faust, Marlowe ignored much of the grotesque, outlandish, and melodramatic scenes in Johann Spies's *Faustbuch* (*Historia von D. Johann Fausten*), published in England in 1587 as *The Damnable Life and Deserved Death of Doctor John Faustus.* Marlowe, in fact, chose to portray Faust ironically for having squandered his soul only to perform trivial acts of magic and pranks; except for the Helen of Troy episode, the play shows him dissipating his unparalleled powers and failing to grasp important opportunities, including opportunities to gain the vast knowledge he had said he sought.

19. As both Peter Gay and Dagmar Barnouw have shown, German creative writers, artists, and intellectuals reached a rapprochement with political and civil authorities regarding the free exercise of their creative prerogatives. For their part, writers, artists, and intellectuals avoided subjects of a controversial nature, being deferential toward authorities and institutions; rather than engaged, they were detached. This modus vivendi left the proponents of culture free from censorship or other forms of intrusion. However, their apparent liberalization has been perceived by Gay and Barnouw as a Faustian bargain that, in time, led to the fall of the Weimar Republic and the institutionalization of the Nazi regime.

20. The *Key of Solomon,* or *Clavicula salomonis,* was a Hebrew magical text that contained the rituals and formulaic words purportedly giving access to the supernatural world and the spirits thereof. It was published in France (as a pamphlet and at an unknown time) as *Les véritables clavicules de Salomon, trésor de sciences occultes suivies [de] grand nombre de secrets, et notamment de la grande Cabale dite du papillon vert.*

21. Tradition has it that to know the name of a person or thing is to have power over it, hence Mephistopheles' reluctance to disclose his identity to Faust. Similarly, the true name of God is hidden from mankind; cabalists try to decipher it by reworking the order and relation of letters and numbers in the Pentateuch, the first five books of the Old Testament. A recent History Channel program, *The Biblical Codes,* has proposed that the Torah predicts future events through the relations of letters and numbers encoded in its texts.

22. This last onomastic derives from the biblical Baal-zebub (2 Kings 1:2), commonly Beelzebub.

23. In *The Divils Charter* (England, ca. 1607) by Barnabe (or Barnaby) Barnes, the protagonist, Pope Alexander VI (Roderigo Borgia), performs a conjuration in his study (act 4, sc. 1) in order to learn of the Devil, who murdered his son and Lucretia's husband. Toward the end of the play (act 5, last scene), the Devil is seated at the pope's desk, having materialized without being conjured; he has come to bear the magician's soul to hell. Alexander tries to exorcise him, but the Devil mocks his attempt, arguing that he gave up his soul's salvation through his own free will. The pope's philosophical pleadings not withstanding, the demonic host carry his soul off to hell triumphantly. His corpse remains in his study.

24. The Welsh magician Owen Glendower appears in *Henry the Fourth, Part 1,* but, as his supernatural machinations antecede the action, they have no importance in the development of the plot. Magic is a prime element in *A Midsummer Night's Dream,* with Titania and Oberon as the principal movers, and in *The Tempest,* where Prospero performs his many feats, while magical operations of other types occur in *Hamlet* and *Macbeth.*

25. In other instances, the magician stands within the circle, using its encryptions as personal protection from the spirits that will become manifest outside its boundaries.

26. Ariel may be modeled on Shrimp, the elflike magician's facilitator in Anthony Munday's *John a Kent and John a Cumber* (England, ca. 1595) (see Reed, 109–10).

27. A Gnostic reading would equate Prospero with the God of Light, his cell/*cella* with the pleroma, and Caliban with the negative supernatural forces outside the pleroma, along with Sycorax and the Devil.

28. The play is based, if loosely, on the English prose romance *The Famous Historie of Fryer Bacon.*

29. For a comment on the subsequent use of magic by Friar Bacon in the play *John of Bordeaux,* see Traister, 86 n. 24.

30. In Munday's play *John a Kent and John a Cumber,* there is a reference to the vault as cave when Griffin asks the magician John a Kent: "Canst thou my freend, from foorth the vaultes beneathe, / call vp the ghosts of those long since deceast?" (act 1, sc. 1, lines 108–9; p. 64). This image may have had currency in Shakespeare's day, or he may have borrowed it from Munday.

31. The incantation translates as follows: "Emperor of the legions of the spirits of the West, mighty Behemoth, appear, appear, attended by Ashtaroth, thy unvanquished lieutenant! I adjure thee by the inscrutable secrets of the Styx, by the irretraceable windings of Hell, be present, O Behemoth, thou for whom the cabinets of the mighty lie open. By the secret depths of Night and Darkness, by the wandering stars, by the stealthy march of the hours and Hecate's deep silence, come! Appear in spiritual form, gleaming, resplendent, lovely" (Chapman/Parrott, 53).

32. The appendix lists numerous court masques that contain occult elements.

33. For an assessment of the evolution of the character Hellequin, its antecedents and its derivates, see chapter 2 above.

34. In time, Théophile repents and prays to the Virgin Mary for redemption. Seeing him truly repentant, Mary wrests the pact from Satan and returns it to Théophile. The miracle play ends with everyone singing the glory of God.

35. For a list of plays on the subject, see Lima, "Spanish Drama," 117–38, or *Dark Prisms,* chap. 9.

36. Celestina performed her Plutonic magic in her house, in a place apart from the prying eyes of all, and her retiring thereto could arguably be interpreted as removal to a basement or some similar underground area appropriate to contact with the pagan Lord of the Underworld (see chapter 3 above).

For instances in the pastoral narrative in which caves are so employed, see de Armas. For a study of Don Quijote's descent into the cave of Montesinos in pt. 2 of Cervantes's novel, see Sullivan.

37. Calderón's play, a favorite in Germany, is held to have been a model for Goethe's *Faust.*

38. The play tells the story of two who would become the early Christian martyrs Saint Cyprian and Saint Justina, Virgin.

39. For another interpretation, see Varey, 255–56.

40. This document was subsumed into the *Crónica general* of 1344 (see Ruiz de la Puerta, 53–54).

41. Another such tradition is extant in La Coruña, in Galicia, with the so-called Tower of Hercules, a Roman lighthouse that still stands. The *Crónica del moro Rasis* (ca. 1344) recounts of Toledo: "[F]ue una de las quatro cibdades que Ercoles pobló en España" (it was one of the four cities that Hercules founded in Spain) (quoted in Carré Alvarellos, 144).

42. In *Crónica general de España de Alfonso X el Sabio* (1275), there is an account of a King Rocas, said to be a descendant of Hercules, who during his travels came on a cave in the area that would become Toledo: "[F]allo y una cueva en ques metio o yazie un dragon muy grand . . . e fizo una torre sobraquella cueva" (Ruiz de la Puerta, 48). Later documents added to or liberally changed the account: in the 1440 rewriting of the *Crónica general de 1344,* the legend has it that it was Hercules himself who made the structure but that it was changed from a tower to "una casa tan maravillosa, e por tal harte, que nunca en el mundo fue ome que verdaderamente sopiere dezir como era fecha" (Ruiz de la Puerta, 49), while, in an Arabic chronicle written by Al-Makkari, it is the Greeks who build the tower as a talisman to protect the city of Toledo, which they founded, from the enemies predicted by their astrological readings. For these and other versions of the legend of the tower, palace, and cave, see Ruiz de la Puerta, 45–63.

43. Virgil's first use of this device occurs in canto 3, lines 94–96, when Charon refuses passage to Dante across Acheron, the first river of hell. Virgil states: "Charon, do not torment yourself. / It is so willed where will and power are one, and ask no more" (49). A second and similar use of the formula occurs in canto 5, lines 22–24, when Minos, the judge who assigns souls their appropriate sector of hell, refuses to let Dante pass. The word of power is used on other occasions as well, as at the opening of canto 7 (lines 8–12), when Pluto bars the way. However, Virgil is impotent before the gates to the city of Dis (canto 8) and must await the arrival of a heavenly messenger, who rebukes the demons and lets Virgil and Dante enter nether hell (canto 9). Only in canto 21, lines 79–84, does he again employ the magical formula, this time in an extended text: "Consider, Malacoda, said my master, / whether you would see me come this far / unstopped by all your hindering / without the will of God and favoring fate? / Let us proceed, for it is willed in Heaven / that I guide another down this savage way" (355).

44. As is true of much of medieval European literature, this collection has been influenced by previous didactic tales, as Fradejas Rueda outlines in his edition (66–80). Likewise, it has influenced subsequent writers. Lope de Vega used the tale "Ejemplo XXV: De lo que conteçió al conde de Provençia, cómmo fue librado de prisión por el consejo quel dió Saladín," in his *La pobreza estimada,* as did Calderón de la Barca in *El Conde Lucanor.*

45. Where here the dean leaves without commenting on what he may have ex-

perienced—the panorama of his entire career in the church—the narrator in Luis Gálvez de Montalvo's *El pastor de Fílida* (1582), where a similar situation develops in the cave of the magician Erión, declares: "No se yo si esto fuere por fuerza de encantamiento o verdadero edificio" (474; I do not know if this came about through the power of enchantment or [is] a real structure). For the uses of the cave in the Spanish pastoral novel, see de Armas.

46. In Cervantes's *Los trabajos de Persiles y Segismunda,* the astrologer-magician Soldino inhabits a cave through which "se descubrió el cielo luciente y claro y se vieron unos amenos y tendidos prados que entretenían la vista y alegraban las almas" (1678) and within which he practices his art through intuitive knowledge: "Aquí estoy, donde sin libros, con sola la esperiencia que he adquirido con el tiempo de mi soledad" (1679).

47. Don Juan Manuel's tale also provided the central character for José de Cañizares's *Don Juan de Espina en Milán* and the duque de Rivas's *El desengaño en un sueño.*

48. Lope de Vega's *Porfiar hasta morir* does not, as some critics would have it, deal with the subject; Enrique de Villena is alluded to only as the master of the poet Macías, protagonist of Lope's *comedia,* but he never appears.

49. Cervantes's *La casa de los celos* contains a serpent cave.

50. A large number of Ruiz de Alarcón's *comedias* are concerned with magic, astrology (or other forms of divination), and various superstitions of an occult nature. Besides the play under consideration, these include most notably *Quien mal anda en mal acaba, El anticristo, La prueba de las promesas, El dueño de las estrellas,* and *La manganilla de Melilla* (see Espantoso Foley).

51. In act 2, sc. 2, Don Diego tells Zamudio what occurred thereafter, revealing that her resolve was so great and her laughter so mocking that he withdrew at the light of dawn, ashamed of his actions. He does not employ the ways of magic again to obtain his desire. Yet, despite his behavior, Doña Clara still loves him, and, when Don Diego inherits a title that guarantees his income, their marriage is assured.

52. Enrico's admission has another dimension, which is both religious and political: it represents the triumph of a learned churchman from Spain over a misguided magician from France; it is also the triumph of the Christian ethos under the aegis of Spain over the obscurantist practices of France that Enrico represents. Spain emerges as the "Defender of the Faith," a title that the nation and its rulers cherished from Ferdinand and Isabel through the Counter-Reformation.

53. The servant is named after an old dance and the tune that accompanies it, but the first part of his name (from the adjective *zambo, zamba*) also implies triply one who is knock-kneed, a half-breed (American Indian and Negro), and a variety of South American monkey. In the list of characters, the role is classified as "estudiante gorrón," which identifies him as a sponger or hanger-on as well as a libertine.

54. The church faced many interpretations of the struggle. Chief among them in the Middle Ages was that promoted by the Manichaeans, followers of the third-century Persian prophet Mani (or Manes) who proclaimed himself a new incarnation of Jesus Christ. Among his doctrines was that of the cosmic battle between the

God of Light and the Lord of Darkness; the former was the Gnostic Supreme Being, the latter was the Demiurge, identified with the Old Testament Yahweh. Mani and other Gnostics held that the Jewish and Christian deity was evil: "It is the Prince of Darkness who spoke with Moses, the Jews, and their priests. Thus the Christians, the Jews and the Pagans are involved in the same error when they worship this god" (Legge, 2:239). In an earlier context, also out of Persia, Mithraism saw the struggle as between the divine twins Ahura Mazda, the solar deity, and Ahriman, the deity of darkness.

Works Cited

Agrippa, Henry Cornelius. *The Philosophy of Natural Magic*. Secaucus, N.J.: University Books, 1974. Originally published as *De occulta philosophiae* (Cologne, 1533).

———. *Of the Vanitie and Uncertaintie of Artes and Sciences.* Translated by James Sanford. London, 1569.

Barnes, Barnabe. *The Divils Charter: A Tragedie.* ca. 1607. See Pogue 1980.

Barnouw, Dagmar. *Weimar Intellectuals and the Threat of Modernity.* Bloomington: Indiana University Press, 1988.

Berg, William. *Early Virgil.* London: Athlone, 1974.

Blake, William. *The Four Zoas.* 1797 (p. 65, v. 241; manuscript held in the British Library). Textual page citation refers to David V. Erdman, ed., *The Complete Poetry and Prose of William Blake.* New York: Doubleday, 1988.

Calderón de la Barca, Pedro. *El mágico prodigioso.* In *Obras completas,* 1:807–45. Madrid: Aguilar, 1959.

Carré Alvarellos, Leandro. *Las leyendas tradicionales gallegas.* Madrid: Espasa-Calpe, 1978.

Cervantes Saavedra, Miguel de. *La cueva de Salamanca.* In *Obras completas,* 587–93. Madrid: Aguilar, 1962.

———. *Los trabajos de Persiles y Segismunda.* In *Obras completas,* 1525–1714. Madrid: Aguilar, 1962.

Chapman, George. *The Plays and Poems of George Chapman.* Edited by T. M. Parrott. Vol. 1. London, 1910.

———. *Bussy d'Ambois.* Edited by Maurice Evans. Mermaid Dramabook. New York: Hill & Wang, 1966. All quotations are taken from this edition.

Cornford, F. M., trans. *Plato's Cosmology: The Timaeus of Plato.* London: Routledge & Kegan Paul, 1952.

Crónica general de España de Alfonso X el Sabio. 1275. Edited by Ramón Menéndez Pidal. Madrid, 1955.

Dante Alighieri. *Inferno.* Translated by Robert Hollander and Jean Hollander. New York: Doubleday, 2000.

Day Lewis, C., trans. *The Aeneid of Virgil.* Garden City, N.Y.: Doubleday/Anchor, 1953.

de Armas, Frederick A. "Caves of Fame and Wisdom in the Spanish Pastoral Novel." *Studies in Philology* (Durham) 82, no. 3 (summer 1985): 332–58.

Don Juan Manuel. *El Conde Lucanor.* Edited by José Manuel Fradejas Rueda. Biblioteca Crítica de Autores Españoles, vol. 27. Barcelona: Plaza & Janes, 1984.

Eliade, Mircea. *Le mythe de l'éterne retour.* Paris: Gallimard, 1949. Translated as *Cosmos and History: The Myth of the Eternal Return* by Willard R. Trask. New York: Harper & Row/Harper Torchbooks, 1959.

Espantoso Foley, Augusta. *Occult Arts and Doctrine in the Theater of Juan Ruiz de Alarcón.* Geneva: Droz, 1972.

Fadrejas Lebrero, José. "Un cuento de Don Juan Manuel y dos comedias del Siglo de Oro." *Revista de Literatura* (Madrid) 8, no. 5 (July–September 1955): 66–80.

The Famous Historie of Fryer Bacon. Edited by William J. Thoms. In *Early English Prose Romances,* vol. 1. New York: AMS, 1970.

Feijoo, Fray Benito Jerónimo. "Cuevas de Salamanca y Toledo, y mágica de España." In *Obras escogidas,* 374–81. Biblioteca de Autores Españoles, vol. 56. Madrid: Perlado, Páez, 1903.

Gálvez de Montalvo, Luis. *El pastor de Fílida.* 1582. In *Historia y antología española,* ed. Federico C. Sainz de Robles, 670–73. Madrid, 1964.

Gay, Peter. *Weimar Culture: The Outsider as Insider.* New York: Harper & Row, 1968.

Goethe, Johann Wolfgang von. *Faust: Part One and Part Two.* Translated, with an introduction and notes, by Charles E. Passage. New York: Bobbs-Merrill, 1965.

Gozzi, Carlo. *The King Stag.* Translated by Carl Wildman. In *The Classic Theatre,* ed. Eric Bentley, vol. 1. New York: Doubleday/Anchor, 1958.

Greene, Robert. *The Honorable History of Friar Bacon and Friar Bungay.* In *An Anthology of English Drama before Shakespeare,* ed. Robert B. Heilman, 167–240. New York: Holt, Rinehart & Winston, 1962.

Halle, Adam de la. *Le jeu de la feuillée.* Edited and translated by Jean Dufournet. Gand: Editions Scientifique, 1977.

Harpur, James. *The Atlas of Sacred Places.* New York: Holt, 1994.

Legge, Francis. *Forerunners and Rivals of Christianity.* 2 vols. New York: University Books, 1964.

Lima, Robert. "Spanish Drama of the Occult through the Eighteenth Century: An Annotated Bibliography of Primary Sources." In "The Occult Arts in the Golden Age," ed. Frederick A. de Armas. Special issue, *Crítica Hispánica* (Pittsburgh) 15, no. 1 (1993): 117–38.

———. *Dark Prisms: Occultism in Hispanic Drama.* Lexington: University Press of Kentucky, 1995.

———. "La Gueule de l'enfer: Iconographie de la damnation dans le théâtre de l'époque médiévale." In *Enfer et paradis: L'au-delà dans l'art et la littérature en Europe,* 205–18. Conques: Les Cahiers de Conques, March 1995. For an English translation, see Lima 1996.

———. "The Mouth of Hell: The Iconography of Damnation on the Stage of the Middle Ages." In *European Iconography East and West,* ed. György E. Szönyi, 35–48. Symbola et Emblemata Series. Leiden: Brill, 1996.

———. "The Arcane Paganism of Celestina: Plutonic Magic versus Satanic Witchcraft in *Tragicomedia de Calixto y Melibea.*" *Neophilologus* (Dordrecht) 82, no. 2 (April 1998): 221–33.

Lope de Vega Carpio, Félix. *Porfiar hasta morir.* In *Obras escogidas,* 3:1003–31. Madrid: Aguilar, 1955.

Marlowe, Christopher. *The Tragedy of Doctor Faustus.* New York: Washington Square, 1965.

The Merry Devil of Edmonton. In *The Shakespeare Apocrypha,* ed. C. F. Tucker Brooke, 265–84. Oxford: Oxford University Press, 1967.

Michell, John. *The Earth Spirit: Its Ways, Shrines and Mysteries.* New York: Crossroad, 1975.

Munday, Anthony. *John a Kent and John a Cumber.* ca. 1595. Edited by Arthur E. Pennell. New York: Garland, 1980.

Niklaus, Thelma. *Harlequin Phoenix; or, The Rise and Fall of a Bergamask Rogue.* London: Bodley Head, [1956]. For the text of *Harlequin Student; or, The Fall of Pantomime, with the Restoration of the Drama* (1741), see 200–207.

Plato. *The Republic.* Translated, with an introduction, by H. D. P. Lee. London: Penguin, 1955.

———. "The Republic, Book VII." In *The Portable Plato,* trans. Benjamin Jowett, ed., with an introduction by, Scott Buchanan, 546–84. New York: Viking, 1957.

———. *The Republic of Plato.* Translated, with an introduction and notes, by Francis MacDonald Cornford. London: Oxford University Press, 1967.

———. *Timaeus.* See Cornford 1952.

Pogue, Jim C., ed. *"The Devil's Charter" by Barnabe Barnes: A Critical Edition.* New York: Garland, 1980.

Reed, Robert R., Jr. *The Occult on the Tudor and Stuart Stage.* Boston: Christopher, 1965.

Rojas Zorrilla, Francisco de. *Lo que quería ver el marqués de Villena.* In *Comedias escogidas de don Francisco de Rojas Zorrilla,* 319–48. Biblioteca de Autores Españoles, 54. Madrid: M. Rivadeneyra, 1866.

Ruiz de Alarcón, Juan. *La Cueva de Salamanca.* In *Obras completas de Juan Ruiz de Alarcón,* 1:383–470. México, D.F.: Fondo de Cultura Económica, 1957.

———. *La prueba de las promesas.* In *Obras completas de Juan Ruiz de Alarcón,* 2:742–825. México, D.F.: Fondo de Cultura Económica, 1957.

Ruiz de la Puerta, Fernando. *La cueva de Hércules y el Palacio encantado de Toledo.* Madrid: Editora Nacional, 1977.

Rutebeuf. *Le miracle de Théophile.* Paris: Librairie Ancienne Edouard Champion, 1925.

Shakespeare, William. *The Works of William Shakespeare Gathered into One Volume.* New York: Oxford University Press, n.d.

Spies, Johann. *Faustbuch.* 1587. Amsterdam: Rodopi, 1970. Also known as *Volksbuch.*

Sullivan, Henry W. "The Beyond in the Here-and-Now: Passing through Purgatory in *Don Quixote, Part Two.*" In "The Occult Arts in the Golden Age," ed. Frederick A. de Armas. Special issue, *Crítica Hispánica* (Pittsburgh) 15, no. 1 (1993): 63–84.

Traister, Barbara Howard. *Heavenly Necromancers: The Magician in English Renaissance Drama.* Columbia: University of Missouri Press, 1984.

Varey, John E. "Calderón y sus trogloditas." In *Cosmovisión y escenografía: El teatro español en el Siglo de Oro,* 249–61. Madrid: Castalia, 1987.

Walker, Barbara G. *The Woman's Encyclopedia of Myths and Secrets.* San Francisco: Harper & Row, 1983.

Appendix

Bibliography of European and American Drama of the Occult

The first list below is of plays from classical Greece and Rome, England, France, Germany, Ireland, Italy, Poland, Russia, Spain, and Sweden as well as other European nations, along with those from the United States, that fall under the broad theme of occultism. The plays are arranged alphabetically by author; for each are given, where known, author's birth and death dates, publication date, and pertinent contents. The second list gathers plays under prominent occult themes or motifs. (While only four plays are listed under the heading *astrology,* the reader should note that almost all Renaissance plays are concerned with astrology to a greater or lesser degree.) Plays from Spain and Spanish America are not listed here if they appear in the comprehensive bibliography in Robert Lima, *Dark Prisms: Occultism in Hispanic Drama* (Lexington: University Press of Kentucky, 1995).

Bibliographies, anthologies, encyclopedias, histories, critical studies, and articles on national literatures and dramatists, sources too numerous to list here in their entirety but most of which appear in the lists of works consulted, have provided the information given in this international compilation; among these are the various Oxford University Press "Companion" volumes; the journals the *Tulane Drama Review* and its sequel the *Drama Review, Modern Drama,* and *Theatre Documentation; The Occult in Language and Literature,* ed. Hermine Riffaterre (New York: New York Literary Forum, 1980); *Chambers Biographical Dictionary,* ed. Magnus Magnusson (Cambridge: Chambers, 1993); *A History of Witchcraft,* by Montague Summers (New York: University Books, 1956); and *The Reader's Encyclopedia of World Drama,* ed. John Gassner and Edward Quinn (New York: Crowell, 1969). Among others, I consulted the following in the field of English drama, by far the most representative in occult content: *Annals of English Drama, 975–1700,* comp. Alfred Harbage, rev. S. Schoenbaum (Philadelphia: University of Pennsylvania Press, 1964); *Chester Plays,* ed. Hermann Deimling, EETS, England, Extra Series, nos. 62 and 115, (London: Early English Text Society, 1893); *The Digby Plays,* ed. F. J. Furnivall, EETS, England, Extra Series, no. 70 (London: Early English Text Society, 1896); *Dodsley's Old English Plays,* ed. W. Carew Hazlitt (London, 1875); *English Drama, 1580–1642,* ed. C. F. Tucker Brooke and N. B. Paradise (Boston, 1933); *The English Mystery Plays,* by Rosemary Woolf (Berkeley: University of California Press, 1972); *Five Elizabe-*

than Tragedies, ed. A. K. McIlwraith (London, 1938); *Five Pre-Shakespearean Comedies,* ed. F. S. Boas (London, 1934); *The Jacobean and Caroline Stage,* by Gerald E. Bentley, 7 vols. (Oxford: Clarendon, 1941–56); *Ludus Conventriae,* ed. J. O. Halliwell, SS, England, no. 4 (London: Shakespeare Society, 1841); *The Macro Plays,* ed. F. J. Furnivall and A. W. Pollard, EETS, England, Extra Series, no. 91 (London: Early English Text Society, 1904); *Religious Drama 2,* ed. E. Martin Browne (New York: Meridian/Living Age, 1958); *A Select Collection of Old Plays,* ed. Robert Dodsley and Isaac Reed (London, 1827); *The Shakespeare Apocrypha,* ed. C. F. Tucker Brooke (Oxford, 1918); *Typical Elizabethan Plays,* ed. F. E. Schelling and M. W. Black (New York, 1949); and *York Plays,* ed. Lucy T. Smith (Oxford, 1885).

I gratefully acknowledge the assistance of my university colleagues Dr. Beno Weiss (modern Italian), Dr. Sherry Roush (Renaissance Italian), Dr. Norris Lacy and Dr. Alan Knight (medieval French), Dr. Judd Arnold (Elizabethan-Jacobean English), Dr. Michael M. Naydan (Ukrainian), Dr. Linda Ivanitz (Russian), Dr. Ernst Schurer (German), and Dr. Jean-Claude Vuillemin (baroque French) in the resolving of some of the lacunae in their respective fields.

Playwrights and Their Plays on Occultist Themes

Addison, Joseph (England, 1672–1719)
The Drummer (England, 1715). Moral prose comedy.

Aeschylus (Greece, ca. 525–ca. 456 B.C.E.)
Agamemnon (Greece, 458 B.C.E.). The sybil Cassandra. Prognostication.
The Eumenides (Greece, 458 B.C.E.). The Furies. Ghost of Clytemnestra. Priestess of Apollo. Athena.
The Persians (Greece, 472 B.C.E.). Ghost of Darius.

Aggio, Felice (Italy, twentieth century)
Il vampiro (Italy, 1925). Vampire.

Aleshin, Samuel (Russia, 1913–)
Togda v Sevill'e (Russia, 1947, 1961). Don Juan.

Alterman, Nathan (Poland-Israel, 1910–70)
Pundak haroochot/The Inn of Ghosts (Poland, 1962). Ghosts.

Amiel, Denys (France, 1884–1977)
Le démon du soir (France).

Anderson, Maxwell (United States, 1888–1959)
Joan of Lorraine (United States, 1947). Joan of Arc.

Anonymous
Abraham and Isaac (Brome, England, ca. 1375–1400). Mystery play. Angel.
Abraham and Isaac (Dublin, Ireland, fifteenth century). Mystery play. Angel.
Abraham and Isaac (St. Dunstan's, England, fifteenth century). Mystery play. Angel.
Adam (England, twelfth century).

Adam and Eve; or, The Creation of Eve, with the Expelling of Adam and Eve out of Paradise (Norwich, England, 1478–ca. 1565). Mystery play. Norwich cycle. Grocers' play. Devil.
Adam and Eve (England, 1528). Tailors' play.
Asfeld Passion Play (Germany, medieval). Lilith as Höllenrücke, the woman who walks on "hell's crutches."
The Annunciation (Lincoln, England, 1389–91). Angel.
The Antichrist (England, medieval). Mystery play.
Appius and Virginia (England, 1575).
Assumption of Mary (Catalan, before 1420). Lucifer. Devils. Mouth of Hell.
The Birth of Merlin (England, ca. 1612). Merlin. Devil.
Blutsauger (Austria, 1997). Multimedia presentation. Vampire.
The Bugbears (England, ca. 1565). Adaptation of Grazzini's *La spiritata.*
The Castell of Perseverance (England, ca. 1425). Morality play. Devil. Mouth of Hell.
Celestina (England, 1598). Lost translation/adaptation of Fernando de Rojas's *Tragicomedia de Calixto y Melibea.* Celestina as witch.
Common Conditions (England, 1576).
Corpus Christi (England, 1415). Moses' brazen serpent. Plays and processions on Corpus Christi day, the second Sunday after Pentecost, were performed throughout England in medieval times, most notably during the fourteenth and fifteenth centuries in such locales as Bungay, Heybridge, Dunmow, Chester, Chelmsford, Kendal, Doncaster, Hereford, Bury St. Edmunds, Canterbury, Coventry, Newcastle, Ipswich, Lincoln, Worcester, York, and King's Lynn.
Corpus Christi (Dublin, fifteenth century).
Corpus Christi (Valencia, Spain, early fifteenth century). Sant Jordi (Saint George) and the Dragon.
The Creation (England, medieval). Mystery play. Towneley cycle. Devil.
The Creation, and the Fall of Lucifer (England, medieval). Mystery play. York cycle. Barkers' pageant play. God. Lucifer. Seraphim. Cherubim. Hell.
The Creation of the Heavenly Beings: The Fall of Lucifer (England, medieval). Mystery play. York cycle, Tanners' play. God. Lucifer. Seraphim. Cherubim. Hell.
Day of Judgment (England, medieval). Mystery play. York cycle. See The Last Judgment, below.
Delphrygus and the King of Fairies (England, 1570). Fairies.
Descensus Christi ad inferos (England, 1486). Mystery play. Hell.
The Devil and Dives (England, 1570). Devil.
The Devil of a Wife (England, 1699). Performed at Bartholomew's Fair.
Doctor Lambe and the Witches (England, 1634). Lost. From an earlier play. Witchcraft.
Doomsday (England, medieval). Mystery play. Towneley cycle. Devil.
Doomsday (England, medieval). Mystery play. Coventry cycle. Weavers' play. Mouth of Hell.
Doomsday (England, 1433). Mystery play. York cycle. Mouth of Hell.
Das Egerer Fronleichnamsspiel (Germany, medieval). Lucifer.
The Fairy Knight; or, Oberon the Second (England, 1638). Fairies. Based on the play by T. Randolph.

The Fall of Man (England, medieval). Mystery play. York cycle. Cowpers' play. Satan. God.
The Fall of the Angels (England, medieval). Mystery play. God. Lucifer. Angels.
La farce de Martin de Cambrai (France, sixteenth century). Feigned Devil.
Le fées ou les contes de ma mère l'oye (France, 1697). Ogres. Fairy.
The Feigned Astrologer (England, 1668). Adaptation of T. Corneille's *Le feint astrologue.*
Festa di S. Giovanni (Florence, 1454). Last Judgment float. Mouth of Hell.
Festo praesentationis Beatae Virginis Mariae (Avignon, France, 1372). Archangel Michael. Lucifer crushed under Mary's foot.
The Ghost; or, The Woman Wears the Breeches (England, 1640).
Grim, the Collier of Croydon (England, ca. 1598).
Harlequin Amulet; or, The Magic of Mona (England, 1800). Pantomime.
Harlequin Dame Trot (England, eighteenth century). Christmas pantomime. Harlequin. Witchcraft.
Harlequin Mother Bunch (England, eighteenth century). Christmas pantomime. Harlequin. Witchcraft.
Harlequin Munchausen; or, The Fountain of Love (England, 1818). Pantomime. Vulcan. Cyclops. Venus. Cupid. Moon-King.
Harlequin Student; or, The Fall of Pantomime, with the Restoration of the Drama (England, 1741). Pantomime. Magician. Cave.
Harlequin's Invasion; or, A Christmas Gambol (England, 1759). Pantomime interpreted by David Garrick. Harlequin as a diabolical figure. Mercury.
The Harrowing of Hell (England, medieval). Mystery play. York cycle. Saddlers' play. Christ. Prophets. Devils. Belzabub. Satan. Belial.
The Harrowing of Hell (England, medieval). Mystery play. Coventry cycle. Cappers' play. Mouth of Hell.
The Harrowing of Hell (England, medieval). Mystery play. Chester pageant of the Cooks and Innkeepers. Jesus. Archangel Michael. Satan. Devils.
Hell's Higher Court of Justice; or, The Trial of the Three Politic Ghosts (England, 1661). Re Oliver Cromwell, the king of Sweden, and Cardinal Mazarin.
Herpetulus the Blue Knight and Perobia (England, 1574). Heroic romance.
Histoire plaisante des faicts et gestes de Harlequin commedien italien (France, 1585). Harlequin's first appearance in a written play. Hades.
Hocus Pocus (England, 1638). Magic.
Le Jeu d'Adam (et Eve)/Ordo representacionis Ade (Anglo-Norman, mid-twelfth century). *Mystère.* Devil. Mouth of Hell.
Judicium (England, medieval). Mystery play. Towneley cycle. Demon Titivillus.
Juttaspiel (Germany, medieval). Secular play. Lilith.
The Knight in the Burning Rock (England).
Lady Alimony (England, printed 1659).
The Last Judgement (England, medieval). Mystery play. York cycle. Mercers' play. God. Devils.
Ludus at virum dictum wildman (Aarau, Switzerland, 1399). Wild Man.
Ludus conventriae (England, ca. 1468). Mystery play. God. Angels. Lucifer.
Ludus de Antichristo (Germany, mid-twelfth century). Devil.
Ludus de Bellyale (Aberdeen, Scotland, 1471). Belial.

Lust's Dominion; or, The Lascivious Queen (England, ca. 1599).
Lusty Juventus (England, medieval). Morality play. Devil.
Magnus ludus de homine salvatico (Padua, Italy, 1208, 1224). Wild Man.
Mankind (England, medieval). Morality play. Devil.
A Marvellous History of Mary of Nimmegen, who for more than seven years lived and had ado with the Devil (Holland, ca. 1520). Devil. Necromancy.
A Mask of Foresters; or, Hunters (England, 1574). Wild Men.
[*Masque*] (England, 1348). Wild Man.
The Maydes Metamorphosis (England, 1600).
Medea (England, early seventeenth century). Medea.
The Merry Devil of Edmonton (England, ca. 1608). Comedy.
Miracle de Nostre Dame de Robert le Dyable/Le Mystère de Robert Le Diable (France, early fourteenth century). Devil. Miracle.
Mother Goose (England). Christmas pantomime. Witchcraft.
Le mystère d'Adam/Repraesentatio Adae (Anglo-Norman, ca. 1146–ca. 1174). Devil.
Le mystère de la Passion (Rouen, France, 1474). Mouth of Hell.
Le mystère de la Passion (Montferrand, France, 1477). Mouth of Hell.
Le mystère de la Passion (Mons, Belgium, 1501). Mouth of Hell.
Le mystère de la Passion (Bozen, France, 1514). Mouth of Hell.
Le mystère de la Passion (Valenciennes, France, 1547). Mouth of Hell.
Le mystère de la Passion (Arras, France, medieval). Mouth of Hell. Charm against enchantment.
Le mystère de Saint Crespin et Saint Crespinien (France, mid-fifteenth century). Mouth of Hell. Devils. Possession.
Le mystère de Saint Laurent (France, 1499). Mouth of Hell. Devils.
Le mystère de Saint Laurent (France, early sixteenth century). Mouth of Hell. Devils.
Le mystère de Saint Remi (France, early sixteenth century). Mouth of Hell. Devils. Possession. Exorcism.
Le mystère de Sainte Apolline/The Martyrdom of Saint Apollonia (France, mid-fifteenth century). Mouth of Hell. Devils.
Le mystère des saints actes des apostres (Bourges, France, 1536). Mouth of Hell.
Le mystère des trois doms (Romans, France, 1509). Mouth of Hell.
Le mystère du chevalier qui doona sa femme au Diable (France, 1505).
Le mystère du Viel Testament (France, early sixteenth century). Lucifer. Devils.
Ordinale de vita Sancti Mereadoci Episcopi et Confessoris/Saint Meriasek (Cornwall, England, 1504). Mouth of Hell.
Ordo representacionis Ade (see *Le jeu d'Adam*).
Origo mundi/The Creation of the World (Penrhyn, Cornwall, England, late fourteenth century).
Osterspiel (Lucerne, Switzerland, 1415). Passion play. Moses' brazen serpent.
Osterspiel (Lucerne, Switzerland, 1583). Passion play. Mouth of Hell.
The Parliament and the Devil (England, 1648).
Passion Play (Vienna, Austria, early fourteenth century). Devils. Lucifer. Mouth of Hell.
Passion Play (Metz, Germany, 1437). Devils. Mouth of Hell.
Passion Play (Frankfurt, Germany, 1450). Devils. Mouth of Hell.
Passion Play (Villingen, Germany, 1585). Devils. Mouth of Hell.

Pope Joan (Germany, 1480). Secular play. Lilith as the Devil's grandmother.
Processus Satanae (England, 1575). Devil.
Purificazione (Florence, fifteenth century). Jonah's whale.
The Puritaine Widdow/The Puritan; or, The Widow of Watling Street (England, 1607).
The Red Knight (England, 1576). Heroic romance.
Le sabbat et la herse infernale (France, 1925–26). Dramatic episode in the Follies Bergère Revue *Un soir de folie.*
Saint George and the Dragon (England, 1686).
Saint Mary Magdalen (Digby, England, late fifteenth century). Mouth of Hell.
Schembartlauf (Nuremberg, Germany, 1539). Hell. Wild Men.
The Second Maiden's Tragedy (England, 1611).
Secunda pastorum/The Second Shepherd's Play (England, mid-fifteenth century). Angel.
La seinte Resurreccion (Anglo-Norman, late twelfth century). Mouth of Hell.
La seinte Resurreccion (Paris, France, 1419). Satan. Mouth of Hell.
The Seven Champions of Christendome (England).
Sir Clyomon and Sir Clamydes (England, 1599). Magician Brian Sansfoy.
The Solitary Knight (England).
Das Spiel von den Klugen und Torichten Jungfrauen (Eisenach, Germany, 1322). Devils. Mouth of Hell.
Sponsus (France, ca. 1096–99). Probably from Saint-Martial de Limoges. Earliest extant example of demons on-stage. Mouth of Hell.
Stella; or, Tres Reges (England, 1222). Liturgical drama. Magi.
Stella; or, Tres Reges (England, 1337). Liturgical drama. Magi.
The Story of Orpheus (England, 1547). Lost. Descent into Hades.
The Temptation of Christ (England, medieval). Mystery play. York cycle. Locksmiths' play. Devil. Jesus. Angels.
Thersites (England, ca. 1537).
Tobias (Lincoln, England, 1564). Mouth of Hell.
The Tragedy of Locrine (England, ca. 1595).
Twelfth Night (England, 1515). Court masque. Eight Wild Men.
The Two Noble Ladies; or, The Converted Conjurer (England, 1622). Magic.
Uther Pendragon (England, 1597). Merlin.
La vie de Saint Martin (France). Mouth of Hell. Devils.
Wars of Cyrus (England). Magic.
The White Witch of Westminster; or, Love in a Lunacy (England, before 1642). Witch.
The Wisdome of Doctor Dodypoll (England, ca. 1600). London. Fairies. Magic ring.
The Wise Woman of Hogsdon (England). Comedy.
The Witch of Islington (England, prior to 1597). Witchcraft.
The Witch Traveller (England, 1623). Erroneous for *The Welsh Traveller.*
A Yorkshire Tragedy (England, ca. 1608). Demonic possession.

Anouilh, Jean (France, 1910–87)
L'Alouette/The Lark (France, 1953). Joan of Arc.
Médée (France, 1946). Medea.

An-Sky, S. (Shloyme Zanvl Rappoport, Russia, 1863–1920)
The Dybbuk (Russia, 1914). Yiddish. Hasidic lore. Dybbuk. Transmigration of soul. Cabala. Possession. Exorcism. Apotheosis.

Apollinaire, Guillaume (Apollinaris Kostrowitsky, Italy, 1880–1918)
Les mamelles de Tirésias / The Breasts of Tiresias (France, 1918). First surrealist play. Metamorphosis: Thérèse to Tiresias. Androgyny.

Archibald, William (1879–1959?)
The Innocents (England, 1950). Based on Henry James's *Turn of the Screw.* Ghosts. Possession.

Ariosto, Ludovico (Italy, 1474–1533)
Il negromante (Italy, 1520; 1528). Maestro Iacherino, a necromancer. Astrology.

Aristophanes (Greece, ca. 448–ca. 388 B.C.E.)
The Birds (Greece, 414 B.C.E.). Greek gods and heroes.
The Frogs (Greece, 405 B.C.E.). Dionysus. Hades.

Armin, Robert (England, ca. 1565–1615)
The Valiant Welshman (England, 1615).

Auden, W. H. (England, 1907–73)
The Ascent of F6 (England, 1935). In collaboration with Christopher Isherwood. "The Demon of the Mountain."
For the Time Being: A Christmas Oratorio (England, 1945). Angel Gabriel. The Three Wise Men.

Audiberti, Jacques (France, 1899–1965)
La hobereaute (France, 1958). Struggle between good and evil.
La logeuse (France, 1954). Circe.
Les naturel de Bordelaiss (France, 1953). Metamorphosis of men into beasts.
Opéra parlé (France, 1956). Pagan goddess of the forest.
Quoat-Quoat (France, 1946). Ancient Mexican god.

Balderston, John L. (United States, 1889–1954)
Dracula (England–United States, 1927). Adaptation of the 1924 Hamilton Deane play. Vampirism.

Bale, John (England, 1495–1563)
The Temptation of Our Lord and Saviour Jesus Christ by Satan (England, 1538). Devil.

Balogh, Zoltan (Hungary, nineteenth century)
Báthory Erzsébet (Hungary, 1882). Vampire. Elizabeth Bathory.

Barjona, Laurentius (Laurence Johnson, England, d. 1582)
Misogonus (England, 1570).

Barker, James Nelson (United States, 1784–1858)
Superstition (United States, 1824). Salem witchcraft.

Barnes, Barnabe (England, 1569–1609)
The Divils Charter (England, 1607). Pope Alexander VI as magician. Devil.

Barnes, Peter (England, 1931–)
The Bewitched (England, 1974). Carlos II of Spain.
Noonday Demons (England, 1969).

Barrie, Sir James M. (England, 1860–1937)
Dear Brutus (England, 1917, 1923). Magic.
Mary Rose (England, 1935). Fairies. Ghost.

Basset, Serge (France, 1865–1917)
Vers le Sabbath (France, 1897). One act. Witchcraft.

Beaumont, Francis (England, 1584–1616)
The Custom of the Country (England, 1628). In collaboration with John Fletcher. Witchcraft.

Behn, Mrs. Aphra (England, 1640–89)
The Luckey Chance; or, An Alderman's Bargain (England, 1686). Feigned magic and witchcraft.

Belasco, David (United States, 1859–1931)
The Return of Peter Grimm (United States, 1911; 1920). Supernatural events.
Van Der Decken (United States, 1915). Flying Dutchman.

Bely, Andrei (Boris Nikolayevich Bugayev, Russia, 1880–1934)
Antichrist (Russia, 1898). Unfinished apocalyptic mystery play. Two parts completed: *Jaws of Night* and *He Who Has Come.*

Benet, Stephen Vincent (United States, 1898–1943)
The Devil and Daniel Webster (United States, 1939). Devil as Mr. Scratch.

Bentivoglio, Ercole (Italy, 1507–73)
I fantasmi (Italy, 1547). Ghosts.

Bergman, Hjalmar Frederik (Sweden, 1883–1931)
En skugga (Sweden, 1918). Doppelgänger.

Berney, William (United States, twentieth century)
Dark of the Moon (United States, 1945). In collaboration with Howard Richardson. Dramatization of "The Ballad of Barbara Allen." Witchcraft.

Betterton, Thomas (England, 1635–1710)
The Prophetess; or, the History of Diocletian (England, 1690). Adaptation of the Fletcher and Massinger work.
The Tempest; or, The Enchanted Island (England, 1674). Adaptation of Shakespeare's play in collaboration with Thomas Shadwell. Magic.

Bingen, Hildegard von (Germany, 1098–1179)
Ordo virtutum (Germany, ca. 1152). Devil. Mary treading on Satan.

Björnson, Bjorn-Stjerne (Norway, 1832–1910)
Over aevne i/Beyond Human Power (Norway, 1883). Faith healing. Miracles.

Blache, François Alexis (France, nineteenth century)
Polichinel vampire (France, 1823). One-act ballet-pantomime. Vampire.

Blake, William (England, 1757–1827)
The Ghost of Abel (England, 1822). Satan.

Bodel, Jean (France, twelfth century)
Le jeu de Saint Nicolas (Arras, France, ca. 1201). Miracle. Pagan god Tervagan.

Bois, Jules (France, 1868–1943)
Les noces de Satan (France, 1892). *Drama ésoterique.* Devil.

Boito, Arrigo (Italy, 1842–1918)
Mefistofele (Italy, 1868). Libretto for the opera. Devil.

Bouchor, Maurice (France, 1855–1929)
[*Asmodee?*]. (France, 1889). Asmodeus's seduction of Sarah, Book of Tobit.

Boucicault, Dion (Ireland, 1822–90)
The Phantom (Ireland, 1856). Revised version of *The Vampire.*
The Vampire (Ireland, 1852). Vampirism.

Braein, Edvard Fliflet (Norway, 1924–76)
Anne Pedersdotter (Norway, 1971). Opera based on the play by Hans Wiers-Jenssen. Witchcraft.

Brandon-Thomas, Jevan (England, 1898–)
The Glory of the Sun (England).

Brazier, Gabriel (France, nineteenth century)
Les trois vampires; ou, Le clair de la lune (France, 1820). One-act vaudeville piece in collaboration with Armand Brazier.

Brecht, Bertolt (Germany, 1898–1956)
Galileo (Germany, 1937). Italian Inquisition.
Der gute Mensch von Setzuan/The Good Woman of Setzuan (Germany, 1938–40). Dream interludes. Three gods.

Brevanne, Roland (France, nineteenth–twentieth century)
Misses noire/Black Masses (France, 1904). Gilles de Rais. Alchemy. Witchcraft. Abbé de Guiborg.

Bridie, James (Osborne Henry Mavor, Scotland, 1888–1951)
Tobias and the Angel (Scotland, 1930). Story from the Apocrypha.

Brome, Richard (England, ca. 1590–ca. 1652)
The Late Lancashire Witches (England, 1634). In collaboration with Thomas Heywood. Witchcraft. Pendle Forest witch trials of 1634.

Browne, William (England, ca. 1591–ca. 1643)
Ulysses and Circe (England, 1615). Inner Temple masque. Circe.

Bruno, Giordano (Italy, 1548–1600)
Il candelaio (Italy, 1582). Alchemist Bartolomeo. Magician Scaramure.

Buchanan, George (England, 1506–82)
Medea (England, 1543). Translation of Euripides' work. Medea.

Burke, J. M. (England)
The Tradgedy of Deardrie and the Sons of Unsa (England).

Byron, George Gordon, Lord (England, 1788–1824)
The Deformed Transformed (England, 1821). Faust.
Cain: A Mystery (England, 1821).
Heaven and Earth (England, 1821; 1823). Angels.

Cahusac, Louis de (France, 1706–59)
Zoroastre (France, 1749). Libretto for the opera by Jean Philippe Rameau.

Campton, David (England, 1924–)
Carmilla (England, 1973). Adaptation of the Le Fanu work.
Frankenstein (England, 1973). Adaptation of the Mary Shelley work.
Usher (England, 1973). Adaptation of the Poe work.
Where Have All the Ghosts Gone? (England, 1969).

Carr, William (England, seventeenth century)
Pluto furens et vinctus; or, The Raging Devil Bound (England, 1669). Devil/Pluto.

Carrington, Leonora (England, 1917–)
Un chemise de nuit de flanelle (England, 1945). Celtic myth. Alchemical symbolism. Cadavers.
Pénélope (England, 1957). Surreal play. Alchemical imagery. Specters. Magic.

Carroll, Paul Vincent (Ireland, 1900–1968)
Shadow and Substance (1937). Visions.

Catina, Ion (Romania, nineteenth century)
Tepes Voda (Romania, 1823). Vlad Tepes.

Césaire, Aimé Fernand (Martinique, 1913–82)
Et les chiens se taisaient (Martinique, 1956). Surreal tragedy. Word alchemy. Madwomen as mediums. Demoniacs.
[*The Tempest*.] (Martinique). Adaptation of Shakespeare's work. Magic.

Chapman, George (England, ca. 1559–1634)
Bussy D'Ambois (England, ca. 1605). Behemoth. Specter.
Caesar and Pompey (England, ca. 1613).
The Revenge of Bussy D'Ambois (England, ca. 1610).

Chayefsky, Paddy (United States, 1923–81)
The Tenth Man (United States, 1960). Cabalist. Dybbuk. Possession. Exorcism.

Chesterton, Gilbert Keith (England, 1874–1936)
Magic (England, 1913). Magic.

Chettle, Henry (England, ca. 1560–1607)
Vayvode (England, 1598). Lost. Possibly about Vlad Tepez, the Impaler.

Cicognini, Iacopo (Italy, 1577–1633)
Il convitato di pietra (Italy, seventeenth century). After Tirso de Molina's *Don Juan Tenorio.* Specters.
La vita é un sogno (Italy, seventeenth century). After Calderón's *La vida es sueño.* Astrology.

Ciercelin, Louis (France, nineteenth century)
Le Diable couturier (France, 1894). Based on Breton legend. Devil.

Claudel, Paul (France, 1868–1955)
L'annonce faite à Marie/The Tidings Brought to Mary (France, 1955). Angelic visitation.
Jeanne d'Arc au bûcher/Joan of Arc at the Stake (France, 1939). Libretto for the opera by Arthur Honegger. Joan of Arc.

Cocteau, Jean (France, 1889–1963)
The Knights of the Round Table (France, 1937). Merlin.
La machine infernale/The Infernal Machine (France, 1934). After Sophocles' *Oedipus.* Sphynx. Olympian gods. Ghost. Anubis.
Orphée (1926). Descent into the underworld. Angel. Talking horse.

Cokayne, Sir Aston (England, 1608–84)
Trappolin creduto principe; or, Trappolin Supposed a Prince (England, 1656). Magic. Familiars.

Corneille, Pierre (France, 1606–84)
L'illusion comique (France, 1636). Magician. Visions.
Médée (France, 1635). Medea.

Corneille, Thomas (France, 1625–1709)
La devineresse; ou, Les faux enchantements/Madame Jobin (France, 1679). In collaboration with Jean Donneau de Vizé. False enchantment. Hand of glory.
Le feint astrologue (France, ca. 1668). Feigned astrology.

Cosmar, Alexander (Germany, 1805–42)
Der Vampyr (Germany, 1828). Vampire.

Coward, Noel (England, 1899–1973)
Blithe Spirit (England, 1941). Spiritualism. Séance. Specters.

Daborne, Robert (England, ca. 1570–1628)
Machiavel and the Devil (England, 1613). Devil.

D'Annunzio, Gabriele (Italy, 1863–1938)
La figlia di Jorio (Italy, 1904). Warlock. Burning at the stake.

D'Avenant, Charles (England, 1656–1714)
Circe (1677). Circe. Magicians. Pluto.
The Tempest; or, The Enchanted Island (England, 1667). Adaptation of Shakespeare's play in collaboration with John Dryden.

D'Avenant, Sir William (England, 1606–68)
The Temple of Love (England, 1634). A masque. Cave. Magicians.

Davenport, Robert (England, 1624–40)
Circe (England, 1676). Circe. Pluto. Magicians.
A New Trick to Cheat the Devil (England, 1625 or 1639)

Day, John (England, ca. 1574–ca. 1640)
Friar Rush and the Proud Woman of Antwerp (England, 1601). In collaboration with William Haughton.

Deane, Hamilton (England, 1880–1958)
Dracula (England, 1924). Dramatization of the novel by Bram Stoker. Vampirism.

De Capitani, Elio, Ida Marinelli, and Gabriele Salvatores (Italy, twentieth century)
Dracula, il vampiro (Italy, 1980). From Bram Stoker's novel. Vampire.

Dekker, Thomas (England, ca. 1570–ca. 1632)
The Fairy Knight (England, 1624). In collaboration with John Ford.
If This Be Not a Good Play, the Devil Is in It (England, 1612). Three minor demons.
Old Fortunatus (England, 1599). Magic.
The Virgin Martyr (England, ca. 1620). In collaboration with Philip Massinger. Angels.
The Witch of Edmonton (England, ca. 1623). In collaboration with William Rowley and John Ford. Witchcraft. Elizabeth Sawyer tried as a black witch. Familiar.
The Whore of Babylon (England, ca. 1607).

Dempsey, John (United States, 1964–)
The Witches of Eastwick (United States, 2000). Musical in collaboration with Dana P. Rowe, based on the novel by John Updike. Witchcraft. Devil.

De Richemont, Eugène, and Leon Frank (France, nineteenth century)
Vampire et loup garou; ou, Le violon de voyage (France, 1870?). One-act operetta. Vampire. Werewolf.

Désaugiers, Marc Antoine Madeleine (France, 1772–1827)
Cadet Buteux, vampire (France, 1820). Vampire.

Dibdin, Charles (England, 1745–1814)
Harlequin in His Element; or, Fire, Water, Earth, and Air (England, 1810). Personification of the four elements.

The Lancashire Witches; or, The Distresses of Harlequin (England, 1782). Burlesque of witchcraft.

Donneau de Vizé, Jean (France, 1638–1710)
La devineresse; ou, Les faux enchantements (France, 1679). In collaboration with Thomas Corneille. False enchantment.

Dorset, St. John (Rev. Hugo John Belfour, England, nineteenth century)
The Vampire: A Tragedy (England, 1821). Vampire.

Drayton, Michael (England, ca. 1563–1631)
The Merry Devil of Edmonton (England, ca. 1599). Magician. Coreb, a devil. Demonic pact.

Dreiser, Theodore (United States, 1871–1945)
Plays of the Natural and the Supernatural (United States, 1916). Contents: *The Girl in the Coffin; The Blue Sphere; Laughing Gas; In the Dark; The Spring Recital; The Light in the Window; Old Ragpicker.*

Dryden, John (England, 1631–1700)
The Duke of Guise (England, 1682). In collaboration with Nathaniel Lee. Damnation of the wizard. Familiar.
An Evening's Love; or, The Mock Astrologer (England, 1668). Feigned astrology.
The Indian Queen (England, 1663). In collaboration with Sir Robert Howard. Spirits. Ismeron the prophet.
Oedipus (England, 1678). In collaboration with Nathaniel Lee. Tiresias the prophet. Ghost.
The State of Innocence, and the Fall of Man/The Fall of Angels and Man in Innocence (England, 1677). Fallen angels.
The Tempest; or, The Enchanted Island (England, 1667). Adaptation of Shakespeare's play in collaboration with Charles D'Avenant.
Tyrannick Love; or, The Royal Martyr (England, 1669). Placidius the magician. Incantations. Cave. Angels.
The Wild Gallant (England, ca. 1662).

Ducange, Victor (France, 1783–1833)
La sorcière; ou, L'orphelia écossais (France, 1821). In collaboration with Frédéric Dupetit-Méré. Witchcraft.

Duffett, Thomas (England, seventeenth century)
The Mock Tempest; or, The Enchanted Castle (England, 1674). Magic.

Dumas, Alexandre, Père (France, 1802–70)
L'alchimiste (France, 1839). Alchemy.
La tour de Nesle (France, 1832).
Urbain Grandier (France, 1850). In collaboration with Auguste Maquet. Possession. Exorcism.
Le vampire (France, 1851). In collaboration with Auguste Maquet. Vampire.

Dunsany, Lord (Edward John Moreton Drax Plunkett, Ireland, 1878–1957)
The Jest of Hahalaba (Ireland, 1928). Alchemy. Magic. Spirit.
A Night at an Inn (Ireland, 1916). Supernatural vengeance. Indian idol comes to life.

Dupetit-Méré, Frédéric (France, 1785–1827)
La sorcière; ou, L'orphelia écossais (France, 1821). In collaboration with Victor Ducange. Witchcraft.

Durrell, Lawrence (England, 1912–90)
An Irish Faust (England, 1963). Faust.

Dürrenmatt, Friedrich (Switzerland, 1921–90)
Ein Engel kommt nach Babylon (Switzerland, 1953). Angel.

Egret, Marie-François (France, twentieth century)
Báthory Erzsébet (France, 1978). Vampire. Elizabeth Bathory.

Ellmenreich, Friederike (Germany, 1775–1845)
Der Vampyr (Germany, 1827). Translation of the play by Scribe.

Erenberg, Il'ia Grigor'yevich (Russia, 1891–1967)
A Fairy Tale (Russia, ca. 1921).

Erskine, Jean (England)
The House of Severn (England).

Erskine, John (United States, 1879–1951)
Adam and Eve, Though He Knew Better (United States, 1927).

Euripides (Greece, ca. 480–406 B.C.E.)
Alcestis (Greece, 438 B.C.E.). Greek gods.
Bacchae (Greece, 405 B.C.E.). Dionysus. Tiresias.
The Cyclops (Greece, ca. 425 B.C.E.). Cyclops. Satyrs. Silenus.
Medea (Greece, 431 B.C.E.). Medea.
The Trojan Women (Greece, 415 B.C.E.). The sybil Cassandra.

Fabre des Essart, Léonce-Eugène Joseph (France, 1848–1917)
Christ the Savior (France). Gnosticism. Satan. Angel.

Fielding, Henry (England, 1707–54)
The Intriguing Chambermaid (England, 1733). Based on Regnard's *Le retour imprevú.*

Fitzball, Edward (England, 1792–1873)
The Lancashire Witches: A Romance of Pendle Forest (England, 1848). Witchcraft.

Fletcher, John (England, 1579–1625)
The Bloody Brother; or, Rollo, Duke of Normandy (England, 1616). Astrology.
The Chances (England, ca. 1618).
The Custom of the Country (England, 1628). In collaboration with Francis Beaumont. Witchcraft.
The Devil of Dowgate; or, Usury Put to Use (England, 1623).

The Faire Maide of the Inne (England, 1626). In collaboration with Philip Massinger. Astrology.
The Faithful Shepherdess (England, ca. 1608). The white witch Clorin.
Monsieur Thomas (England, ca. 1612).
Night-Walker; or, The Little Thief (England, 1634). In collaboration with James Shirley.
The Prophetess (England, 1622). In collaboration with Philip Massinger. Delphia, white witch of Diocletian's Rome. Lucifera.

Ford, John (England, 1586–ca. 1640)
The Fairy Knight (England, 1624). In collaboration with Thomas Dekker.
The Witch of Edmonton (England, ca. 1621). In collaboration with Thomas Dekker and William Rowley. Witchcraft. Elizabeth Sawyer tried as a black witch. Familiar.

Forster, William (England, 1818–82)
The Weirwolf: A Tragedy (England, 1876). Lycanthropy.

Fossé, Pierre de la (France, nineteenth century)
Le vampire (France, 1820). Melodrama. Vampire.

Fry, Christopher (England, 1907–)
The Lady's Not for Burning (England, 1947). Comedy. Witchcraft.

Fulwel, Ulpian (England, ca. 1546–78)
Like Will to Like (England, 1568).

Gabory, Emile (France, 1872–1954)
L'an mille (France). The first millennium. Satan.

Gager, William (England, 1555–1622)
Oedipus (England,1584). Tiresias the prophet.

Gaines, Frederick (United States, twentieth century)
Dracula (United States). Vampirism.

Garay, János (Hungary, 1812–53)
Bátori Erzsébet (Hungary, 1840). Vampire. Elizabeth Bathory.

Garnier, Robert (France, ca. 1545–90)
Les Juifves/The Hebrew Women (France, 1583). Tragedy. Biblical prophecy. Clairvoyance.

Gascoigne, George (England, ca. 1539–78)
The Savage Man and Echo (England, 1575). Court masque. Wild Man?

Ghelderode, Michel de (Belgium, 1898–1962)
Fastes d'enfer/Chronicles of Hell (Belgium, 1947). Medieval beliefs.

Ghéon, Henri (France, 1875–1944)
The Marvelous History of St. Bernard (France, 1924). Devil.
Parade at Devil's Bridge (France). Legend of Saint Cado and the Devil.

Ghilan, Eddy (France, twentieth century)
La sorcière (France, 1962). One act. Gypsy witchcraft.

Giraudoux, Jean (France, 1882–1944)
Intermezzo (France, 1933). Magic. Ghost.
Ondine (France, 1939). Water sprite of German legend.

Goethe, Johann Wolfgang von (Germany, 1749–1832)
Faust (Germany, 1808 [pt. 1], 1832 [pt. 2]). Faust. Mephistopheles. Magic. Walpurgisnacht. Lilith.

Goldfaden, Abraham (Russia, 1840–1908)
Di Kishef-Makharin/The Sorceress (Russia, 1879). Yiddish.

Gordin, Jacob (Russia, 1853–1909)
Got, Mentsh, un Tayvl/God, Man, and the Devil (Russia, 1900). Yiddish.

Gourmont, Remy de (France, 1858–1915)
Lilith (France, 1892). Lilith, first consort of Adam.

Gozzi, Count Carlo (Italy, 1720–1806)
Fiaba dell'amore delle tre melarance/The Love of Three Oranges (Italy, 1761). Fata Morgana.
Il re cervo/The King Stag (Italy, 1762). Durandarte the magician. Prognostication by a plaster head. Transformations.

Grabbe, Christian Dietrich (Germany, 1801–36)
Scherz, Satire, Ironie und tiefere Bedeutung/Hest, Satire, Irony, and Deeper Significance (Germany, 1822). Devil.

Grangé, Eugene (France, ca. 1812–87)
Les diables roses (France, ca. 1863). In collaboration with Lambert Thiboust. Comedy.

Granville, George (England, 1667–1735)
The British Enchanters (England, 1706).

Grazzini, Antonfrancesco (Italy, 1503–83)
La spiritata (Italy, 1564).

Greene, Graham (England, 1904–91)
The Potting Shed (England, 1957).

Greene, Robert (England, 1560–92)
The Comicall Historie of Alphonsus, King of Arragon (England, 1599). Sybil named Medea. Conjuration. Brazen head.
The Honorable History of Friar Bacon and Friar Bungay (England, ca. 1589). Magic. Conjurations. Behemoth.
A Looking Glasse for London and England (England, ca. 1590). In collaboration with Thomas Lodge. Good angel. Evil angel. Devil.
Orlando furioso (England, 1592). Melissa, an enchantress.

The Scottish Historie of James the Fourth, Slaine at Flodden (England, ca. 1591). Oberon, King of the Faeries.

Grillparzer, Franz (Austria, 1791–1872)
Des Meeres und der Liebe Wellen/Hero and Leander (Austria, 1831). Greek mythology.

Guarnieri, Flamminio (Italy, sixteenth century)
Il mago (Italy, 1569). Magic.

Gwinne, Matthew (England, ca. 1558–1627)
Tres sibyllae (England, 1605). Sibyls.

Halle, Adam de la (Adam le Bossu, France, ca. 1250–ca. 1288)
Le jeu de la feuillée (Li jus Adan ou de la feuillie)/Play of the Bower (France, ca. 1276). Demon Crokesot. Herlequin/Hellequin. Fairies.

Haughton, William (England, ca. 1575–1605)
The Devil and His Dame (England, 1600). Published in 1662 as *Grim the Collier of Croydon; or, The Devil and His Dame.*
Friar Rush and the Proud Woman of Antwerp (England, 1601). In collaboration with John Day.

Hauptmann, Gerhart (Germany, 1862–1946)
Hannels Himmelfahrt/Little Hanne's Journey to Heaven (Germany, 1893). Ghost. Visions.
Hexenritt/The Witches Ride (Germany, 1929). Witchcraft.
Die versunkene Glocke/The Sunken Bell (Germany, 1896). Elves. Fauns.

Hausted, Peter (England, ca. 1605–44)
The Rival Friends (England, 1632).

Hauteroche, Noel (see Noel Lebreton de Hauteroche)
Gyges und sein Ring/Gyges and His Ring (Germany, 1856). Magic ring. Invisibility.
Hebbel, Friedrich (Germany, 1813–63).

Heiberg, Johan Ludvig (Denmark, 1791–1860)
Elverhoj/Elf Hill (Denmark, 1828). Fantasy.

Heigel, Cäsar Max (Germany)
Der Vampyr (Germany, 1828). Adapted from Byron's and Polidori's work.
Ein Uhr! (Germany, 1822). Vampire.

Heijermans, Herman (Holland, 1864–1924)
Eva Bonheur/The Devil to Pay (Holland, 1916)

Herman, George (United States 1928–)
The Devil of the Second Stairs (United States, 1967). Ghosts. Diabolical possession.

Heywood, John (England, ca. 1497–ca. 1580)
The Playe Called the Foure PP (England, ca. 1523; published 1545). Hell. Devils.

Heywood, Thomas (England, ca. 1575–1641)
The English Traveler (England, 1633).
The Late Lancashire Witches (England, 1634). In collaboration with Richard Brome. Witchcraft. Pendle Forest witch trials of 1634.
The Wise-Woman of Hogsdon (England, ca. 1604). Witchcraft as quackery.

Hildegard von Bingen (see Bingen, Hildegard von)

Hobbes, Thomas (England, 1588–1679)
Medea (England, 1602). Translation of Euripides' work. Medea.

Hochwälder, Fritz (Austria-Switzerland, 1911–76)
Donnerstag (Switzerland). Mystery play. Demonic pact.
Die Herberge (Switzerland, 1956).

Hofmannsthal, Hugo von (Austria, 1874–1929)
Jedermann/Everyman (Austria, 1910). Morality play. Devil.

Holden, John (England, seventeenth century)
The Ghosts (England, 1665).

Holland, Samuel (England, seventeenth century)
The Enchanted Grove (England, 1656). Court masque.

Hovey, Richard (United States, 1864–1900)
The Holy Grail (United States, published posthumously in 1907). Unfinished.
The Quest of Merlin (United States, 1891). A lyrical masque; part of *Launcelot and Guenevere: A Poem in Five Dramas.* Magic. Merlin.

Hughes, Richard (England, 1900–1976)
A Comedy of Good and Evil (England, 1924).

Hughes, Thomas (England, prior to 1571–1618)
The Misfortunes of King Arthur (England, 1587). Court masque influenced by Seneca. Ghost.

Hugo, Victor (France, 1802–85)
Torquemada (France, 1882). Spanish Inquisition.

Ibsen, Henrik (Norway, 1828–1906)
Peer Gynt (Norway, 1867). Fantasy. Trolls.

I.C. (England, seventeenth century)
A Pleasant Comedie Called the Two Merry Milk-Maids (England, ca. 1610).

Inglelend (Ingelend), Thomas (England, sixteenth century)
The Disobedient Child (England, ca. 1550). Devil.

Irwin, Margaret (England, 1889–1967)
Madame Fears the Dark (England, 1936). One act.

Isherwood, Christopher (England, 1904–86)
The Ascent of F6 (England, 1935). In collaboration with W. H. Auden. "The Demon of the Mountain."

Ivsic, Radovan (Croatia, 1921–)
Airia (Croatia, 1960). Surreal play. Word alchemy. The spirit Airia. Water, the element.
Le Roi Gordogane (Croatia, 1968). Surreal play. Tarot imagery.
Vané (Croatia, 1963). Surreal play. Metamorphoses.

Jeffers, Robinson (United States, 1887–1962)
Medea (United States, 1946). Medea.
The Tower beyond Tragedy (United States, 1925). Based on the Oresteia. The sybil Cassandra.

Jelinek, Elfriede (Austria, 1946–)
Krankheit oder moderne Frauen (Austria, 1987). Vampire.

Jevon, Thomas (England, 1652–88)
The Devil of a Wife; or, A Comical Transformation (England, 1686).

Jodelle, Estienne (France, ca. 1532–73)
Cléopâtre captive (France, 1553). Ghost.

Jonson, Ben (England, 1572–1637)
The Alchemist (England, 1610). Pseudoalchemy.
Bartholomew Fair (England, 1614). Cupid. Ghost of Dionysus.
Cynthia's Revels; or, The Fountain of Self-Love (England, 1600). A masque. Magic fountain. Cupid. Mercury.
The Devil Is an Ass (England, 1616). Comedy. Pug, a minor devil.
The Entertainment at Althrope (England, 1603).
The Fortunate Isles (England, 1624).
Gipsies Metamorphosed (England, 1621).
Love Restored (England, 1612).
The Masque of Queenes (England, 1609). Twelve black witches.
Mercury Vindicated from the Alchemists at Court (England, 1616). A masque. Alchemy.
Oberon, the Faerie King (England, 1611). Satyrs. Faeries.
The Poetaster (England, 1601).
The Sad Shepherd (England, ca. 1637). Black witch, Mother Maudlin. Puck as the Devil. Left unfinished at Jonson's death.
The Satyr (England, 1603).
A Tale of a Tub (England, 1633).

Jordan, William (England, sixteenth–seventeenth century)
Gwryans an bys/The Creation of the World, with Noah's Flood (Cornwall, England, 1611). Cornish mystery play. Adaptation of the anonymous fourteenth-century *Origo Mundi.*

Kallen, Horace Meyer (United States, 1882–1974)
The Tragedy of Job (United States). God. Satan.

Keigwyn, John (England, 1641–1716)
The Creation of the World, with Noah's Flood (England, 1693). Translation of Jordan's Cornish mystery play of the same title.

Kirke, John (England, ca. 1563–1638)
The Seven Champions of Christendome (England, 1638). The black witch Calib. The devil Tarpax. Three spirits. Five ghosts. Two magicians. Seven saints.

Kleist, Heinrich von (Germany, 1777–1811)
Das Kätchen von Heilbronn oder die Feuerprobe/Cathy from Heilbronn; or, The Trial by Fire (Germany, 1808). Dream. Witch.

Krasinski, Zygmunt (Poland, 1812–59)
Irydion (Poland, 1836). Pact with the Devil.

Kyd, Thomas (England, 1558–94)
The Spanish Tragedy; or, Hieronimo Is Mad Againe! (England, ca. 1586). Specter.

L., Emile B. (France, nineteenth century).
Encore un vampire (France, 1820). Vampire.

Lagerkvist, Pär (Sweden, 1891–1974)
Lat manniskan leva/Let Man Live (Sweden, 1949). Giordano Bruno. Joan of Arc. Witch.
The Sibyl (Sweden, 1956). Greek and Judaic myths.

Laloue, Ferdinand (France, d. 1850)
Les pilules du Diable (France, 1831). In collaboration with Anicet Bourgeois and Laurent.

Larivey, Pierre de (France, ca. 1540–1619)
Les esprits (ca. 1574). Sorcerer. Feigned haunting of a house. Feigned Devil. Feigned exorcism. Adapted from Lorenzino de Medici's *Aridosia* (1536).

Lebreton de Hauteroche, Noel (France, 1617–1707)
L'esprit folet; ou, La dame invisible (France, 1684). Translation of Calderón's *La dama duende.* Feigned invisibility.

Lee, Nathaniel (England, 1651–92)
The Duke of Guise (England, 1682). In collaboration with John Dryden.
Oedipus (England, 1678). In collaboration with John Dryden. Tiresias the prophet.
Sophonisba (England, 1675). Cultish rites. Possession. Spirits.

Leivick, H. (Leivick Halpern, Russia, 1888–1962)
The Golem (Russia, 1921). Magic. Jewish legend.

Le Metel d'Ouville, Antoine (France, d. 1657)
L'esprit folet (France, 1642). Translation of Calderón's *La dama duende.* Feigned invisibility.

Lenau (Nikolaus Franz Niembsch von Strehlenau, Austria-Hungary, 1802–50)
Faust (Austria, 1835). Faust. Devil.

Lenormand, Henri-René (France, 1882–1951)
A l'ombre du mal/In the Shadow of Evil (France, 1924).
La dent rouge/The Red Tooth (France, 1922). Swiss peasant superstitions.
L'homme et ses fantômes/Man and His Phantoms (France, 1924). Don Juan. Medium. Phantoms.
The Magician Love (France).

LeSage, Alain René (France, 1668–1747)
Turcaret (France, 1709). Comedy. Magic.

Lessing, Gotthold Ephraim (Germany, 1729–81)
Nathan der Weise/Nathan the Wise (Germany, 1779). Magic ring.

Levy, Benn Wolfe (England, 1900–1974)
The Devil Passes/The Devil (England, 1931). Devil.

Lewis, Matthew Gregory (England, 1775–1818)
The Castle Spectre (England, 1797). Ghost.
The Wood Daemon (England, 1807). Gothic horror.

Lodge, Thomas (England, ca. 1558–1625)
A Looking Glasse for London (England, ca. 1590). In collaboration with Robert Greene.

Longfellow, Henry Wadsworth (United States, 1807–82)
Christus: A Mystery (United States, 1872). Influenced by the German *Der Arme Heinrich.* Three parts: 1. *The Divine Tragedy* (Gospel, miracle play "The Nativity"); 2. *The Golden Legend* (Lucifer); 3. *The New England Tragedies* (Salem witchcraft).
Giles Corey of the Salem Farms (United States). Salem witch trials.

Longford, Frank Pakenham, Earl of (England, 1905–)
Carmilla (England, 1932). Adapted from Joseph Sheridan Le Fanu's "In a Glass Darkly." Vampirism.

Loquin, Anatole (France, 1834–1903)
Les Basques; ou, La sorcière d'espelette (France, 1892). In collaboration with Mégret de Belligny. Witchcraft.

Lortz, Richard (United States, 1917–80)
Voices (United States, 1972). Ghosts.

Lower, Sir William (England 1600–62)
The Enchanted Lovers (England, 1658).

Lunacharskii, Anatolii (Russia, 1875–1933)
Faust i gorod/Faust and the City (Russia, 1918). Faust.
Magi (Russia, 1919). Magi.

Lyly, John (England, 1554–1606)
Endimion (England, 1585). Faeries introduced into English drama.
Gallathea (England, 1584).
Mother Bombie (England, ca. 1590). White witch. Fortune-telling.

Mabbe, James (England, 1572–1642)
The Spanish Bawd (England, 1631). Translation of Fernando de Rojas's *Tragicomedia de Calixto y Melibea.* Celestina. Magic.

Machiavelli, Niccolò (Italy, 1469–1527)
La mandragola/The Mandrake (Italy, ca. 1518). Feigned magic.

MacKaye, Percy Wallace (United States, 1875–1956)
Jeanne d'Arc (United States, 1906). Joan of Arc.
The Scarecrow (United States, 1908). Devil. Witch. Scarecrow comes to life.

MacLeish, Archibald (United States, 1892–1982)
JB (United States, 1958). Devil. Job.

Maeterlinck, Maurice (Belgium, 1862–1949)
Soeur Beatrice/Sister Beatrice (Belgium, 1901). Virgin Mary takes the place of the absent nun of the title.

Magre, Maurice (France, 1877–1941)
L'an mille (France). The first millennium. Satan.

Maittare, Michael (England, 1668–1747)
Inferno navigatio (England, 1699). Adaptation of Virgil. Hell.

Maquet, Auguste (France, 1813–86)
Le Vampire (France, 1851). In collaboration with Alexandre Dumas père. Vampire.

Marivaux, Pierre Carlet de Chamblain de (France, 1688–1763)
Arlequin poli par l'amour (France, 1720). Harlequin.

Marlowe, Christopher (England, 1564–93)
The Jew of Malta (England, ca. 1592). Ghost of Machiavel. Barabas parodies Medea's incantation in Seneca's tragedy.
Tamburlaine I, II (England). Renaissance hermetic philosophy, especially that of Giordano Bruno. Magic.
The Tragical History of the Life and Death of Doctor Faustus (England, ca. 1592). Faust. Devil. Demonic pact. Damnation scene.

Marschner, Heinrich (Germany, 1795–1861)
The Vampire (1997). Translated by Jutta Romero.
Der Vampyr (Germany, 1828). Opera libretto. Vampire.

Marston, John (England, 1575–1634)
Antonio's Revenge (England, 1602). Specter.
The Mountebank's Masque (England, 1618).
The Tragedie of Sophonisba (England, ca. 1606). The classical witch Erictho.

Martainville/Marteinville, A. Alphonse (France, 1776–1830)
Le pied de mouton (France, 1807). In collaboration with Ribié.

Martinet (France, nineteenth century)
Le vampire (France, 1820). Vampire.

Masefield, John (England, 1878–1967)
The Witch (England, 1910). Adapted from H. Wiers-Jennsen's *Anne Pedersdotter.* Witchcraft.

Masquellier, Albert (France)
Le vampire de la rue (France, n.d.). Vampire.

Massinger, Philip (England, 1583–1640)
The Faire Maide of the Inne (England, 1626). In collaboration with John Fletcher. Astrology.
The Prophetess (England, 1622). In collaboration with John Fletcher. Delphia, white witch of Diocletian's Rome. Lucifera.
The Unnatural Combat (England, ca. 1621).
The Virgin Martyr (England, ca. 1620). In collaboration with Thomas Dekker. Angels.

Master S (William Stevenson?) (England, ca. 1521–75)
Gammer Gurton's Needle (England, ca. 1553; published 1575). Attempted conjuring of the Devil.

Mathews, Cornelius (United States, 1817–89)
Witchcraft; or, The Martyrs of Salem (United States, 1846). Salem witchcraft.

Mavrodollu, G. (Romania, nineteenth century)
Vlada Tsepeshu, drama istorica în cinci acte (Romania, 1858). Vlad Tepes.

McNally, Terrence (United States, 1939–)
And Things That Go Bump in the Night (United States, 1964). Ghost.
There Is Something out There (United States, 1962). One-act predecessor of *And Things That Go Bump in the Night.* Ghost.

McPherson, Conor (Ireland, 1971–)
The Weir (Ireland, 1997). Suggested ghost.

Medici, Lorenzino de (Italy, 1513–48)
Aridosia (Italy, 1536). Sorcerer. Feigned haunting of a house. Feigned Devil. Feigned exorcism.

Mengals, Martin Joseph (Belgium, 1784–1851)
Le vampire (Belgium, 1826). Comic opera.

Menotti, Gian Carlo (Italy, 1911–)
The Medium (Italy, 1946). Libretto for an opera in one act. Medium. Séance.

Mewe, William (England, ca. 1602–ca. 1669)
Pseudomagia (England, 1626). Magic.

Micinski, Tadeusz (Poland, 1873–1918)
Basilissa teophano/In the Shades of the Golden Palace (Poland). Occult iconography. Pagan cults.
Revolt of the Potemkin (Poland). Lucifer. Magical effects. Ghost.

Mickiewicz, Adam (Poland, 1798–1855)
Forefathers' Eve (II, IV) (Poland, 1823). Pagan ancestor worship. Spirits.

Middleton, Thomas (England, ca. 1570–1627)
Blurt, Master-Constable (England, 1602).
The Changeling (England, 1622). In collaboration with William Rowley. Changeling lore used as comic subplot.
A Courtly Masque: The Device Called, the World Tost at Tennis (England, 1620). In collaboration with William Rowley. Devil.
A Game at Chess (England, 1624).
A Mad World, My Masters (England, 1608).
The Phoenix (England, 1607).
The Witch (England, ca. 1612). Black witches named Hecate, Stadlin, Hoppo, Puckle, and Hellwain. Familiar.

Miller, Arthur (United States, 1915–2005)
Clara (United States, 1987). One act. Ghost.
The Crucible (United States, 1953). New England witchcraft. Protestant Inquisition.

Milton, John (England, 1608–74)
Maske of Comus (England, 1634; published 1637). A masque. Magic. Spirit.

Molière (Jean-Baptiste Poquelin, France, 1622–73)
Les amants magnifiques (France, 1670). Astrology.
Amphitryon (1668). Jupiter. Mercury. Transformations. Influenced by Rotrou's *Les Sosies.*
Le festin de pierre (France, 1665). Don Juan. Based on Tirso de Molina's *El burlador de Sevilla* (Spain).

Molnár, Ferenc (Hungary, 1878–1952)
The Devil (Hungary, 1907).
Liliom (Hungary, 1909). Heaven. Return to life after death.

Montfleury, Antoine Jacob de (France, ca. 1639–85)
Le comédien poète (France, 1678).

Montherlant, Henri de (France, 1896–1972)
Don Juan (France, 1958). Don Juan.

Moody, William Vaughn (United States, 1869–1910)
The Faith Healer (United States, 1909). Faith healing. Miracle.
The Fire Bringer (United States, 1904). Prometheus.
The Masque of Judgment (United States, 1900). The archangel Raphael. Serpent.

Moretti, Mario (Italy, twentieth century)
Dracula, esercizio sul terrore (Italy, 1983). Vampire.

Morlock, Frank J. (United States, 1941–)
Urbain Grandier (United States, 2000). Adaptation of the play by Alexandre Dumas père and Auguste Maquet. Possession.
The Vampire (United States, 1999). Adaptation of the play by Alexandre Dumas père. Vampire.

Mountfort, William (England, ca. 1664–92)
Doctor Faustus, with the Humours of Harlequin and Scaramouche (England, 1686). Adaptation of Marlowe's play. Faust. Exorcism.
The Vampire (United States, 1999). Adaptation of the play by Alexandre Dumas père and Auguste Maquet. Vampire.

Munday, Anthony (England, 1553–1633)
Fedele and Fortunio; or, The Two Italian Gentlemen (England, 1585).
John a Kent and John a Cumber (England, ca. 1595). Magic.

Nemerov, Howard (United States 1920–91)
Endor (United States, 1961). Drama in one act. Biblical Witch of Endor. Ghost.

Nerval, Gérard de (Gérard Labrunie, France, 1808–55)
Faust (France, 1828). Translation of the second part of Goethe's work. Faust.
La main de gloire (France, 1832). Based on story by Hoffman. Hand of glory.
Le prince des sots (France, 1830). Devil. Angel.

Neville, Alexander (England, 1544–1614)
Oedipus (England, 1563). Tiresias the prophet.

Nodier, Charles (France, 1780–1844)
Infernalia (France, 1822). Vampirism.
Le vampire (France, 1820). Vampirism.

Norton, Thomas (England, 1532–84)
Gorboduc; or, Ferrex and Porrex (England, 1561). In collaboration with Thomas Sackville. Wild Men as ancient Britons. Three Furies from hell.

O'Casey, Sean (Ireland, 1884–1964)
Cock-a-Doodle-Dandy (Ireland, 1948). Irish superstitions. Exorcism.

Olson, Elder (United States, 1909–92)
Faust: A Masque (United States, n.d.). Faust. Demonic pact.

O'Neill, Eugene (United States, 1888–1953)
The Emperor Jones (United States, 1920; 1921). Voodoo. Apparitions.
Exorcism (United States, 1920). One-act play.

Orrery, Roger Boyle, Earl of (Ireland, 1621–79)
The Tragedy of Zoroastres (Ireland, 1676). Zoroaster. Magic. Spirits.

Otway, Thomas (England, 1652–85)
The History and Fall of Caius Marius (England, 1679). Syrian witch Martha. Spirits.

Ourry, Maurice (France, 1776–1843)
Le loup-garou (France, 1807). In collaboration with Francis Ourry. Werewolf.

Payne, Henry Neville (England, ca. 1648–1705)
The Fatal Jealousie (England, 1672). Witchcraft. Imps. Devils.

Peabody, Josephine Preston (United States, 1874–1922)
The Piper (United States, 1909; 1910). Devil.

Peele, George (England, ca. 1557–96)
The Arraignment of Paris (England, ca. 1584). Pan. Pluto. Numerous other Greek deities.
The Battle of Alcazar (England, ca. 1594).
The Old Wives' Tale (England, ca. 1593). Magic. Warlock Sacripant.
Sir Clyomon and Sir Clamydes (England, ca. 1575). Magician Brian Sansfoy.

Percy, William (England, 1575–1648)
The Fairy Pastoral; or, Forest of Elves/The Fairy Chase; or, Forest of Elves (England, 1603). Fairies.
Necromantes; or, The Two Supposed Heads (England, 1632). Magic.

Phelps, Lyon (United States, 1923–)
The Gospel Witch: A Poetic Drama (United States, 1952). Salem witchcraft.

Pichette, Henri (France, 1924–2000)
Les epiphanies (France, 1948; 1969). Surreal play. Word alchemy. L'Illuminé. Devil.

Pikerynge, John (England, 1544–96)
A Newe Enterlude of Vice Conteyninge the Historye of Horestes (England, 1567). Morality play. Orestes.

Planché, James Robinson (England, 1796–1880)
The Vampire; or, The Bride of the Isles (England, 1820). Vampire.

Plautus, Titus Macc(i)us (Rome, 250–184 B.C.E.)
Amphitryon (Rome, ca. 186 B.C.E.). Greek gods. Transformation.
Mostellaria/The Haunted House (Rome, early second century B.C.E.). Feigned haunting.

Porter, Thomas (England, 1636–80)
The French Conjurer (England, 1677). Magic.

Pottecher, Maurice (France, 1867–1960)
Chacun cherche son trésor (France, 1899). Comedy. Sorcery.
Le reine de l'esprit (France, 1891).

Potter, Dennis (England, 1935–94)
Brimstone and Treacle (England, ca. 1976).

Powell, George (England, 1659–1714)
The Imposture Defeated; or, A Trick to Cheat the Devil (England, 1697).

Preston, Thomas (England, 1537–98?)
A Lamentable Tragedie, Mixed Full of Pleasant Mirth, Containing the Life of Cambises, King of Percia (England, ca. 1569). Morality play. Greek deities.

Provost, Serge (Canada, 1952–)
Le vampire et la nymphomane (Canada, n.d.). Vampire.

Przybyzewski, Stanislaw (Poland, 1868–1927)
Goscie/Visitors (Poland, 1901). One-act play. Double. Diabolic powers.

Pushkin, Alexander Sergeyevich (Russia, 1799–1837)
Kamyenni gost'/The Stone Guest (Russia, 1837). Don Juan.
Rusalka/The Water Nymph (Russia, 1832). Unfinished play. Female spirit.

Quinault, Philippe (France, 1635–88)
Amadis (France, 1684). Chivalric fantasy.
Le fantôme amoureux/The Amorous Ghost (France, 1656). Based on a Spanish *comedia.* Ghost.

Racine, Jean (France, 1639–99)
Iphigénie (France, 1674). Based on Euripides. Oracle.

Raimund, Ferdinand (Austria, 1790–1836)
Moisasurs Zauberfluch (Austria, 1827). Magic.

Randolph, Thomas (England, 1605–35)
Amyntas; or, The Impossible Diary (England, 1633).
The Fary Knight (England, ca. 1623).

Rastell, John (England, ca. 1475–1536)
Calisto and Melebea (England, 1527). Translation/adaptation of part of Fernando de Rojas's *Tragicomedia de Calixto y Melibea.*

Ravenscroft, Edward (England, ca. 1643–1707)
Dame Dobson; or, The Cunning Woman (England, 1683). Adapted from the Corneille and Donneau play *La devineresse; ou, Les faux enchantements.* Witchcraft.
Scaramouch a Philosopher; Harlequin as Schoolboy, Bravo, Merchant and Magician (England, 1677). Harlequin. Magic.

Raynouard, François-Just Marie (France, 1761–1836)
Les Templiers (France, 1805). Templars. Sorcery.

Regnard, Jean-François (France, 1655–1709)
Le retour imprévu (France, 1700). One-act comedy.

Ribié, César (France, 1755–1830)
Le pied de mouton (France, 1807). In collaboration with A. Alphonse Martainville.

Rich, John (England, ca. 1682–1761)
Harlequin Necromancer and Dr. Faustus (England, 1723). Staged by John Rich at Lincoln's Inn Fields. Harlequin. Faust.

Harlequin Sorcerer (England, 1717). First pantomime. Magic.
Orpheus and Eurydice (England, 1739). Underworld. Harlequin. Serpent.

Richards, Ivor Armstrong (England, 1893–1979)
Tomorrow Morning, Faustus! (England, 1962). Faust in a business setting.

Richardson, Howard (United States, 1917–85)
Dark of the Moon (United States, 1945). In collaboration with William Berney. A dramatization of "The Ballad of Barbara Allen." Witchcraft.

Ritter, L. (Germany, nineteenth century)
Der Vampyr oder die Todten-Braut (Germany, 1822). Vampire. After Lord Byron.

Robert, Clémence (France, b. 1735)
Le Diable dans un bénitier (France). Devil.

Rojas, Fernando de (Spain, 1470–1540)
Tragicomedia de Calixto y Melibea (Spain, 1499, 1502). Attributed. Celestina. Magic.

Rotrou, Jean (France, 1609–50)
Les sosies (France, 1638). Influenced by Plautus's *Amphitryon*. Jupiter's seduction of Alcmène.

Rowe, Dana P. (United States, twentieth century)
The Witches of Eastwick (United States, 2000). Musical in collaboration with John Dempsey, based on the novel by John Updike. Witchcraft. Devil.

Rowley, William (England, ca. 1585–ca. 1642)
The Birth of Merlin; or, The Childe Hath Found His Father (England, 1608, published 1662). Merlin. Magic. Devil.
The Changeling (England, 1622). In collaboration with Thomas Middleton. Changeling lore used as comic subplot.
A Courtly Masque: The Device Called, the World Tost at Tennis (England, 1620). In collaboration with Thomas Middleton. Devil.
The Witch of Edmonton (England, ca. 1621). In collaboration with John Ford and Thomas Dekker. Witchcraft. Elizabeth Sawyer tried as a black witch. Familiar.

Rudkin, David (England, 1936–)
Afore Night Come (England, 1962). Ritual sacrifice.

Rutebeuf (France, ca. 1230–86)
Miracle de Théophile (France, ca. 1261). Prototype of the Devil pact in drama.

Sackville, Thomas (England, 1536–1608)
Gorboduc; or, Ferrex and Porrex (England, 1561). In collaboration with Thomas Norton. Wild Men as ancient Britons.

Sardou, Victorien (France, 1831–1908)
Les diables noirs (France, ca. 1863). Devil.
La sorcière (France, 1903). Witchcraft. Spanish Inquisition.
Spiritisme (France, 1897). Spiritism.

Sartre, Jean Paul (France, 1905–80)
Le Diable et le bon Dieu (France, 1951). Devil.
Huis clos (France, 1944). Hell. Devil.

Sayers, Dorothy (England, 1893–1957)
The Devil to Pay (England, 1939). Faust.
The Zeal of Thy House (England, 1937). Archangels.

Schafranek, Dorothea (Austria, 1938–)
Der Blutsauger (Austria, 1988). Vampire.

Schildt, Runar (Finland, 1888–1925)
Galgamannen: En midvintersaga/The Gallows Man: A Midwinter Story (Finland, 1922). One act. Gallows Man, a magic talisman.

Schiller, Friedrich (Germany, 1759–1805)
Don Carlos (Germany, 1787). Spanish Inquisition.

Scott, Sir Walter (England, 1771–1832)
Erl-King (England, 1797). Translation of the work by Goethe. Green Man or Wild Man. Herleking.
Guy Mannering; or, The Astrologer (England, 1815). Astrology.

Scribe, Eugène (France, 1791–1861)
Cagliostro (France, ca. 1833). Magic.
Le domino noir (France, 1837).
La fée aux roses (France, 1849).
Fra Diavolo (France). Libretto for the opera.
Le loup-garou (France, 1827). Libretto with Mazères for an "opéra-comique." Werewolf.
Le philtre (France, 1831). Potion.
Robert le Diable (France, 1831). Libretto for the opera by Meyerbeer. Haunted convent.
Le vampire (France, 1820). One-act "comédie-vaudeville" in collaboration with Mélesville. Vampirism.

Seneca, Lucius Annaeus (Rome, ca. 4 B.C.E.–ca. 65 C.E.)
Medea (Rome). Medea as a witch.

Settle, Elkanah (England, 1648–1724)
The Fairy Queen (England, 1692). Adaptation of Shakespeare's *A Midsummer Night's Dream.* Fairies.

Shadwell, Thomas (England, ca. 1642–92)
The Lancashire Witches and Tegue O'Divelly, the Irish Priest (England, 1682). Based on Heywood and Brome's play. Witchcraft.
The Tempest; or, The Enchanted Island (England, 1674). Adaptation of Shakespeare's play in collaboration with Thomas Betterton. Magic.

Shakespeare, William (England, 1564–1616)
The Comedy of Errors (England, ca. 1597). Adapted from Plautus' *The Twin Menaechmi* (Greece, third century B.C.E.). Wizard.

Hamlet, Prince of Denmark (England, ca. 1600). Specter.
Julius Caesar (England, ca. 1598). Prognostication.
King Henry the Fourth, Part 1 (England, ca. 1597).
King Henry the Sixth, Part 1 (England, ca. 1591). Joan of Arc as Joan la Poucelle, a black witch. Fiend.
King Henry the Sixth, Part 2 (England, ca. 1591). Witchcraft by Margery Jourdain. Magic by Roger Bolinbroke. Spirit Asmath.
King Lear (England, ca. 1605).
Macbeth (England, ca. 1606). Witchcraft and prognostications by the Weird Sisters. Hecate. Ghost.
The Merry Wives of Windsor (England, ca. 1598).
A Midsummer Night's Dream (England, ca. 1595). Transformations. Puck. Oberon. Titania. Fairies.
Richard III (England, 1592).
Romeo and Juliet (England, ca. 1595).
The Tempest (England, ca. 1612). Magic. Witchcraft. Ariel. Caliban.

Sharp, William (pseudonym Fiona Macleod, Scotland, 1855–1905)
The Black Madonna (Scotland). Isis.
The Passing of Lilith (Scotland, 1886; 1893). Lilith, first consort of Adam.

Shaw, George Bernard (Ireland, 1856–1950)
Back to Methusaleh (Ireland, 1921). Lilith.
Don Juan in Hell (Ireland, 1903). Don Juan. Hell. Devil.
Saint Joan (Ireland, 1923). Joan of Arc. Inquisition. Witchcraft.

Shelley, Percy Bysshe (England, 1792–1822)
Prometheus Unbound (England, 1818–19; 1820). Greek mythology.

Sheppard, Samuel (England, ca. 1624–ca. 1655)
The Jovial Crew; or, The Devil Turned Ranter (England, 1651).

Sherburne, Sir Edward (England, 1618–1702)
Medea (England, 1648). Translation of Seneca's work. Medea.

Shirley, James (England, 1596–1666)
The Lady of Pleasure (England, 1635). Talk of a witch.
Night-Walker; or, The Little Thief (England, 1634). In collaboration with John Fletcher.
Saint Patrick for Ireland (England, 1639). Archimagus and other Druids.

Skelton, John (England, 1460–1529)
Nigramansir (England, ca. 1504). Devil. Magic.

Sophocles (Greece, ca. 496–405 B.C.E.)
Antigone (Greece, ca. 441 B.C.E.). The seer Tiresias. Prognostication.
Oedipus the King (Greece, ca. 430 B.C.E.). The seer Tiresias. Prognostication.
Philoctetes (Greece, ca. 409 B.C.E.). Magic bow. Heracles.

Spire, André (France, 1868–1966)
Samael (France, 1921). Gnostic deity.

Steinman, Jim (Austria, twentieth century).
Tanz der Vampire: Das Musical (Austria, 1988). Vampire.

Strindberg, August (Sweden, 1849–1912)
Charles XII (Sweden). Swedenborg as a seer.
Ett drömspel/A Dream Play (Sweden, 1901–2). Dream imagery. Daughter of the god Indra.
Spöksonaten/The Ghost Sonata (Sweden, 1907). Symbolic ghosts. Symbolic vampire.
Till Damaskus/To Damascus (Sweden, 1898–1904). Trilogy with occult and Swedenborgian mysticism.

Studley, John (England, ca. 1545–ca. 1590)
Medea (England, 1566). Translation of Seneca's work. Medea.

Suckling, Sir John (England, 1609–42)
The Goblins (England, 1638). Influenced by Shakespeare's *The Tempest.*

Svevo, Italo (Ettore Schmitz, Italy, 1861–1928)
Terzetto spezzato/Broken Triangle (Italy, ca. 1920). Spiritism. Séance. Ghost.

Synge, John Millington (Ireland, 1871–1909)
The Well of the Saints (Ireland, 1905). Miracle. Saint.

Taille, J. de la (France, ca. 1540–ca. 1607)
Le négromant (ca. 1562). Magic.

Tate, Nathum (Ireland, 1652–1715)
Brutus of Alba; or, The Enchanted Lovers (Ireland, 1678). Ragussa, the sorceress.
Dido and Aeneas (Ireland, 1689). Libretto for the opera by Henry Purcell. Witchcraft.
Duke and No Duke (Ireland, 1684). Version of Cokayne's *Trappolin creduto principe.*

Tavan, Alphonse (France, 1833–1905)
Les mascs (France, 1897). Sorcery.

Taylor, Bayard (United States, 1825–78)
Faust (United States, 1870–71). Translation of Goethe's work. Faust.

Tennyson, Alfred (England, 1809–92)
The Devil and the Lady (ca. 1823; published 1930). Devil.
The Foresters (England, 1892). Woodland masque. Robin Hood.

Thiboust, Lambert (France, 1826–67)
Les diables roses (France, ca. 1863). In collaboration with E. Grangé. Comedy.

Thies, Eva-Maria (Germany, twentieth century)
Kein Blut für Dracula: Eine Grusel-Krimi-Parodie (Germany, 1994). Vampire.

Thomas, Augustus (United States, 1857–1934)
The Witching Hour (United States, 1907). Hypnotism.

T[homson], T[homas] (England)
The Life of Mother Shipton (England, 1670). Witchcraft. Pluto. Proserpina. Devils.

Thurmond, John (England, fl. 1724–49)
Harlequin Doctor Faustus (England, 1723). Pantomime. Faust.

Tolstoy, Count Leo (Russia, 1828–1910)
Pervyi vinokur/The First Distiller (Russia, 1886). Morality play. Devil.

Tourneur, Cyril (England, ca. 1580–1626)
The Atheist's Tragedie (England, ca. 1611). Specter.

Ukrainka, Lesia (Ukraine, 1871–1913)
Forest Song (Ukraine, 1912). Fairies.

Ustinov, Peter (England, 1921–2004)
The Love of Four Colonels (England, 1951). The Evil Fairy.

Van Druten, John (United States, 1901–57)
Bell, Book, and Candle (United States, 1948). Modern witchcraft.

Vane, Sutton (England, 1888–1963)
Outward Bound (England, 1923). Ghosts.

Veiller, Bayard (England, 1869–1943)
The Thirteenth Chair (1916). Spirits.

Vigne, André de la (France, ca. 1457–ca. 1527)
La farce du Meunier (France). Devils.

Villiers de l'Isle-Adam, Jean Marie, Comte de (France, 1838–89)
Axel (France, 1890). Occultism based on Eliphas Levi. Rosicrucianism.

Vivie, Aurélian (France, nineteenth century)
La sorcière Canidie (France, 1888). One act. Witchcraft.

Voltaire, François Marie Arouet de (France, 1694–1778)
Oedipe (France, 1718). Tiresias the prophet.
Tanis et Zelide (France). Magician.

Vondel, Joost van den (Holland, 1587–1679)
Lucifer (Holland, 1654). Devil. Fall of the angels.

Vroncourt de la Ville, Raymond (France, b. 1883)
The Mystery Play of Love (France). Lucifer.

Walpole, Horace (England, 1717–97)
The Castle of Otranto (England, ca. 1764). Version of the novel. Gothic.

Webster, John (England, ca. 1575–ca. 1634)
The Devil's Law Case (England, 1617).

Wedekind, Frank (Germany, 1864–1918)
Die Büchse der Pandora/Pandora's Box (Germany, 1902). Sequel to *Earth Spirit*. Jack the Ripper.

Erdgeist/Earth Spirit (Germany, 1895). Snake-woman, sex incarnate.
Frühlings Erwachen/Spring's Awakening (Germany, 1891). Ghost.

Werfel, Franz (Czechoslovakia, 1890–1945)
Bocksgesang/Goat Song (Czechoslovakia, 1926). Changeling. Dionysus.
The Song of Bernadette (United States, 1941). Visions.

Wever, Richard (England, ca. 1500–1560)
Lusty Juventus (England, ca. 1550). Sathan the Deuyll.

Whiting, John (England, 1917–63)
The Devils (England, 1961). Based on *The Devils of Loudun* by Aldous Huxley. Possession. Exorcism.

Widmann, Joseph Viktor (Germany, 1842–1911)
Der heilege und die tiere (Germany, 1912). Puppet play. Lilith. Asasel.

Wiers-Jenssen, Hans (Norway, 1866–1925)
Anne Pedersdotter (Norway). Translated as *The Witch* by John Masefield. Witchcraft.

Williams, Charles (England, 1886–1945)
Grab and Grace; or, It's the Second Step (England). Morality play. Sequel to *The House by the Stable.* Hell personified.
The House by the Stable: A Christmas Play (England). Morality play. Hell personified.

Wilmer, Lambert A. (United States, 1805–63)
Merlin (United States, 1827). Magic. Merlin. Spirits. Furies.

Wilmot, Robert (England, 1566–1608)
Tancred and Gismunda (England, ca. 1568).

Wilson, John (England, 1627–96)
Belphegor; or, The Marriage of the Devil (England, ca. 1690). Comedy. Devils.

Wohlbrück, Wilhelm August (Germany, 1796–1861)
Der Vampyr (Germany, 1828). Opera libretto. Music by Heinrich Marschner.

Woodes, Nathaniel (England, b. ca. 1550)
The Conflict of Conscience (England, 1568). Morality play.

Wulfingen, Bock von (Germany, late nineteenth, early twentieth century).
Ein Vampir unsere Tage (Germany, 1910). Vampire.

Wyspianski, Stanislaw (Poland, 1869–1930)
Acropolis (Poland, 1903). Syncretic mythology.
Noc listopadowa/November Night (Poland). Eleusinian mystery. Greek mythology.

Yeats, William Butler (Ireland, 1865–1939)
At the Hawk's Well (Ireland, 1917). Suggested witch, the Guardian of the Well. Changeling lore.
The Countess Cathleen (Ireland, 1892). Demons. Angels.

The Green Helmet (Ireland, 1910). A spirit, Red Man, with horns. Cat-headed Black Men. Cuchulain.
The Herne's Egg (Ireland, 1938). Herne. The god's priestess, Attracta. Trance.
The Hourglass (Ireland, 1914). Angel as herald of death.
The Land of Heart's Desire (Ireland, 1894). One act. Fairy child.
The Only Jealousy of Emer (Ireland, 1919). Ghost of Cuchulain. Sidhe. Changeling lore.
The Words upon the Window-Pane (Ireland, 1934). Spiritualism. Séance.

Zuckmayer, Carl (Germany, 1896–1977)
Des Teufel General/The Devil's General (Germany, 1946). Hitler as Devil.

Recurrent Major Occult Motifs in Western Drama

Alchemy
The Alchemist (England, 1610) by Ben Jonson.
L'alchimiste (France, 1839) by Alexandre Dumas père.
Il candelaio (Italy, 1582) by Giordano Bruno.
The Jest of Hahalaba (Ireland, 1928) by Lord Dunsany.
Mercury Vindicated from the Alchemists at Court (England, 1616) by Ben Jonson.

Astrology
An Evening's Love; or, The Mock Astrologer (England, 1668) by John Dryden.
The Faire Maide of the Inne (England, 1626) by John Fletcher and Philip Massinger.
The Feigned Astrologer (England, 1668, anonymous).
Le feint astrologue (France, ca. 1668) by Thomas Corneille.

Cassandra/Sibyls
Agamemnon (Greece, 458 B.C.E.) by Aeschylus.
The Sibyl (Sweden, 1956) by Pär Lagerkvist.
The Tower beyond Tragedy (United States, 1925) by Robinson Jeffers.
Tres sibyllae (England, 1605) by Matthew Gwinne.
The Trojan Women (Greece, 415 B.C.E.) by Euripides.

Cave
Il re cervo/The King Stag (Italy, 1762) by Count Carlo Gozzi.
The Temple of Love (England, 1634) by Sir William D'Avenant.

Circe
Circe (England, 1676) by Robert Davenport.
Circe (England, 1677) by Charles D'Avenant.
Ulysses and Circe (England, 1615) by William Browne.

Demonic Pact
The Devils (England, 1961) by John Whiting.
Donnerstag (Switzerland) by Fritz Hochwälder.
Faust (Germany, 1808 [pt. 1], 1832 [pt. 2]) by Johann Wolfgang von Goethe.

Faust: A Masque (United States, n.d.) by Elder Olson.
Irydion (Poland, 1836) by Zygmunt Krasinski.
Le Miracle de Théophile (France, ca. 1261) by Rutebeuf.
Tomorrow Morning, Faustus! (England, 1962) by I. A. Richards.
The Tragical History of the Life and Death of Doctor Faustus (England, ca. 1592) by Christopher Marlowe.

Devil

L'an mille (France) by Maurice Magre.
Belphagor; or, The Marriage of the Devil (England, ca. 1690) by John Wilson.
A Courtly Masque: The Device Called, the World Tost at Tennis (England, 1620) by Thomas Middleton and William Rowley.
The Creation, and the Fall of Lucifer (England, medieval, anonymous).
The Devil (Hungary, 1907) by Ferenc Molnár.
The Devil and Daniel Webster (United States, 1939) by Stephen Vincent Benet.
The Devil and Dives (England, 1570, anonymous).
The Devil and the Lady (ca. 1823; published 1930) by Alfred Tennyson.
The Devil of the Second Stairs (United States, 1967) by George Herman.
Le Diable couturier (France, 1894) by Louis Ciercelin.
Le Diable dans un bénitier (France, 185?) by Clémence Robert.
Le Diable et le bon Dieu (France, 1951) by Jean Paul Sartre.
Les diables noirs (France, ca. 1863) by Victorien Sardou.
Les epiphanies (France, 1948; 1969) by Henri Pichette.
The Ghost of Abel (England, 1822) by William Blake.
Der heilege und die tiere (Germany, 1912) by Joseph Viktor Widmann.
Huis clos (France, 1944) by Jean Paul Sartre.
JB (United States, 1958) by Archibald MacLeish.
Jedermann/Everyman (Austria, 1910) by Hugo von Hofmannsthal.
Le jeu de la feuillée (France, ca. 1276) by Adam de la Halle.
Lucifer (Holland, 1654) by Joost van den Vondel.
Machiavel and the Devil (England, 1613) by Robert Daborne.
A Marvellous History of Mary of Nimmegen, who for more than seven years lived and had ado with the Devil (Holland, ca. 1520, anonymous).
The Marvelous History of St. Bernard (France, 1924) by Henri Ghéon.
Mefistofele (Italy, 1868) by Arrigo Boito.
The Merry Devil of Edmonton (England, ca. 1608, anonymous).
Le miracle de Théophile (France, ca. 1261) by Rutebeuf.
A New Trick to Cheat the Devil (England, 1625) by Robert Davenport.
Nigramansir (England, ca. 1504) by John Skelton.
Les noces de Satan (France, 1892) by Jules Bois.
Parade at Devil's Bridge (France) by Henri Ghéon.
Pervyi vinokur/The First Distiller (Russia, 1886) by Count Leo Tolstoy.
The Piper (United States, 1909; 1910) by Josephine Preston Peabody.
The Playe Called the Foure PP (England, ca. 1523; published 1545) by John Heywood.
Pluto furens et vinctus; or, The Raging Devil Bound (England, 1669) by William Carr.
Processus Satanae (England, 1575, anonymous).

The Scarecrow (United States, 1908) by Percy Wallace MacKaye.
Scherz, Satire, Ironie und tiefere Bedeutung/Hest, Satire, Irony, and Deeper Significance (Germany, 1822) by Christian Dietrich Grabbe.
The State of Innocence, and the Fall of Man/The Fall of Angels and Man in Innocence (England, 1677) by John Dryden.
The Tragedy of Job (United States) by Horace Meyer Kallen.
The Witches of Eastwick (United States, 2000) by John Dempsey and Dana P. Rowe.

Don Juan
Il convitato di pietra (Italy, seventeenth century) by Iacopo Cicognini.
Don Juan (France, 1958) by Henri de Montherlant.
Don Juan in Hell (Ireland, 1903) by George Bernard Shaw.
Le festin de pierre (France, 1665) by Molière.
L'homme et ses fantômes/Man and His Phantoms (France, 1924) by Henri-René Lenormand.
Kamyenni gost'/The Stone Guest (Russia, 1837) by Alexander Sergeyevich Pushkin.
Togda v Sevill'e (Russia, 1947, 1961) by Samuel Aleshin.

Fairies
Delphrygus and the King of Fairies (England, 1570, anonymous).
Endimion (England, 1585) by John Lyly.
The Faire Maide of the Inne (England, 1626) by Philip Massinger and John Fletcher.
The Fairy Knight (England, 1624) by Thomas Dekker and John Ford.
The Fairy Knight; or, Oberon the Second (England, 1638, anonymous).
The Fairy Pastoral; or, Forest of Elves/The Fairy Chase; or, Forest of Elves (England, 1603) by William Percy.
The Fairy Queen (England, 1692) by Elkanah Settle.
A Fairy Tale (Russia, ca. 1921) by Il'ia Erenberg.
The Fary Knight (England, ca. 1623) by Thomas Randolph.
Le fées ou les contes de ma mère l'oye (France, 1697, anonymous).
Fiaba dell'amore delle tre melarance/The Love of Three Oranges (Italy, 1761) by Carlo Gozzi.
Forest Song (Ukraine, 1912) by Lesia Ukrainka.
The Land of Heart's Desire (Ireland, 1894) by William Butler Yeats.
The Love of Four Colonels (England, 1951) by Peter Ustinov.
Mary Rose (England, 1935) by Sir James M. Barrie.
A Midsummer Night's Dream (England, ca. 1595) by William Shakespeare.
Oberon, the Faerie King (England, 1611) by Ben Jonson.
Ondine (France, 1939) by Jean Giraudoux.
Die versunkene Glocke/The Sunken Bell (Germany, 1896) by Gerhart Hauptmann.

Faust
The Deformed Transformed (England, 1821) by George Gordon, Lord Byron.
The Devil to Pay (England, 1939) by Dorothy Sayers.
Doctor Faustus, with the Humours of Harlequin and Scaramouche (England, 1686) by William Mountfort.
Faust (Germany, 1808 [pt. 1], 1832 [pt. 2]) by Johann Wolfgang von Goethe.

Faust (France, 1828) by Gérard de Nerval.
Faust (Austria, 1835) by Nikolaus Lenau.
Faust (United States, 1870–71) by Bayard Taylor.
Faust: A Masque (United States, n.d.) by Elder Olson.
Faust i gorod/Faust and the City (Russia, 1918) by Anatolii Lunacharskii.
Harlequin Doctor Faustus (England, 1723) by John Thurmond.
Harlequin Necromancer and Dr. Faustus (England, 1723) by John Rich.
An Irish Faust (England, 1963) by Lawrence Durrell.
Tomorrow Morning, Faustus! (England, 1962) by I. A. Richards.
The Tragical History of the Life and Death of Doctor Faustus (England, ca. 1592) by Christopher Marlowe.

Ghosts, Specters, Séances, and Spiritism
And Things That Go Bump in the Night (United States, 1964) by Terrence MacNally.
Blithe Spirit (England, 1941) by Noel Coward.
Clara (United States, 1987) by Arthur Miller.
The Devil of the Second Stairs (United States, 1967) by George Herman.
I fantasmi (Italy, 1547) by Ercole Bentivoglio.
Frühlings Erwachen/Spring's Awakening (Germany, 1891) by Frank Wedekind.
The Ghost; or, The Woman Wears the Breeches (England, 1640, anonymous).
The Ghosts (England, 1665) by John Holden.
The Goblins (England, 1638) by Sir John Suckling.
Hamlet, Prince of Denmark (England, ca. 1600) by William Shakespeare.
Hannels Himmelfahrt/Little Hanne's Journey to Heaven (Germany, 1893) by Gerhart Hauptmann.
L'homme et ses fantômes/Man and His Phantoms (France, 1924) by Henri-René Lenormand.
The Innocents (England, 1950) by William Archibald.
Intermezzo (France, 1933) by Jean Giraudoux.
The Jew of Malta (England, ca. 1592) by Christopher Marlowe.
The Medium (Italy, 1946) by Gian Carlo Menotti.
The Only Jealousy of Emer (Ireland, 1919) by William Butler Yeats.
Pundak haroochot/The Inn of Ghosts (Poland, 1962) by Nathan Alterman.
Terzetto spezzato/Broken Triangle (Italy, ca. 1920) by Italo Svevo.
There Is Something Out There (United States, 1962) by Terrence MacNally.
The Thirteenth Chair (1916) by Bayard Veiller.
The Weir (Ireland, 1999) by Conor McPherson.
The Words upon the Window-Pane (Ireland, 1934) by William Butler Yeats.

Harlequin
Arlequin, Empereur dans la Lune (France, 1684, anonymous).
Arlequin poli par l'amour (France, 1720) by Pierre Carlet de Chamblain de Marivaux.
Doctor Faustus, with the Humours of Harlequin and Scaramouche (England, 1686) by William Mountfort.
Le fées ou les contes de ma mère l'oye (France, 1697, anonymous).
Harlequin Amulet; or, The Magic of Mona (England, 1800, anonymous).
Harlequin Dame Trot (England, eighteenth century, anonymous).

Harlequin Doctor Faustus (England, 1723) by John Thurmond.
Harlequin in His Element; or, Fire, Water, Earth, and Air (England, 1810) by Charles Dibdin.
Harlequin Mother Bunch (England, eighteenth century, anonymous).
Harlequin Munchausen; or, The Fountain of Love (England, 1818, anonymous).
Harlequin Necromancer and Dr. Faustus (England, 1723) by John Rich.
Harlequin Sorcerer (England, 1717) by John Rich.
Harlequin Student, or, The Fall of Pantomime, with the Restoration of the Drama (England, 1741, anonymous).
Harlequin's Invasion; or, A Christmas Gambol (England, 1759, anonymous).
Histoire plaisante des faicts et gestes de Harlequin commedien italien (France, 1585, anonymous).
Le jeu de la feuillée/Play of the Bower (France, ca. 1276) by Adam de la Halle.
The Lancashire Witches; or, The Distresses of Harlequin (England, 1782) by Charles Dibdin.
Orpheus and Eurydice (England, 1739) by John Rich.
Scaramouch a Philosopher; Harlequin as Schoolboy, Bravo, Merchant and Magician (England, 1677) by Edward Ravenscroft.

Joan of Arc
L'alouette/The Lark (France, 1953) by Jean Anouilh.
Jeanne d'Arc (United States, 1906) by Percy Wallace MacKaye.
Jeanne d'Arc au bûcher/Joan of Arc at the Stake (France, 1939) by Paul Claudel.
Joan of Lorraine (United States, 1947) by Maxwell Anderson.
King Henry the Sixth, Part 1 (England, ca. 1591) by William Shakespeare.
Lat manniskan leva/Let Man Live (Sweden, 1949) by Pär Lagerkvist.
Saint Joan (Ireland, 1923) by George Bernard Shaw.

Last Judgment
Day of Judgment (York, England, medieval, anonymous).
Doomsday (Coventry, England, medieval, anonymous).
Doomsday (Towneley, England, medieval, anonymous).
Doomsday (York, England, 1433, anonymous).
The Last Judgement (York, England, medieval, anonymous).

Lilith
Adam and Eve (United States, 1927) by John Erskine.
Asfeld Passion Play (Germany, medieval, anonymous).
Back to Methusaleh (Ireland, 1921) by George Bernard Shaw.
Faust (Germany, 1808 [pt. 1], 1832 [pt. 2]) by Johann Wolfgang von Goethe.
Der heilege und die tiere (Germany, 1912) by Joseph Viktor Widmann.
Juttaspiel (Germany, medieval, anonymous).
Lilith (France, 1892) by Remy de Gourmont.
The Passing of Lilith (England, 1886; 1893) by William Sharp.
Pope Joan (Germany, 1480, anonymous).

Lycanthropy
Báthori Erzsébet (Hungary, 1840) by János Garay.
Báthory Erzsébet (Hungary, 1882) by Zoltan Balogh.

Báthory Erzsébet (France, 1978) by Marie-François Egret.
Der Blutsauger (Austria, 1988) by Dorothea Schafranek.
Blutsauger (Austria, 1997). Multimedia presentation.
Cadet Buteux, vampire (France, 1820) by Marc Antoine Madeleine Désaugiers.
Carmilla (England, 1932) by Frank Pakenham, Earl of Longford.
Dracula (England, 1927) by Hamilton Deane.
Dracula (United States) by Frederick Gaines.
Dracula, esercizio sul terrore (Italy, 1983) by Mario Moretti.
Dracula, il vampiro (Italy, 1980) by Elio De Capitani, Ida Marinelli, and Gabriele Salvatores.
Encore un vampire (France, 1820) by Emile B. L.
Infernalia (France, 1822) by Charles Nodier.
Kein Blut für Dracula: Eine Grusel-Krimi-Parodie (Germany, 1994) by Eva-Maria Thies.
Krankheit oder moderne Frauen (Austria, 1987) by Elfriede Jelinek.
Le loup-garou (France, 1807) by Maurice Ourry.
Le loup-garou (France, 1827) by Eugène Scribe.
The Phantom (Ireland, 1856) by Dion Boucicault.
Polichinel vampire (France, 1823) by François Alexis Blache.
Tanz der Vampire: Das Musical (Austria, 1988) by Jim Steinman.
Tepes Voda (Romania, 1823) by Ion Catina.
Les trois vampires; ou, Le clair de la lune (France, 1820) by Gabriel and Armand Brazier.
Ein Uhr! (Germany, 1822) by Cäsar Max Heigel.
Ein Vampir unsere Tage (Germany, 1910) by Bock von Wulfingen.
Le vampire (France, 1820) by Pierre de la Fossé.
Le vampire (France, 1820) by Martinet.
Le vampire (France, 1820) by Charles Nodier.
Le vampire (France, 1820) by Eugène Scribe.
Le vampire (Belgium, 1826) by Martin Joseph Mengals.
Le vampire (France, 1851) by Alexandre Dumas and Auguste Maquet.
The Vampire (Ireland, 1852) by Dion Boucicault.
Le vampire de la rue (France, n.d.) by Albert Masquellier.
Le vampire et la nymphomane (Canada, n.d.) by Serge Provost.
Vampire et loup garou; ou, Le violon de voyage (France, 1870?) by Eugène De Richemont and Leon Frank.
Der Vampyr (Germany, 1827) by Friederike Ellmenreich.
Der Vampyr (Germany, 1828) by Alexander Cosmar.
Der Vampyr (Germany, 1828) by C. M. Heigel.
Der Vampyr (Germany, 1828) by Heinrich Marschner.
Der Vampyr (Germany, 1828) by Wilhelm August Wohlbrück.
Der Vampyr oder die Todten-Braut (Germany, 1822) by L. Ritter.
The Vampire: A Tragedy (England, 1821) by St. John Dorset.
The Vampire; or, The Bride of the Isles (England, 1820) by James Robinson Planché.
Vayvode (England, 1598) by Henry Chettle.
Vladu Tsepeshu, drama istorica în cinci acte (Romania, 1858) by G. Mavrodollu.
The Weirwolf: A Tragedy (England, 1876) by William Forster.

Magic

Cagliostro (France, ca. 1833) by Eugène Scribe.
Il candelaio (Italy, 1582) by Giordano Bruno.
Dear Brutus (England, 1917, 1923) by Sir James M. Barrie.
The Divils Charter (England, 1607) by Barnabe Barnes.
The French Conjurer (England, 1677) by Thomas Porter.
Harlequin Necromancer and Dr. Faustus (England, 1723) by John Rich.
Harlequin Sorcerer (England, 1717) by John Rich.
Harlequin Student; or, The Fall of Pantomime, with the Restoration of the Drama (England, 1741, anonymous).
Hocus Pocus (England, 1638, anonymous).
The Honorable History of Friar Bacon and Friar Bungay (England, ca. 1589) by Robert Greene.
L'illusion comique (France, 1636) by Pierre Corneille.
Intermezzo (France, 1933) by Jean Giraudoux.
The Jest of Hahalaba (Ireland, 1928) by Lord Dunsany.
John a Kent and John a Cumber (England, ca. 1595) by Anthony Munday.
King Henry the Sixth, Part 2 (England, ca. 1591) by William Shakespeare.
Il mago (Italy, 1569) by Flamminio Guarnieri.
The Merry Devil of Edmonton (England, ca. 1599) by Michael Drayton.
Moisasurs Zauberfluch (Austria, 1827) by Ferdinand Raimund.
Necromantes; or, The Two Supposed Heads (England, 1632) by William Percy.
Le négromant (France, ca. 1562) by J. de la Taille.
Il negromante (Italy, 1520; 1528) by Ludovico Ariosto.
Nigramansir (England, ca. 1504) by John Skelton.
The Old Wives' Tale (England, ca. 1593) by George Peele.
Le prince des sots (France, 1830) by Gérard de Nerval.
Pseudomagia (England, 1626) by William Mewe.
Il re cervo/The King Stag (Italy, 1762) by Count Carlo Gozzi.
Scaramouch a Philosopher; Harlequin as Schoolboy, Bravo, Merchant and Magician (England, 1677) by Edward Ravenscroft.
The Spanish Bawd (England, 1631) by James Mabbe.
Tanis et Zelide (France) by François Marie Arouet de Voltaire.
The Tempest (England, ca. 1612) by William Shakespeare.
[*The Tempest*] (Martinique) by Aimé Fernand Césaire.
The Tempest; or, The Enchanted Island (England, 1667) by Charles D'Avenant and John Dryden.
The Tempest; or, The Enchanted Island (England, 1674) by Thomas Shadwell and Thomas Betterton.
The Temple of Love (England, 1634) by Sir William D'Avenant.
The Tragedy of Zoroastres (Ireland, 1676) by Roger Boyle, Earl of Orrery.
Tragicomedia de Calixto y Melibea (Spain, 1499, 1502) by Fernando de Rojas.
Trappolin creduto principe; or, Trappolin Supposed a Prince (England, 1656) by Sir Aston Cokayne.
Zoroastre (France, 1749) by Louis de Cahusac.

Medea
Medea (Greece, 431 B.C.E.) by Euripides.
Medea (Rome) by Lucius Annaeus Seneca.
Medea (England, 1543) by George Buchanan.
Medea (England, 1566) by John Studley.
Medea (England, 1602) by Thomas Hobbes.
Medea (England, early seventeenth century, anonymous).
Medea (England, 1648) by Sir Edward Sherburne.
Medea (United States, 1946) by Robinson Jeffers.
Médée (France, 1635) by Pierre Corneille.
Médée (France, 1946) by Jean Anouilh.

Merlin
The Birth of Merlin (England, ca. 1612, anonymous).
The Birth of Merlin; or, The Childe Hath Found His Father (England, 1608, published 1662) by William Rowley.
The Knights of the Round Table (France, 1937) by Jean Cocteau.
Merlin (United States, 1827) by Lambert A. Wilmer.
The Quest of Merlin (United States, 1891) by Richard Hovey.
Uther Pendragon (England, 1597, anonymous).

Mouth of Hell
Assumption of Mary (Catalan, before 1420, anonymous).
The Castell of Perseverance (England, ca. 1425, anonymous).
Doomsday (England, medieval, anonymous).
Festa di S. Giovanni (Florence, 1454, anonymous).
The Harrowing of Hell (England, medieval, anonymous).
Le jeu d'Adam (et Eve)/Ordo representacionis Ade (Anglo-Norman, mid-twelfth century, anonymous).
Le mystère de la Passion (Rouen, France, 1474, anonymous).
Le mystère de la Passion (Montferrand, France, 1477, anonymous).
Le mystère de la Passion (Mons, Belgium, 1501, anonymous).
Le mystère de la Passion (Bozen, France, 1514, anonymous).
Le mystère de la Passion (Valenciennes, France, 1547, anonymous).
Le mystère de Sainte Apolline/The Martyrdom of Saint Apollonia (France, mid-fifteenth century, anonymous).
Le mystère de Saint Crespin et Saint Crespinien (France, mid-fifteenth century, anonymous).
Le mystère des saints actes des apostres (Bourges, France, 1536, anonymous).
Le mystère des trois doms (Romans, France, 1509, anonymous).
Ordinale de vita Sancti Mereadoci Episcopi et Confessoris/Saint Meriasek (Cornwall, England, 1504, anonymous).
Osterspiel (Lucerne, Switzerland, 1583, anonymous).
Passion Play (Vienna, Austria, early fourteenth century, anonymous).
Passion Play (Metz, Germany, 1437, anonymous).
Passion Play (Frankfurt, Germany, 1450, anonymous).

Passion Play (Villingen, Germany, 1585, anonymous).
Saint Laurence (France, 1499, anonymous).
Saint Mary Magdalen (Digby, England, late fifteenth century, anonymous).
La seinte Resurreccion (Anglo-Norman, late twelfth century, anonymous).
La seinte Resurreccion (Paris, France, 1419, anonymous).
Das Spiel von den Klugen und Torichten Jungfrauen (Eisenach, Germany, 1322, anonymous).
Sponsus (France, ca. 1096–99, anonymous).
Tobias (Lincoln, England, 1564, anonymous).

Possession and Exorcism
Cock-a-Doodle-Dandy (Ireland, 1948) by Sean O'Casey.
The Devil of the Second Stairs (United States, 1967) by George Herman.
The Devils (England, 1961) by John Whiting.
The Dybbuk (Russia, 1914) by S. An-Sky.
Et les chiens se taisaient (Martinique, 1956) by Aimé Fernand Césaire.
Exorcism (United States, 1920) by Eugene O'Neill.
The Innocents (England, 1950) by William Archibald.
Les possédés (France, 1909) by Henri-René Lenormand.
The Tenth Man (United States, 1960) by Paddy Chayefsky.
Urbain Grandier (France, 1850) by Alexandre Dumas père.

Tiresias
Antigone (Greece, ca. 441 B.C.E.) by Sophocles.
Bacchae (Greece, 405 B.C.E.) by Euripides.
Les mamelles de Tirésias / The Breasts of Tiresias (France, 1918) by Guillaume Apollinaire.
Oedipe (France, 1718) by François Marie Arouet de Voltaire.
Oedipus (England, 1563) by Alexander Neville.
Oedipus (England, 1584) by William Gager.
Oedipus (England, 1678) by John Dryden and Nathaniel Lee.
Oedipus the King (Greece, ca. 430 B.C.E.) by Sophocles.

Vampirism (see Lycanthropy)

Wild Man
Erl-King (England, 1797) by Sir Walter Scott.
Gorboduc; or, Ferrex and Porrex (England, 1561) by Thomas Norton and Thomas Sackville.
Ludus at virum dictum wildman (Aarau, Switzerland, 1399, anonymous).
Magnus ludus de homine salvatico (Padua, Italy, 1208, 1224, anonymous).
A Mask of Foresters; or, Hunters (England 1574, anonymous).
[*Masque*] (England, 1348, anonymous).
The Savage Man and Echo (England, 1575) by George Gascoigne.
Schembartlauf (Nuremberg, Germany, 1539, anonymous).
Twelfth Night (England, 1515, anonymous).

Witchcraft
Anne Pedersdotter (Norway) by Hans Wiers-Jenssen.

Les Basques; ou, La sorcière d'espelette (France, 1892) by Anatole Loquin and Mégret de Belligny.
Bell, Book, and Candle (United States, 1948) by John Van Druten.
The Crucible (United States, 1953) by Arthur Miller.
The Custom of the Country (England, 1628) by Francis Beaumont and John Fletcher.
Dame Dobson; or, The Cunning Woman (England, 1683) by Edward Ravenscroft.
Dark of the Moon (United States, 1945) by Howard Richardson and William Berney.
La devineresse; ou, Les faux enchantements (France, 1679) by Thomas Corneille and Jean Donneau de Vizé.
Doctor Lambe and the Witches (England, 1634, anonymous).
Endor (United States, 1961) by Howard Nemerov.
The Faithful Shepherdess (England, ca. 1608) by John Fletcher.
The Fatal Jealousie (England, 1672) by Henry Neville Payne.
Giles Corey of the Salem Farms (United States) by Henry Wadsworth Longfellow.
The Gospel Witch: A Poetic Drama (United States, 1952) by Lyon Phelps.
King Henry the Sixth, Part 2 (England, ca. 1591) by William Shakespeare.
The Lancashire Witches: A Romance of Pendle Forest (England, 1848) by Edward Fitzball.
The Lancashire Witches and Tegue O'Divelly, the Irish Priest (England, 1682) by Thomas Shadwell.
The Lancashire Witches; or, The Distresses of Harlequin (England, 1782) by Charles Dibdin.
Lat manniskan leva/Let Man Live (Sweden, 1949) by Pär Lagerkvist.
The Late Lancashire Witches (England, 1634) by Thomas Heywood and Richard Brome.
The Life of Mother Shipton (England, 1670) by Thomas Thomson.
Macbeth (England, ca. 1606) by William Shakespeare.
The Masque of Queenes (England, 1609) by Ben Jonson.
Mother Bombie (England, ca. 1590) by John Lyly.
The Prophetess (England, 1622) by John Fletcher and Philip Massinger.
The Sad Shepherd (England, ca. 1637) by Ben Jonson.
The Scarecrow (United States, 1908) by Percy Wallace MacKaye.
The Seven Champions of Christendome (England, 1638) by John Kirke.
The Seven Champions of Christendom (England, anonymous).
La sorcière (France, 1903) by Victorien Sardou.
La sorcière (France, 1962) by Eddy Ghilan.
La sorcière Canidie (France, 1888) by Aurélian Vivie.
La sorcière; ou, L'orphelia écossais (France, 1821) by Frédéric Dupetit-Méré and Victor Ducange.
The Spanish Bawd (England, 1631) by James Mabbe.
Superstition (United States, 1824) by James Nelson Barker.
The Tragedie of Sophonisba (England, ca. 1606) by John Marston.
Vers le Sabbath (France, 1897) by Serge Basset.
The White Witch of Westminster; or, Love in a Lunacy (England, before 1642, anonymous).
The Wise-Woman of Hogsdon (England, ca. 1604) by Thomas Heywood.
The Witch (England, ca. 1612) by Thomas Middleton.
The Witch (England, 1910) by John Masefield.
The Witch of Edmonton (England, ca. 1621) by Thomas Dekker, William Rowley, and John Ford.

The Witch of Islington (England, prior to 1597, anonymous).
Witchcraft; or, The Martyrs of Salem (United States, 1846) by Cornelius Mathews.
The Witches of Eastwick (United States, 2000) by John Dempsey and Dana P. Rowe.

Index

The authors and works listed in the appendix are not indexed here unless they are also mentioned in the text proper.